THE
VLADIMIROV
DIARIES

YENAN, CHINA: 1942–1945

THE VLADIMIROV DIARIES

YENAN, CHINA: 1942–1945

PETER VLADIMIROV

DOUBLEDAY & COMPANY, INC.
GARDEN CITY, NEW YORK
1975

ISBN: 0-385-00928-3
Library of Congress Catalog Card Number: 74-27591
Copyright © 1975 by Novosti Press Agency

CONTENTS

PUBLISHER'S NOTE

The publisher has not read the original Russian-language version of *The Vladimirov Diaries*. The text has been edited from an English translation supplied by the Novosti Press Agency Publishing House in Moscow. In the opinion of experts who have read the manuscript, it is perhaps most valuable as an insight into Sino-Soviet relations during the period 1942–45, as described by Mr. Vladimirov, a Tass correspondent and Comintern agent assigned to the Chinese Communist area in Yenan. The publisher wishes to point out that the text contains certain inconsistencies and that new "explanatory" material may have been added. The book should therefore be read as both a historical and a contemporary document.

THE
VLADIMIROV
DIARIES
YENAN, CHINA: 1942–1945

Peter (Pyotr Parfenovich) Vladimirov was born in 1905. His first job was a fitter's apprentice at the Voronezh farm implements plant. Later he worked as a fitter at the locomotive repair works in Tikhoretsk. In 1927 he joined the All-Union Communist Party of the Bolsheviks. In 1931 he was called up for military service. Back from the Red Army, he entered the Narimanov Institute of Oriental Studies in Moscow, which he finished with honors.

From May 1938 until the middle of 1940 P. P. Vladimirov was a Tass correspondent in China. From April until August 1941 he was in China again on an assignment from Tass.

In May 1942 he was sent to Yenan (Special Area) as a liaison officer of the Comintern at the Headquarters of the Central Committee of the Chinese Communist Party and doubled as a military correspondent for Tass. He remained there till November 1945.

In 1946 he took a job at the Ministry for Foreign Affairs of the Soviet Union.

From 1948 until 1951 he was Soviet consul general in Shanghai and in 1952 was appointed Soviet ambassador to Burma.

He died in Moscow on September 10, 1953, as the result of a severe illness.

In his diaries Vladimirov recorded both his personal impressions and extracts from official correspondence. He did that because of the constant shadowing by Kang Sheng, head of the punitive bodies of the Special Area. The notebooks and diaries, therefore, were the only convenient and secure place for keeping copies of translations, documents of the Executive Committee of the Comintern, articles, reports, business telegrams, etc.

Vladimirov's Yenan diaries, which were prepared for publication by Y. P. Vlasov, are in an abridged form.

Most of the photographs in the book were taken by Peter Vladimirov.

———————

Most Chinese personal and place names have been rendered in the Wade-Giles romanization system, as modified by Matthews' Chinese-English Dictionary. All diacritical marks, including the aspirate, have been deleted except where essential for reasons of clarity. Exceptions have been made for the more familiar place names, which are given in the customary Chinese Postal Atlas system, and for personal names in cases where the individual is known to prefer a particular English rendering (e.g., T. V. Soong).

1942

May 1942

May 10, 1942

We are in Lanchow, the fourth night at Chinese airports after we took off in Alma-Ata in our TB-3 plane. We spent one night in Kuldja, then in Urumchi, then in Hami. Our destination is the city of Yenan, where I shall represent the Comintern and hold a job as a war correspondent for Tass. I have been a military man since July 1941. . . .

May 11, 1942

Our plane is heavily overloaded, and we had a hard time taking off at Hami, leaving a thick trail of dust behind. . . .

At first we had a clear blue sky all around us, then sailed into a thick ragged bank of fog. But after that the plane ducked out into the serene blue again and kept strictly on course. Half an hour later, though, we sailed into a lulu of a cloud! We climbed as high up as we could, but failed to get out into the clear. We tried a lower altitude, but to no avail. . . . There were occasional clear patches through which we glimpsed mountain peaks, deep gullies, and cliffs. Sometimes we came so close to them—a mere fifty to one hundred meters away!

The flight commander was grumbling: "What is that fog doing here at this time of the year? The weather must have gone crazy!" A quarter of an hour later he turned the plane 180°, but we were still flying blind. Every two or three minutes the flight commander said, "Bearings, pilot!"

Finally we got out of the "soup."

If the commander or the pilot had less experience, I would not be writing these lines now. . . .

I had managed to arrange for Maria [the wife of Peter Vladimirov] to come to Alma-Ata. I had not seen her since July 1941. We met at Alma-Ata Airport and there we parted. She must by now have returned to our sons, to Leninsk-Kuznetsky.

I can't imagine Nikolai [a friend of Peter Vladimirov's] dead. I really can't! This news came to me as a terrible shock. There is only one consolation: His death was quick. Nikolai was firing at the enemy from a blazing armored car when it was hit by an artillery shell. The shock wave threw Nikolai out on the road, and the Germans shot him dead on the spot. . . .

Now all this, as many other things, is in the past. But how tragic and painful this past is! It will never vanish; it is here with us forever.

The second hour in flight . . . We are making the slowest possible headway, for visibility is poor. The bomb rack is filled with cargo. The passenger compartment is also cluttered with boxes, containers, and metal tanks with gasoline. The boxes and containers are filled with medical supplies for the Chinese hospital in Yenan, spare parts for the radio station, and a new power generator. That radio station in Yenan is so old, it can give up the ghost at any time. The gasoline is for the station's engine. It consumes two barrels per year! At this rate the supply could well last several years. It is not known when another plane will come. And if Japan attacks the Soviet Union, we shall find ourselves blocked off in the Shensi mountains. . . .

By "we" I mean Orlov, Rimmar, and our friends in Yenan.

Andrei Yakovlevich Orlov, who has been assigned as surgeon to the Yenan hospital, is a short, thin man. Before his trip to Yenan Andrei Yakovlevich taught at the Medical Military Academy named after Kirov. We were yet to get better acquainted.

Nikolai Nikolayevich Rimmar, or Kolya as we called him, is a radio operator, who is to help our radio operator Dolmatov in Yenan.

We are dressed in fur-lined overalls, our teeth loudly chattering with cold. We looked out of the porthole feeling uneasy at the thought that we might still be meeting with Japanese fighter planes. After all we were well within their operation range. Our patched and repatched TB-3 was a poor match for new powerful Japanese fighter planes. From time to time the gunner takes a critical look at his SHKAS [a

1.62-mm-caliber aircraft gun], but actually we are completely de-
fenseless in case of a Japanese attack and could very easily get shot
down. We are not flying but sneaking to Yenan literally hugging the
earth.

Below are mountains, mountains . . . mountains everywhere.

The sky at dawn is blue and clear. . . .

I am turning over in my mind my meetings with Chu Teh, Kang
Sheng, and Peng Teh-huai. . . .

The pilot is busy with his map. . . .

I am writing these notes at night on our arrival at Yenan.

The TB-3 landed in a river valley between mountain slopes. There
we were met by Dolmatov, Aleyev, and some Chinese comrades.

"I am glad to salute our dear Soviet friends," said Mao Tse-
tung, holding my hand. He inquired after my health, said hello to my
colleagues and the crew. Then he remarked: "I shall be able to receive you soon. Maybe tomorrow . . ."

His manners are simple. He asked questions slowly, smiled wearily,
and listened carefully to each of us. His clothes, just like the clothes of
all the other Chinese comrades, consisted of a cotton jerkin and pants
of similar material. He wore slippers of twined string. Clothes of this
sort are called *tan-i*.

I know some Chinese comrades from my previous visit: in Lanchow and Sian. Most of them come from the old party guard which
had gone through the crucible of the Civil War. Almost all of them
had been wounded in battle, lost relatives. . . .

Kang Sheng embraced and kissed me while others were looking on.
I could not say I was delighted. When I was in Lanchow, he treated
the Soviet people with great disrespect. Our boys fought in China's
sky, sustained heavy losses, while the Japanese were losing twice and
even three times as many men and machines. Wherever Soviet fighter
planes appeared, Japanese bombers could not reach their targets. But
on the ground Kang Sheng's agents spied on every Soviet citizen. I
could never shake off the impression that this man, disguised as an important official, was an enemy of the Chinese Communists. Kang
Sheng was cautious, but his deeds spoke more than words. I do not
doubt, though, that sooner or later the Chinese comrades will see
through him.

Kang Sheng's kiss is a kiss of Judas. But, being a guest, I cannot betray my feelings. Mao Tse-tung lit up a cigarette and fell to talking with the crew, while Kang Sheng, with a frozen smile playing at his lips, hissed into my ear: "We are great brothers. . . ."

Mao Tse-tung said good-by and made for his car, followed by young men with Mauser pistols in their hands. The chauffeur started the engine and the car trundled off. That was an old ambulance of British or American make. The broad backs of the guards concealed Mao from view. . . .

I was introduced to the Tass group. Boris Vassilyevich Aleyev, the official translator, Leonid Vassilyevich Dolmatov (or Li Wen), a radio operator. He also wore the *tan-i* and showed off string slippers. Igor Vassilyevich Yuzhin was not among the welcoming party: He was away on duty at the radio station.

The day turned out to be bright and sunny. Our TB-3 left Yenan soon after unloading.

I am writing about all this sitting with Dolmatov in a room taken up by the radio station. Dolmatov is ticking off a message to Moscow about our successful arrival. The gasoline engine is rattling outside. Rimmar is studying the radio facilities. In the neighboring room Yuzhin and Orlov are setting the holiday table. The burning candles in the room have made the atmosphere cozy. . . .

We shall live in this cottage, too. All of us except Orlov, who will move to a place near the hospital. Dolmatov told me that the hospital is housed in several caves dug out in a hillside.

Everybody is excited: we because of our arrival in Yenan, and Yuzhin, Dolmatov, and Aleyev because of the fresh news from Russia and the letters from their relatives.

Our Yenanian old-timers understand the situation in the world much better than we. The radio station Dolmatov had set up makes it possible to listen in practically day and night.

May 12, 1942

The year 1927 saw the establishment of the Kuomintang [Nationalist Party, headed by Chiang Kai-shek] dictatorship. However, peasant unrest continued in the country. Using the peasant movement, the Chinese Communist Party began setting up its bases.

Mao Tse-tung headed one of the armed units which later entrenched itself in the mountains of Chingkangshan. He was soon joined by Chu Teh. The joint army units were called the IV Corps of the Red Army, with Chu Teh as commander and Mao Tse-tung as political commissar. In January 1929 the IV Corps effected a breakthrough to the town of Tui-chin. The central revolutionary base began to function in the province of Kiangsu.

In the course of the Civil War the Red Army suffered heavy losses, and its strength shrank from 300,000 to 25,000. It was now a matter of vital necessity to unite all the split-up sections of the Red Army and to choose a more suitable place for its central base.

As the result of the Long March, the dispersed Red Army units were banded together in the northwestern part of China at the end of 1935. The territory which was formerly occupied by the troops of Marshal Chang Hsueh-liang and local militarists was turned into the Liberated Area, with the administrative center at Yenan.

At that time about 25,000 commanders and soldiers—all that was left after the Long March—made their way to Yenan. Later they were joined by smaller units.

Local people call Yenan Fu-shih.

I was interrupted at my writing by a visit from Kang Sheng and his secretary, Hsiao Li.

I made hurried preparations for receiving my guests in the dining room.

All information for our news bureau—events in China, the situation on war fronts, relations with the Kuomintang, events in the Special Area, the situation in Manchuria—we shall from now on officially receive from Kang Sheng or his assistants, as, in fact, has been the case so far.

Moreover, I am supposed to advise the Comintern of the situation—and this side of my activities requires personal contacts with Mao Tse-tung, members of the Politburo, and other high-ranking party officials. My arrival was co-ordinated with the leadership of the Chinese Communist Party.

Kang Sheng asked detailed questions about the situation on the Soviet-German front, stressing now and then that he wished us an early victory over the Nazis.

Kang Sheng, or Kang Hsing, as he is also called, has a shrill and hissing voice. He speaks Russian with an accent, without conjugating verbs. His vocabulary is very poor, but he understands Russian well.

Kang Sheng always smiles. It seems that the smile has been glued to his thin, bilious face. When he listens, he inhales the air noisily, in a Japanese manner, to show that he is glad to hear the voice of his interlocutor. He has not changed in the years I have not seen him, and has remained the way I have always known him—gnarled of features and energetic in a nervous way. The impression he gives of himself is that of a wooden puppet suspended on strings. . . .

Kang Sheng described the situation in the Special Area, which includes the provinces of Shensi, Kansu, and Ningsia. On the northwest the area is blockaded by the Ma brothers, two militarist generals who do not obey anybody and who ply a brisk trade with the Japanese. One can expect any dirty trick from these generals because of their large number of well-armed troops.

On the side of the Shansi province, the Special Area has been invested by the troops of militarist marshal Yen Hsi-shan who obeys the Central Government in Chungking. This warlord is famous for having collected taxes thirty-two years in advance, a kind of highway robbery! Those routes to the Special Area which have not been occupied by the Japanese are all blocked with Kuomintang troops. Kang Sheng says that "Chiang Kai-shek does not give a damn about the united front and is looking for a pretext to start military operations against it."

Thus the situation within and without the Special Area is very complicated. . . .

I am tied down to my home, for I am expecting an invitation from Mao Tse-tung at any time.

After dinner I made another entry in my diary and then went out for a look-around. Our house is perched on the hillside next to a big mountain with a plateau top. Below is the valley of the Hsiu and Yang rivers. The valley is flanked by elevated plateaus covered with shrub and stunted trees. The valley and the foothills are studded with green square-shaped farm fields. There are but few trees in the valley. Below us is a large estate with several houses and a lush peach orchard belonging to some local landlord. Now this mansion houses Kang Sheng's office known as the Information Service, or Tsao-yuan.

Our house is made of light gray bricks with windows pasted over with paper. The windows themselves look like beehives. Only the window in the radio room has one of its quarter sections glassed in, affording the view of the courtyard.

All the housekeeping is done by Cheng, an old Chinese who lived in the Far East. He can speak tolerable Russian. He is helped by two lads and a Chinese cook. All of them are on our payroll. . . . The cook is sloppy and dirty. He has been assigned to us by Kang Sheng. . . .

The mountain plateau is roughly eight to twelve hundred meters above sea level. A person not used to living at such an altitude finds it difficult to walk uphill.

I am writing this long past midnight.

In the evening Orlov, Rimmar, Aleyev, and myself were invited to visit Mao Tse-tung. He received us in his cave, which opens out into a narrow precipice over a river. In the dry season the river looks like a shallow brook and can easily be forded. The village near Mao Tse-tung's cave is called Yang-chia-lin. The cave and the approaches to it are heavily guarded by strapping Mauser-toting men.

With Mao Tse-tung were Kang Sheng and other members of the Politburo. After the customary exchange of courtesy, Mao Tse-tung proceeded to ask us about the situation at the Soviet-German front. He was particularly interested in knowing about the stability of our front. We tried to answer all his questions. After that Mao Tse-tung said that the Chinese Communist Party is loyal to the principles of internationalism, to the policy of a united anti-Japanese front, and to cooperation with the Kuomintang.

"Sun Yat-sen's teachings are summed up in three principles: national independence, democratic freedoms, people's welfare," remarked Mao Tse-tung. "All these principles of the father of the Chinese Revolution are sacred elements of our party program. . . ."

He rummaged in his pockets absent-mindedly and took out a crumpled pack of cigarettes. He slowly lit up. "The main thing is support by the people," said Mao Tse-tung. "The enemy can be fought even without technology, just with sticks and stones, if you win the support of the masses. That is why we must fight for the betterment of the economic position of the masses; otherwise the people will not support us. . . ."

Mao Tse-tung's living quarters consist of two adjacent caves carefully lined with shingle. Deep inside the cave on a brick floor stands his desk piled with books, papers, and candlesticks. Mao Tse-tung stoops a little, his eyes are circled with tiny wrinkles. He speaks in the rough Hunan dialect. Everything in him bespeaks a long line of peasant ancestry.

At the end of the official part of the reception Mao Tse-tung promised to help us in every way and praised the wisdom of Comrade Stalin and the Comintern leadership.

Jen Pi-shih, a member of the Politburo and the Secretariat of the Central Committee of the Chinese Communist Party, is of short build, with a weak voice and a good-natured bewhiskered face. He is about forty. . . .

Wang Chia-hsiang, a member of the Politburo, is a bit taller than the average and thin of build. His hair, just like Mao Tse-tung's, is lighter than usual.

Mao Tse-tung was served Dutch gin while we were treated to *khanja* [local homemade alcoholic beverage]. He came up to each member of our group, inquiring politely after our health. He wore the same patched-up *tan-i* and held a glass of gin in his hand. Sipping the gin and chewing ground nuts, he asked detailed questions about Stalin and Dimitrov.

Mao Tse-tung introduced us to his wife, Chiang Ching, a thin woman with a lithe figure and dark clever eyes, who looked very fragile next to her husband's stocky figure. . . .

She treats him very gently and tries to please him in every way.

Meanwhile Kang Sheng told us about attempts on Mao Tse-tung's life, all of which had failed. It turned out that a mere glance cast by Mao at the conspirators was enough to make them confess their intentions. There had been three such cases. . . .

Mao Tse-tung fell silent, sitting in his lounge and inhaling tobacco smoke and shaking off the ashes onto the floor. We interpreted that as a signal to show us the reception was over. We got up and said goodby to our hosts. Mao Tse-tung walked us down to the entrance. Pressing my hand, he repeated that he was glad to see us in China, that he appreciates the work and the concern shown by the Comintern and Comrade Stalin, and again promised to help us in our work. Kang Sheng noisily inhaled the air through his teeth and smiled. . . .

The foliage of the one remaining tree in the courtyard is rustling gently, and the flame of the candle is flickering in the wind. . . . In his room Yuzhin is listening to his radio set. Now he strikes a match and lights up a cigarette.

Everything around us here—the candle, the papered window, the shrill barking of the jackals in the hills—all this somehow seems unreal. Come to think of it, just a few weeks ago I was walking the streets of Moscow.

May 13, 1942

In the morning I was awakened by the bright sunshine, the dazzling brilliancy of which was intensified by the rarefied air of the mountains.

The molten disk peered from behind the nearby peak. The valley below was still shrouded in the dark. The mist-whipped craggy cliffs suddenly took on a bluish tinge. . . . That glorious dawn in the mountains, this riot of light and shade, is something to behold, something to marvel at.

The folds of craggy rocks rise sheer from the valley, while the valley itself looks green with farm fields. The mountains here look surprisingly like crouching animals.

The Hsiu is a narrow shallow river from two to seven meters wide. Running down the valley, its waters flow into the Yang River.

The Yang River is a fast mountain stream about fifty meters wide. In some places it forms creeks and tiny waterfalls. . . .

The Yang River takes its rise in the spur of the Payushan Range and flows into the Yellow River, east of Yenan.

In these rivers local residents wash their clothes and dry them on stones. The sun is blazing hot here, so the clothes dry up in just a few minutes.

The loess slopes are dotted with hundreds of caves—the homes of students, former city-dwellers, military and party workers. The peasant population of the area also largely resides in these caves. I took a peek into one of them by permission of its owner. Stretching the length of the cave is a *kang,* which in wintertime is heated from the chimney. Near the cave I saw some pigs which looked scared of something. They were black, thin and agile like dogs. Their pendant bellies all but touched the ground.

The loess soil is soft like face powder. On roads and footpaths, though, the loess is rather well packed.

The boys and young men employed as messengers, officer's attendants, waiters at taverns, etc., are called here *hsiao-kueis* ("little devils").

Besides the information we receive from the Kang Sheng bureau, from our trips to the front line, from meetings with the leaders of the Chinese Communist Party and with ordinary Chinese civilians, we also receive fresh news from the radio, which we use mostly at night. Broadcasts from Chungking, which is 850 kilometers away, can best be heard in the evening.

Besides, our group has two-way radio contact with Moscow. The connection is most dependable in the dead of night or on a bright sunny day, but, thanks to Dolmatov's skill, radio contact was maintained practically all the time, except in July when, because of the ionospheric changes, the contact was cut off between noon and five o'clock local time.

We also have a reserve storage-battery power supply ready to be used in case of emergency. We keep it mainly against the possibility of a Japanese breakthrough. . . .

About ten kilometers to the west was the Chinese radio station controlled by Po Ku. He is also in charge of the newspaper *Liberation Daily* and the Hsinhua News Agency and in general all other printed news media.

The Central Committee of the Chinese Communist Party has a radio station of its own. Since 1936 Yenan has maintained constant radio contact with the leading bodies of the Comintern.

Po Ku (Chin Pang-hsien) is a member of the Politburo of the CCP Central Committee. From September 1931 to January 1935 he headed the Provisional Central Committee of the CCP. After the conference at Tsunyi in January 1935, the Central Committee of the party is headed by Mao Tse-tung.

May 14, 1942

Yenan as a city is practically nonexistent. Winding among the ruins are narrow streets cleared of debris. The Japanese bombed out Yenan in 1940. The only structures left standing are the city wall and several houses. One of the houses spared by the bombings, a solid brick house, is the bank of the Special Area. The chairman of the board of directors of the bank is Li Fu-chun. The bank notes, or *pien-pi,* are red papers which look like playing cards.

Li Fu-chun, a member of the Central Committee of the CCP, has been put in charge of economic and fiscal matters of the Special Area.

Lin Po-chu, the chairman of the government of the Special Area—

the provinces of Shensi, Kansu, and Ningsia—is a polite, kindly looking elderly man.

Some people are still huddling in small shacks built amid the ruins, but for the most part the city looks derelict. Outside the Southern Gate people have dug out hundreds of caves. The valley is alive with a multitude of small shops, ramshackle houses, and a newly opened market.

The city wall is about eight meters high and one and a half meters thick. In the crevices and hollows of the crenelated wall swallows have built their nests. The city gates are in the traditional Chinese style; the most attractive of them is the Southern Gate. . . .

Most of the people around Yenan are outsiders, with only a sprinkling of local residents.

The administrative center of the province is Sian, which I have visited several times. Sian lies at the crossroad of central China and central Asia, northern China and the southwestern provinces. In the past it was the capital of the imperial dynasties: the Chou, the Ch'in, the Sui, the Tang. . . . The ancient name of Sian is Chang-an.

The Red Army came to Shensi in 1935.

———

The main armed forces of the Chinese Communist Party converged on Shensi in 1935, at a time when there had already been formed a Soviet district headed by Communists Liu Chih-tan and Kao Kang.

Liu Chih-tan died in 1936 in a battle with the Kuomintang troops.

Now Kao Kang is the chief secretary of the northwestern bureau of the Central Committee of the Chinese Communist Party; the party has also entrusted him with the solution of complicated nationalities questions in the Special Area.

There are more than fifty non-Chinese nationalities in China, making up a population of several dozen million. This makes the nationalities policy of the Chinese Communist Party most important.

For ages various national and religious groups have been engaged in bitter fighting in the provinces which are now the Special Area. From time immemorial Moslems have been moving from Sinkiang via Kansu. They were assimilated by the local Chinese population. This assimilated part of the population has long since been called Dungans, or Chinese Moslems. Before the war they numbered about eight million, while in Shensi alone there were more than one million of them. There are also many Mongols in the provinces of the Special Area. In Kansu also live Tibetans. . . .

Yuzhin told us that the Chinese and the Dungans have until recently been engaged in armed clashes, both showing extreme cruelty.

Kao Kang is a very experienced man with a thorough knowledge of the nationalities and religious problems of various ethnic groups and their relations. After 1935 he all but put a stop to the national and religious massacres in the provinces of the Special Area. This is his great service to the Chinese Communist Party.

———————

In March, Chiang Kai-shek, the head of the Central Government, visited India. That was one of the most important foreign-policy actions of the Central Government.

This visit was undoubtedly dictated by the tremendous importance of the communications between India and China, since it was the most important route along which military cargoes were delivered to the Chinese troops. The Japanese fought fiercely to capture these land routes. Bitter fighting was going on in Burma and Yunnan.

The visit ended on March 21.

Chiang Kai-shek and Nehru made a joint statement:

—The Indian and Chinese people will exert every effort in the name of freedom and humanity.

—The peoples of India and China constitute half of the world's population.

—The history of the cultural and economic relations between the two nations is two thousand years old; China and India have never engaged in military conflicts; no other country knows such peaceful interstate relations.

—The world is being threatened by brutal fascist violence which makes it imperative that we rally our nations still closer in the joint struggle against it; we must fight shoulder to shoulder in one single anti-imperialist front. Therein lies the main conditions for world peace, and for this noble cause our peoples are prepared to accept any sacrifice.

At a press conference Chiang Kai-shek expressed hope that Britain would finally give India genuine, and not fictitious, political rights.

Chiang Kai-shek's visit was primarily aimed at ensuring the safety of the communications between India and China.

The point is that the maritime provinces of China have been occupied by the Japanese from the sea, while the adjacent water area is dominated by the Japanese Navy and Air Force. On the north the country has been almost completely blockaded by the occupationists. The only communications link was through Burma.

The industrial areas of China have been either captured or destroyed by the Japanese. The only hope of getting arms is by this road.

In these conditions the air bridge between the Soviet Union and China (across Sinkiang) for shipment of war matériel in line with the 1937 agreement has definite importance.

Of special significance is the resistance put up by the Chinese people! The unity of the anti-Japanese front is a task of foremost importance. The anti-Japanese bloc provides for the unity of all social forces (the Communist Party, the Kuomintang, the Democratic League of China, and other patriotic groups).

May 15, 1942

A wide campaign was launched in Yenan in the winter for the "rectification of the three styles of work," that is, the style of party work, the style of public education, and the style of writing. This month, too, Mao Tse-tung spoke several times at various conferences on questions of literature and the arts. This campaign began with his speech in February. . . .

May 16, 1942

The whole of March and April the Japanese were pulling up their troops toward the Soviet border in the Khanka, Suifenho, and Hanchun sectors (in the Maritime Province). From the South Seas area airborne troops were being lifted to Manchuria. The Japanese were especially active in the Maritime direction. The antiaircraft means in Manchuria have been alerted, and the civilians are being rapidly moved into the interior areas.

It's night again, and again the candlelight is flickering on my desk, and the torn paper in the window is rustling, and the dog Mashka is whining outside.

This dog was brought to us by our housekeeper Cheng. It soon became everybody's pet here in our colony. . . .

At the end of May or at the beginning of June Yuzhin and Aleyev will go to the Eighth Route Army, to the front line. Tass wants news stories about the front-line life of the Chinese Communists.

May 17, 1942

The rumors about the attack of the Kuomintang troops against the Special Area have caused panic in Yenan. People are making hasty preparations for departure, running around hysterically, and shouting like mad. This is a sign of a poor political education among the population and, which is still more important, the weakness of the Communist Party leadership.

Today I met a certain Ma Hai-te [George Hatem] at Kang Sheng's office. This odd-looking individual is a naturalized Jew. He is a physician by profession and is working at the Chinese hospital to which Orlov has been assigned. He is of medium size, dark of complexion, and sturdy of build. His pitch-black hair is streaked with gray. . . .

May 18, 1942

Meetings are being held to acclaim Mao Tse-tung's recent speeches. I attended several such meetings. I have not yet received their printed copies, but I shall for sure ask the Chinese comrades to provide me with them.

In the evening I discussed the content of these speeches with Yuzhin. I was surprised to see that in the conditions of a long-drawn-out war with the Japanese, when China's very life was at stake, Mao Tse-tung dwelled on such problems as "rectification of the style of party work," which, necessary as it might be, was undoubtedly a question of secondary importance.

It was also not without a feeling of bitterness that I learned from Yuzhin that Soviet citizens are as a rule not invited to hear the speeches of the CCP leaders. In fact, each invitation is an exception. Yuzhin and Aleyev were invited only once to hear Mao Tse-tung speak in February. Yuzhin is still very much surprised at the content of that speech. Mao Tse-tung suddenly turned against sectarians, dogmatists, empiricists, and subjectivists and called them the worst enemies of the Communist Party. He failed to mention even a single name in this invective. Toward the end Mao Tse-tung's speech grew very confusing and incoherent. He warned somebody and then criticized somebody, but could not make himself clear, although his entire tone was threatening. . . .

All this is very strange and deserves the closest scrutiny.

The Comintern is worried at what is going on in the leadership of the Chinese Communist Party.

May 19, 1942

The campaigns for "rectification of the three styles of work" and against the "conservative patterns of work in the party" are called the *cheng-feng yun-tung*. The leadership of the CCP seems to have attached foremost importance to these campaigns. This is the only reason it calls so many meetings in Yenan. The cheng-feng is undoubtedly a political campaign but its meaning is still obscure. . . .

May 22, 1942

Yuzhin recalls with a touch of irony his arrival in Yenan. Right from the airport he, Dolmatov, and Aleyev were taken to Yang-chia-lin. The mouth of the precipice was guarded by two uniformed men with huge swords at the ready. The guests were led into the cave to Jen Pi-shih. One by one in came Mao Tse-tung, Chu Teh, Wang Chia-hsiang, Teng Fa, and others. After the customary ceremony of greeting, Jen Pi-shih said bluntly, "Tell Stalin: We need weapons! We shall use them against the Japanese!"

"You will soon have a chance to see for yourself how they are fighting," Yuzhin added.

Yuzhin was known among the Chinese comrades as Yu Jen. They have dubbed me Sung Ping.

Teng Fa is the director of the Higher Party School in Yenan.

Wang Ming (Chen Shao-yu) is a member of the Politburo and the director of the Women's University. There are more than fifteen hundred students there. Wang Ming is thirty-eight.

Jen Pi-shih is Mao Tse-tung's assistant for civil administration.

May 23, 1942

Kang Sheng told us about the military situation at the front around the Special Area:

1. The northern front: 110 infantry divisions, 11 cavalry divisions.

This accounts for about 1.2 million servicemen. Out of this number 28 divisions, or 300,000 troops, have invested the Special Area. About 25,000 troops have been concentrated on the approaches to Sinkiang.

2. The central front: 136 infantry divisions, 3 cavalry divisions. This makes up about 1.4 million troops.

3. The southern front: 52 infantry divisions, 11 infantry brigades. Altogether about 700,000 troops.

4. The Burmese front: 3 infantry divisions: about 32,000 troops.

Because of the rivalry between the Chinese Communist Party and the Kuomintang, twenty-eight divisions have been diverted from operations against the Japanese and are now investing the Special Area! This plays into the hands of the Japanese, who apparently have taken advantage of the mutual distrust of the two most influential political forces of China. . . .

Chiang Kai-shek's attitude toward the Special Area can hardly be termed friendly by reason of class antagonism. And on top of that Chiang Kai-shek obviously wants to cash in on a possible conflict between the Soviet Union and Japan.

May 24, 1942

I have been trying to find the reasons for the cold and often hostile attitude of some Chinese party workers. As the result of my talks with the leaders of the party, talks which I found highly distasteful, I have become convinced that the unfriendly attitude to the Soviet community is only a reflection of their hostility toward the Soviet Union.

May 25, 1942

As the German troops neared Moscow in the second half of 1941, the attitude of the CCP leaders to the Soviet community became still more inimical and, toward the end of November of that year, grew outright hostile. The senior workers of the Chinese Communist Party stopped meeting us. Under the pretext of being busy Mao Tse-tung did not receive Soviet journalists once, while Kang Sheng put a tail on us. . . .

In this unfriendly situation it was my task to build up relations with the Chinese comrades without going back on our ideological principles. The job was a difficult one, considering the growing influence of Kang Sheng in the CCP.

May 27, 1942

I have met Ma Hai-te several times, sometimes at Kang Sheng's office, sometimes in the company of Jen Pi-shih . . . at Wan-chia-ping, at Nan-men-wai. . . .

He is always seen with the ranking officials of the Special Area. My Soviet colleagues say that he loves to entertain guests, throw parties, and always sees to it that alcohol will have its desired effect on his guests, although he himself drinks moderately and very cautiously.

I asked Kang Sheng about this man and was told that Ma Hai-te is a skilled physician, has been working in the Pei-yang River hospital for a long time, and is a loyal comrade. Ma Hai-te came to the Special Area in 1937, although some name an earlier date.

According to Kang Sheng, Ma Hai-te came to the Special Area because of his internationalist convictions. As a medical man, he renders disinterested assistance to the Chinese Communists, he added. Being Jewish by nationality, he is a citizen of New Zealand. He was born in the Near East, and his name is Mahmud. In China it was modified to Ma Hai-te. I wondered where he had received his medical education.

"He has a very fundamental education," said Kang Sheng. "He took his studies in the United States."

My colleagues in the news bureau are sure that this New Zealand citizen receives good wages, which go to his fat bank account in the United States, and believe that he is a professional intelligence officer.

May 28, 1942

There is one idea which cuts across the current cascade of Mao Tse-tung's speeches: One should not blindly follow other people's views. Although this idea is not altogether incorrect in theory, it negates in substance the ideological values of revolutionary philosophy. I am convinced of this; life will show whether I am right or not.

I've based my conclusions on Mao's speech made on February 1, 1942, "For the Rectification of the Style of Work in the Party."

Here is what he said in part:

"A Communist should never fail to ask why about anything; he should always use his brains and think hard how far it is real and what, if any, is the reason for it, and should never follow blindly or advocate slavish obedience.

"How can we integrate Marxist-Leninist theory with the practice of the Chinese Revolution? To put it in common parlance, we should 'shoot the arrow at the target.' Marxism-Leninism bears the same relation to the Chinese Revolution as the arrow to the target. Some comrades, however, are shooting their arrows at no target. . . ."

This means that Mao Tse-tung's speech was directed against a certain category of party workers. We will yet have to see which category. . . .

May 29, 1942

The cheng-feng campaign is assuming mass character. Not only party members but even soldiers and civilians are now required to cram Mao Tse-tung's speeches on the questions of culture, the "rectification of the three styles of work," and so on. . . .

All that, in the conditions of arduous war and economic difficulties, and finally in the face of the open preparation of Japan for an attack on the Soviet Union, looks ridiculous.

The cheng-feng campaign is undoubtedly meant to cover up something very serious, something that Mao Tse-tung needs very badly. It is he who has initiated this campaign. . . .

May 30, 1942

The Japanese radio is busy broadcasting allegations that the Soviet border installations are threatening Japan and demands that "offensive defense" be started from Manchukuo. . . .

A law has been passed in Manchukuo on the registration of workers and on assigning them permanently to their place of work.

The Kwantung Army command has announced that from now on all young people in Manchukuo will have to undergo military training.

There is no ignoring the fact that should a war break out the Manchukuo Army, 250,000 strong, could be used in sectors of secondary importance.

I am trying to make out the essence of cheng-feng. However, the inner life of the CCP is largely a secret and can be judged only from the atmosphere that prevails at open party meetings. All other facts are carefully hidden from us. No explanations can be obtained from Kang Sheng on this question. As a rule, he greets me with smiles, says he has no secrets from Soviet people. After that he flies into a rage and begins to gesticulate feverishly. He holds forth with pathos, as if he were addressing a large audience. Sometimes he stumbles and, panting, tries to catch his breath noiselessly with his mouth.

June 1942

June 3, 1942

The Japanese have stepped up their military operations in areas controlled by the Eighth Route Army. They are seeking to secure the rears of their groupings which are to operate against the Mongolian People's Republic from Inner Mongolia, as well as to make their communications lines in Manchuria and North China safe in the event of a war against the Soviet Union.

After the German defeat near Moscow, Hitler's government undoubtedly has exerted and continues to exert every possible political effort to involve Japan in the war against the Soviet Union.

Japan has scored tremendous successes. The unpreparedness of the United States for military operations is obvious. Now Japan faces no real force, except the Soviet Union and the Chinese armies, which do not compare to our Red Army in fighting efficiency.

Regarding action by the Eighth Route Army to counter the onslaught of Japanese troops: Kang Sheng demagogically talks of the CCP's loyalty to its internationalist duty, speechifies with fervor, in his custom of not looking at his interlocutor, with his head lowered. But these are only words, words, words. . . .

June 7, 1942

Yesterday Orlov officially started his work in the main hospital.
He said about the hospital: "This disease-breeder must be cleaned

up. Tidiness and sterility above all. Then I shall organize the training of surgical nurses and surgeons. We shall be performing operations as they do in the best clinics. . . ."

Well, good luck to you, Andrei Yakovlevich! . . .

The logic of events leads to the definite conclusion that the CCP leadership with Mao Tse-tung at the head are deliberately ignoring the Soviet correspondents. It is extremely difficult to meet with Mao Tse-tung.

Nor had I expected such an attitude to myself, for that matter. After all, I have been sent here by the Comintern, an international revolutionary organization that has been giving the CCP disinterested assistance for years.

The role of the Comintern in the history of the CCP is extremely great. It was with the Comintern's support and assistance that the first Marxist circles appeared in the country, from which the CCP was formed in July 1921.

The Chinese Communist Party developed under the influence of the national liberation movement, in which the bourgeoisie had the overwhelming preponderance. The Chinese working class does not form even 1 per cent of the population. It absolutely dissolves in the peasant and petty-bourgeois elements.

It can certainly be held that the CCP emerged at a time when the Chinese working class had not yet constituted itself as a class. This led to the most serious ideological errors of the party leadership. In this context the guiding role of the Comintern is extremely great and has been proved by the lessons of history. . . .

The Comintern has repeatedly helped the CCP to overcome various leftist and opportunist trends.

It is striking that here, in Yenan, nobody ever recalls Li Ta-chao, Chu Chiu-pai, and other remarkable Chinese Marxist-internationalists. Chance is to be ruled out in such situations. All this is the result of definite tactics.

Eighth Route Army units, instead of active military operations to hold the Japanese interventionists in check, limit themselves to sluggish defensive fighting of local importance. Whenever fighting starts on the enemy's initiative, the Eighth Route Army rolls back to the mountains, avoiding clashes. Thus, practically the Japanese are preparing their rear echelons for a war against the Soviet Union without hindrance.

An agreement has been signed between the United States and China. The United States commits itself to continue to render military and technical aid to China as a world area of vital importance to American defense.

June 10, 1942

From my conversations with Chinese comrades I become convinced that in the CCP leadership, which outwardly is monolithic, a fierce struggle has been going on.

Yesterday I was received by the Chairman of the Central Committee of the CCP.

As defined by Mao himself, there are three groups in the CCP:

1. The Right group believes the Central Committee's policy toward the Kuomintang to be too crude and dangerous and is working for co-operation with the Kuomintang within the framework of an anti-Japanese united front.

2. The Left group proposes that the policy of co-operation with the Kuomintang be totally abandoned and an absolutely independent political line be adopted, without fearing a break with Chiang Kai-shek.

3. The third group is made up of "subjectivists who have lost the perspective of the Chinese Revolution."

Mao Tse-tung did not give names, but it appears that Chou En-lai leads the third group.

It turns out that the cheng-feng campaign is not so innocuous a talking shop. This campaign is the result of the internal political divisions in the CCP leadership. Ideologically the campaign is led by Mao Tse-tung.

This is so serious that it wholly absorbs my attention. I am trying to gain an understanding of the political situation in the CCP. Yes, just trying, since they are concealing everything from me, and the ECCI [Executive Committee of the Communist International] must know the truth.

June 11, 1942

It seems that Mao Tse-tung thinks the Comintern's line toward China to be erroneous. Wang Ming [Chen Shao-yu] adheres to the Comintern's positions. He, Po Ku, Lo Fu, and others are for the policy of proletarian internationalism and fraternal co-operation with the

AUCP(B) [All-Union Communist Party of the Bolsheviks, the name of which was changed in 1952 to the Communist Party of the Soviet Union]. . . .

The atmosphere in the CCP leadership is not good. I still know too little about it to form a full judgment. I am clearly being ignored. But in the rare meetings we have Mao Tse-tung tries to charm me with his courtesies. . . .

June 12, 1942

In May new Japanese units and combat equipment kept arriving in Manchuria. The Japanese radio has been reiterating about the "offensive defensive" by Manchukuo: "Manchuria is the lifeline of Japan! We shall defend the possession gained by the blood of our fathers and grandfathers! Manchuria is the front line of defense of our empire!"

A special representative of the Emperor, Prince Takamatsu, the Emperor's brother, visited Manchuria from May 25 to June 2. The prince had a number of meetings with General Yoshijiro Umezu, the commander of the Kwantung Army. . . .

Even without military operations this state of tension in the Far East alone is no doubt advantageous to Germany, since it diverts dozens of Soviet divisions to protect the frontiers.

June 15, 1942

Yuzhin thus sums up the practice of party meetings in Yenan:

Party meetings are fixed by an order from above. No "unscheduled" initiative is tolerated. The chairman of a cell delivers an obligatory opening speech, stating the essence of the agenda of the meeting—that is, predetermining the nature and content of speeches.

Party discipline is based on absurdly cruel forms of criticism and self-criticism. The chairman of a cell points out who is to be criticized at each meeting and for what. As a rule, one Communist is "flogged" at each meeting. Everyone takes part in the "flogging." He has to.

The "flogged" has only one right: to confess his "mistakes." But if he doesn't and thinks himself innocent or if he has "confessed" not enough (as may have seemed to the chairman or any of the party members), "flogging" is resumed.

Meetings are numerous. Speeches are long, high-sounding, and roughly of the same content. A real psychological drill . . .

Minor faults, even small infringements of the daily routine, usually come in for "flogging."

I eyewitnessed how severely a lad was being criticized for having talked with a girl, although nobody knew what they had talked about. But in general attempts are being made to bar us from party meetings.

Another time a girl was abused unashamedly. During leisure hours she had dared to put on a house dress which remained since the old days. The speakers ranted and raved about her "bourgeois nationalism" and did not stint dirty epithets.

But one is under the impression that it is only a psychological drill, nothing more. Somewhere deep in their hearts people remain people. They jump up, they speak—and here their obligations end. Then many sit like graven images or openly doze it away. . . .

June 17, 1942

The attitude to the Soviet group has sharply changed after the military setbacks of our troops on the Soviet-German front, and particularly after it became clear that because of the war against fascist Germany our government cannot meet the demand of the CCP leadership for immediate and extensive arms supplies.

The CCP leaders refuse to understand that arms are vital to us and that we ourselves are badly in need of them. The leaders of the CCP regard as nonsense the fact that if the Soviet Union loses the war, there will be neither Special Area nor Communist troops. They will be crushed by either the Kuomintang or the Japanese.

In my opinion the CCP leaders had hoped to get arms not for the armed struggle against the aggressors, but for unleashing a conflict with the Kuomintang. How pleased the men in Tokyo would have been! . . .

However, on behalf of the CCP leadership, Kang Sheng has assured me of the resolve of the troops of the CCP to fight against Japan. Other CCP officials have also assured me of this. Is it an unserious game or double-dealing? Or double-dealing that is already a policy?

June 18, 1942

The Japanese are completing the military construction on the Soviet-Manchurian border which they started last November.

The flow of ammunition and equipment from Japan has sharply

increased in the last few weeks. New infantry units (according to prisoners) are being urgently formed in the mother country.

Infantry divisions are being hastily reorganized into motorized in the Japanese Army. Four-regiment divisions are made three-regiment. The latest types of large heavy tanks are arriving in Manchuria.

No more than ten infantry divisions of the samurai are active in China and some twenty more in the South Seas area, and over fifty divisions are so far in reserve, intended, no doubt, for military actions against the Soviet Union.

There are many rumors that Japan intended to attack the Soviet Union this spring. Beyond question, under pressure from the Germans and in view of the creation of a "New Asia"—that is, the destruction of any real military force in the East which would be capable of opposing imperial Japan—the fascist Cabinet of Tojo does not rule out a war against the Soviet Union. An indisputable fact, but it so much depends on the situation on the Soviet-German front.

Kang Sheng's secretary, Hsiao Li, very often calls on us, preferably when we have a meal. After having his fill, he turns philosophical. Today, picking his teeth, he said: "What did you white people do thousands of years ago? . . . You used bows to shoot. And we had powder. Already then we built canals, dikes, fortresses, and were able to make porcelain, silk, writing paper, India ink, while white people still subsisted on raw meat. We had an outstanding philosophy, while white people just tried to devise their alphabet. Our culture has nourished the East. It is the original mother of world culture. . . ."

Dolmatov flushed with anger. Parting, we just smiled polite smiles. . . .

The high ancient civilization gave rise to the view of feudal China as the first world power. For dozens of centuries this idea was carefully cultivated in Chinese society. Regrettably, certain members of the Communist Party are not free from it to this day.

June 20, 1942

In the CCP leadership Mao Tse-tung's group is gaining the upper hand. This expresses itself in the leadership's policy of coming closer to a break with the Kuomintang, despite the harm this does to the cause of the liberation war. Such actions not only play into the hands of the Japanese but jeopardize the very existence of the Special Area and the CCP. The Kuomintang, having an enormous numerical superiority, can easily destroy the few army units stationed in the Special Area and then crush the state and party machinery of the CCP. The policy of the CCP leadership is surprising!

June 23, 1942

The material of the Information Department of the Central Committee of the CCP, supplied by Kang Sheng, is so muddled and contradictory and, most important, so tendentious, particularly on the questions of the domestic and foreign policies of the Kuomintang, that it takes great pains to restore the approximate truth.

We are trying to overcome a double blockade: the Japanese one, which cuts us off from the outside world, and Kang Sheng's, which cuts us off from the CCP leadership.

Kang Sheng and his entourage are exploiting the fact of the timely information about the planned attack by Germany on the Soviet Union. They keep dinning it into my and my comrades' ears. . . .

Dolmatov told us how a few days before the outbreak of the war the Soviet group in Yenan was warned about the impending attack by Germany on the Soviet Union. Some time later we learned about the telegram of Chou En-lai from Chungking.

On June 18 Chou En-lai reported that Chiang Kai-shek had been informed that Germany would attack the Soviet Union on the night of June 21, and so Chiang Kai-shek was urgently planning a general campaign against the Special Area. Chiang Kai-shek was informed by Kuomintang's ambassador in Berlin, Cheng Chia, and Military Attaché Wei Yung-ching.

Kang Sheng spends days and nights at Mao Tse-tung's. Yesterday Kang Sheng tried hard to bring it home to me how great Mao Tse-tung's services were in creating the "most modern tactics of revolutionary wars" (not just the revolutionary war in China, but such wars in general!). He claimed that all the Chinese, even the enemies, acknowledged his innovation in applying "maneuver tactics." Thanks to these tactics, "we used to beat Chiang Kai-shek's troops and are now smashing the Japanese."

The maneuver tactics of small forces or guerrillas are as old as wars themselves. Incidentally, they also ascribe to Mao Tse-tung the honor of the "discovery" of many other truths which are absolutely obvious and which long ago were enunciated by other people. The present Mao "maneuver tactics" by small forces are the tactics of evasion of any actions against the occupationists altogether. . . .

June 25, 1942

Ma Hai-te too often "happens" to appear where I am. His polite impertinence already sickens me. I have learned by heart the sharp features of his face, his big nose, his deep-seated lively eyes. He has a remarkable command of the Chinese language and speaks many of its dialects.

Ma Hai-te is "free" from the guardianship of Kang Sheng's men, which cannot be said of us. He moves alone to any place in Yenan and the Special Area. He has firm connections with CCP functionaries. He is received as a guest of honor. He uses the need of medical assistance as a cover for his visits.

June 27, 1942

The talk of some of the CCP leaders of their amicability, which the warning about Germany's attack supposedly expressed, is openly speculative. The reality is the hidden hostility of Kang Sheng and, perhaps, even the Chairman of the CCP Central Committee—Mao Tse-tung. . . .

Hostility of Mao Tse-tung?! No, for me now the thought is not so heretical at all. There are many insignificant and significant details which change my idea of this man. Do I encounter here in Yenan in the person of Mao Tse-tung political errors or deliberate tactics?! This keeps constantly nagging me.

I must, I am duty-bound to make out the substance of the policy of the leadership of the CCP. Not the sham policy, but the real one. My arrival seems to have coincided with its definite transformation. An enormous responsibility to my party and the Comintern rests with me.

June 29, 1942

Mao Tse-tung pursues a policy that runs counter to the line and principles of the Comintern. But what guides him?!

On the eve of the day I flew to Yenan I was acquainted in Moscow with the decision of the ECCI to create an anti-Japanese united front.

The main tasks of the CCP: termination of the Civil War, joint actions with the Kuomintang, and unification of all the forces of the Chinese people to protect the integrity and independence of China against the aggression. The policy of the CCP must be subordinated to this task. Here is the meaning of this document: the view that the CCP's alliance with the Kuomintang is supposedly a capitulation to Chiang Kai-shek brings grist to the pro-Japanese elements' mill and facilitates the fomenting of an internal internecine war. The most serious attention must be devoted to the designs of Trotskyist elements, which by their provocative activity in China are seeking to wreck the cause of an anti-Japanese united front and are the servitors of the Japanese invaders. . . .

July 1942

July 1, 1942

The laboratory of the central hospital is wretchedly equipped. Many hospital sections are headed by doctors without a higher medical education, the result being frequent mistakes and death of patients. The death rate in the hospital is intolerably high. There are several medical books in Chinese and English, but they are outdated. There is no Russian medical literature. It is twice, thrice more difficult for Orlov, who doesn't know Chinese. And yet he manages, and how! . . .

———

From the hilltop one gets a view of the grayish-yellow pleateau cut by gorges. Only the dark rocks which break through the loess deposits disrupt this gray-and-yellow harmony.

Overhead is the fathomless blue space. The shadows of eagles skim noiselessly over the rocky screes and drop abruptly into the gorges.

Thorny shrubs and dwarf trees giving refuge to pheasants cover the sides of the gorges and the hill slopes. At sunset and sunrise one hears the perky clucking of the pheasant cocks.

Everywhere one stumbles across the Chinese acacia, beaten down and gnarled by the winds. The rocks are burning hot. The scorching sun looms large overhead.

July 5, 1942

The Soviet Informburo reported the death of Evgeni Petrov, who was at the front as war correspondent.

Petrov was only forty. I met him several times in the *Pravda* editorial office. In my memory his image is always associated with sunshine.

Journalists Edgar Snow, Anna Louise Strong, and Agnes Smedley have given Mao Tse-tung the reputation of "avowed genius" of the Chinese Revolution.

Mao Tse-tung has done everything for the arrival of these journalists, who are of a liberal and semi-anarchist frame of mind. He has spared no efforts to create a favorable impression of himself. In his interviews the Chairman of the Central Committee spoke rather modestly of the Chinese Revolution and more than enough of himself. . . .

Mao Tse-tung's confession to Edgar Snow about the political views of his youth has always astonished me. Mao Tse-tung spoke of them as "hotchpotch" of utopian socialism, liberalism, and democratism.

His outlook was influenced most of all by his seminary teacher, Yang Chang-chi, who was educated in England. According to Mao Tse-tung, his mentor was a confirmed idealist.

Mao Tse-tung's first wife was the daughter of Yang Chang-chi. Her name was Yang Kai-kuei.

July 8, 1942

All our business relations are confined to Kang Sheng. It is not easy to meet Mao Tse-tung. He leads the life of a hermit in his cave in Yang-chia-lin.

Kang Sheng tries to isolate us from all the prominent CCP members. Incidentally, the Chinese comrades also avoid us: Kang Sheng has taken care of that.

When Mao Tse-tung does receive us, it is invariably in the presence of Politburo members, and the official character of this meeting is made clear to us. Twice he paid us a visit, but with the same entourage.

Only Kang Sheng drops in whenever he thinks fit, as does his secretary, Hsiao Li.

July 9, 1942

Yuzhin and Aleyev have come back from their tour. They are depressed by what they have seen.

The troops of the Eighth Route Army (and the New Fourth Army, of course) have long been abstaining from both active and passive action against the aggressors. Nor has the situation changed now, despite the frenzied samurai onslaught in Southeast China and the threat of Japan's aggression against the Soviet Union.

CCP detachments offer no resistance to the present actions of the Japanese to clear the areas from CCP troops; they leave for the mountains or beyond the Yellow River.

The CCP leadership regards the Kuomintang its main enemy and spares no efforts to gain hold of territories under the control of the Central Government. This is achieved by hook or by crook.

These clearly sectarian activities harm the liberation movement of the Chinese people against the invaders, increase the sacrifices made by the Chinese people, and are fraught with military clashes with the Kuomintang, which at the present moment is immeasurably stronger than the CCP in every respect.

July 10, 1942

Page by page I gradually translate the speech of Mao Tse-tung at the conference on art and literature.

The introduction is his speech of May 2. But his concluding speech at the conference on May 23 is actually a political report and, as it seems to me, with a great undercurrent. Here is a noteworthy page:

"Take, for example, the sectarian tendencies in artistic and literary circles. This is also a question of principle. The sectarian tendencies can be eradicated only by putting forward the slogans 'Serve the workers and peasants,' 'Serve the Eighth and New Fourth armies,' and 'Go into the midst of the masses' and by carrying them out. Otherwise it is absolutely impossible to do away with the sectarian tendencies. Lu Hsun once said: 'The necessary condition for the united front is a common aim. . . . The fact that we lack unity shows that we are not agreed on the aim, some pursuing narrow group interests and others working only for their own ends. If we make it our goal to serve the broad masses of workers and peasants, our front will of course be united.' The same problem cropped up in Shanghai just as it now crops up in Chungking. There it is as hard to solve the problem thoroughly as it was in Shanghai because the rulers there oppressed and continue to oppress the revolutionary artists and writers and deprive them of the freedom to go into the midst of the masses of workers, peasants, and soldiers. But here among us the situation is entirely different. Here we encourage revolutionary artists and writers to get actively into contact with the workers, peasants, and soldiers, and give them full freedom to go into their midst, to create genuinely revolutionary art and literature. The problem here is therefore nearing solution. Yet to be nearing the solution is not the same as to arrive at a complete and thorough solution, and it is for this complete and thorough solution that we say we must study Marxism and society. By Marxism we mean the living Marxism that can have practical bearing on the life and struggle of the masses, and not Marxism in words. When Marxism in words is transformed into Marxism in practical life, there will be no more sectarianism. It will be possible not only to do away with sectarianism but to solve many other problems as well."

It is clear that the report is aimed against a definite group of CCP workers.

According to Mao Tse-tung, everything is not well in the party: In party ideology "living Marxism" has been replaced by "dogmas." If it is transformed into "Marxism in practical life, there will be no more sectarianism."

Thus the problem of "Marxism in practical life" is on the agenda in the CCP.

July 13, 1942

Yesterday Kang Sheng gave me a record of Mao Tse-tung's talks with Edgar Snow: I had left at home the copy published in Moscow. I am reading some parts over again. Kang always grants such requests quite willingly.

The radio gives a lot of hullabaloo about a military defeat of the Soviet Union. From morning till night the Japanese radio is rehashing Goebbels' reports.

I am uneasy. One thing is clear—something has happened at home. . . .

————————

I was suddenly invited to Mao Tse-tung's. It was already late when I arrived. He was alone. We exchanged civilities.

Mao Tse-tung asked me in detail about the situation on the Soviet-German front. I told him what I knew. He listened in silence turning to the map several times. I helped him to find the points whose names were unknown to him.

Smoke has penetrated into every object inside the cave. Cigarette butts lie all over the place. The Chairman offered me a chair, took one across from me, and said that the Soviet Government had no cause for worry, that the worries of Stalin and the Soviet people were understood by him and the Chinese people, and that is why "I have given orders to get ready for combat operations against the Japanese fascists. Just let them violate the Soviet Union's frontier! Don't you worry. The Eighth Route Army is making the necessary redislocation."

July 14, 1942

Mao Tse-tung is moving from Yang-chia-lin to Chiao-yuan. Officially this is explained by the need to ensure Mao Tse-tung's safety in view of the activization of the Kuomintang intelligence.

While building caves for Mao Tse-tung in Chiao-yuan, the destruction capacities of the largest caliber were taken into consideration. Calculations were made by military engineers.

Sometimes Mao Tse-tung quotes Confucius from memory. He is well versed in the Four Books.

Confucianism is the cult of the supreme ruler and the superiority of everything Chinese. Confucianism is responsible to a great measure for China's spiritual paralysis and cultural backwardness. This religious-philosophical system is categorical, aggressive, and dogmatic.

It is with pain in one's heart that one observes the behavior of the CCP leadership. The situation is critical for the Soviet Union, but the CCP leaders are indifferent to this. Their activity, or rather inactivity, is obviously spurring the samurai to step up military preparations on our frontiers. Bearing in mind the latest developments on the Soviet-German front, such a policy on the part of the CCP leadership is more than simply shortsighted.

––––––––––

Ma Hai-te poses as a friend of the Chinese Communists, flaunting his allegedly progressive views. He is highly educated and therefore easily worms himself into people's confidence. He keeps company with the workers of the general staff of the CCP armies. He tries to win everyone's favor by entertaining. Ma Hai-te is well informed about all the major military and party events.

July 16, 1942

According to Yuzhin, in July 1941 the Soviet command informed the CCP of the transportation to the mainland of full-strength units from Japan proper and their concentration along the Soviet frontier.

The Soviet command proposed that the Eighth Route Army break up the concentration of Japanese troops in the Peiping-Kalgan and Paotow directions and thus help the Soviet Union in the critical situation.

"It is particularly important," ran the request, "to disrupt normal railway communications leading to the mentioned points. . . ."

The CCP leaders did not grant this or any other request.

The CCP Central Committee stopped passing over the usual information on international issues, and the party's internal life was made secret.

July 18, 1942

Dolmatov has added to Yuzhin's story.

How depressed all of our comrades were that when answering the question of a Soviet comrade, Mao Tse-tung, in the presence of Wang Chia-hsiang and Kang Sheng, said in an irritated voice, "In case the Japanese declare war on the Soviet Union, we shall conduct only minor operations, without introducing large forces, so as to preserve our own. In the course of the war we shall act depending on the situation. . . ."

Wang Chia-hsiang added not without malevolence: "We don't need Manchuria. It's Russia that's interested!" (Of course, Russia is interested. It is there, in Manchuria, that the Kwantung Army is mustering forces and White Guard bands are popping up.)

"Depending on the situation! . . ." Dolmatov fumed. "As if they would survive if we lost the war. They would be crushed here, in the Special Area, in a month's time by the Japanese or the Kuomintang, or perhaps by both together. They are alive because the Soviet Union is alive."

The CCP leaders are least of all concerned about the future of the world revolutionary movement. The main thing is that there is the opportunity to sit it all out in the Special Area. But they do not care what the price of this opportunity is nor where the future of the world revolutionary movement or their own future, for that matter, is being solved. It's a fact.

I have once again called on Wang Ming. He says that if Japan attacks the Soviet Union, the CCP is most likely to take into account the balance of forces, its own and the enemy's. That is why the Soviet Union ought not take the Eighth Route Army into account without knowing the exact policy of the CCP leadership. . . .

July 20, 1942

After supper I sat up with Aleyev. He has much to recall.

"Our group of correspondents," he said, "always displayed exceptional tact. Nevertheless, the attitude toward us becomes worse every day. In the last few months all civilities have been cast aside; all that remains is blatant caddishness and insolent efforts to undermine our prestige among the population. I am absolutely sure that in case of a Japanese-Soviet war it is useless to count on the help of the CCP armed forces. A hostile group is secretly operating in the Special Area."

"A hostile group is secretly operating"—this is much too vague to make any sense to me. It is necessary to find out the aims, the tasks, of this group, its role and influence in the CCP. To all appearance, this "group" is exerting an ever increasing influence on the line of the CCP.

In my opinion our military setbacks have set loose the hostility toward our country that had been smoldering among some of the CCP leaders. Take Kang Sheng, for example, whose informers watch our every step.

These last few days he has been foisting upon me a teacher of Russian whom I should accept as a pupil. I have never seen a Chinese girl of such striking beauty. The girl doesn't give us a day's peace. . . .

July 22, 1942

Yuzhin described his trip to the front lines:

". . . Covered hundreds of kilometers of the Special Area but saw no troops anywhere: this was explained by competent camouflage. Actually no one is engaged in combat training. Like everywhere in the Special Area, meetings are the only form of work carried on in the army units. In the summer this is supplemented to some extent with the laying-in of farm produce. . . .

"In the staff of the front-line division men killed time by playing cards and gossiping. Visited the headquarters of the 19th Regiment. The chief of staff remarked that the Japanese had opened fire on them that day, that there were casualties. An hour later the regiment commander sold me the same story as a minor victory over the Japanese. . . .

"I was unable to reach Wu-tai [a town in the northwestern part of Shansi]. Although the situation on the front lines was quite tolerable, I was prevented from seeing the actual state of things at the front; my presence was quite a burden. . . ."

July 24, 1942

At home the events are taking a tragic turn. The fascists are already on the approaches to Novocherkassk and Tsimlyanskaya. Our troops are recoiling to the Volga and the Caucasus.

The Chinese troops have recovered Jui-an (Chekiang province), and in Shansi, according to secondhand information, the city of Lin-chuan.

Probably to raise the fighting spirit of the population, the Japanese radio once again relished the recent victories: ". . . On February 8, 1942, under cover of night and supported by the Air Force, the glorious Army of the Emperor began the landing of troops on Singapore Island. On February 15 the biggest naval fortress of the British was seized!"

The Japanese divisions were under the command of General Tomoyuki Yamashita, the idol of the Japanese military.

The discord between Mao Tse-tung and his opponents, whom he sarcastically calls the "Moscow group" or "Muscovites" becomes more evident. The "Moscow group" does not agree with Mao Tse-tung's political line.

Kang Sheng supports Mao Tse-tung with every means—this fact alone puts one on the alert. Wherever you find Kang, there is no respect for the Soviet people or the Comintern.

Wang Ming and Po Ku stand for a policy of loyalty to internationalism and friendship with the Soviet Union.

While listening to the radio, I put my hand on Dolmatov's back. Leonid Vassilyevich started.

It turned out that he had been a volunteer in Spain: For three months he had headed the communications service under the chief adviser for naval affairs, Admiral Nikolai Kuznetsov in Cartagena, then was appointed radio operator under the chief military adviser, Stern, in Valencia.

"I was wounded on October 5, 1937, near Saragossa on the Ebro River," said Dolmatov. "Four days before my twenty-fifth birthday. It was a lovely sunny day. Suddenly a group of Messerschmitts came out in a low flying attack. There was a blast, another blast, and a burst of machine-gun fire. A wild pain, fire racked my whole body, and me crying, crying with all my might: 'Mamma!' "

July 27, 1942

The tactics of a single anti-Japanese front, approved by the Comintern, is first of all in the interests of China's national independence. However, the alliance of the CCP with the Kuomintang against the Japanese invaders also means support for the world's first socialist state which is defending in its struggle against fascism the interests of all the working people.

Ma Hai-te's family is here in Yenan: his wife—a Chinese woman, Su Fei by name—and a son, Yu Ma. Su Fei, a graceful woman, is very feminine. She is very tender with the men. Uses all her charms to make friends with our radiomen. She has a slightly ingratiating voice of a soft velvety texture.

I never get enough sleep. The Japanese, British, and American broadcasts are coherent only in the night hours. And one is so eager to learn as soon as possible what is going on in the world and at home.

Communication with Moscow—6,000 kilometers—is maintained only by Dolmatov's skill. He has resoldered the transmitter and is now keen on setting up a "Zeppelin" type of aerial which should put an end to all interruptions in our communications. There are no spare crystals. He takes care of the apparatus as if it were the dearest thing in the world.

What is going on at home? Where will they finally stop the Germans?

July 29, 1942

The Chairman of the CCP Central Committee speaks scornfully of the Soviet leaders. Thus without concealing his contempt he said of I. V. Stalin: "He doesn't know and cannot know China, yet he pokes his nose into all matters. All of his so-called theses on our revolution are but rancid nonsense. And those in the Comintern are blabbing the same thing. . . ."

The Chairman has an extremely hazy idea of the Soviet Union. The word "republic", and nothing more, is his only knowledge of the subject.

He has the most perverted ideas about the Soviet Union which have emerged not without the influence of Kang Sheng.

And what is most amazing of all is that he never asks us about the Soviet Union. He lacks interest in what is taking place in our country. The only thing he takes interest in is the situation on the Soviet-German front.

When the battle for Moscow in October–December of the previous year was at its height, the Chairman stated: "See what Stalin's babbling has brought him to. That's the limit! I'd like to see the leader babbling now, there, in Moscow. . . ."

And the news from Moscow becomes more and more tragic.

August 1942

August 2, 1942

Mao Tse-tung invited Yuzhin to his quarters: wanted to teach him how to play Mah-Jongg. During the game Yuzhin asked: "Comrade Mao Tse-tung, how can it be that the peasants living in the Special Area used to be punished for the illegal traffic in opium, and now even troops and institutions headed by Communists openly engage in opium production?"

Mao Tse-tung vouchsafed no reply. The question was answered by Teng Fa: "The Special Area previously exported only salt and soda to the Kuomintang provinces. We fitted out caravans loaded with salt and brought back an undernourished purse. And only one! Now we send along an undernourished bag of opium and bring back a caravan loaded with money. The money is used for buying weapons from the Kuomintang, and with it we'll knock down the same Kuomintang!"

The Central Committee of the CCP keeps in touch with the Comintern (Executive Committee) by means of radio stations run by Po Ku. All communications are coded.

Po Ku is among the few comrades who hold their ground. If he does not agree with someone, he will say so or will just give one of his smiles. And this smile of his speaks better than words.

At suppertime we were graced with a call from Hsiao Li, who ate with good appetite and then broke the latest news: "Your troops are giving up the Kuban area to the Germans. . . ." His words were soaked with malice.

There is no system of money remuneration in the Special Area. Industrial and office workers, students and military men, are issued uniforms and food.

In army units 1.5 catties of millet is issued per man, while at offices and educational establishments it is a mere 1 catty and 3 Chinese ounces.

Every student and office worker is entitled to a change of underclothes, one change of summer clothes, and one change of winter clothes a year. The quota is slightly higher in the Army.

Officially every citizen is supposed to have 3 pounds of meat, 16 ounces of oil, 1 pound of salt, and 260 local dollars for spice every month.

This is nothing but a declaration, for in actual fact they eat millet porridge twice a day. Meat products are given only to high-ranking party and military officials.

I have never been in the tropics, but this must be what tropical rain is like. The fluffy clouds are touching the barren mountaintops. There are clouds coming in from everywhere. Thunderbolts split the sky and release a Niagara of water which turns the loess dust into a sea of mud.

I feel grateful to our short robust ponies, which gingerly carry us up and down the steep mountain roads. I am smelling strongly of horse sweat.

August 5, 1942

Hsiao Li was right. The Germans have invaded the Kuban area. . . .

No second front in sight. Just like in China, the Allies prefer to engage in air combat only. So let the Russians, the Chinese, and the partisans in the occupied countries spill their blood. . . .

In an effort to strengthen his position Kang Sheng surrounded himself with his own men. His secretary, Hsiao Li, is rabidly anti-Soviet, and his deputy, Li Ko-nung, came here in 1941 from the Kuomintang area where he had been chief of the intelligence and counterintelligence of the Kuomintang. Li Ko-nung is undoubtedly a bitter enemy of the Soviet Union.

The special department is headed by Peng Chen.

According to Yuzhin, Peng Chen brought with him Liu Shao-chi from the New Fourth Army in spring. Liu Shao-chi was a military commissar in the New Fourth Army.

Incidentally, Li Ko-nung has a heart condition, and he went to see Orlov about it. Some man Li Ko-nung—first puts him under surveillance and then seeks medical advice from him!

Li Ko-nung is a gloomy individual; rough, despotic. He is extremely careful that nobody will see who comes to see him.

August 6, 1942

Transportation facilities are being moved to Manchuria, and water-crossing means to the Maritime Province.

At their meetings with Russian counterrevolutionary leaders the samurai openly speak about a future war against the Soviet Union and about the creation of a buffer state.

The Japanese radio is ranting about "stamping out the threat from the north." With every passing day the tone of its broadcasts is becoming more and more virulent.

Moscow reports fifteen violations of the Soviet border by Japanese servicemen and Japanese aircraft in May and June. This was how the Nazis began the war in 1941!

Preparations have been under way, since the beginning of the year, for the Seventh Congress of the CCP. The congress was expected to be held earlier, but the routing of the New Fourth Army was used as a pretext for postponement.

Some of the delegates from the remote liberated areas have already arrived in Yenan. More delegates are coming. . . .

We believe that the true reason for the postponement of the congress is the fact that, in the conditions of strife within the leadership of the CCP, Mao Tse-tung does not want to risk speaking openly before the congress.

The cheng-feng campaign seems to have a direct bearing on the coming congress.

August 9, 1942

Aleyev and I may soon be going to the Eighth Route Army at the front, most likely in the middle of September. There we shall be able to compare the words of the CCP leadership with their policy.

Kang Sheng is trying to put the members of the Central Committee of the CCP against the alliance with the Kuomintang in an effort to provoke an armed clash with the Japanese at any cost. The question suggests itself whether Kang Sheng is not a Japanese agent. He is decidedly opposed to an active struggle against the occupationists and is inciting Mao Tse-tung to withdraw all troops from the Japanese front into the rear.

The leading members of the CCP are treating us with disparagement, and now that the Soviet Army is retreating, their attitude to us is nothing short of hostile.

Kang Sheng has ordered his staff to maintain no relations with us whatsoever. They prevent us from knowing anything about local life, we are not allowed to go to the theater or to musical and literary soirees. They are even trying to conceal the existence of Moscow newspapers in the Special Area. . . .

Kang Sheng is hypocritical. Outwardly polite as before. Promises much but does nothing. Since I am an "old acquaintance" of his, he greets me with a hissing and a profusion of smiles.

Today Aleyev could tolerate this no longer and gave a whole speech. We were sitting at the table after breakfast when he said: "We have a lot of facts, big and small, to show that we are among enemies! There is nothing here that we could call friendly!"

It's damn easy to lose your peace of mind here!

After a glass of *pai-kan* and ample refreshment Hsiao Li blabbed out his patron's order. Kang Sheng had told the men who had returned from the Soviet Union: "Forget that you have ever worked there! This is China. You must work Chinese-style! Remember that you were spoiled there, not taught! I forbid you to hobnob with the Soviets!" The contempt in which Hsiao Li holds our *hsiao-kuei*s defies description.

We are under the surveillance of Kang Sheng's staff wherever we go. Be that the pretty teacher or our former cook. There is a good score of informers watching our every step: Kang Sheng's ubiquitous men are amazingly light of foot. Their very presence clams shut the mouths of anyone we want to talk with. Kang Sheng himself decides who is to talk and with whom. And naturally, all these people have been indoctrinated properly. . . .

August 13, 1942

Mao Tse-tung suddenly remembered Ma Hai-te in Yuzhin's presence: "Ma Hai-te is a foreign national who has voluntarily come to serve the Chinese Revolution. Abiding by our internationalist duty we welcome foreign volunteers."

Judging by the short remarks he always exchanges with us, Ma Hai-te knows all there is to know about the state of affairs in Yenan.

The members of the Central Committee of the CCP can be roughly divided into four groups:

1. Mao Tse-tung, Kang Sheng (one of the most powerful men in the Special Area and in the CCP), and Liu Shao-chi (who is not a member of the Politburo, but who is slowly arrogating power to himself and is coming into prominence).

2. Wang Chia-hsiang, Chen Yun, Chu Teh, who more or less adhere to the principles of Marxism-Leninism, but who are not strong on theory and are often unable to defend their views.

3. The so-called Moscow group, which is the main opposition to the opportunism of Mao Tse-tung and his supporters: Wang Ming, Po Ku, Lo Fu.

4. Jen Pi-shih belongs to the so-called bog. He is easily swayed by whoever is the stronger at the moment.

Teng Fa follows a neutral line.

Chou En-lai represents the CCP in Chungking and is actually kept outside the struggle in the party.

Wang Chia-hsiang was born in Anhwei province in 1907. Graduated from the Sun Yat-sen University in Moscow. Returned to China in May 1930. At present chief of the Political Department of the CCP armed forces.

Chen Yun was born in the province of Kiangsu in 1905. After

finishing school he sold newspapers in Shanghai. Educated in the Soviet Union. Heads the Joint Financial and Economic Department of the Special Area. Chief of the Organizational Department of the Central Committee of the CCP. His pseudonym is Liao Chen-yun.

Chu Teh was born in Szechwan in a poor farmer's family in 1886. Finished a military school. In 1922 he went to Germany, where he studied at Göttingen University. While abroad he met Chou En-lai. His political activities led to his ouster from Germany back to China via the Soviet Union. In 1927 he was in command of troops which took part in the uprising in Nanchang. In 1928 he joined the peasant armed units of Mao Tse-tung in the Chingkangshan Mountains and was put in command of the joint Army—a beginning of the Chinese Red Army.

Lo Fu (Chang Wen-tien) was born in 1900, in the family of a well-to-do local official in Kiangsu province. Finished an engineering school in Nanking and later paid his way through the University of California in the United States. On his return from the United States he took up translation into Chinese of Western and Russian classical writers. In 1925 he joined the CCP on the recommendation of Chen Yun. In 1926 he went to the Sun Yat-sen University in Moscow. In 1930 he returned to China. A member of the Politburo since January 1931. In Yenan he is the chief lecturer of the CCP Central Committee in the local Higher Party School. A capable journalist. As general secretary of the Central Committee, he is, officially, Mao Tse-tung's deputy in the party leadership.

Chou En-lai was born in Chekiang province in the family of a big landowner in 1898. Studied at Waseda University in Tokyo and later in Tientsin. He spent six months in jail for taking part in anti-Japanese demonstrations. In 1920 Chou En-lai went to France to advance his education. Here he set up the Paris section of the CCP and took part in the organization of the Union of the Socialist Youth. Visited Britain and studied in Germany for a year. In 1924 Chou En-lai returned to China. A member of the Politburo of the CCP Central Committee since April 1927.

August 16, 1942

While Aleyev and I were waiting for an Informburo front-line news at night, Aleyev said:

"I think that the best of the young people left the Special Area before 1940. Most of those remaining here are college students of petty-bourgeois origin, who came here in 1936 to 1938 when they were not yet twenty. They came to Yenan being bitten by the bug of romanticism and short-lived fanaticism at a time when the anti-Japanese movement was at its highest. Some of the students who were totally unfit for life came here in the hope of being given a chance to study in Yenan for many years and thus be able to lead a secure, though poor, life. Many of the young people joined the CCP in the belief that they would be able to ride the tide of events, that the Communist Party would grow stronger, and that they would thus be able to climb fast.

"In colleges young men and women are getting a taste for long useless meetings and aimless criticism, which often degenerate to mud-slinging. They can make rambling, utterly senseless speeches for hours on end, or spend whole days gossiping.

"Even among themselves, in discussing any subject, they repeat invariably: 'The party has sent me here to do this job. I must do it. I am ready to make any sacrifice in the name of the Chinese Revolution!'

"The students receive no practical knowledge, and their idea of political subjects, foggy as it is, is limited to a set of quotations. In fact, they love to discourse about Marxism-Leninism, quoting passages from their textbooks, without knowing the essence of it.

"Their idea of the history of China and the revolutionary movement is either very foggy or completely nonexistent.

"They know next to nothing even about the Soviet Union: There all people are provided with porridge free of charge, allowed to study at college as long as they wish to, and are not required to work. Many Chinese young men and women are dreaming about going to the Soviet Union in order to study for ten or more years there.

"In spite of their rudimentary knowledge, especially of political and economic disciplines, they love to discourse on any subject and are nursing the hope of taking important posts. At the same time they show contempt for routine work. Few of them would dare to join medical courses or radio operators' courses, for these offer but very scanty prospects for a fast advance.

"Once they find themselves in the Special Area, people are compelled to sever all family and social ties. Correspondence is frowned upon, and, in fact, very few people would dare to correspond with their relatives. Family attachments are regarded as something to be ashamed of and are carefully concealed. With time men grow out of the habit of associating with women. The sight of a man walking and conversing with a woman is an extraordinary occurrence here. A man is allowed to marry only a 'girl from the party.' Married couples do not live together, for each of them is 'registered' at the place of work. They can meet only on Saturdays and often by special permission of the party organization.

"Being carried away by cheap romanticism or by a 'Left' revolutionary phraseology, the young people reject the culture and traditions of the people.

"The time-honored politeness of the Chinese has completely disappeared, giving way to a kind of language and expressions which are not used elsewhere in the country. This jargon is poor, artificial, and rough.

"As a result, working skills are gradually forgotten, except for the compulsory knitting of socks and warm clothes and making patches. It looks like no working habits are necessary if everyone is provided with millet porridge regardless of what he does—works, studies, or just wags his tongue. . . .

"In actual fact, young people receive no speciality after staying in Yenan for many years.

"Putting it mildly, the party cadres brought up in the Special Area have a low standard of basic knowledge. Even the students not always can tell the time; they are on bad terms with arithmetic. Most of the future party workers have no practical experience, have no profession, and suffer from general backwardness. Having a bourgeois mentality, they are dreaming about guiding others and of nothing else.

"People here are apt to hold forth about 'self-sacrifice, the Kuomintang perfidy, and the Japanese bandits,' and are prepared to wait for months until some five-ten Japanese soldiers deign to get out."

All this infuriates Boris Vassilyevich. Nevertheless, I don't share his categorical judgment. I believe that there are many young people in Yenan who are dedicated to the ideals of the revolution, but who have, unfortunately, been indoctrinated with stultifying, mind-boggling propaganda and are doomed to indolence. I feel sick seeing these young people being compelled to do so much useless cramming which paralyzes any independent thinking.

Had they found themselves in another situation, they would have shown feats of heroism and would do any hard work for the good of their country without a murmur.

I saw for myself how courageously the Chinese Army fought against the Japanese in the first years of the war.

Poorly trained and corrupted by the roguery of the officials and generals, with no arms to speak of, the Army managed to stand up to the Japanese. It was thanks to the pressure of the best part of the Chinese population that the united anti-Japanese front had been formed then.

It is clear to me that most of the young people in Yenan are truly devoted to their country. As for corruption, this kind of filth can breed in any conditions.

August 18, 1942

In July one more Japanese infantry division was moved to Manchuria. The flow of arms and matériel for the Kwantung Army is continuing, and so is the air lift of troops toward the Soviet border. Work has begun on the construction of the Dairen-Harbin highway. Highways and dirt roads in the border area are being repaired.

A tank army unit is being formed there.

In some sectors the Japanese are bringing their troops directly to the Soviet border.

Thus the Kwantung Army is being enlarged and strengthened.

Instead of the customary morning greeting, Hsiao Li exclaimed from the threshold: "At this rate your troops will soon be pushed back right to the Urals!" He ran up to me and smiling unctuously, began to question me about when the Russians were going to stop the German advance.

I said: "Comrade Hsiao Li, it was no easy job to rout the Germans at Moscow in 1941, either, but we did it. I am sure that we shall stand up to their pressure this time, too. The Germans have their front line and their communications stretched dangerously thin. On its retreat the Soviet Army is preparing the necessary conditions for the future decisive rout of the Nazis. . . ."

There was nothing else I could say. I do not doubt even for a moment that the victory will be ours, but men like Hsiao Li have every reason for being spiteful. As a matter of fact, he and others of his ilk are likewise indifferent to the woes of their own people. . . .

Yuzhin, Aleyev, and I have decided to move to Ta-pien-kou (which is the Chinese for "great comfort"). This will save us much time. We will be close to Yang-chia-lin (the residence of the Chairman of the CCP Central Committee) and to the city itself.

Kang Sheng has satisfied our request. By the beginning of October we shall have caves dug out for us there.

August 22, 1942

American General Joseph Stilwell has been appointed chief of staff of the allied armed forces in the Far East. The generals in Chungking are thoroughly displeased with the Americans nosing in the affairs of their general staff. The strongest opposition to Stilwell comes from Ho Ying-chin, the War Minister of the Central Government.

Ho Ying-chin has been Chiang Kai-shek's close assistant for many years. He received his military education in Japan.

August 28, 1942

In today's news from the front Stalingrad has been mentioned for the first time. The Germans have made it to the Volga after all. Fierce fighting has broken out in the northwestern part of the city.

———

Su Fei, Ma Hai-te's wife, and Chiang Ching, Mao Tse-tung's wife, are friends. I often see them walking together. Su Fei spends much time in Chiang Ching's quarters.

Chiang Ching loves horseback riding.

———

Chen Po-ta is Mao Tse-tung's secretary. He is an uncouth-looking individual with glasses, running to fat, with incongruously large ears and deep-set eyes. From my personal observations and also from what I hear from my friends, Chen Po-ta is a clever and talented person. Unlike Kang Sheng, he is sociable and has many friends. He can create an impression of benevolence and affability.

Chen Po-ta was born in the province of Fukien in 1904. In the 1920s he completed his studies at the Sun Yat-sen University in Moscow. Being endowed with outstanding literary talents, he wrote many articles on the theory of Marxism in the 1930s and taught philosophy in Peiping. Chen Po-ta is also the author of a number of books.

In 1937 he came to Yenan where he has remained since, lecturing at the local Party School. For a poorly educated man like Mao Tse-tung, Chen Po-ta is invaluable, especially because Chen Po-ta can "digest" and present in suitable form any of his patron's ideas.

August 30, 1942

Despite the many years of civil war, the weakness of the proletariat, and the opportunistic mistakes of some of its leaders, the Chinese Communist Party was still at the head of the revolutionary movement. This is the result of the influence exerted by the ideas of the October Revolution, the result of the heroic struggle of the Chinese Communists. In the face of the difficult conditions the CCP continued to fight for the liberation of its people from feudal, capitalist, and foreign domination. The working people of China regard the CCP as an exponent of the principles of the October Revolution. They have faith in the party. . . .

I have noticed that at all my meetings with Mao Tse-tung his retinue tries hard to look gay and at the same time courageous in a naïve sort of way when they pass judgment on the complicated events of the day. In this respect, nobody could beat Teng Fa, Jen Pi-shih, and Hsiao Ching-kuang.

Their brash behavior offsets the stiff modesty of Mao Tse-tung. On such occasions he is always in the midst of this noisy crowd, listening silently to whatever is taking place around him.

In the evening Mao Tse-tung invited Aleyev and myself to call on him. Judging by the flushed faces of the members of the Politburo, I realized that they had just been in conference and that the session had been far from peaceful. The invitation struck me as unusual because it was not accompanied by the usual dry official ceremonies.

Besides the stiff bearing which is meant to inspire awe in the visitors, Mao Tse-tung has another, purely Chinese way about him. This time he asked us solicitously about our health and about our needs, seated me into the leather armchair which is usually reserved for guests of honor, then he himself brought rice, khanja, and tea. Chiang Ching moved up the beach chair and he stretched on it by our side. The guard handed him a cup of khanja, and Chiang Ching dropped a few peanuts into his hand.

We asked him what he thought about a possible Japanese attack on the Soviet Union and about the CCP's attitude to such a war. Mao Tse-tung replied absent-mindedly, "Of course we shall conduct operations against the Japanese."

The question obviously rubbed him the wrong way. Mao Tse-tung tried to conceal his irritation with a vagrant smile and proceeded to expound the current tasks of the CCP:

"All that does not contribute to unity must be destroyed. We must banish complaisance and excoriate the unhealthy style." (He failed to elucidate this point.) "It is necessary to check on the probity of the personnel and to judge it on the merit of their work," etc.

Sitting left of me was Kang Sheng. From time to time I looked at this bespectacled man with a receding hairline and thin tightly pressed lips and thought about the tremendous power he had and the authority he exercised over so many human lives. . . .

Mao Tse-tung suddenly fell silent and ordered that pimiento pepper be brought in. We took it as a sign that the official part of the meeting was over. Mao Tse-tung pointed at me, and a plate loaded with red pimientos was passed to me first. A similar plate was given to Mao Tse-tung.

Mao Tse-tung bolted the pepper and, stretching in his chair, threw his questions: "Is Stalin a revolutionary? Does he like red pepper? A genuine revolutionary must eat red pepper. . . ." He sipped out of his jug and remarked, "Alexander the Great adored red pepper for sure. He was a great man and a revolutionary in his own right. As for Stalin, he surely eats pepper, too. You must also eat pepper, Sung Ping. Come on, do, if you are a revolutionary. . . ."

Mao Tse-tung put away one pod after another, washing it down with khanja. One must admire his strong head, which can carry so much alcohol.

Kang Sheng was in raptures over Mao Tse-tung. Squirming and smiling from cheek to cheek he noisily inhaled the air. . . .

After a while Mao Tse-tung's face became as red as the pepper on our plates. . . .

Chiang Ching kept putting on Gramophone records. . . .

We were joined by Wang Chia-hsiang. The conversation now drifted to the current events.

Wang Chia-hsiang and Kang Sheng took a jibe at our often fruitless efforts to study their information, which by all standards can hardly satisfy anyone: scant and false. . . .

About an hour and a half later Mao Tse-tung turned logy. He

yawned and stretched in his beach chair. Chiang Ching put on a Gramophone record of an ancient Chinese opera—Mao Tse-tung nodded approval and began clapping his hands by way of accompaniment. His slow and measured clapping gradually put him to sleep.

September 1942

September 1, 1942

Orlov insists on the building of a new operating room: a stone annex in front of the cave. He avails himself of the fact that all prominent CCP workers are under his medical observation. Chiang Ching is an enthusiastic patient of his. He tries to convince everyone of the need for a new operating room. . . .

Due to the shortage of instruments, laboratory equipment, and medicines, Orlov has to make the most of his skill, the more so that the Chinese doctors envy him and are reluctant to help.

Yet, Orlov hopes to overcome this atmosphere of mistrust and train skilled surgeons and nurses. . . .

September 2, 1942

Disconcerting news from Moscow. All of us have lost peace of mind. One constantly hears Dolmatov being pestered with questions: "What are the reports?" "How's Stalingrad?"

A difficult summer. Seems there is no end to grief and misfortune. . . .

Foreign broadcasts are chary of information on China. Here this is attributed to severe censorship by Chiang Kai-shek. . . .

The Tokyo radio calls the Chungking Government "nationalistic," and Chiang Kai-shek a "nationalist."

A tank army comprising three tank divisions has been formed in Manchuria. This is the first tank army of the Japanese.

Yang Shang-kun is one of Wang Ming's adherents. A former secretary of the North China Bureau of the CCP Central Committee (1934), he now heads the United Front Department of the Central Committee. A native of Szechwan.

Against the cheng-feng background, the ideological struggle in the Politburo acquires a specific character. Mao Tse-tung accuses Wang Ming, Po Ku, Lo Fu, and others of "dogmatism"—the mechanical transferring of the experience of Marxism-Leninism without consideration for Chinese reality. Chu Teh and Lin Po-chu share in the main the views of the "Moscow opposition." Unfortunately no details are known about this struggle. . . .

Among "dogmatists" Mao Tse-tung includes Communists who had studied in the Soviet Union and who were responsible for political work in the party, as well as party intellectuals guided in their work by the experience of the AUCP(B).

Cheng-feng acquires an embittered character. Now people not only learn documents coming from above by rote but also abuse "dogmatists," although their names are concealed from the rank-and-file party members.

September 6, 1942

The rear of the Japanese Army is oriented not on Japan, but on the war arsenal of Manchuria. This turns the Kwantung troops into a mighty independent force.

The Japanese military youth are subjected to intensive indoctrination in the spirit of the ancient *bushido* ("way of the warrior")—the ethical code of Japanese in war. All Japanese military instructions, directions, and regulations, and the behavior of a soldier in general, are determined by the commandments of this medieval code.

Bushido plays a decisive role in developing the moral make-up of the Japanese soldier. One of *bushido*'s main commandments is absolute obedience and scorn for death.

To be taken prisoner is not only a disgrace to a soldier. A war prisoner disgraces his entire nation and, of course, his Mikado.

In most cases Japanese war prisoners refuse to admit that they were captured. They "lost their way" or "were prevented from offering resistance," while they themselves did not "lay down arms," etc.

The city of Hsinking is the capital of the Manchukuo state. Hsinking is also the site of Kwantung Army headquarters.

Manchuria is a huge proving ground. Untrained contingents of soldiers arriving from Japan are constantly trained here. From here trained troops are sent to the South Seas and new troops arrive in their stead.

Now the Kwantung force is in top combat readiness.

According to Aleyev, some enemy grouping is operating in the Special Area. I think the matter is much more serious. Besides, I cannot be satisfied with such a vague definition. If this is a hostile grouping, then what are its composition, aims, and methods of operation?

Cheng-feng extols, in every possible way, the services of Mao Tse-tung. Thanks to Mao Tse-tung, "The party holds high the banner of the revolution," "The chief revolutionary bases and the cadre of the party have been preserved," "A single anti-Japanese front has been set up," and "A new revolutionary theory has been worked out" (this refers to Mao Tse-tung's work *On New Democracy*); that is, "The role of the party in the present historical stage has been correctly defined."

At meetings people are told that:

Mao Tse-tung "has defined the new role of the petty and middle national bourgeoisie as a patriotic element and formulated the principles of new democratism."

Mao Tse-tung "saved the Red Army from being defeated by the Kuomintang," etc.

September 9, 1942

Liberation Daily has published an editorial attributed to Mao Tse-tung. Evidently, it has been put together as usual by his scholarly secretary Chen Po-ta. In his time Chen Po-ta had incurred a penalty from the Comintern Executive Committee for propagating Trotskyism. . . .

September 12, 1942

I have translated an article from *Liberation Daily* entitled "A Political Measure of Exceptional Importance." This is an appeal to engage with greater enthusiasm in cheng-feng, and not only in the Special Area, but at all the Communist bases. The report abounds in quotations from ancient Chinese classical authors (the "classical" style of Mao Tse-tung, precisely mastered by Chen Po-ta) and discourse on the necessity of routing the Japanese.

I take down another document which was handed over to me by the Comintern Executive Committee for correct orientation in the Yenan situation:

"In January 1930 the Comintern Executive Committee received the report of Ching Yi-sung, 'On the Discussion About the Red Army of Chu Teh and Mao Tse-tung':

"Chu Teh was subjected to severe criticism (for the defeat in south Hunan), and Mao Tse-tung, knowing that the defeat had greatly impaired Chu Teh's prestige, tried to capitalize on this to give Chu Teh's authority a final blow. . . .

"Mao Tse-tung wants to concentrate all power in his own hands, and, of course, being keen on this, he cannot cope with the situation. As for Chu Teh, he is fully aware of this but does not want to interfere with Mao. . . .

"Chu Teh declares that Mao Tse-tung is to blame for everything. It is difficult to say who is right and who is wrong, but it should be noted that the masses at any rate are not satisfied with Mao Tse-tung. . . .

"Mao Tse-tung has a definite view on many points. As for Chu Teh, his views often change. . . .

"Mao Tse-tung's negative features: not popular with the masses and is maneuvering in the party . . ."

Chu Teh is much too popular. And Mao Tse-tung has been looking for a chance to discredit him. However, this is not a matter of likes and dislikes. Power over the Army—this was the aim of Mao Tse-tung. This becomes clear when one compares the documents of the Comintern Executive Committee with real facts.

Mao Tse-tung could not vie with Chu Teh's military talent, for he himself had none. Besides, Mao Tse-tung cuts a poor figure side by side with the famous commander. That sends him trying to promote new military leaders in every way. Thus, Lin Piao has been promoted from a company commander to a corps commander within a few years.

According to Mao Tse-tung himself, *Great Heroes of the World* was one of his favorite books in his youth. He admires famous conquerors, kings, and all who were able to gain a firm foothold at the top of the "human pyramid."

September 14, 1942

Judging by its disposition, the Japanese tank army is intended for action in the Primorye Line (to seize Khabarovsk). General Yoshida is in command of the Army.

Headquarters of the Kwantung Army has been transformed into Front Headquarters with three sectors to mind (Transbaikalia, Primorye, and along the Sungari River).

General Yamashita, one of the most experienced Japanese military commanders, noted for his seizure of Singapore and other successful operations in the South Seas, is to command one of the key sectors. This fact is highly significant.

Manchuria is crammed with Japanese troops and matériel.

The Kurils, Sakhalins, and Manchuria—a gigantic line of Japanese forces deployed against the Soviet Union. And this deployment has been completed.

Kenji Doihara is a notorious Japanese agent, one of the most sinister figures in the world history of intelligence service. A cruel, cunning, and insidious organizer of literally all the provocations against the Soviet Union.

His aim in life is to weaken the might of the Soviet Union. All the eastern Russian lands between the ocean and the Urals must belong to Japan—this is the political credo of this Lawrence of Japan. He has reared and guides the activities of the White Guard bands of Semyonov, Kiselev, Radziyevsky, and Ukhtomsky. Through these bands he actively recruits his agents. . . .

This is the Doihara who during the years of the Civil War left a bloody trail in our Far East.

And like a watchdog, nearly all his life the general hangs around the Soviet borders.

I have seen Doihara's photo. A smug butcher, of middle height, thick-set, wears glasses . . .

September 15, 1942

From the way things stand the Germans aim their main blow at Stalingrad.

Foreign radio stations repeat Hitler's braggadocio that the city on the Volga will succumb to the German soldier within the next twenty-four hours. Many commentators link this with the final defeat of the Soviet Union and the establishing of a bastard state similar to Vichy France.

The Chinese fronts show no essential changes. Evidently both sides consider that the summer campaign is over. Separate encounters take place for more advantageous positions.

The British radio continues to express anxiety about the disorders in India. The police constantly employ arms to break up demonstrations. Gandhi is anathematized by the colonialists. . . .

We keep diaries, memo books, and papers in the radio room. I don't trust our guards and the superintendent Cheng.

Our opinions of Cheng have divided. Yuzhin thinks he is an honest man. Dolmatov, Rimmar, Orlov, and I are sure that the superintendent is Kang Sheng's informer.

We keep the radio room locked, and one of us is always in the house.

I am astonished at the endurance of the radiomen. The boys transmit our exceptionally long reports sometimes for hours on end.

Everything here in Yenan convinces me that the secret political processes in the CCP leadership have entered a new phase. This political phase is stimulated by the weakening of Comintern's role due to the World War and the difficult situation of the Soviet Union. One should not be hasty with conclusions. I can be completely frank only with my diary. Facts first of all, then analysis. However, the trend of the analysis is already becoming clear.

When dawn breaks, I leave for the front with Aleyev. It is necessary to verify on the spot the nature of combat operations of the Eighth Route Army.

September 1942

It took us ten days to reach Ho Lung's headquarters.

Here and there the path was so narrow that we had to dismount and lead the horses by the bridle. Frail bridges were thrown across precipices. The path was strewn with rock debris. Rockfalls kill many people in these parts.

The only way to get to some temples is by steps hewn in rock. These steeply ascending pathways are hundreds of meters long.

On the way, we startled hares, foxes, wild hogs, wild goats, and jackals. Herds of wild hogs took to flight. . . .

I preferred sleeping outdoors. The mountains were full of bandits and it was cold there, but at least there were no vermin. Mats in roadside eating places were crawling with lice and fleas. The itching was a curse. We would buy *pai-kan* and rub it on to relieve the itch. Sleep was out of the question.

The place had more than its share of bandits and other riffraff. Many gangs pass themselves off as guerrillas. These gangs, like the Japanese, terrorize the population.

The organization of the partisan movement is poor. Many large partisan detachments still have no reliable contact with the center, although the war has been raging for many years.

The poverty and illiteracy of the peasants are astounding. Requisitions, the war, the tiny plots of land, do not let them make both ends meet. A hand-to-mouth existence. All their meager possessions are in ramshackle huts. They sleep naked on a kang and cover themselves with lice-ridden rags. There is hardly a family that does not stupefy itself with opium. Literally all children suffer from worms, gastric diseases, rickets, and terrifying skin diseases.

I saw villages whose entire population was infected with trachoma, leprosy, syphilis. We bypassed regions swept by smallpox and typhus.

Superstition is rife. Sorcery is a respected profession, and amulets to exorcise devils are in general use.

Marriage of persons far apart in age is legal. Their purpose is to get more working hands. I saw an eight-year-old bridegroom and a twenty-year-old bride.

Confucius preached obedience to the father, the husband, and the elder son if there is no father. The obedience of children is beyond question. The Chinese family is a domestic community. The heritage is equally allotted to the sons.

Buffalo is the main draft animal in the village. It is used for riding, plowing land, and carrying loads.

The hardiness of the Chinese is incredible. The peasants labor all day long without a break, on poor nourishment. Death at thirty to forty is commonplace. Drudgery has been the lot of everyone since childhood.

I also visited places where peasants had forgotten when they had had enough food. The most common food is the dish called *ku-tsai*.

Over the relatively small territory comprising the Special Area there is a confusion of religions: Catholicism, Buddhism, Taoism, Islam. . . . What a tremendous variety of nationalities: the Chinese, the Kirghiz, the Uigurs, the Mongols, the Tibetans . . .

Confucianism has had a tremendous influence on the mentality and way of thinking of the Chinese people. Its simplest practical application is the edifying inscriptions on the walls of temples.

Confucianism is a chauvinistic philosophy. Government officials, teachers, emperors, historians, and poets have been brought up on the famous Four Books of Confucius. . . .

I saw streams with a lot of oil in the water. People scooped up the water with discarded tins to filter off some of the oil. The oil so obtained is used in lamps. Candles are a luxury which only the party functionaries in Yenan can afford.

There are over 2 million acres of arable land in the Special Area. The harvest is 14 million poods of cereals and legumes. The extraction of salt in lakes is a considerable help. Small spinning and papermaking mills and coal mines employ more than four thousand workers.

Support of the population for the CCP is feeble and directly depends on the land policy. The political work among the masses is formal and primitive. Even in Yenan I saw people readily fall for sensational and provocative rumors. The situation is even worse in the Godforsaken localities we are passing through. . . .

The refugees have reached the outer limits of exhaustion. They go about begging, offering a daughter or a sister for a tiny measure of rice. There is despair in their eyes. . . . Some are digging for edible roots. . . .

I will never forget an old peasant. The Japanese destroyed his village and killed off the population. He managed to escape with his grandson by sheer chance.

"Why don't their mothers lose milk?" he asked whenever there was mention of the Japanese.

The Army doesn't get a cent from Yenan, and it doesn't provide any supplies. Besides the troops and territories they control, Ho Lung, Liu Po-cheng, Nieh Jung-chen, Cheng Kuang, and Hsiao Ko have their own industrial arsenals and issue their own money. Each commander imposes his own tax on the peasants. There is no single system of taxation.

Old arms are repaired here in workshops; several discarded rifles are taken to pieces to assemble one good rifle. Production of grenades and mines is well organized. Metal for their casings is produced in primitive furnaces.

Army leadership is not free from feudal survivals. I got acquainted with a commander who has two very young wives, almost girls. And no one seems to be outraged.

The commanders and their deputies report to Yenan by telegraph to the extent they consider fit. Directives issued by the center are discussed from the viewpoint of their expediency, and not as to whether they should be fulfilled. The commanders disdainfully refer to the leading Yenan comrades as "scribblers."

Among the troops there is an atmosphere of indolence, waiting for the events to take their course. No one sincerely helped us get information about the combat actions. We were met affably, but then they immediately sought to get rid of us. . . .

The Eighth Route Army peaceably coexists with the enemy. The Japanese had comfortably settled for the winter in built-up areas (we stayed well out of their reach as we went by). Meanwhile, the Eighth Army's units idled their time away in the vicinity.

In the area of Hsin-hsiang very small Japanese garrisons, of five to forty soldiers, occupy villages which are invested by the numerically superior forces of Ho Lung. I asked why they did not recapture the villages, since it was easy to destroy the punitive forces. The men of the Eighth Route Army watched them have a good time. I was corrected: "They have four hundred soldiers there, not four!"

We dismounted, had a smoke with the men, and they admitted, "We are told not to touch them. If we destroy the garrison, they tell us, the Japanese will bring in reinforcements. What's to be done then? So we do not touch them and they don't touch us. . . ."

The men wear puttees, caps, service jackets, or short coats. They are sun-tanned and lean. Courageous, energetic faces . . .

The Mauser pistol is everybody's favorite weapon.

The invaders carry part of the harvest to Japan; they also ship out industrial raw materials, obviously without paying for anything.

The Japanese have the run of the place. They treat the Chinese as an inferior race. Use them as draft cattle. The Japanese rape women and force them to live with them. They maltreat the people with impunity, kill them for the slightest disobedience.

Rear areas are dotted with brothels, swarming with black marketeers and bandits.

Race propaganda has taken root in the mentality of the Japanese youth. Everything that is not Japanese is ruthlessly destroyed and ruined here. Even in the brothels catering for the occupiers the race principle is strictly observed. The women provided for the soldiers are all Japanese.

The war against the invaders is of a markedly passive character.

One cannot help feeling that the Eighth Route Army awaits the outcome of the struggle between Nazi Germany and the Soviet Union and that here, in the Special Area, people are indifferent to the struggle of the Soviet people.

The CCP leadership do not take effective measures to tie down the Japanese expeditionary force in the north of the country. This is an indisputable fact. All requests by Moscow to the CCP leadership to use any means to impede Japan's preparations for war against the Soviet Union went unheeded. The policy of Yenan is the same: to reduce the scope of operations by the Eighth Route Army's regular units.

As we could see, the Kuomintang forces are the main concern of the Eighth Route Army. Propaganda in the units is spearheaded against them; combat actions are also expected against them in the future. Consequently, nearly all operations undertaken by the Japanese are successful. Yenan has ordered the preservation of the personnel of the Eighth Route Army at all costs, so the Army is backing away, although the forces of the advancing enemy are insignificant.

Mao Tse-tung doctrine: The war is waged to preserve his own man power, not to exterminate the enemy. It is achieved by slackening resistance to the enemy and by yielding more territory.

The years of inactivity have had a degrading influence on the armed forces of the CCP. Discipline is slack, and cases of desertion have become more frequent. The men neglect their weapons. Training in the units and in staffs is not organized. Co-operation between the units is not organized. Staff officers play cards and gossip. Operational orders are issued in the presence of peasants.

Here, in the mountains of northern China, the fighting spirit is incomparably below that of our Red Army. The military specifics and the fighting ability of the Chinese soldier are not in question; courage and endurance have always been his mark. The reckless policy of unleashing a civil war is to blame. The armed forces of the CCP are at present unable to fight the vastly superior Kuomintang forces.

The tearful talk about the stringent blockade of the Special Area is a propaganda hoax started by Kang Sheng. It is very easy to cross both the front line and the border of the Special Area. We have seen this for ourselves. By talking of severe isolation the CCP leadership add fictitious difficulties to real ones.

A trip to the front left me firmly convinced that the CCP leadership do not intend to fight the Japanese; they regard the war as an opportune period for setting up their own bases. And not by their forces, but by those of the other contending parties: the Japanese and the Kuomintang.

If the Japanese inflict a defeat on the Kuomintang and the power of the Central Government is undermined, the Eighth Route Army's units immediately penetrate the area in question. If necessary, they finish off their comrades-in-arms in the single anti-Japanese front and seize power.

Retreating in face of the invaders, Mao Tse-tung is looking for a chance to turn the clashes between the forces of the Central Government and the Japanese to his advantage. At a time of national disaster, when the people suffer privation and make untold sacrifices, and when the country is subjugated by the fascists, this tactic is more than perfidious.

Of what internationalist policy can one speak to Mao Tse-tung when even his own people are merely tools in the struggle for power! Blood and suffering, woes and tribulations of millions, are to him abstract notions.

Oh, the role of an individual in history! How often do we oversimplify it.

October 1942

October 21, 1942

Wang Ming is sick. Orlov is worried.

Wang Chia-hsiang has also fallen ill.

Wang Chia-hsiang is drawn by Mao Tse-tung's group, but he can't stand Kang Sheng. He is not at all kind to us.

Wang Chia-hsiang's friend Chen Yun is also being increasingly influenced by Kang Sheng. "Influenced" is not the word—both are clearly being terrorized by Kang Sheng!

The role played by Liu Shao-chi is growing fast. Once an obscure military commissar in the New Fourth Army, he is now becoming second to Mao Tse-tung and the actual conductor of Mao's ideas in cheng-feng. He drafts the most important documents. He has to be reckoned with by the Politburo members and high-ranking military officials.

There is an article on the battle of Stalingrad in *Liberation Daily*. Though ascribed to Mao Tse-tung, it is sure to have been written, as usual, by Chen Po-ta. . . .

If Russia holds out and routs Germany, this will also affect the situation in the Far East—such is the essence of the article.

". . . Anyone who is pessimistic in his appraisal of the international situation must change his point of view," admits the author.

So, keep in alignment with the Soviet Union—just in case!

From now on, Yuzhin, Aleyev, and I shall be living in caves, like all local Chinese.

As one climbs up the narrow steep footpath, one reaches the first ledge with the caves of party functionaries, students, and military men.

Our "suite" is on the next ledge. Beyond the ledge is a deep gorge.

The footpath goes on to the last tier of caves. The poet Emi Siao and other Chinese comrades live there.

Emi Siao was Mao Tse-tung's classmate at the district school in Hsiang-tang.

Mao Tse-tung includes in the "party opposition" both the "dogmatists" and the "empiricists." The difference between "empiricists" and "dogmatists" is hard to grasp, even when Mao Tse-tung explains it. Mao Tse-tung regards as "empiricists" Liu Po-cheng, Peng Teh-huai, Yeh Chien-ying, Chou En-lai, Nieh Jung-chen. . . .

Sports contests were held here in September. Among their organizers were Yeh Chien-ying, Hsu Teh-li, Wang Shih-tai, Wang Ho-shou, and Li Fu-chun (a zealous football player in his time).

October 22, 1942

The agrarian policy at this stage:

—Refusal for the time being to expropriate the landlords' property. Land is requisitioned only from traitors to the country.

—The organization of liberated areas in the rear of the Japanese, if this does not involve major military actions.

—Reduction of rent for land and interest on loans in all liberated areas.

Mao Tse-tung says that the united anti-Japanese front should be strengthened, exposing at the same time the treacherous acts of the Chungking reactionaries.

According to Mao Tse-tung, it was in the interests of the united anti-Japanese front that the Communist Party replaced the slogan of a democratic republic of workers and peasants with the slogan of a people's republic in which power will be in the hands of the workers, peasants, and national bourgeoisie. This is in the interests of the anti-Japanese struggle.

As far as I know this is the tactic of the Communist International, the very tactic which Mao Tse-tung is clearly subverting now.

It was on the Comintern's recommendation that an agreement between the Chinese Communist Party and the Kuomintang was concluded in September 1937.

These recommendations of the Comintern also took account of the fact that the national bourgeoisie was frightened by the Japanese aggression and began to fight it.

Mao Tse-tung uses the outwardly correct analysis and recommendations of the Comintern to cover up his efforts to break up the united anti-Japanese front. In word he is for unity, yet in deed unity is rejected, military actions are curtailed, and anti-Kuomintang slogans are put forward.

October 23, 1942

In September Ho Lung openly spoke at a meeting of the inevitability of a breakup with the Kuomintang and the need to prepare for action, for capturing territory and valuables; this, he said, is not realized by the "dogmatists" "who have partly received their due and who should be finally brought to heel. . . ."

Ho Lung is politically illiterate. He had been instructed by Mao Tse-tung.

Ho Lung is commander of the 120th Infantry Division, a hero and very popular in the Army. He comes from the same province as Mao Tse-tung and enjoys his trust.

Ho Lung is kind but morbidly ambitious, and Mao Tse-tung uses this to his own advantage.

In point of fact Ho Lung is a local militarist, and he makes no secret of it. At present he is chief of the joint staff of the Special Area troops and is quartered on the other side of Yenan, near the Western Gates.

Li Feng is military commissar of the 120th Infantry Division.

Chou En-lai is listed with the "empiricists." He spends all his time in Chungking.

Our caves are a row of large burrows in the mountain.

The entrance is boarded up, with a cloth curtain in place of a door and the windows pasted up with paper.

The storage of my notes presents quite a problem.

I suffer from exhausting stomach pains after the amoebic dysentery which I had during my trip to Ho Lung's 120th Infantry Division. I am writing with my vision blurred.

October 25, 1942

Comparison of data produces most disheartening results. There is no active military action on the part of the Eighth Route Army! What is more, such actions are strictly prohibited.

The leadership of the Chinese Communist Party continues to deceive Moscow by feigning readiness to fight the Japanese.

In his struggle with his political opponents Mao Tse-tung makes use of his work *On New Democracy,* which serves as a kind of platform for a whole group of his adherents. At this stage one can definitely speak of the division of political forces. Jen Pi-shih, Li Feng, Chen Yun, Wang Chia-hsiang, and, of course, Kang Sheng (here I mention only the most prominent representatives of the group) in general follow the line of the Chairman of the Central Committee of the Chinese Communist Party, as laid down in his work *On New Democracy.*

A thorough analysis of this work leaves no doubt that the Chairman of the Central Committee is against an anti-Japanese bloc and the adjustment of relations with the Chungking Government. Mao Tse-tung's position weakens the resistance to the aggressor and fragmentizes the forces.

That is why anti-Kuomintang propaganda is being constantly conducted in the Special Area.

All these circumstances make one take a fresh view of the tragic end of the New Fourth Army and the unceasing discord between the Communist Party and the Kuomintang.

The views of the Chairman of the CCP Central Committee are not shared by everyone. Some time ago Wang Ming, the prominent internationalist and leader of the Chinese delegation at the Comintern Executive, rallied round himself Chu Teh, Chou En-lai, Po Ku, Lo Fu, and, I think, a number of prominent military officials who are now in the active Army. . . .

The Kuomintang's proposals are rejected under various pretexts. Chiang Kai-shek's proposal of July 14 about a meeting with Mao Tse-tung has in effect been declined.

In military matters Mao Tse-tung and his entourage are for the "man power preservation" tactics, which means curtailment of the combat actions.

October 26, 1942

Mao Tse-tung is getting more and more rude to his opponents.

When, during an argument, one of them referred to an article by Stalin, Mao Tse-tung cried, "It's just like you, 'Muscovites'—if Stalin chooses to break wind, you are prepared to sniff and admire it!"

But in our presence Mao lavishes praise on Stalin. There is a reason for this—he hopes that I will pass it on to Moscow. Stalin's favor spells great benefits for Mao Tse-tung in the future.

I got acquainted with Wang Cheng. He suffers from a stomach condition and takes treatment from Orlov.

Wang Cheng is commander of the 359th Infantry Brigade and the temporary commandant of the city of Yenan. This young and capable commander initiated the introduction of a constant combat training in the Army. His troops are the best in the Special Area.

Wang Ming is in very poor health. His wife is worried.

Wang Ming is under observation of the Chinese doctors who attend to the leading figures of the CCP Central Committee.

October 30, 1942

Mao Tse-tung and his followers underestimate the military might of the Soviet Union and overestimate Germany's successes. Hence their conclusions on the possible defeat of the Soviet Union and, as a consequence, the refusal of the Eighth Route and New Fourth armies to fight the Japanese; they imply that their views are another proof of the correctness of the theory of preserving man power at any cost. Even at the cost of treachery, it seems.

Everybody is cramming party documents and indulges in self-flagellation, which is both tragic and comical. . . .

Mao Tse-tung explained to me that "empiricists" in the Chinese Communist Party are practical workers from among industrial workers and peasants who share to a varying extent the views of the "dogmatic grouping of Wang Ming and Po Ku." As he said that, he was obviously irritated.

Wang Ming is representative of the Central Committee of the Chinese Communist Party at the Comintern and member of the

Comintern Executive Presidium. To attack him openly would mean to disparage the Comintern's line. This ticklish situation makes Mao Tsetung angry. He would have crushed another opponent long ago.

Mao Tse-tung can hardly stand Po Ku, especially for the latter's indifference to Mao's "services to the party" and his independent manner.

The label of "dogmatism" helps to settle accounts with the "Wang Ming–Po Ku group" without formally attacking the Comintern's policy.

The freshly dug cave smells of damp and mold. The light barely filters in through the tiny papered-up window. . . .

I go outside to shave. Our cook, a young *hsiao-kuei,* is pottering around our improvised stoves, a huge Mauser pistol dangling from his belt.

November 1942

November 4, 1942

During our night vigil at the radio set Aleyev once again spoke much and with resentment.

"All of us are under observation," he said. "The superintendent and the interpreters are Kang Sheng's informers. They spy on us in the house and shadow us in the streets.

"Ever since our arrival the attitude toward us has been one of condescension, and now it is hostile. At first this was veiled by a show of politeness; now we come up against open insolence. Kang Sheng has a hand in this: Everyone fears him and tries to please him.

"They reckoned with us when we came here. The CCP leadership was out to get the latest armaments and other equipment from the Soviet Union. Then the Great Patriotic War broke out. There were not enough arms for our Red Army. Relations immediately grew cold and, after our military failures, became openly hostile and rude. . . ."

November 8, 1942

Stalingrad! Radio stations all over the world are lauding its fortitude.

Americans have landed in northern Africa. The road to Berlin is far from short. . . .

The Kwantung Army is marking time. To think of all our cadre divisions that are tied down, when each Red Army soldier counts.

November 11, 1942

From seemingly harmless ideological statements cheng-feng develops into a violent political campaign. Allegedly aimed against "subjectivism," "dogmatism," and "stereotype patterns," it is actually used by Mao Tse-tung's group to suppress all those in the CCP leadership who disagree with its policy.

The movement for the "study of party history" is added to the movement for the "rectification of the three styles." Mao Tse-tung directs his chief blow against the "Moscow group."

Pressure is increased upon all who had worked or studied in Moscow and particularly against those who had been linked with the Comintern. . . .

The working atmosphere becomes more complicated with each hour. In many cases people refuse to talk to us and start back as if we were contagious.

Kang Sheng mockingly palms off false information.

Mao Tse-tung is, as always, polite, cordial, and lavish with promises.

November 12, 1942

Again I have spent several hours looking around Yenan. The day has been drab, windy, and dusty. The outlines of pagodas on the mountaintops were hardly visible, but the central pagoda on the hill near the town wall could be clearly seen from the distance. It is a ten-tier tower in which every tier is crowned with a smartly curved tiled roof.

In times of old, Yenan was a hard nut for its enemies. It is not witnessed by legends only. The town is hidden behind hardly accessible mountains, located in a valley on a rather steep height, and surrounded by a strong wall. Many approaches to the wall are blocked by a mountain river, and the terrain around is smooth.

There are very few trees, with only small gardens in some places which used to belong to the local rich.

The peasants satisfied my curiosity and willingly showed me their meager possessions. Buddhism is a prevailing religious denomination here. There are primitive altars in almost every house. Among various bodhisattvas and buddhas I saw many small bronze figures of the main

Buddha—Sakyamuni—which were extremely elaborately made. I would not resist the temptation and bought one of the figures.

Yang-chia-lin, the current residence of the CCP leadership, was a remote village near Yenan. Outwardly it is the same now.

The first years after the Long March Mao Tse-tung made his appearance in this village or near it. But now we hardly ever see him. . . .

November 14, 1942

The struggle in the CCP between Mao Tse-tung and the "Moscow group" began during the Civil War in China.

At that time Po Ku stood at the head of the party, and Li Teh (Otto Braun) headed the Army.

Profiting by the mistakes made by certain commanders during the Long March, Mao Tse-tung accused Po Ku and Li Teh of these mistakes, succeeded in removing them from their posts, and took charge of the Army, foisting his will upon Chu Teh.

The post of general secretary was given to the more complaisant Lo Fu.

Upon returning from Moscow Wang Ming reported to the Central Committee of the CCP on the need to go over to single-front tactics with the Kuomintang against Japan.

The CCP Central Committee unanimously approved Wang Ming's proposal.

One can assume that from that day Mao Tse-tung has regarded Wang Ming as political adversary number one.

At first the path leading to our caves held me in a state of constant nervous tension. A single meter lay between me and the abyss. I am used to it now and no longer take notice. . . .

The hospital is slightly more than an hour's walk from our caves. It takes less than an hour to get to the radio station. . . .

Ma Hai-te is my neighbor now, and we meet several times a day.

November 19, 1942

Kang Sheng (Kang Hsing) was born in 1899 in Tsingtao in the family of a small landowner and teacher. Completed secondary school.

Member of the CCP from 1924. In 1920 he was a student of the preparatory course at Tsingtao University.

Beginning with the end of 1920 and up till 1923 he worked as a teacher in a rural school in Chu-chiang county (Shantung province). Later a student of Shanghai University. Simultaneously attended extension courses for party leaders set up by the CCP Central Committee. Since 1926 he was secretary of the central and then northern district committee of the CCP in Shanghai.

In March 1927 Kang Sheng headed workers' street fighting during the armed uprising in Shanghai on the eve of the Eighth Route Army's entry into the city.

Beginning with 1928—department chief of the Kiangsu Provincial Committee and member of the Auditing Commission of the CCP Central Committee.

Between 1930 and 1931—chief of Organization Department of the CCP Central Committee.

In 1931 was co-opted into the Central Committee and Politburo of the CCP at the fourth plenum of the CCP Central Committee. Up to 1933 was secretary of the Central Committee and chief of Organization Department of the CCP Central Committee.

In 1933 Kang Sheng attended the plenum of the Comintern Executive. In 1935 was a delegate to the Seventh Comintern Congress.

Between 1933 and 1937 was a permanent member of the CCP delegation to the Comintern Executive.

One begins to understand Mao Tse-tung's enmity to Chen Yun, Hsu Hsien-nien, Li Hsien-nien, and Chen Chang-hao. . . .

They had witnessed Mao's "strategic talents" during the Long March. . . .

November 24, 1942

Kang Sheng holds the post of chief of Ching-pao-chu—head of the Department of Information Service in the Liberated Areas of China, which combines the functions of the intelligence and counterintelligence, justice, the court and the Procurator's Office, and information services. By 1941 Kang Sheng had turned the department into a powerful service, having included into its work many functions of the General Headquarters. The General Headquarters, headed by Yeh Chien-ying, is to a certain extent but a nominal organization.

Kang Sheng heads the Commission for the Review of Party Cadres and Nonparty Personnel. The work of the commission fused with the cheng-feng campaign acquires the most perverted form.

Members of the Commission for the Review of Party Cadres and Nonparty Personnel—Kao Kang, Peng Chen, and Chen Yun—are wholly in the hands and under the influence of Kang. . . .

Today I have been strolling around Yenan with my camera. The entire new district of the town is actually situated between the fortress wall and the river. It is an incredible mixture of shacks, small shops, and chow rooms—all of them made from the remnants of old town structures. Everything here is impregnated with smells of garlic, sheepskin, and all kinds of broths made in chow rooms or right in the street.

I climbed the mountaintops to see the pagodas which surround Yenan like delicate summer houses. The central pagoda, which is a large ten-tier tower, can be easily seen from any spot in the valley. For how many centuries it has been standing above the ancient Yenan!

I am anxious about my family. But I am sure of Maria. We were brought up in poverty. She will see that nothing happens to the children. . . .

I had brought a small volume of Pushkin from Moscow. There was no room for more. That is why there are no other Russian books except for the selected works of Gogol brought here by Dolmatov. Yuzhin never parts with Clausewitz, whom he holds in great esteem. But for the soul there are only the much-worn Pushkin and Gogol.

My eyes smart from the weak light. . . . But I cannot keep from leafing through Pushkin, the only thing to remind me here of my country. . . .

November 25, 1942

Wedges are driven farther and farther into the German rear. If only the fascists would stay put in the "caldron"!

The communiqué reported the particular role of the Sixty-second Army, the direct defender of Stalingrad. V. I. Chuikov is the army commander.

This is the same Chuikov who until recently was Military Attaché in Chungking.

———

In the evenings we reread the theses of the Comintern Executive "On the Military and Political Situation in China as of December 22, 1930." I have brought the document from Moscow.

History repeats itself before our eyes. Not all of us are sure of this, and there is much argument.

. . . Of late a highly critical situation has arisen inside the Chinese Communist Party. According to an assessment made by the Presidium of the Comintern Executive, the history of the Comintern knows no equal precedents for deviations of the kind that have appeared inside the CCP. The subject of the matter is that the Politburo of the CCP Central Committee, following in the tracks of their leader Li Li-san, adopted a position radically different from the general line of the Comintern.

Li Li-san contemplates the victory of the Chinese Revolution only if the revolution succeeds on a world scale. Proceeding from this premise, he demanded that in the interests of the quickest implementation of socialism, the Soviet Union should immediately launch war against Japan, that Mongolia should immediately move its troops against China, and the Soviet Union should arm hundreds of thousands of Chinese workers in Siberia and also send them against China. Simultaneously Li Li-san called for an uprising in all the Chinese cities. With this purpose trade unions, Komsomol, and party organizations were abolished throughout China. Instead, committees of action were set up for the implementation of the uprising.

Despite the defeat of the Red Army at Changsha in August 1930, it was ordered to advance on Changsha, Hankow, and Nanchang.

Protesting against the decisions of the Comintern which denounced such a provocative and anarchist policy, Li Li-san declared that he would speak in a different tone to the Comintern when the Red Army occupied Hankow.

On the decision of the Comintern Executive Committee the third plenum of the CCP Central Committee was convened in October of this year.

Although the members of the Chinese delegation to the Comintern were acquainted with the Comintern's decisions and called Li Li-san a madman, on their return to China they not only refused to uphold the Comintern line, but immediately took up Li Li-san's point of view, explaining their former criticism of his policy by supposedly technical differences with the Comintern's views. . . .

No matter how Maria may have been used to poverty, I am constantly worried. Absolutely alone, in a new place, with two boys on her hands. It was only recently that she had recovered from tuberculosis. If only she would have enough strength to go through all the hardships.

When holidays come, Moscow cables only two phrases: "Your families are alive and well. Send their best wishes."

But what lies behind these words—none of us in Yenan can know. . . .

November 29, 1942

By chance I have seen the "Instructions for Work with Secret Societies," elaborately written by brush, in the possession of Li Ko-nung.

Secret societies embrace both the wealthy strata of urban dwellers and the rural poor. They form a network of well-camouflaged organizations which extends far beyond the borders of China, where its members are Chinese emigrants.

Kang Sheng uses these organizations to perpetrate acts of terrorism, diversion, and espionage. Severe discipline reigns in the secret organizations, and apostates are almost always put to death.

Li Ko-nung arrived in Yenan at the same time as Liu Shao-chi, that is, in 1942 and not in 1941, as I was told before.

In Yenan he leads a secluded life, holding secret meetings and interrogations during the nights. Numerically his guards are second only to those of Mao Tse-tung.

He is a typical feudal lord by nature. When his son happened to disobey him, he drove him from home and never inquired after him again.

Li Ko-nung is a sturdy, heavily built man of middle height, an excellent cavalryman. Yuzhin is acquainted with his daughter.

My meetings with Li Ko-nung leave me with a feeling of discomfort. Such a man is capable of any cruelty.

With the help of his subordinates Kang Sheng keeps all the prominent party and army leaders shadowed and makes wide use of the service personnel as informants and spies.

Heavy frosts and snowstorms rage in Siberia. How is my family getting on?

I know what the Siberian winter is like. In that hungry summer of

1921 we ate grass, oil cake, and roots. My body wasted away until I was all skin and bones. Somehow we managed to reach Siberia. My father sent me out to work as a farm hand for a rich peasant in the village of Bayevo.

My employer would not let me into the house. I slept with the cattle, burying myself into the hay to keep warm. Freezing from the cold, I would get up and nestle up to the cow. How many times the animals had trampled me. . . .

I was covered with boils from head to foot. I suffered from the cold. My voice was hoarse. I was racked by a cough and could not get warm either in the daytime or at night. But I did not dare quit. To quit would mean to starve to death.

December 1942

December 3, 1942

Wang Ming lives near the Women's University. We call his Chinese wife Rosa Vladimirovna, as Russians do.

Po Ku lives near his printing shop, beyond the Eastern Gate. Lo Fu and Wang Chia-hsiang, in Yang-chia-lin, and Chu Teh and Yeh Chien-ying, in Wan-chia-ping.

Kai Feng is the secretary of the Party Bureau of Northwestern Shansi. Is anti-Soviet. A rather eccentric person . . .

Chiang Ching is very friendly. She calls on us and invites us to go horseback riding.

Her original name was Li Yun-hao and her stage name Lan Ping.

She told us, by the way, that she had been born in 1912 in Chucheng (Shantung) in a poor family. Her father had died early and her mother had to hire out as a maid. Her mother adored her and on her miserly earnings managed to provide for her daughter's primary education.

Chiang Ching was seventeen when she entered the Shantung Provincial School under a new name of Lieh Chu-chia. In 1929 she transferred to Tsingtao Institute, determined on a theatrical career. . . .

As far as is known, Chiang Ching was helped along in her career by influential patrons.

Thus, in 1934 she moved with the wealthy Huang Ching to Peiping, where, after meeting Peng Chen, she became involved in revolutionary activities. She acted the part of poor peasant women in plays by contemporary Chinese writers.

Then with Professor Wang Lai-tien of the Shantung Theater School she went to Shanghai.

The professor arranged for her engagement with the Ming Hsing film studios. She appeared in patriotic anti-Japanese films.

Chiang Ching had changed four patrons before she became Mao Tse-tung's consort. Each meant a step higher up the ladder of social hierarchy.

But anyway this is unconfirmed information and possibly inaccurate. . . .

Chiang Ching is always kindly and talkative.

We have formed a definite idea of her, not the one she is trying to impose on us.

Extreme purposefulness is her outstanding quality. She disposes of all the obstacles and is stubbornly climbing to an honorable position in society. Her mind has the upper hand over her temperament. She drives herself without mercy, and her career is her only concern. She is in a hurry to achieve her ends while she is still young. . . .

In 1937 Chiang Ching moved to Chungking with a group of actors. And in 1938 she turned up in Yenan. Here she was treated as no other but a real film star, and here she made her greatest success. . . .

Her husband's whole secret correspondence is in her hands now. She knows all his plans and is worshiped by Kang Sheng. In short, she runs her husband's home office.

We're still having bright, cloudless days. I sweat in my quilted jacket in the sun and freeze in the shade.

At night the temperature drops below zero. The air is crisp and clear. . . .

There is a bottle of alcohol in the far end of my cave. The fiery liquid is for our guests. To preserve it I have to close it with sealing wax every time we use it.

This is nightmare—the level in the sealed bottle drops steadily. . . .

December 6, 1942

The "dogmatists" are accused of the desire to shift the brunt of the revolutionary struggle from the village on to the town and win victory "through the towns."

According to Mao Tse-tung, this is the basic mistake of the "dogmatists."

Mao Tse-tung believes that counterrevolutionary forces have extremely strong positions in the town and therefore the Chinese Red Army can have no access to it. This is one of the reasons behind the failure of the revolution in China. The towns must be walled in by the victorious peasant revolution, headed by the CCP, and seized as the citadels of counterrevolution.

This theory of Mao Tse-tung's in fact implies that the village is the base of the revolution and that the peasant elements are the CCP cadres. The peasantry and the peasantry alone are the support of the revolution.

The results of this theory are already plain—the drastic slowdown of revolutionary activities in towns and the party's loss of contact with the working class.

Mao Tse-tung names Po Ku, Wang Ming, and Li Li-san among the ideological chieftains of the "dogmatists" and refers to the Comintern as their base.

He deliberately associated Li Li-san's "left opportunism" with Po Ku, Wang Ming, and the others. . . .

Li Li-san has already been condemned by the party. Hence Po Ku, Wang Ming, and the others fall under the condemnation automatically. A clever move!

Mao Tse-tung calls Po Ku and Wang Ming "left opportunists," the people who were the cause of the party's smashing defeats in the revolutionary struggle.

Mao Tse-tung maintains that the decisions of the enlarged sitting of the CCP Central Committee Politburo of January 1935 in Tsunyi removed the "left opportunist leadership of the Communist Party." The question on the agenda now is the ideological uprooting of all and any traces of "dogmatism."

December 7, 1942

The secret societies in China are several millenniums old. Different epochs brought forth different societies: Yellow Turbans, Red Eyebrows, Bronze Horses, White Lilies, Red Lances, White Lotus, Swords, Society of Universal Goodness, Triads, Elder Brothers. . . .

The secret societies united the village poor. Nationalist and religious rites and trumpery concealed their antifeudal character. The societies were fought down by the imperial officialdom.

In a not-too-distant past the landlords succeeded in forcing the secret societies to serve their counterrevolutionary ends.

The Red Lances peasant society, far-flung even today, is a branch of the ancient society of the White Lilies. Since no rifles are available, the peasants arm themselves with lances adorned with red tassels at the points.

The Communists are trying to infiltrate the Red Lances and the Swords in order to win the people over to their side.

The leaders of the secret societies play on the ignorance of the popular masses. That is why the societies have a marked religious-mystical coloring.

Secret-society leaders try to convince the city and village poor that the various religious ceremonies and incantations protect them from misfortune. Very often such societies degrade into gangster groups, selling opium, smuggling goods, robbing, running dives and brothels.

What was once the White Lotus, the oldest religious community, is still surviving.

Sun Yat-sen met with a leader of the Triads in an attempt to win his support.

These societies have a membership of millions, representing all sections of Chinese society.

Kang Sheng has established contact with the secret organizations and is supplied by a wealth of data on literally all the people and events that interest him.

Kang Sheng's power is in his knowledge of the country and his ability to put any situation to his own practical use. A policy Kang Sheng-style is to be squeamish about nothing. . . .

December 13, 1942

The Informburo report speaks of significant events: 105 planes have been seized, 1,510 tanks, 2,134 guns of different caliber; 72,400 Nazi soldiers have been imprisoned. And on top of that what man power and matériel have been destroyed!

The American ambassador to the Soviet Union has published an article in an American magazine, which was broadcast over the radio. I remembered the ambassador's words: "Immortal traits of a really great people. . . ."

Lin Po-chu has been head of the Special Area Government since 1937.

Comes from the same part of the country as Mao Tse-tung but is eleven years his senior. CCP member since 1921. Took part in the Nanchang uprising of 1927. Later studied in Moscow. Attended the conference on romanization of the Chinese written language in Vladivostok. Participant in the Long March.

Lin Po-chu's expression is one of pained bewilderment. He is completely gray. Strikes one as being an emotional person. His manners are pleasant and refined.

Kao Kang is a pleasant exception among those close to Kang Sheng. He is friendly and sincere with us. Holds himself independently.

Kao Kang is tall, with pock-marked face and hair combed back; speaks in a hollow voice. Unhurried walk. A capable and strong-willed worker.

December 22, 1942

This is what Mao Tse-tung thinks about cheng-feng.

Numerous kulak, bourgeois-intellectual, and lumpen proletarian elements have made their way into the party. They have entrenched themselves even in the leading posts.

Criticism and self-criticism are the basis of everyday work. The party must make an end of "dogmatism," a dangerous form of opportunism, once and for all. Left opportunism has taken root in the political, organizational, and military activities of the party.

The conference in Tsunyi has saved the party—is the main postulate of this campaign.

Wang Ming is under strong pressure to admit the "fallaciousness of his course." His resistance irritates the CCP Central Committee Chairman.

December 28, 1942

The victories at Stalingrad have been noted at Yenan.

We have been invited to the conference of the Special Area activists.

Mao Tse-tung made a verbose speech. Once more he tried to convince everybody of the expediency of cheng-feng. Only this time he gave the campaign different names—now it was the struggle to reduce the Army, now the struggle against bureaucratization, now the struggle for a correct solution of all economic and financial questions. . . .

He called on the Communists to develop agricultural production locally and said that "according to Marx's teaching, to live and fight it is above all necessary that something should go in here"—Mao Tse-tung indicated his wide-open mouth—"and something should come out here"—he showed exactly what he meant. . . .

A fine piece of civilized behavior! What deep thought!

———

Winter in Yenan is peculiar. If no wind is blowing, it is so warm in the daytime that it is possible to go in shirt sleeves. But in the shade or after sunset the cold is biting. . . .

When I'm alone at night, silence overcomes me. Even my steps on the earth floor are noiseless.

I'm writing and listening to the scratching of my pen. In the still night the scratching seems very loud, as though coming from the river valley below. . . .

December 30, 1942

The critical moments of World War II reveal Mao Tse-tung's political image. In his struggle for power he has chosen the way of political gambling. It is a fact.

He tries to have as much as possible from his "class brothers" and has no scruples about parading patches on his *tan-i*. And he doesn't give a damn that his "class brothers" are bleeding to death.

All our comrades share this view in one way or another.

Yuzhin, who allows for Mao Tse-tung's "faults," considers him a Communist with leftist deviations. Igor Vassilyevich defines all the ideological struggle in the CCP as a typical wrangle for power and nothing else!

———

I've called on Orlov. Though we live in a group, he is all alone. For days on end he has no one to speak a word of Russian to. . . . He enjoys extraordinary respect of the Chinese comrades. . . .

Wang Ming's condition is worse every day. Andrei Yakovlevich fears for his life. . . .

There are several foreign doctors working in the hospitals in Yenan.

By the way, Orlov said that Ma Hai-te has a very vague idea about medicine. He tries his best to avoid contact with Orlov—his arrival puts him in an awkward position.

Ma Hai-te has enough money to live comfortably and throw parties for military and party workers. . . .

1943

January 1943

In the Stalingrad and northern Caucasus areas battles are being fought with a view to annihilating the Hitlerites.

In the Red Army they have a new insignia of grade—shoulder straps. . . .

Thirty-three fascist agitators have been brought to trial in the United States. . . .

The Japanese are advancing in Hupeh and Anhwei. . . .

A telegram has been sent to Chungking asking that an experienced therapeutist be sent to Yenan. The telegram was preceded by the following events.

The doctors of the main hospital drew up a telegram on Wang Ming's illness and the need to take him for treatment to Chengtu or the Soviet Union.

The telegram was drawn up after a sharp worsening of Wang Ming's health. His disease has taken a new dangerous turn. Wang Ming's life is at stake now. His liver and kidneys are failing him. He complains of agonizing headaches and a general weakness.

At a meeting of leading medical specialists the question was raised of the need to wire Chiang Kai-shek for a plane for the patient. The Chairman of the CCP Central Committee crossed out the text of the doctors' telegram and sent his own instead: asking Chungking to send an experienced therapeutist to Yenan for consultation—and nothing more!

I must show no leniency toward myself. I must write only truth. I must not lie to myself or seek ways to compromise. Whether my reports will be published or not and how my reports will be treated in Moscow—this must not concern me. My duty is to write the truth. I owe it the thousands of people who die in the struggle against fascism.

January 14, 1943

The scheming around Wang Ming continues among Mao Tse-tung's entourage. Mao Tse-tung for the second time refused to send a telegram to Chiang Kai-shek despite doctors' insistence on the immediate evacuation of the patient.

Because Wang Ming is a member of the ECCI Secretariat, Wang Chia-hsiang and Jen Pi-shih advise Mao Tse-tung to forestall events, rather than wait for intervention by Dimitrov.

Wang Ming has been terrorized by Kang Sheng and fears our visits. Through Orlov he conveyed to me his request to help him go to the Soviet Union for treatment, but to arrange this so that he could escape Mao Tse-tung's vengeance.

Often, too often, I find myself wondering how Mao Tse-tung, coming out actually against Marxism-Leninism, has established himself and continues to consolidate his position as the leader of the Communist Party. Well, treachery, cruelty, but what next?

All that is not so simple, of course. In his own way he is clever—in fact, much more intelligent than his opponents. Not all of them, to be sure.

He is aware of the fact that the revolution will develop in China and is building up his personal position. He cannot all the time conceal the antiparty and opportunist nature of his actions. Both the Chinese Communist Party and the Communist parties of other countries have never regarded these actions as deliberately anti-Communist. They are rather interpreted as "mistakes," "deviations," but always within the framework of the Marxist ideology. It is worthy of note that in the past Mao Tse-tung did not "open up" so demonstratively and he was much more cautious than now. As a matter of fact, all his actions hostile to the ideology of Marxism-Leninism were taken for mistakes, some more and some less serious miscalculations made by a Communist who in all respects was loyal to the cause of the revolution. Both in the Comintern and in the Chinese Communist Party these mistakes were looked upon as errors of judgment which would be gradually overcome by the very logic of the revolution, as the still young CCP and its leaders matured and gained experience. The conditions in which the CCP came into existence and in which it exists today have always been much too complicated.

However, as far as I can see, this view of the "activities" of the Chairman of the Central Committee of the CCP has proved wrong.

In that case I can see my way clear to the task I yet have to perform. . . .

January 17, 1943

The spiteful attitude of highly placed CCP functionaries to the Soviet Union and their gloating over its ordeal gives way to a forced well-wishing: The Red Army is on the offensive. For many here this has come as a surprise.

Discreetly Mao Tse-tung did not permit himself to gibe at our military setback in public. Only among his close associates he was less reserved. . . .

But Kang Sheng and some others did not stand on ceremony. The more striking is the change in their behavior. . . .

January 19, 1943

The blockade of Leningrad has been broken south of the Ladoga Lake! Children, old people, and women will no longer die from hunger at last.

According to the information of Kang Sheng, the occupationists are retreating in the southern part of Hupeh province. . . .

––––––––

Every person who has visited the Soviet Union is declared in the Special Area a "dogmatist."

Mao Tse-tung does not bother himself even with meeting these party workers. To him the Chinese comrades who have studied in the Soviet Union are "dogmatists" and the target for vicious punitive actions by Kang Sheng and other cheng-feng leaders.

Mao Tse-tung yesterday remarked to me that "the experience of the AUCP(B) is unsuitable and harmful for the CCP." The conversation was long and unpleasant, full of awkward subterfuges and crude flatteries on his part. . . .

Clearly, each country has its own historical and national peculiarities, and a Marxist party must take them into account, but not to trust the AUCP(B), to disregard its experience, and, even worse, to punish people for their sympathies with the AUCP(B) is the sign not so much of the political immaturity of the CCP leadership as of its hostility to revolutionary Marxism.

Mao Tse-tung is seeking a civil war. He totally disregards the present political situation and has been artificially speeding events. I involuntarily remember the words of Victor Hugo: You can't speed up time by pushing forward the hand of the clock. . . .

_____

The brazier emits a crimson light in the corner. Behind it are the bed curtains. And beyond is the frosty night. . . .

The candlelight throws my long shadow on the wall. And so we while away night hours over the diary or document translations—I and my shadow. . . .

January 26, 1943

The condition of Wang Ming is unenviable. Bedridden for a long time, he has grown very weak. Kang Sheng has isolated him from the outside world. Dr. Ching treats Wang Ming.

_____

At a New Year meeting of the activists Mao Tse-tung spoke with hatred about the vitality of "dogmatism" and gave a call to fight against it.

". . . The present leadership of the CCP," declared Mao Tse-tung, "believes that the purges carried out in the past in the AUCP(B) were erroneous. What is necessary is the 'spiritual purges' that are now being conducted in the Special Area."

According to Mao Tse-tung, this means that each must publicly confess his sins.

Kang Sheng hastily declared that he himself "studied nothing in the Soviet Union," otherwise he would also "have sunk into 'dogmatism.' "

Even before my arrival in Yenan, Kang Sheng in his speeches in the Politburo of the CCP Central Committee declared that the stay of Soviet people in Yenan is undesirable and slandered my comrades and the Soviet Union.

The sympathies of the Chinese Communists for the AUCP(B) are firm and well grounded. And this questions the exclusive authority of the Chairman of the CCP Central Committee. His aims do not accord with the policy of the Comintern. Now a blow is being dealt to the links between the CCP and the AUCP(B).

Any friendly feelings for the country of the first socialist state are subject to suppression. The results of such a policy can easily be foreseen: For the CCP there will be no other authority and "thoughts" more comprehensive and profound than the "thoughts of Mao Tse-tung."

January 29, 1943

The liberated areas represent a strange picture. No less strange is the picture represented by the military units of the CCP. All of them are trading as much as possible with Japanese rear detachments.

Everywhere illicit opium traffic is going on. Thus, in Tsai-ling, at the rear-most headquarters of the 120th Infantry Division they have allotted a premise where raw materials are processed and from where opium as finished product goes to markets.

In northwestern Shansi, virtually all the counties have been flooded with the most diverse Japanese goods. These goods are supplied directly from Japanese rear depots.

In the headquarters of the 120th Division, discussions center not on combat missions, operations, and other military matters, but on commercial deals and profits.

All this is the result of certain instructions. Thus, all the units of the Eighth Route and New Fourth armies have been strictly ordered not to undertake any vigorous operations or actions against the Japanese. In a word, not to engage in any combat actions. This includes retreating under an attack and seeking, if possible, a truce.

The best combat units of the CCP are being redeployed. They are leaving the North China region. The new location is the Special Area. In the main these units are being concentrated in the direction of Sian.

I know precisely that the troops of the Central Government are billeted in their old quarters and stationed along the southern border of the Special Area.

February 1943

The destruction of Nazi troops in the Stalingrad area has been completed. Scores of German divisions have been routed. The number of prisoners is enormous. Among them are twenty-four generals, including General Field Marshal Friedrich von Paulus.

I was not mistaken in my previous conclusions. Kang Sheng has a strong influence on the Chairman's moods.

Mao Tse-tung is indifferent to practical problems of socialism. He is crammed with Kang Sheng's inaccurate stories about our country; in this case this is the only source of his information. As for Kang Sheng, he is only too glad to slander us. He is a rabid enemy of the Soviet Union, he sullies the Bolshevik Party and spares no efforts to prevent the Chinese Communist Party from consolidating ideologically. Kang Sheng acts not only as an enemy of the Soviet Union, but also as an enemy of his party, for he impedes its organizational unity. Chairman Mao comes out against the opportunist perversions and leftism of Chen Tu-hsiu and Li Li-san only in words. Actually he is under the influence of their petty-bourgeois theories. Kang Sheng is perfectly aware of this and puts his heart and soul into the cultivation of this ideologically dangerous deviation of the Chairman.

Kang Sheng cannot be called anything but a "fall minister" [an image from ancient Chinese literature meaning a minister who sows death among his people].

The objective demands of the Chinese Revolution are deliberately perverted. This is presented as development of Marxism and is disguised as Marxism. And, of course, it serves a definite political purpose.

One can feel the malicious will of the Fall Minister in Mao Tsetung's attacks on the Comintern.

Comintern's policy is dictated by the principles of the Communist doctrine and program, and not by the will of Moscow, as Kang Sheng tries to present it.

In between the Comintern congresses the international workers' movement is headed by the Comintern Executive Committee. Among its members are Dimitrov, Togliatti (Ercole), Gottwald, Manuilsky, Pieck, Wang Ming, Thorez, Koplenig. Thus the policy of the Comintern Executive is mapped out by representatives of the international workers' movement.

February 5, 1943

To mark the Stalingrad victory our group held a reception for the CCP leadership. Among the guests were Mao Tse-tung, the Fall Minister, Chiang Ching, Wang Chia-hsiang, Jen Pi-shih. . . .

The banquet was arranged in our house. Tables seating four were put up. I produced my sealed bottle of alcohol which turned out to be emptied to a half in a mysterious way.

The Fall Minister, having consumed a good quantity of alcohol in Aleyev's company, tried to make him reveal the content of our reports. . . . He is greatly worried about our attitude toward him and his department. . . .

Andrei Yakovievich was responsible for the "evaporation" of the alcohol. He gave the boys the idea of withdrawing the alcohol by means of a veterinary syringe and then rub out the needle mark with one's finger. All evening long I was the object of his jokes. . . .

February 7, 1943

A return banquet was given by the Fall Minister. It is impossible to enumerate all of the seventy dishes served to the guests.

Hors d'oeuvres and drinks were in abundance. There were salads, cabbage, ducks, meat with different sauces, delicacies of sea-weed. . . . Then different aromatic soups were served. . . .

One had to see how Mao Tse-tung started up when a dish of trepangs was brought in, how carefully and ceremoniously he helped himself to the dish, and how solemnly he stood eating them as if he were taking an oath. . . .

The favorite Chinese dish, sugared chicken, was served. Then came all kinds of porridges, cooked over steam without salt; puffs of wheat flour, very light; and fat pork in sugar powder. . . .

Kang Sheng's senior chef was a cook of the last Chinese Emperor, Pu-yi, now the Emperor of the puppet Manchukuo state.

Mao gave an amiable smile to everyone who talked to him and taught Dolmatov how to eat red pepper: One had to stick the pod deep in one's throat and swallow it instead of placing it on the tongue. . . .

Mao Tse-tung has a soft voice. When he speaks, everyone stops talking. He retains this manner when speaking in public. One has to get used to his southern dialect. . . .

Mao Tse-tung is a chain smoker. He holds the cigarette between his thumb and forefinger. He is a heavy drinker, too.

Mao Tse-tung astonishes one with his condescendingly scornful atti-tude to culture, which speaks of his narrow-mindedness. He enjoys making people fear him and regards such people with favor.

In the atmosphere of backwardness characteristic of the population of the Special Area, Mao Tse-tung's "erudition" makes him almost a prophet.

February 9, 1943

The results of the Stalingrad victory are felt in Yenan. The Kwantung Army has already moved to winter quarters. The comrades from the Central Committee have become more complaisant. . . .

The other day Hsiao Li asked not without malice: "Comrade Sung Ping, the Soviet Union is supplying arms to Chiang Kai-shek. These arms are handed out to Kuomintang divisions. And these divisions are blocking us from the south. How is this to be understood?"

I said: "There is a common antifascist front in the world. Fascism is the chief enemy of Communists in all countries. Fascist Japan is ravag-ing China. The main forces fighting against Japan are the Kuomintang armies, who numerically are several times superior to the Eighth Route and New Fourth armies."

"Well, we'll cope with our enemies somehow," Hsiao Li replied.

I said, "By its agreement with the Central Government and the dependence of this government on armament deliveries the Soviet Union is exerting a checking influence on Chungking."

Hsiao Li left.

Dolmatov flung open the door and grumbled, "Have to air the room. . . ."

———

The Fall Minister gets a part of his information from the bosses of secret societies. He has reliable connections there.

Kang Sheng takes into consideration the national peculiarities of his country. This gives him priority in the struggle against his political adversaries, and there are more than enough of them in the CCP. . . .

Li Ko-nung takes charge of the Fall Minister's ties with secret societies. He heads the operations dealing with the production and marketing of opium. Here the services of the secret societies are invaluable. Currency pours into the hands of the Ching-pao-chu chief.

February 17, 1943

The role of Chiang Ching in all the political backstage intrigues is extremely shady. The more I think of the Mao–Chiang Ching–Kang Sheng alliance, the more apparent become the following dynamics of the events.

The chief of the Ching-pao-chu, who is quite inconspicuous in the party, decides to link his career with an actress from Chungking. He chooses her not only for her charms but also for her intellect, tact, and will. It is he who introduces Chiang Ching to Mao Tse-tung, who is already in his third marriage and still a great enthusiast of sexual amusements.

From this moment Kang Sheng begins to play for high stakes. Having discerned in the Chairman of the CCP Central Committee kindred views, Kang Sheng goes all out for a place at his side.

It is the chief of Ching-pao-chu's professional duty to discern human vices and weaknesses and to use them to his benefit. Not an honorable occupation, but one that gives power over people.

His stake on Chiang Ching is justified. After Chiang Ching's marriage to Mao Tse-tung, Kang Sheng becomes nearer to the Chairman and close contacts are established between them.

Spurred on by ambition and self-seeking interests, Chiang Ching and Mao Tse-tung become closely bound to each other. Their feelings are spurred on by their allied natures. In the person of Chiang Ching Mao Tse-tung finds a reliable assistant, adviser, and comrade in the struggle for power.

It is curious that Liu Shao-chi makes his appearance in Yenan with none other than Peng Chen, an old acquaintance of Chiang Ching's. Here the stake is also made on personal relationships.

It is not only Chiang Ching and Mao Tse-tung who profit by their marriage. It is also big gain for the Fall Minister, and probably for Liu Shao-chi, who has rightly placed his bet on Peng Chen.

The marriage of Mao Tse-tung and Chiang Ching took place against the will of the Central Committee. The bride turned out to be a lady of dubious reputation. However, the Fall Minister was able to win over the discontented. . . .

Not only is Chiang Ching the personal secretary of the Chairman, she also takes charge of all his secret correspondence. . . .

———

Ho Lung, Commander of the 120th Infantry Division, is at present the head of the Joint Staff Forces of the Special Area. He is a sturdy, smartly dressed military man, who loves the good things of life. The soldiers adore Ho Lung.

———

Wang Ming is bedridden. Kang Sheng makes use of this fact to keep him in strict isolation. It is impossible to meet Wang Ming and we make no attempts to do so, so as not to rouse censure on the part of the CCP leadership.

February 22, 1943

Mao Tse-tung knows no foreign languages. He is well versed in ancient Chinese literature and is always ready to flaunt his knowledge. He takes charge of military affairs himself and has a reputation of being an expert in guerrilla warfare.

Mao Tse-tung is convinced that he is a talented historian, poet, and writer.

He stays in his residential quarters as if in confinement. Nobody remembers the Chairman to have paid a visit to an industrial enterprise or military unit.

February 27, 1943

The educational establishments of Yenan do not give proper schooling. Marxism and political economy are not included in the curriculum. Instead the reading of old-time novels, such as *San Kuo Chih* ["Romance of the Three Kingdoms"], *Hung Lou Meng* ["Dream of the Red Chamber"], and *Shui Hu Chuan* ["The Story of the Water Margin"] is strongly recommended.

For more than a year already all studies have been called off in all the educational establishments. This is the result of the cheng-feng campaign. Many offices also barely function and are open only half the day. Everyone is occupied at meetings or is studying "The Twenty-two Documents."

In the press and speeches Mao Tse-tung is extolled and the "dogmatists" are branded. While Wang Chia-hsiang, Jen Pi-shih, and Li Feng and others who are aware of the harmful effect of all this sometimes raise their voices in weak protest, Kang Sheng gives his wholehearted support to the Chairman.

Mao Tse-tung reckons only with Kang Sheng.

All these "buds" of the cheng-feng campaign flourish in all their splendor in the apparatus of the Fall Minister. Cramming, criticism, and self-flagellation to hysterics are rife there.

Actions of this kind are meant to make the rank-and-file party members believe that Mao Tse-tung's "ideas" are the acme of world culture, the summit of revolutionary Marxism. And cheng-feng turns these "ideas" into the sole spiritual and political nourishment of the party.

It is hard to expect creative initiative from the party cadres and rank-and-file Communists. The administration implants a system of cramming and dogmatism.

March 1943

March 4, 1943

A sturdy pavilion has been built in Yang-chia-lin for the Central Committee meetings. On Saturday evenings and on holidays opera performances are given there.

Liu Shao-chi is indifferent to opera, but he often comes to Mao Tsetung with papers during the performance.

"Here comes this lout again!" Chiang Ching whispers loudly in such cases, shrugging her delicate shoulders with disgust.

"Spiritual purge"—each man must come and confess his sins. One's stay in the Soviet Union and one's connection with Wang Ming are obvious "crimes against the party." Patriotism and loyalty to Mao Tsetung are identified.

Fall Minister sets the junior cadres against the leading cadres, sows mutual distrust, and causes general irritation by providing bad material and everyday life conditions and making any association with women, even one's wife, impossible.

Orlov has grown much thinner. Puny as he is, he now looks like an adolescent. And he has grown a beard and mustache not to look like one, perhaps.

March 10, 1943

The Japanese failed to encircle the Kuomintang troops in the Huai-an–Yen-cheng area, though the Chinese suffered considerable losses. Now the samurai are hurriedly organizing their offensive operations to be launched from their springboard on the southern bank of the Yangtze.

The situation in the economically feeble China that has lived through many years of destructive war is deteriorating catastrophically. The richest maritime provinces have been lost fully or partially, inflation is raging, the population is impoverished, the troops feel an acute shortage of munitions, weapons, commanders, etc.

The CCP leaders are all worked up about Wang Ming's planned departure to Moscow.

Mao Tse-tung is afraid that Wang Ming will report to the Comintern Executive Committee on the actual situation in the CCP.

Our contacts with the Chinese comrades give Mao Tse-tung reason to believe that Moscow is sufficiently well informed. This embitters him. Our contacts with people are restricted. Kang Sheng feels somewhat dejected, fearing exposure by the Comintern.

Mao Tse-tung is frantically searching for a way out. In the meantime, he has forbidden Wang Ming to leave. . . .

March 14, 1943

The situation has changed sharply. Now, whenever different problems to be solved are discussed, the members of the so-called Moscow opposition are practically ignored. The CCP Central Committee Chairman and Kang Sheng have defamed them sufficiently. The situation in all the supreme organs of the Communist Party is tense. Up until recently the Chairman of the CCP Central Committee mainly relied on Chen Yun, Kang Sheng, and his apparatus of advisers (learned secretaries) headed by the experienced demagogue Chen Po-ta.

I have formed an impression that the CCP Central Committee Chairman does not see eye to eye with Li Fu-chun, Wang Chia-hsiang, and Jen Pi-shih. They disagreed on such important problems as conducting military operations on the Eighth Route Army and the New Fourth Army fronts, the single anti-Japanese front and inner party life. It seems to me that they still disagree with each other on these questions. However, the cheng-feng methods have a terrorizing effect on everybody. And these most authoritative party functionaries prefer to keep mum. Even if they express their dissatisfaction, they never do it in public or at official meetings. They fear Mao Tse-tung; that is why they would hardly gather enough courage to criticize his political line. Thus, the positions of the CCP Central Committee Chairman are being strengthened.

The "Muscovites" have been defamed, while others just keep mum. Only Kang Sheng and other supporters of Mao mold political opinion.

All this creates the false impression that Mao Tse-tung enjoys the unanimous support of the CCP Central Committee and that the policy he pursues is infallible, though it contradicts the Comintern policy. It is physically impossible for the Chinese comrades to report to the Comintern Executive Committee on differences within the party, since all the channels of communication have been blocked by the Fall Minister.

March 16, 1943

The decisions of the CCP Central Committee adopted last year and this year, Mao Tse-tung's speeches, several speeches by Liu Shao-chi, etc., have been included in "The Twenty-two Documents," which the CCP Central Committee Chairman ordered to be learned by rote.

The study of novels is compulsory.

The novel San Kuo Chih ["Romance of the Three Kingdoms"] was written by Lo Kuan-chung in the second half of the fourteenth century.

Lo Kuan-chung's heroic epic is based on the documentary records of the court historiographer Chen Shou, which the author skillfully combined with folk legends.

We read San Kuo Chih at the institute. The novel is written in the old classical language and abounds in idioms. To understand its content correctly one must grasp the meaning of the philosophy of that bygone epoch.

The novel Hung Lou Meng ["Dream of the Red Chamber"] is about the spiritual disintegration of the nobility of old China.

The novel Shui Hu Chuan ["The Story of the Water Margin"] tells about the struggle against the feudal lords waged by the Chinese people six hundred years ago.

Reading novels . . . The purpose of this seemingly innocent pastime is to stir up nationalistic feelings in the party.

March 22, 1943

Orlov visited Wang Ming.

When the prescription given by Dr. Ching, who treated Wang Ming, was taken to a pharmacy, the pharmacist on duty was amazed at the unusual composition of the preparation. The nurse who looked after Wang Ming said the same.

Ching wrote this prescription before Wang Ming developed a serious kidney and liver condition.

Rosa Vladimirovna immediately went to the doctor who prescribed the medication, and Ching confirmed the necessity of taking the drug even when it changed color (to dark green) in time.

At Ching's insistence the patient continues to take the medicine.

Orlov copied Ching's prescription and resolutely forbade the patient to take the medicine.

Andrei Yakovlevich explained to me that outwardly the prescription looked correct, but with time the mixture disintegrates and becomes toxic.

March 23, 1943

The CCP Central Committee Chairman, fearing publicity and disclosure by the Comintern, is trying to "persuade" Wang Ming. For this purpose he "detailed" Jen Pi-shih, Wang Chia-hsiang, and Liu Shao-chi to conduct negotiations. . . .

Wang Ming refused to negotiate, pleading poor health. He declared, however, that Mao Tse-tung pursued his own policy, unapproved by anybody, in dealing with literally all the problems of party life and in his relations with the Kuomintang.

Mao Tse-tung suggested holding the Politburo meeting at Wang Ming's home. The latter refused again. But since the doctors insist that Wang Ming should go and get prolonged treatment at a hospital, Mao Tse-tung gave up and decided to send Wang Chia-hsiang with him to Moscow as official reporter of the CCP Central Committee and Wang Ming's opponent.

Wang Chia-hsiang is energetically preparing for the forthcoming visit to Moscow.

March 25, 1943

A radiogram from Moscow reads: "Preparation composed correctly though with certain deviations harmful for health. When kept for some time calomel disintegrates into sublimate and mercury. . . . Prolonged use of such decomposed medicine causes slow poisoning and results in mercurialism. In grave cases it leads to death preceded by acute anemia."

Trying to protect himself from exposure by the Comintern, the CCP Central Committee Chairman takes most energetic measures. One of such measures is rallying leading workers in the party organs around him. Mao Tse-tung relies upon Chou En-lai's help. That is why he insisted on calling Chou En-lai to the Special Area. Chou, as the CCP permanent representative at Kuomintang (I think he shares the post with Tung Pi-wu) never leaves Chungking. In the circle of his associates the CCP Central Committee Chairman expressed a supposition which allows one to draw the conclusion that he does not doubt that Chou En-lai fully supports his policy.

Mao Tse-tung shows a special attitude to Wang Ming. The Chairman's hostile attitude to him has grown into hatred. Wang Ming is, perhaps, the biggest obstacle on his way to uncontrolled power in the party. Here Kang and Mao and all their supporters lay themselves out to isolate Wang Ming, to create the impression that Wang Ming is alone in the party and that Wang Ming's views are alien to the national specifics of the Chinese Revolution, and, consequently, to the Chinese Communist Party. So far it has not been openly expressed. But Kang Sheng and Mao's entire activity, practically, boils down to it. How else can Lo Fu's sudden return be interpreted? Lo Fu is Wang Ming's ideological follower. In any case Lo Fu approved of the Comintern's activity. He was one of those upon whom Mao inflicted his blow in Tsunyi. True, he still holds a very important post, which seems hard to explain. Obviously, Mao had some reason to keep Lo Fu. However, in the current campaign Lo Fu really catches it as a "dogmatist."

And here is a picture in the Mao style: Lo Fu is treated with special courtesy and attention, and they keep whispering all kinds of vile things about Wang Ming into his ear.

They have forgiven Lo Fu everything—his "dogmatism" and his intransigence.

Before that the Fall Minister expelled Lo Fu from Yenan with the single purpose of breaking up the "Moscow group," isolating Wang Ming, intimidating and confusing all of them, one by one.

Now Mao and Kang are trying to crush Wang Ming ideologically with the help of the "Moscow group" members. If they succeed, Wang Ming will be a political corpse not only to Mao Tse-tung.

March 26, 1943

Wang Ming has been taking calomel for about six months. As the result of it he developed liver and kidney trouble and began losing teeth. Dr. Ching urged his patient to take the mixture precisely when its color changed to dark green.

The prescription got into the hands of Dr. Fu, head of the Central Committee medical service, and he said that calomel in such doses and in such a combination was most toxic.

Dr. Fu immediately reported the case to the Central Committee.

March 28, 1943

Thus, the "prescription affair" came about.

Wang Chia-hsiang kept asking Orlov about the application of calomel, explaining his interest by the fact that his wife is a doctor.

Orlov, without betraying his knowledge of Ching's prescription, explained to him that calomel in big doses and in combination with alkalis and salts produces a toxic effect, affecting the liver and kidneys and destroying teeth.

In the evening Chiang Ching came to see me quite unexpectedly. She talked at length about the "unreliability of Dr. Ching, who is, probably, a Kuomintang agent." . . .

Yet, despite all the maneuvers of Mao and Kang, the unanimity they desire is absent in the leading party organs. Even such a prominent man as Liu Shao-chi is obviously irritated by the methods employed by the Commission for the Review of Party Cadres and Nonparty Personnel. To him the methods employed by this commission headed by Kang Sheng are inadmissible from the point of view of party line standards.

He personally told me that he regards the criticism of Wang Ming and a number of other comrades as a mistake.

Liu Shao-chi advised Wang Ming to insist on the discussion of this question with the analysis of the activity of the commission and, personally, Kang Sheng, as its chairman, at a Politburo meeting. It should be noted that Liu Shao-chi did not even mention Mao.

March 30, 1943

Kang Sheng invited us to see three Kuomintang spies—three emaciated lads.

Yuzhin says that such "shows" have been staged before. The CCP leaders resort to such methods in order to convince us that their anti-Kuomintang propaganda is justified.

Yuzhin is sure that the three lads will be shot. The CCP leadership need proof of Kuomintang's intrigues. Whether the lads are spies or not, it does not interest Kang Sheng a bit. Effective shows, that's what really matters.

April 1943

Mao Tse-tung is trying to frustrate, by hook or by crook, the departure of Wang Ming.

In case the latter does leave for medical treatment in Moscow, a group of party workers is being hastily prepared. It includes Kai Feng, who is being intensively coached by Kang Sheng.

Kai Feng will evidently be the eyes and ears of the Ching-pao-chu chief.

Everybody here knows about the Yenan comrades' forthcoming flight to Moscow. At Mao Tse-tung's instructions this news is being assiduously spread by the Fall Minister's office. The plan is simple enough: In Chungking they will nose it out and will not let a Soviet plane go through at any cost. Chiang Kai-shek is not a fool, and he is vitally interested in preserving tensions in the CCP leadership. . . .

It is impossible to get to Wang Ming except through persons trusted by the Chairman of the CCP Central Committee. . . .

April 6, 1943

Mao Tse-tung and Kang Sheng are sure that we know what is behind the "case of the prescription" that is premeditated poisoning of Wang Ming. . . .

This compelled them to give up the idea of murdering Wang Ming: Chinese doctors can be bullied, but what about us?

Chiang Ching's visits, importunate talks about the prescription, and the intensified shadowing of us corroborate this conclusion. . . .

April 8, 1943

In a talk with me Po Ku used sharp words about Kang Sheng. He called him "a politically alien figure" in the Chinese Communist Party. He was outraged with the surveillance system introduced by Kang Sheng.

Po Ku spoke of Liu Shao-chi with ill-concealed bitterness.

It turned out that Liu is changing his views radically. He does his best to come to terms with Kang Sheng. He even tries to flatter him. Apparently this is why Liu Shao-chi has been left in the new Secretariat of the CCP Central Committee. The Secretariat membership has been reduced. Mao wants to have effective control over the activities of all the higher party bodies. The Secretariat now includes Liu Shao-chi, Jen Pi-shih, and Mao Tse-tung himself. I don't think this is the final choice. There are only three persons in this body of the CCP Central Committee as yet. . . .

April 9, 1943

Something must be done to invigorate and exonerate the campaign of the "spiritual purification and screening of cadres." That is why the Chairman of the CCP Central Committee has advanced a new thesis: The intelligentsia needs both purification and screening. Of course, not the entire intelligentsia but that part of it which has remained here since 1938. The Chairman believes, and seriously at that, that it is risky to trust these comrades, that they should be first reformed ideologically ("spiritually") and then put through Kang's commission. There, the alien element will be pinpointed and subjected to collective reforming. Naturally enough Mao's entourage also keeps to this point of view. Nobody in the CCP leadership is taken aback by the fact that out of the veteran cadres (those who came to Yenan during the Long March) only a few hundred comrades are still alive and that the backbone of the cadres are young people, novices who number at least thirty thousand.

The Chairman of the CCP Central Committee refers to the few

hundred old cadres as his "own" people. This reference has outlawed, as it were, the remaining thousands upon thousands of party workers. They can and should be suspected, tested, and reformed.

Thus, all who came to Yenan after the Long March are in an exceptionally difficult position. Arrests are a consequence of this latest directive of the Chairman.

Chiang Kai-shek, or a group of the Kuomintang big shots headed by Hu Tsu-nan, is expected here every day now. Martial law has been introduced, although it is hard to understand its expediency. This has also caused a wave of arrests.

Asked Kang about the arrests. He clearly disliked the talk. However, he said that the "order to isolate Kuomintang and Japanese henchmen has been given by the CCP leadership."

Arrests are being made in a planned manner. People are taken away at night.

Following Mao's statement concerning political distrust in the intelligentsia and cadre workers, everyone is regarded as a Kuomintang or a Japanese agent. . . .

April 10, 1943

Although "The Twenty-two Documents" does not contain openly anti-Soviet or anti-Marxist statements, it is compiled in such a way that along with Chinese novels compulsory for study, it fosters nationalist haughtiness and a negative attitude to the Soviet Union. The notion "dogmatist" incarnates open dislike for the Soviet Union and for Marxism-Leninism and internationalism.

One of the aims of the CCP is the national liberation of the country, but this struggle should not make it a party for which nationalism is the main aim, and an end in itself.

At the stage of national liberation the Communist Party should unite all more or less revolutionary-minded strata of society, including the middle bourgeoisie, and provide leadership for this struggle. However, the national liberation of the country is only a stage and should not be an end in the policy of the Communist Party.

April 15, 1943

At the insistent request of Rosa Vladimirovna I went to see Wang Ming. He feels very bad. What's wearing him down is not so much his physical ailment as moral suffering.

Rosa Vladimirovna warned me that she hadn't told her husband about the fanatic persecution of the "Moscow group."

Wang Ming told me bitterly about Kang Sheng's behavior in Moscow. In Moscow the future Fall Minister was officially subordinated to Wang Ming. He went out of his way to please him and all noted workers of the Executive Committee of the Communist International.

Wang Ming recalled that at that time at all meetings Kang Sheng was the first to jump to his feet, warmly applaud, and ecstatically shout "Long live . . . !"

April 23, 1943

Cheng-feng and the "spy" arrests are aggravating the general tension in Yenan.

Chiang Kai-shek proposes settling disputes through talks. The CCP leadership sabotages all proposals coming from Chungking.

The united anti-Japanese front does not mean a rejection of Marxist ideology, but a determination of the CCP's right place at the current stage of the revolution. Legalization of the Communist Party will open up broad opportunities for the CCP organizational and propaganda activities. However, the party leadership is inclined to unleash an armed conflict with the Kuomintang.

April 28, 1943

Despite the past and present extremes in the development of Soviet power, the prestige of the party is exceedingly high throughout China. The party is the only force to have come out against foreign and domestic oppressors. Tens of thousands of Communists gave their lives for this cause.

Mao Tse-tung says that "dogmatism" must be crushed, and the party, believing him, stigmatizes "dogmatists." The most regrettable thing is that the "Moscow group" has had no possibility to expound its views. This was precluded.

Mao Tse-tung's strength is not only in that he does not disdain to use any means in this struggle. It is also in his thorough knowledge of the psychology of the Chinese peasants, the petty-bourgeoisie, the customs and mores of the people. This cannot be said of the "Moscow group," whose members are too often pure theoreticians, even though sincerely devoted to the revolution.

Mao's demagogy takes into account national peculiarities, and that is why it is flexible, cleverly camouflaged, and much easier to bring home. Mao plays on the national feeling injured by foreign oppression and speculates on the popularity of Marxism-Leninism. . . .

I cannot relax for a moment—there are meetings, shouting, posters cursing "dogmatists" and the Kuomintang, and nervous and worn-out people. . . .

May 1943

May 7, 1943

The following resolution of the Presidium of the Executive Committee of the Communist International has been transmitted from Moscow for our information:

The historic role of the Communist International, which was set up in 1919 as the result of political bankruptcy of most of the pre-war revolutionary parties, is that it safeguarded Marxism from vulgarization and distortion by opportunist elements in the working-class movement; it promoted the alliance of progressive workers in genuinely workers' parties and helped them to mobilize the masses of working people to defend their economic and political interests, to fight against fascism and the war it was hatching, and to support the Soviet Union as the bulwark in the struggle against fascism. . . .

But even before the war it became increasingly clear that as the domestic and international situation of individual countries grew more and more aggravated, the solution of problems of the working-class movement of each individual country by an international center would meet with insurmountable difficulties. The fact that the working class of individual countries is faced with different tasks is to be explained by several reasons: the profound differences in the historical development of the various countries of the world, the different and even contradictory nature of their social systems, the difference in the level and rate of their social and political development, and finally the difference in the level of working-class awareness and organization. . . .

Guided by the teaching of the founders of Marxism-Leninism, the Communists have never advocated preservation of outdated organizational forms; they have always subjected the forms of working-class organization and the methods of this organization to the basic political interests of the working-class movement as a whole, the distinctive features of the given concrete historical situation, and the tasks directly stemming from this situation. They remember great Marx and the example he set when he united progressive workers in the International Workingmen's Association, and after that when the First International had fulfilled its historical task, having laid the foundations for the development of workers' parties in the countries of Europe and America, how he dissolved it because the situation was ripe for the setting up of mass national workers' parties, and in its form the First International could no longer cope with this task. . . .

The Presidium of the Executive Committee of the Communist International has no opportunity of calling a congress of the Communist International when there is a world war going on. Therefore, it takes it upon itself to submit for approval by the sections of the Communist International the following propositions: The Communist International as the leading center of the working-class movement should be dissolved and its sections should be relieved of their duties set forth by the rules and decisions of the congresses of the Communist International.

The Presidium of the Executive Committee calls on all the supporters of the Communist International to concentrate on all-round support for and active participation in the liberation war of the peoples and states of the anti-Hitler coalition for the earliest defeat of the enemy of the working people—German fascism and its allies and vassals.

Members of the Presidium of the Executive Committee of the Communist International: Gottwald, Dimitrov, Zhdanov, Kolarov, Koplenig, Kuusinen, Manuilsky, Pieck, Thorez, Ercole. . . .

May 29, 1943

I had expected that the news of the dissolution of the Comintern would be a very joyous piece of information for the Mao group. But what really happened surpassed my wildest surmises.

But all in good time.

The minute the CCP Central Committee Chairman received the telegram on the resolution of the Presidium of the Comintern Executive on the dissolution of the Comintern, all the Politburo members were called. They were literally aroused by alarm.

The telegram caused no bewilderment or speculations on Mao's part—he had it all thought out.

The sitting of the Politburo was chaired by Mao. He read out the telegram and declared that the Presidium resolution was perfectly justified and correct, since the Comintern had long since outlived itself as the leading body of the international working-class movement and for that reason had been interfering with it and harming it by its misunderstanding of the essence and peculiarities of the activities of the Chinese Communist Party.

When Po Ku was telling me about that emergency sitting, his very voice and all his gestures conveyed Mao's elation. As a matter of fact, Mao himself did not conceal his triumph as he talked with me the following day.

At the same sitting the Chairman asked the Politburo members if Marxism-Leninism was needed at all. "What do we need Marxism-Leninism for? Is there any real need in its propaganda?"

Having asked these questions, he made a pause and replied that there could be no doubt as to that, for, of course, Marxism-Leninism was needed but it was absolutely essential to adopt it to the strictly Chinese national requirements and national conditions. And the Chairman formulated the following task facing every responsible party worker: It is necessary steadfastly and consistently to fight for a genuinely national and independent character of the CCP.

The Chairman laid a special stress on relationships between the CCP and the Kuomintang. According to him, it was necessary to take into consideration the various situations that could evolve from the dissolution of the Comintern, but that first of all a great sense of responsibility should be displayed. No matter what difficulties could materialize, it was necessary to remember about explanatory work. In this case explanatory work was absolutely necessary, it would be impossible to do without it, for a part of the Communists, a part of party workers, would not comprehend the historical necessity of the given resolution of the Presidium of the Comintern Executive.

Mao Tse-tung drew the Politburo's special attention to those people in the Communist Party for whom it was not the Central Committee of the CCP, but the Comintern and its workers, that was the most authoritative body. Those Chinese comrades did always listen to the Comintern alone.

At this point the CCP Chairman began to act in such a way that it became obvious that those who should display any independent thinking (and possibly those who have already displayed it) would be punished in a most cruel way, perhaps even expelled from the party. Of course, Mao meant the "dogmatists" and the "Moscow group" with Wang Ming, Po Ku, and the members of the "military opposition" in the lead. Mao did not give any names, but everything was clear anyway.

The Chairman warned against underestimation of the activities of the hostile and opportunist elements in party ranks. Those elements could develop clandestine activities and could use the fact of the Comintern's self-dissolution for active propaganda.

A rigorous, principled campaign is needed against such Communists.

Cheered by his yes-men and accompanied by shouts of admiration, Mao Tse-tung announced to the Politburo that now the time had come and "it is possible and necessary to convene the long-awaited party congress" without any second thoughts.

The atmosphere at the Politburo was elated, almost festive. The supporters of the Central Committee Chairman behaved as though they felt their hands had been finally untied. That was my impression after meeting with several members of the Politburo. True, they were not distinguished for their Marxist views before either. But now it looked like they had lost even the natural feeling of moral responsibility.

Liu Shao-chi took the floor next. Where did his former displeasure with the highhanded Kang Sheng commission on personnel check-up and his sympathies with Wang Ming vanish?

Liu Shao-chi repeated the main points of Mao's speech. They boiled down to the following: The Comintern had outlived itself; it was lagging behind and making bad mistakes; it did not appreciate the difficulties of the Chinese Revolution (difficulties of a purely national, Chinese character); and therefore it did harm. . . .

No comment.

June 1943

June 2, 1943

It looks as if the relations between the Communist Party and the Kuomintang will sharply deteriorate. Thus, shortly before the decision of the Presidium of the Comintern Executive Committee to dissolve the Comintern, an important telegram came from the Comintern Executive to the Central Committee of the CCP.

Among other things, the telegram recommended that the Chairman of the CCP Central Committee and the entire leadership preserve, as far as possible, businesslike and normal relations with their partner in the anti-Japanese united front. Yet at the last meeting of the Politburo of the CCP Central Committee no mention at all was made of the specific character of the policy of the Communist Party toward the Kuomintang, of the attitude to the single anti-Japanese bloc, and of joint resistance to the Japanese fascists.

It may be expected that the tactics of covertly breaking the alliance with the Kuomintang will become the official course of the CCP leadership. The fate of the Comintern Executive telegram can be adduced as a proof. According to an established practice, they passed their own resolution on it. This resolution ordered all Communist Party military centers to refrain from any action whatsoever against the units of the Central Government and categorically prohibited independent actions, in order to avoid a conflict with the Kuomintang.

To be sure, this did not agree with the point of view of Mao Tse-tung. As soon as the meeting of the Politburo to discuss the ECCI Presidium decision to dissolve the Comintern took place, Mao Tse-tung ordered that the resolution of the Central Committee's Politburo on the all-out preservation of normal relations with the Kuomintang not be sent to the bases. This resolution was later declared null and void and was revoked.

June 3, 1943

The Soviet Union helped China in repulsing Japanese aggression by providing not only military supplies and loans but also her air power. Many Soviet fighter and bomber squadrons fought in the Chinese skies. Those were Soviet aircraft manned by Soviet personnel. This assistance was particularly valuable, as at the time of the formation of the united anti-Japanese front the Chinese Air Force was practically destroyed (and so was its flying personnel). The Soviet aircraft assumed the air defense of individual sectors of the Sino-Japanese front. Heavy losses were inflicted on the Japanese in a very short time (take, for example, the famous raid of our Tupolev bombers on Formosa—the main base of the Japanese Air Force).

My first mission proved to be in China when the united anti-Japanese front had just emerged and strengthened. I recall with what enthusiasm the news about it was received by the Chinese public. The most energetic measures were being taken to overcome the enmity between the Kuomintang and the Communist Party, friendly contacts were being established, and the Japanese were immediately dealt a number of telling joint blows which impeded the occupation of the country by the aggressor.

I remember the national enthusiasm that seized China, the slogans of the anti-Japanese united front, the desire to join forces for a rebuff to the enemy, the measures taken to overcome capitulationist sentiments and reorganize the armed forces.

The progressive world public hailed the creation of the united anti-Japanese national front in China. This was, no doubt, an effective measure to check the mounting aggression of Japanese imperialism clearly intent on establishing its rule in Asia by the bayonet and gallows.

I remember what it meant at that time for a soldier of the Eighth Route Army or a Chinese Communist to meet a person from the Soviet Union or receive a Soviet badge as a gift. . . .

Much has changed since then. The cheng-feng campaign has a patently anti-Soviet flavor.

June 4, 1943

The CCP Central Committee passed a resolution "On the Methods of Leadership"—one of the legislative foundations for cheng-feng. As usual, the references to Marxism in this resolution are just a cover.

June 12, 1943

The Fall Minister does not at all act behind the back of the Chairman of the CCP Central Committee—here there is an identity of views on all points, and deceit is certainly not present.

The triumph of Kang Sheng consists in that he has succeeded in discerning the true aspirations of Mao Tse-tung and becoming his shadow, his will, his desire. . . .

Wang Ming is living through a real tragedy. Kang Sheng's toady Ching (I cannot write "Dr. Ching," for he's a murderer, not a doctor!) by his "treatment" did irreparable damage to the health of Wang Ming. If it were not for the "prescription affair," he would not have much time left to live. At the age of thirty-nine Wang Ming is chronically ill. He is bedridden to this day. He is very weak. . . .

But the physical sufferings are only a part of the tragedy. Wang Ming experiences all the effects of the suppression by Mao Tse-tung of the internationalist wing in the CCP. Mao regards Wang Ming as the main "dogmatist," a "follower of opportunists Chen Tu-hsiu and Li Li-san," an "extreme deviationist who has no experience of revolutionary struggle." This has led to the isolation of Wang Ming. Under these conditions almost no one dares to maintain even the simplest human relations with him.

As I write these lines, I see Mao in my mind's eye. I hear his soft, unhurried steps. I feel his clasp—a warm soft hand. I see him sit down, his body spreading in the armchair. I feel and see his keen guarded look, softened by an absent-minded smile. And he himself beneath his jacket—flabby, soft, relaxed. And around him—a thick tobacco smell . . . It is always cool in his rooms. He avoids warm premises. How easily he gets excited! How often dirty words escape his lips! And how rude he is when something displeases him! . . .

June 15, 1943

I dare not brush aside the questions which virtually every day are posed before me by the sad reality of Yenan.

I dare not lie or resort to compromises. I rigidly check my every word and read my manuscripts dozens of times.

I am too fixed in my approach to events. An approach developed over many years . . .

No doubt, Mao Tse-tung fights shy of the experience of the AUCP(B).

He fears the principle of democratic centralism which puts him on a par with all Communists. Herein also lies one of the causes of his dislike of Marxism-Leninism, expressed in the contemptuous word "dogmatism."

So long as playing upon Marxism ensured his ascent to power, Mao Tse-tung outwardly accepted it. But hardly had Marxism begun to restrict his power, he declared war on it. So far a secret war . . .

He does not feel he has enough strength, intellect, and culture to run the party on a democratic basis. "Dogmatism" (in Mao Tse-tung's view) condemns him to constant anxiety for power, and this the Chairman of the Central Committee does not dare to allow and will not allow to happen.

The eradication of "dogmatism" means the domination of Mao Tse-tung in the party and the soldierlike submission of all party members—this is the aim of the cheng-feng and the reason behind the constant postponements of the Seventh Party Congress. Mao Tse-tung destroys Marxism by nationalism with the pseudorevolutionary zeal of a petty-bourgeois anarchist. Our meetings in the course of almost fourteen months give me a sufficient idea of him. His learning is sham. Behind it is emptiness. . . .

June 22, 1943

A second year of the singlehanded war against Hitler's Germany, not counting the operations by meager allied forces in Africa and allied air raids on Germany.

Hundreds of German divisions are fighting in Russia. Many million people die at the vast front extending from the Barents Sea to the Black Sea. . . .

The announcer of a Japanese radio spoke about allied air raids on the Japanese islands proper: ". . . There was not and there could not be any panic or confusion among our people! It is with an indomitable belief in our sacred country, with its unprecedented ancient traditions, that everybody in the rear is courageously and resolutely working for the sake of victory. . . ."

———————

Jen Pi-shih reduces any conversation to his ailments and the need to go to the Soviet Union for treatment. As far as political questions are concerned, he shows no independence. He agrees with Mao Tse-tung in everything. . . . In short, an opportunist and no more . . .

Chu Teh remains friendly to Soviet people. He is amiable and ready to do everything lest he should offend his guest or friend. He always wants to know the news from our front and about the political and economic life of the Soviet Union. Unlike Mao Tse-tung, he is not punctillious. He is not afraid that he will lose his dignity by playing volleyball or by his simple manners. He wouldn't mind dancing or playing cards with friends. And how competent he is in military matters. . . .

Now he, too, is being "spiritually purged." . . .

June 24, 1943

Kuomintang spies are being arrested. How many spies are there here?

And who gives Mao Tse-tung the right to suspect any Communist of treason? And what sort of right is it, the right to the supreme wisdom? These claims to infallibility, this inclination for mentorship, show in virtually everything.

How difficult it is to deal with people enamored of their wisdom! How subtle must be the cruelty that is wrapped in courteousness, genteel gestures, and peaceful chatter! . . .

June 30, 1943

Kang Sheng displays a special attitude to all kinds of shady characters. There is the impression that no danger threatens the real Japanese, Kuomintang, and other agents in the Special Area, if they respect Kang. How many dubious characters of all kinds enjoy the confidence and protection of leading CCP functionaries! But honest Communists are not among those whom the Fall Minister's department favors.

The work of party, military, and civil institutions has been paralyzed. An atmosphere of animosity and mutual distrust prevails everywhere. The repressive activity of Kang Sheng's commission fevers the whole party indeed. This embitters the Communists. Some seek by "orthodox" statements to ward off disaster from themselves, while others want to become inconspicuous to survive the troubled days.

Kang Sheng is unpopular in the party, but he has planted his people there, too. Secret reports as well as denunciations through "exposing speeches" at meetings—this is all the intraparty life of the CCP.

———

A political scandal has flared up in Chungking over the abandonment by CCP units of front-line positions and their movement to the area of contact with Kuomintang divisions.

A number of organizations in China have demanded the unconditional transfer of control over the Special Area and CCP armies to the head of the Central Government. Chungking speaks with anger about the perfidy of the Communists who are surrendering the country to the Japanese occupationists. And yet anti-Kuomintang passions are being fanned in the Special Area with an even greater recklessness. Mao Tse-tung is in high spirits. . . .

July 1943

July 3, 1943

Lin Piao, former commander of the 115th Infantry Division. He visited the Soviet Union on several occasions. A good military specialist, he is taking part in the drafting of a military reform.

There was a time when Lin Piao voiced his displeasure with the work of the Kang Sheng commission and adhered to Wang Ming's opposition. Later, however, he apparently became aware of Mao Tsetung's strength and what stood behind his actions and withdrew into silence. He has been assigned to Chu Teh's staff, but holds no post there. Lin Piao is looking for ways to find reconciliation with the Chairman of the Central Committee of the CCP and with Kang Sheng.

Lin Piao was born in 1907. Graduated from the Whampoa Military Academy. Commanded a battalion during the Northern Expedition of 1926–27.

Lean of figure, unsociable, and of taciturn disposition. Has little say with the military authorities. Nevertheless, he is a person not to be discounted.

Lin Piao is slow of movement and speech. Very phlegmatic, although businesslike and active in work. I know a few instances when he acted as a resolute and merciless man. . . .

July 5, 1943

Po Ku is a well-groomed, stocky man with a waddling gait and smooth gestures. His face is round and his lips fat. Unruffled and good-natured. His dialect betrays his northern origin.

When we are alone, he sharply criticizes the regime in the Special Area, despises Mao Tse-tung, and is keenly aware that the latter holds all the levers of power in his hands.

Looks frightened. While we were talking, he looked around cautiously and even stepped out several times for fear of being overheard.

July 7, 1943

Alarming news about the concentration of Kuomintang troops in the south of the Special Area.

The Kuomintang is surely looking for a chance to move against the Special Area. It can also be expected that the militarist groupings of the Ma brothers, the Shansi and Shensi groupings, will not stand on the sidelines. To benefit from this situation will be the Japanese and no one else.

The situation is getting very serious indeed. We have packed up, prepared our belongings and the radio station for an emergency evacuation, and the stationary equipment for demolition.

Mao Tse-tung, Kang Sheng, and others do not want to see their dirty linen washed in public. Their anxiety is not completely groundless, for the Soviet group is the only witness of the political machinations of the CCP leadership.

For his part Hsiao Li makes no bones about the undesirability of our further stay in Yenan. . . .

Being involuntary witnesses of what is going on here, we have become a great source of irritation for the CCP leaders and tie up their activities. We are given to understand this in a way humiliating to our dignity. We are shadowed, debarred from social life, gossiped about, and fed scanty information from local newspapers.

July 9, 1943

A great battle is raging at Kursk. No comparison to the Kharkov tragedy—the Soviet defenses are impenetrable. Three hundred and four Nazi tanks were destroyed in a single day!

Confusion and panic are reigning in Yenan. Everybody is expecting an invasion by the Kuomintang and militarist troops, though the latter prefer to have dealings with the Japanese rather than risk an invasion.

We were invited to Mao Tse-tung's, where he spoke at length about patriotism, about the CCP being loyal to the united front tactics, and about the treacherous policies of the Kuomintang which "is undermining the liberation struggle of the Chinese people."

All of a sudden he remembered the Comintern and informed us that though "this body of the militant union of proletarian parties" was dissolved, in this grim hour the CCP leadership had placed great hopes on an intervention by Comrade Dimitrov, the "loyal friend of the Chinese Communists."

On instructions from the Chairman of the CCP Central Committee preparations have been made for calling a meeting. Leaflets have been printed specially for this purpose. Printed in huge characters were appeals demanding that the Central Government headed by Chiang Kai-shek immediately stop concentrating Kuomintang troops around the Special Area and transferring Kuomintang front-line detachments from the front to the borders of the Special Area. There were also appeals and slogans calling for strengthening the joint anti-Japanese bloc for the defeat of the fascist barbarians, and imprecations against Japan.

Some of the leaflets demand that all people rise for the defense of the Communist Party, "our Eighth Route Army," and the whole of the Special Area.

Large bundles of these appeals had been brought before the meeting was officially opened. I took one such leaflet for future reference. The thin semitranslucent sheet bore the text of an appeal to the Kuomintang. It described any civil war that might break out as criminal and inadmissible.

The meeting was attended by all the CCP leaders. All the leading members of the party took the floor, except the Chairman of the Central Committee, who looked very much put out. The speakers fulminated about the Japanese aggressors, swore their support for the Central Government in Chungking headed by the "Commander in Chief and President Chiang Kai-shek," then suddenly each one of the speakers recalled the injustices they had suffered from Chiang Kai-shek, and that in a tearful and plaintive tone of voice. All the speakers assured Chiang Kai-shek that no one in the Special Area was even thinking about starting a civil war, that all the forces and resources of the Special Area would be used for the struggle against Japanese aggression, that all the units of the Eighth Route Army would mount resistance and would staunchly defend the native soil. The meeting was also addressed by peasants, workers, and soldiers.

According to Kang Sheng, no fewer than fifteen thousand people were present.

Leaflets were passed around.

All this demonstration of good will which was meant for Chungking was playacted seriously and conscientiously.

I took a few shots of the meeting with my camera.

I immediately sent a radio message to Moscow about the critical situation on the southern border of the Special Area and about the need for urgent measures. The rout of the Special Area could be prevented only by speedy interference from the Soviet Union.

July 13, 1943

The Soviet Government has declared to Chungking that its military assistance is aimed at furthering the national liberation struggle of the Chinese people and not for unleashing a civil war, and took a resolute stand in defense of the CCP and the Special Area.

July 15, 1943

In an obvious effort to mend fences with us, the CCP leadership has unexpectedly invited us to attend a meeting of the party activists in Yang-chia-lin. We accepted the invitation, and Yuzhin and I went to Yang-chia-lin.

Crowding the pavilion were about a thousand Communists. The meeting was opened by Peng Chen. He informed the Communists about the seriousness of the situation and said that a large number of "Kuomintang spies" had been exposed and arrested.

"The special department cannot catch all the agents teeming in Yenan. That is why the department has appealed to the Communists for help in this matter of great importance," said Peng Chen. After that several contrite "spies" trooped onto the stage.

They told about their actions, most of which sounded foolish and naïve. They begged forgiveness and swore that they would serve faithfully in the Eighth Route Army under the leadership of Mao Tse-tung. Altogether twelve such "spies" addressed the meeting.

Peng Chen told how Kuomintang agents could be identified and added that all those who have made a clean breast of it would be set free: "All they have to do is to repent fearlessly and not be afraid of giving themselves up to the special department!"

Peng Chen's tall figure dominated the scene, his face flushed, making him look like a butcher.

The next speaker was Kang Sheng. The chief of the Ching-pao-chu was wild with anger. He bared his front teeth, waved his hands wildly, and shouted:

"You know perfectly well that many of your friends are under arrest! No sooner have you left this hall than you'll find many more of you missing! Don't get too much surprised if many of those present here today will be put away tomorrow!"

Kang Sheng then began to implore the participants in the meeting and all the Communists of Yenan to save the Special Area from spies.

"All of you here are spies for the Kuomintang!" shouted Kang Sheng. "Why do you want our destruction? What wrong have we done to you? For you have everything: shelter, food rations. . . . Why do you want us dead? Repent and we shall forgive you, but you must also remember that repentance is not always sincere! . . . and that re-education is a long process!"

Kang Sheng's speech had a terrorizing effect. An oppressive silence descended on the hall and the visibly frightened audience.

People suddenly became aware of what unlimited power the Ching-pao-chu chief wielded and what would become of anyone who dared to raise his voice in defense of truth.

Peng Chen was about to declare the meeting closed when Chu Teh unexpectedly mounted the stage. Judging by the expression on his face, this meeting of party "activists" was news to him as a member of the Politburo.

"Do you mean to say that after this meeting I should lose faith in my friends and comrades-in-arms?" asked Chu Teh in a calm tone of voice. "Does this mean that from now on I should live in fear of arrest or expect to see my friends arrested? How dare you treat the party activists in this way, the best men of the party and its backbone?"

Chu Teh turned around sharply and resumed his seat.

Peng Chen declared the meeting closed. The Communists dispersed in silence. . . .

July 16, 1943

On Mao Tse-tung's instructions Chu Teh sent a telegram to Hu Tsunan, assistant commander of the Kuomintang-held area south of the Special Area:

After your inspection of the border between Lo-chuan and I-chuan the situation in the area has become nothing short of warlike. Rumors are circulating that the Central Government wants to take advantage of the dissolution of the Comintern and has decided to put an end to the Chinese Communist Party. It is also rumored that large contingents are being moved from the area south of the Yellow River in a westerly direction. Large amounts of ammunition and food are being shipped in the same direction. The threat of civil war is imminent.

At this crucial moment of the liberation struggle it is necessary to cement our unity. A civil war would be highly damaging to the cause of the liberation war and the consolidation of the state. Only Japan would stand to gain from this, while our own country would find itself in a dangerous situation. This would also inflict great damage to the military objectives of our allies—Britain, the United States, and the Soviet Union.

Home guards maintain a high order of discipline, ensure production and public education, all of which has greatly changed the situation for the better.

The deployment of your troops shows that you are making preparations for an offensive against us. We are surprised and bewildered by these developments.

We are expecting a reply to this message.

Chu Teh

July 17, 1943

The number of spies who have been caught and who have repented their activities has markedly increased. . . .

The participants in the meeting of the city activists held on July 15 were closely watched by men specially appointed for this purpose by the Department of Information Service in the Liberated Areas. Those in the audience who showed discontent or doubt were "noted."

This calls to memory Mao Tse-tung's words from his "Talks at the Conference on Art and Literature" last year: "To treat one's friends as an enemy is to act from the positions of the enemy."

The suspects are not only arrested but are also victimized. . . .

July 18, 1943

The idea that Wang Ming might go to Moscow keeps Mao Tse-tung on tenterhooks. The fuss over his sickness and his "treatment" continues. . . .

Moscow has taken measures.

The Kuomintang leaders have announced that they have no intention of invading the Special Area. The concentration and deployment of troops on the southern border of the Special Area have discontinued.

July 19, 1943

Delegates to the congress have long since arrived. The cheng-feng not only morally suppresses Mao Tse-tung's opponents and ranges the entire party against them, but is also designed to put them into a certain frame of mind. . . . It would be reasonable to expect that all of them will be "spiritually purified" before the congress.

Ma Hai-te is in a huddle with the most taciturn and close-mouthed person in the Special Area—Li Ko-nung. It looks like Ma Hai-te has the most detailed information about the state of affairs in the leadership of the CCP.

July 20, 1943

The events of the past year have unexpected, albeit logical, results. The Politburo has vested Mao Tse-tung with unlimited powers. From now on the Chairman of the Central Committee of the CCP has the decisive vote at the Secretariat of the Central Committee. This means that Mao Tse-tung will have the last word in everything. As he decides, so will it happen. In fact, the party organs now discharge purely technical functions at his side.

The anti-Kuomintang campaign has drawn to a successful conclusion in Yenan, and the Chairman of the CCP Central Committee has in a way made his mark. In the first place he has managed to transfer large military contingents of the Eighth Route Army to the Special Area. They have quietly moved in from the eastern bank of the Yellow River and taken positions near the border.

The Chairman of the CCP Central Committee realizes that the danger has passed and that the Central Government will not risk retaliation to the anti-Kuomintang propaganda campaign. Another wave of anti-Chiang Kai-shek hysteria. Mao Tse-tung is trying to make the best of the existing situation, acting in the belief that Moscow will step in on his behalf, if necessary.

Vituperation is being heaped on the Chungking Government, and Chiang Kai-shek's entire regime is called fascist.

Mao Tse-tung openly takes credit for the recent conflict with the Kuomintang. He says that a firm stand should have been taken with regard to Chiang Kai-shek much earlier. This firmness, he insists, would have made it possible to avoid the debacle of the New Fourth Army and would secure some other political and material advantages. Thus, the anti-Kuomintang policy has been declared correct and necessary, and all of Mao's actions are described as a farsighted analysis amounting to a great prophecy.

Mao Tse-tung says that the Comintern tactics in this situation would be nearsighted, unrealistic, and divorced from the concrete conditions in the country.

These statements are meant to discredit the internationalist wing of the CCP and are in fact spearheaded against it. In the eyes of the party, Lo Fu, Po Ku, Wang Ming, and other supporters of the Comintern principles are defeatists.

Mao Tse-tung told me all this tête-à-tête. He panned the "dogmatists" who had done so much harm to the party by their capitulatory policy with respect to the Kuomintang, and called them nearsighted theoreticians, Chiang Kai-shek's yes-men.

At another meeting the Chairman of the CCP Central Committee (he was there with Kang Sheng and with one of his secretaries) again cracked down on Po Ku and Wang Ming for their leniency to Chiang Kai-shek. He accused them of all possible "dogmatic" fallacies. Carried away by his own performance, Mao Tse-tung had all but lost his self-control. He paced the floor, speaking in a voice far above its usual pitch, his suffused face turned dark red, while his jibes grew rougher and more bilious every minute.

Kang Sheng fixed me with a silent stare. At one point, when Mao's harangue was at its most acrid, Kang Sheng sent away the secretary with a curt expressive gesture.

In expounding his views Mao sought to make an impression upon me in the hope that I would impart the same impression to Moscow. He wants to bring me around to his point of view, to have me under his influence, so that I shall see the events through his eyes.

He wants to have Moscow believe that his actions are but a practical application of Marxism to concrete reality, and trust and support him. His candor was meant to illicit a similarly candid response from me. He thus wanted to know how Moscow viewed his political "line" and how far he could go in his efforts to suppress the internationalists in the CCP without arousing suspicion.

Pondering over these events, I have come to still another conclusion: The Chairman of the CCP Central Committee is playing a long-range policy and is seeking to create a precongress atmosphere suitable for his designs. And this is the most important thing. . . .

It is in this direction that Mao has bent all his actions. For example, he had Lo Fu, Po Ku, Chou En-lai, Wang Ming, Wang Chia-hsiang, Chen Yun, and Kang Sheng removed from the Secretariat of the Politburo. Mao had secured this decision at an extended meeting of the Politburo. Thus the Chairman of the CCP Central Committee has removed from the Secretariat not only his opponents but also his supporters. This move helped Mao to camouflage the open dispersal of his political opponents, because at the same meeting a new three-man Secretariat was formed under Mao's pressure: Jen Pi-shih, Liu Shao-chi, and Chairman Mao himself. Now Mao can always expect support and understanding from this crew. . . .

The flickering candle, the squeaking pen, the well-worn pages of my notebook . . . I cannot get used to the candle. It is difficult to read and write by its dim shaky light. Or perhaps I am just tired? . . .

July 23, 1943

The CCP leaders are trying to make the best of the situation created by the conflict with the Kuomintang. The administrative, military, and party apparatus of the Special Area are engaged in the daily pursuit of catching Chiang Kai-shek's spies.

In this operation Kang Sheng is aided by a host of social workers who at numerous meetings urge all agents of Japan and Chiang Kai-shek to confess, and threaten that otherwise they will have their heads chopped off. These are not meetings in the usual sense of the word but some sort of raving mad powwows. Everybody is required to listen to the semiliterate hodgepodge of cheng-feng bosses.

Today about six hundred persons have been brought to confession. The number of repenters is growing all the time. People turn up in droves confessing their guilt—mostly students and petty employees. . . .

The next stage of cheng-feng is to expose "spies" in the middle link of the CCP and later in the leading echelon of the party. Thus Mao Tse-tung has identified "dogmatism" in the party with treachery and with kowtowing to the Kuomintang. He is setting the masses against the "dogmatists" and is obviously bent on their physical destruction.

Mao Tse-tung told me with satisfaction that he was planning to carry on this campaign until the next year.

The wave of suicide has not subsided in Yenan.

The city looks like a concentration camp. For the fourth month now no one is allowed to leave offices and schools. The crippling discipline that shackles people is similar to that of a prison.

Many of the arrested have been released, but none from among the "dogmatists" or those who have "stained their reputation with sympathy for the Soviet Union, with association with Wang Ming or the Comintern. . . ."

July 24, 1943

Wang Ming was receiving poisonous drugs.

It is clear that Wang Ming was being poisoned and that Mao Tse-tung and Kang Sheng were involved. It was impossible to kill openly the leader of the internationalists in the CCP, member of the Executive Committee of the Communist International, a man who was loved and respected in the Comintern. Nevertheless, according to the CCP Chairman, the pressure of time was great. The situation was highly favorable for stamping out recalcitrance: a raging war in the world, the Comintern dissolved, Yenan far removed and hard to get to. . . .

A medical council was held. It was attended by all twelve of the Yenan doctors who had spent two weeks at the CCP Central Committee in Yang-chia-lin where, as might be expected, they had received a good dose of "spiritual training."

Mao Tse-tung and Kang Sheng have no doubts that we know of the deliberate poisoning of Wang Ming and that Moscow is therefore also aware of the fact. So this esteemed council of medicos was called entirely for the purpose of hoodwinking those who suspected the worst.

July 26, 1943

While studying the case history the medical council came across the mention of calomel.

The doctors demanded an explanation from Ching. The matter had gone so far that the Central Committee Chairman forbade any more questions to be asked of Ching and interrupted the session. . . .

The doctors felt that some high-ranking officials were involved. At the next meeting some of the pundits announced that they had nothing to say on the matter, and still others even began to support Ching, in defiance of all common sense.

Unexpectedly Rosa Vladimirovna produced several calomel prescriptions and other drugs which Ching had written and which she had put away for future reference.

I wonder what will happen now!

July 27, 1943

Hsu Teh-li is one of the most respected men in Yenan.

This man has a truly unusual biography.

He was born in 1877 into a poor farmer's family; went to a school for poor children. Visited Japan several times where he studied for several years. Taught at a seminary where Mao Tse-tung studied between 1912 and 1918.

Once when Mao Tse-tung was threatened with expulsion, Hsu

Teh-li and Yang Chang-chi stood up for him. At that time Yang Chang-chi, Mao's future father-in-law, was teaching ethics. Thanks to their protection, Mao Tse-tung finished the seminary.

After that Hsu Teh-li studied at the universities of Paris and Lyons for about four years.

In France Hsu Teh-li met Li Li-san and Chou En-lai, who had set up a foreign division of the CCP there.

At that time many Chinese went to college in France under a contract with the Sino-French educational society.

Later Hsu Teh-li worked at factories in Germany and Belgium for a short time.

Back in China, he joined the Kuomintang in 1925. In 1927 he joined the CCP. In the same year he took part in the Nanchang uprising.

In the late 1920s Hsu Teh-li studied at the Sun Yat-sen University in Moscow.

After that he worked, together with Mao Tse-tung, in the government of the Central Soviet Area.

He took part in the Long March. Some time ago, at the age of sixty-four, he took part in a swimming competition. . . .

Although Hsu Teh-li is an old man and looks it, he is still strong and hale.

Mao Tse-tung has profound respect for his former teacher.

The CCP leaders are deathly afraid that Wang Ming might tell the former Comintern leaders in Moscow about the actual state of affairs in the CCP. It is true that they would hardly relish the idea of losing Moscow's support and being left face to face with Chiang Kai-shek.

July 29, 1943

The cheng-feng campaign is clearly aimed at bureaucratizing the party in order to reduce the ardor and initiative of every Communist to naught. Instead of establishing discipline among like-minded people welded together by one great goal, the CCP leaders are trying to instill in them blind servility based on fear. Fear, fear, and again fear sums up the general atmosphere in Yenan.

Kang Sheng's henchmen are so cruel and merciless that they stop at nothing, even at arresting pregnant women. This has put me to thinking about the moral make-up of these "people."

One need not be very observant to see that all of them are akin in their philosophy of life, which is as crude and primitive as a kick in the pants. All of them are on the make, with little in the way of actual achievement to their credit, in most cases. It is worthy of note that these culturally backward mediocrities, corrupted and intellectually hollow creatures, hold down jobs at various punitive organizations here. Their readiness to commit violence and perjury, carry out executions, and write denunciations ensures them slow but steady promotion and, what is still more important, keeps them above poverty. Turpitude is vain and it clings to satiety and pleasure more than anything else.

August 1943

A state of siege has been unofficially introduced in the city. All the offices and educational establishments have been fenced. Guards stand at the gates. Married men are strictly forbidden to see their families on threat of arrest. Private conversation between any two persons also involves an obvious risk.

Many of the "exposed" have been ordered to stay at their places of employment, since there are not enough cells in the prison.

Different organizations communicate with each other through special messengers from the Kang Sheng department.

The "reformation of the exposed" and the vigorous indoctrination of those whose turn will come soon are going on everywhere. Mao Tse-tung admits that he attaches "particular importance" to this campaign.

The activity of the leading party bodies in Yenan and Soviet organs depends on Mao Tse-tung's mood. When he gets tired, any work—conferences and even important reports—is canceled.

A festive novelty at home—artillery salute to mark our Red Army's victories. Yesterday, Moscow saluted in honor of the liberation of Orel and Belgorod.

Liu Shao-chi is reshuffling the members of the leading CCP bodies, not without Mao Tse-tung's knowledge.

Eighty per cent of Kang Sheng's apparatus workers have pleaded guilty of espionage.

Mournful silence reigns in the city and its environs at night; not a voice is heard, no laughter, no lights.

I walked out of my cave a minute ago and looked at the valley—nothing but impenetrable darkness of the night. The footsteps and calls of the guards in Ta-pien-kou are not heard, but all the roads are patrolled.

August 7, 1943

Considering Mao Tse-tung's secret hostility toward me and my comrades, I decided to act absolutely officially. I asked Mao Tse-tung for an audience.

The CCP Central Committee Chairman did not keep me waiting. But in his invitation he asked me to come alone, which made me uncomfortable.

Mao received me in the customary room. He seated me in the leather armchair meant for the guests of honor, offered me some tea. He smiled and joked. After an exchange of traditional polite phrases he asked me on whose initiative I undertook my political and economic study. I answered that it would be too much to call my essays a study and said that I only wanted to enrich my knowledge, to get a better idea of the economic transformations which the CCP was carrying out or is going to carry out. Then I said that the period of the CCP history from 1928 to 1938 and, especially, the importance of the Tsunyi Conference (its proceedings, the delegates' speeches, etc.) were not adequately covered in the party and historical literature.

Mao Tse-tung asked me whether I was doing it at Moscow's instructions or at my own initiative. I told him once again that it was my own initiative dictated by my sincere interest in facts of great political and social importance.

Mao nodded, got up, and paced the room for some time. Then he said: "All right. I shall take it upon myself to elucidate the main questions. I think that I am the only person who can help you there. All right, all right . . ." He suggested that we get down to work right away.

I took out my notebook and hardly had time to get ready when he started dictating. I could see that Mao was used to giving orders and dictating.

I wrote down the plan of work and its starting points.

Mao knows how to work. In not more than ten minutes he was giving me a real lecture on what should be emphasized in the study and what should be avoided.

I tried to mention my own plan, but he wouldn't even hear about it.

The essence of all his arguments is the following: "I am the main participant in and the witness of the events in question and I am the best judge."

Then Mao laid down a condition which had to be observed by all means—he must read my work when I finish it and put his signature everywhere, thus making it authentic and more significant, so to speak. In other words I must write under his strict control or else he refuses to help me with explanations, etc.

It all looked rather childish, but I had no alternative to agreeing.

The CCP Central Committee Chairman will keep the question of the party, its development, ideological clashes within the party, etc., under his personal control, and I am to get the facts and the explanations of the facts only from him. At this point Mao declared categorically that I shouldn't try to discuss these questions with anybody else. He even said that he would warn everybody about it so that the comrades wouldn't give me any consultations without his consent.

That was not funny at all. The nature of relations within the CCP leadership became as plain as daylight: strict obedience of all to the CCP Central Committee Chairman.

When it came to the organization and development of the Red Army of China, the CCP Central Committee Chairman just offered to give me a lecture. He peremptorily labeled any other sources "incompetent" and "pernicious." In this case, too, Mao wouldn't allow any consultations with anybody else.

When we were parting, Mao Tse-tung said that nobody should know about our talks. I was to come alone. He said I did not need the services of Aleyev, the interpreter, since I knew Chinese well enough to understand everything. "Witnesses would only complicate our work," Mao said.

But he did not stop at that. He started flattering me and, at the same time, hinted that he did not trust my comrades. I expressed my surprise. Mao objected to me in such a rude and harsh way that I was taken aback at first. Mao was almost screaming telling me that there, in Yenan, nobody could be trusted, and, especially, my Soviet colleagues, for they were aliens here, etc. And then he went on to praise the Comintern leadership and Comrade Stalin.

But that was not all, either. When I was leaving, he gave out with abuse aimed against Po Ku, Wang Ming, and "other dogmatists, who tied the CCP hand and foot in front of Chiang Kai-shek." He hotly persuaded me that Po Ku and Wang Ming ideologically continued the Chen Tu-hsiu and Li Li-san line, that "those who inspire the dogmatists are essentially alien to the party, are splitters, opportunists," etc. . . .

His lectures will be something on such subjects as: "Mao Tse-tung and the CCP" and "Mao Tse-tung and the Struggle Against the Petty-Bourgeois Trends in the CCP."

This half-comic and half-sad scene clearly showed how touchy Mao was in matters of prestige, merits, and power. He wants to be absolutely right in everything, now and in the future, too.

Well, let's hear what he has to say. . . .

August 9, 1943

Jen Pi-shih does not dare to make independent decisions, though he has the right to such decisions on a number of questions. He even avoids putting his signature to already approved documents without the additional personal endorsement by Mao Tse-tung, whose every word he echoes obsequiously. Kang Sheng capitalizes on this widely.

Jen Pi-shih works in the daytime, always with intervals for rest. If Mao Tse-tung does not call meetings, he goes to bed before dark. He enjoys his food and likes to talk of his ailments. He drinks little and smokes very moderately.

Jen Pi-shih has a twelve-year-old daughter. His wife plays the role of his nurse and private secretary.

His attitude to the Soviet people is not hostile, but he is afraid to compromise himself by any friendly relations with them. That is why he is strictly official.

Mao Tse-tung uses him to keep in touch with me.

August 11, 1943

Nine out of ten central hospital workers have been accused of espionage. Orlov is stunned. . . .

August 17, 1943

Cheng-feng is a real calamity. Lu Hsun's words aptly express the utter bitterness of these agonizing summer months: ". . . even the trees that do not fear cold have long stood naked. . . ."

The evil of these months has not bypassed anybody.

August 19, 1943

The group of CCP representatives in Kuomintang headed by Wang Ming stayed in Hankow in 1938 while Mao Tse-tung stayed in Yenan where he was busy strengthening his positions for a fight against the "Moscow group."

Both groups of the CCP leadership believed that they had every right to pursue an independent policy.

The policy pursued by the Wang Ming group was the policy of pursuing the tactics of a united front with Kuomintang and active military operations against the Japanese invaders. This policy was based on and guided by the Comintern Executive Committee decisions.

Mao Tse-tung did everything to evade the struggle against the invaders and was preparing his Army for civil war against the Kuomintang.

The differences between the CCP Central Committee Chairman and Wang Ming grew especially sharp at the end of 1941, when Mao, believing that the Soviet Union was doomed, put aside all political camouflage and got down to the reconstruction of the party to suit his own ends, though the struggle between them had begun much earlier. At that time Kang Sheng, who succeeded in gaining exclusive power with Chiang Ching's help, began to play an especially sinister role. This secretive, invariably polite, very high-strung, and energetic Chinese brought back with him from the Soviet Union deep hostility to everything that is Soviet. Kang Sheng sided with Mao Tse-tung, upon which he became the Fall Minister of the Chinese Communist Party, Mao Tse-tung's "claws and teeth." He knows everything about everyone and is ruthless. This is what the CCP Central Committee Chairman has always needed most of all.

At that time Chu Teh actively supported the "Moscow group"; Liu Shao-chi was in the New Fourth Army; and Chou En-lai was in Chungking.

Kang Sheng not only got the post of the chief of Ching-pao-chu but also took under his control the Eighth Route Army and the New Fourth Army intelligence.

It was Kang Sheng who assured the CCP Central Committee of the absolute political loyalty of the actress Chiang Ching.

August 21, 1943

In many organizations the number of exposed Kuomintang and Japanese "agents" comes to 100 per cent, and it is not less than 90 in all the rest—Kang Sheng is master of his word.

Thus 90 per cent of the select party cadre are "spies." What a bitter mockery!

Liu Shao-chi is the direct conductor of the ideas of the CCP Central Committee Chairman; Jen Pi-shih is their technical executor; and Kang Sheng, the reprisals man.

The situation is bad. Prices are climbing. A considerable part of our monthly pay issued from Moscow goes to the CCP fund as our personal contributions to the Chinese people's struggle. . . .

August 26, 1943

The arrival of the Soviet plane in Yenan broke the routine of Yenan life. It was necessary to part with the sick Wang Ming, but Mao Tse-tung couldn't risk it. The doctors were called to the leading executives again and again. They were told to say that Wang Ming was gravely ill and Wang Chia-hsiang was unwell, too, and that they both couldn't endure the strain of flight, that they should not be disturbed, etc.

Mao does not show his anxiety, though he looks worried. But Kang Sheng is most active. There is no doubt that he would never let Wang Ming go. Wang Ming is his sworn enemy.

Kang Sheng's activity amounted to collecting all kinds of arguments against Wang Ming's departure. He literally wrests these arguments out of all those who are connected with Wang Ming in some way or other. . . .

August 28, 1943

Po Ku says that the CCP Central Committee keeps showering Moscow with telegrams camouflaging the actual situation in the Special Area and in the CCP, distorting the essence of cheng-feng, the tactics in relation to Chungking, and the nature of differences with Wang Ming.

The CCP Central Committee Chairman would have long severed relations with the former Comintern leaders if he had not hoped for Moscow's assistance in the future and had not feared Kuomintang. Desiring a conflict with Kuomintang, Mao Tse-tung plans to involve the Soviet Union and in this way to solve the problem of power in China.

At the present stage the Chinese Revolution must be aimed first of all at the foreign enemy and enslaver, Japanese imperialism. But these are mere words to Mao. . . .

He skillfully disguises all kinds of political intrigues and actions as campaigns under innocent-sounding slogans. The "rectification of the three styles of work" campaign is nothing but badgering the "dogmatists" and the "Moscow group." The "spies' exposure" campaign is a pretext for physical reprisals.

The CCP Central Committee Chairman has completely recovered from the shock caused by the threat of invasion of the Special Area by the Kuomintang troops and forgotten his pleas addressed to Moscow and Chungking. He no longer speaks about a "liberation war" or "allied commitments."

Yenan is bristling up. It curses "dogmatists," "spies," and the Kuomintang. Fanatical hatred is written on all faces . . . and fatigue, too.

August 30, 1943

Wang Ming stayed in Yenan. Our plane's crew kept delaying the flight as long as they could, but the CCP Central Committee Chairman finally got what he wanted.

Kang Sheng may pause for breath now. Wang Ming is under his supervision, rendered harmless, so to speak.

Kang Sheng made a report at a rather representative party meeting in Yenan. His report was devoted to the struggle against the Chiang Kai-shek and Japanese agents in the Special Area, the results of this campaign, and the new tasks. The obvious connection between the "spies' exposure" campaign and cheng-feng was revealed in this report for the first time.

Kang Sheng devoted his report mostly to a criticism (if only it were just criticism) of the international wing of the Communist Party. Internationalists to him are capitulators, the followers of Chen Tu-hsiu and Li Li-san, and opportunists of the worst petty-bourgeois kind. And, in general, all the evil in the party comes from the internationalists. These "Comintern idealists in the CCP have planted illusions in the minds of Communists that it is possible to co-operate with Chiang Kai-shek. The internationalists began this double-dealing activity as early as the Wuhan period [1938]. They have done great harm to the Communist Party. The damage caused by the activity of the 'capitulators' and 'conciliators' is truly immeasurable."

As the result, the report had a strongly pronounced anti-Kuomintang nature. At the same time Kang Sheng vigorously condemned the "criminal illusions, adventurism, and shortsightedness" of the "Moscow group" members and other party "dogmatists."

The Ching-pao-chu chief avoided mentioning names, but it was clear to everybody whom he had in mind. Later the names of Chou En-lai, Po Ku, Wang Ming, and Lo Fu were mentioned frequently in all the conversations. All the other members of the said groupings who held less important posts in the party were also subjected to a severe tongue-lashing.

The chief of Ching-pao-chu avoided any frank and direct conversation (undoubtedly, he followed Mao's instructions, since all his people speak in the same way). For example, he did not say anything about the anti-Japanese bloc as such, but, again, he made it perfectly clear to everybody that neither the party nor the Special Area would have suffered such a colossal damage but for the above-mentioned "illusions," that the Chiang Kai-shek and other agents thrived in such an atmosphere of complacency and undermined the unity of the Communist Party unhampered, disorganizing the base areas' economy and weakening the armed forces.

Kang set party activists against the "dogmatists" and other "opportunists." He spoke of terror as a revolutionary necessity, justified punitive actions, and extolled the achievements of cheng-feng.

It is significant that this frankly pogromist speech contained information on a detailed discussion of mistakes by "capitulatory elements, opportunists," and all the "dogmatists" in general to be held in the party organizations. The Ching-pao-chu chief listed the main "charges." They included inundation of the base areas with Kuomintang and Japanese agents, and the capitulators' activity that precipitated the rout of the New Fourth Army.

Liberation Daily published material on the participation of the Central Government troops and the CCP troops in the war against Japan. The comparative data of this kind has been published for the first time. This was done with a definite purpose. As far as I know, the CCP Central Committee Chairman is busy searching for contacts with the Americans. This is exactly the data supplied to the American embassy in Chungking at Mao Tse-tung's order.

According to this data, 58 per cent of all the Japanese troops in China and 90 per cent of the bandit puppet troops are allegedly tied up by the Eighth Route Army and the New Fourth Army units. The data is overstated, to say the least.

August 31, 1943

I don't know what happened, but the discussion of the activity of "dogmatists" and "Moscow opposition" ("the left-opportunists," "conciliators," "capitulators") which was promised by Kang Sheng has been postponed. I asked Kang Sheng for when the campaign in question was being planned, and he said that it had been postponed indefinitely at the CCP Central Committee Chairman's instructions.

Mao Tse-tung gambles skillfully on the existing situation. There is hostility between the CCP and Kuomintang—has he not cautioned against it? Have not all his previous statements been brilliantly confirmed by the current events that have almost become tragic for the CCP?

This demagogy is being energetically drummed into the heads of all party members. Mao Tse-tung appears in the role of some prophet without whom CCP would have inevitably pined away. And not a word is said about the Soviet Union's intercession which saved the Special Area.

Mao Tse-tung's influence is growing. He already has become a leader whose wisdom is beyond any doubt.

In his statements Chou En-lai expressed, though very timidly, the idea of the desirability of a peaceful settlement with Chungking. Chou does not dare to speak about it openly, but his innuendo is this: It is necessary to look for an opportunity of a peaceful settlement of the crisis; relations with Kuomintang should not be aggravated. In everything else, however, Chou readily and uncompromisingly yields to Mao Tse-tung. He does not conceal that he has admitted to himself the erroneousness of his policy in the Wuhan period. He defines his mistakes as "capitulatory and right-opportunist." He is going to make statements on these issues. But even now he never misses a chance to say over and over again that he admits his mistakes.

I have not had a chance to see Po Ku lately. I don't know what his present position is.

Most likely he will also change his position. People are placed in a difficult situation. It is hard to hold out. Political deception by Mao Tse-tung is based on the Soviets' and party apparatus of the Special Area. Mao's opponents have no opportunity to appeal to the party membership. All the channels are blocked. Information flows only one way—Mao's supporters are conducting the shameless indoctrination of the party and the Soviets' activists. As the result, the Wang Ming group and internationalists in general are depicted before the party as enemies of the revolution and of the people who are "responsible" for the rout of the New Fourth Army. Everything is blamed on them—the death of their comrades-in-arms, famine, calamities, and epidemics. . . . Not everybody can withstand the condemnation of a collective such as the party. And this is exactly what things are coming to.

September 1943

September 3, 1943

Yura went to the first form and Borya to the third this year. I am afraid my boys will grow up without me. I was away from home for most of 1938, 1939, 1940, and 1941. And now this trip. Who knows how long it will continue?

September 6, 1943

In June, July, and August the drill of "The Twenty-two Documents" was pushed to the background. Everyone—young and old—was busy "spy"-hunting or exposing himself.

A "spy"-reforming campaign has now been launched at the instructions of Mao Tse-tung and Kang Sheng. They will be reformed with the aid of the same "Twenty-two Documents."

Yenan party and military cadres cram these documents with renewed energy.

Mao Tse-tung told me: "You foreigners have a poor knowledge of the soul of the Chinese people." He recommended that I follow Yuzhin's example and read more old Chinese novels. This would help me evaluate correctly the cheng-feng and other developments in the Special Area. . . .

———

Ma Hai-te is correct with us and doesn't mind pretending that he is one of "ours."

His wife, Su Fei, is very frivolous, although it is hard to say whether she owes it to her own temperament or follows the instructions of her husband. She is a success with men and responds to their advances. At present she is flirting with our radio operator.

September 9, 1943

Until this July Chou En-lai headed the CCP mission in Chungking. For his allegiance to Wang Ming's group he has been removed from work. In the past weeks he has been making repentant speeches, vowing his devotion to "Chairman Mao."

With the exception of Wang Ming and several other comrades the "repentance epidemic" has afflicted all party functionaries and CCP military leaders who have suffered from criticism in one way or another.

September 11, 1943

The CCP Central Committee's Politburo was in session all through the end of August and the beginning of September.

Right at the beginning Mao Tse-tung set the tune for the work of this supreme body of the party by saying at its first meeting (which he opened) that the Comintern had been dissolved by decision of its Executive Committee, that it had no longer existed as an organization and therefore it was not necessary to be careful, to conceal things, etc. Emphasizing these facts, Mao Tse-tung urged the audience to speak openly.

Chou En-lai gave a big report. His report, as well as the debate, was devoted to the Communist Party's policy during the national anti-Japanese war (from its beginning to the present day).

The appeal of the Chairman of the CCP Central Committee met with response. The debate clearly pointed to the two main directions: While the political course of the Chairman had preserved and strengthened the Communist Party, the policy of Po Ku, Chou En-lai, Lo Fu, and Wang Ming had been disintegrating the party and threatening it with death.

Almost all Politburo members spoke in this spirit. They called Mao's policy wise, creatively mature, wonderful, etc. At the same time, the policy of Po Ku, Chou En-lai, Wang Ming, and Lo Fu was discredited in every way and they themselves were reproached for their views, alien to the national aspirations of the Chinese people and the interests of the party. Nobody objected when the internationalists' policy was called pernicious, if not criminal. . . .

This campaign was mean also because the bedridden Wang Ming was not present at the sittings and could not say anything in his defense. All dirt was flung at him in his absence.

The main accusations were associated with Wang Ming. Other persons were mentioned only in passing. This was a deliberate tactic of the Chairman of the CCP Central Committee—there were no special reasons for worry, you had all been led astray by Comintern supporter Wang Ming, he was the man to blame, he had confused you and put you in a difficult position, he had nearly turned you into enemies of the party. This tactic of Mao's split the internationalists. It set them free of all moral and political "responsibility before the party," and they supported it with readiness and relief. At the same time Wang Ming's former comrades and adherents resorted to abuse and accusations to "atone for their own sins." As far as I know, Po Ku was the only one not to fall so low. Wang Ming is cursed shamelessly with frenzied spite. He is called a "capitulationist," a "petty-bourgeois opportunist," a "revolutionary without experience," and somebody even labeled him a "figure with elements and ways of a fascistlike ideology"!

The Chairman of the CCP Central Committee has achieved his end. He has isolated Wang Ming politically and spiritually. Simultaneously, he has drawn Wang Ming's former associates to his side.

In this way, the burden of all accusations was laid on Wang Ming's shoulders. And there is a special point in it. Wang Ming was a noted figure in the Comintern. Mao Tse-tung strikes at Wang Ming, having the Comintern in mind. Here Wang Ming personifies the spirit and ideas of the Comintern, and Mao broadly intimates what little weight these ideas carry with him now. The more so as nobody doubts that Wang Ming and Po Ku are "beaten up" precisely for their devotion to the Comintern and the Comintern line in the CCP.

Wang Ming is chastised primarily as a representative of the international Communist organization in the CCP in order to show sincere or ostensible dislike for the Executive Committee of the Communist International.

Wang Ming's "exposure" also promotes another aim of Mao's—negation of the validity of the Bolshevik Party's experience for the

Chinese Communist Party and the Chinese Revolution. This is easy to see if the real meaning of the Chairman's favorite word, "dogmatist," is analyzed.

Besides, Mao hates the Comintern from purely egoistic considerations. For him the Comintern is the force which challenges his right to the undivided leadership of the party, the force which, using its authority, dares to challenge his, Mao Tse-tung's, wisdom! Really, Mao is not one to share his power. . . .

The most important thing for him now is to get rid of Wang Ming. In talks with me the Chairman does not conceal his joy—Wang Ming and his supporters have been "exposed"! Abuse in the address of Wang Ming and Po Ku follows as usual. . . .

What surprises me is Mao's naïveté—he thinks he has camouflaged his actions so well that nobody will be able to see the real reasons behind the struggle. He sees that we have withstood in the war, that we are winning it now. Consequently, we are not shadows in this world. Doesn't he understand that we cannot fail to see something else in all this—evident and growing anti-Sovietism? Naïveté? Does he think we are politically blind? Or maybe he hopes that political speculation and demagogy will help him, as they have already done more than once. . . .

September 15, 1943

The current recess in the work of the CCP Central Committee's Politburo evidently will not continue for long. I think this anti-Comintern action will culminate in adopting a number of organizational measures to put an end to the influence of the international wing's representatives on the party policy.

The first aim, the "ideological defeat" of the "dogmatists" and the "Moscow group," has been achieved.

Mao has got what he was after. In the closing days of the Politburo's work Wang Ming was made fully responsible for the political course of the Executive Committee of the Communist International. Wang Ming had been disintegrating the party by his alien, petty-bourgeois, and capitulationist ideas—this was the main point of nearly all speeches. Everybody spoke on several occasions, defaming the Comintern (without a direct reference to this international organization) and justifying themselves. Judging by what Po Ku and Jen Pi-shih told me, Wang Ming was damned mercilessly and crudely.

My family has returned to Moscow. It will be easier for them at home. I fear for Maria constantly. I am afraid she may have a relapse of tuberculosis because of the bad and insufficient food. . . .

September 19, 1943

Kang Sheng continues to set Central Committee members against Wang Ming. . . .

Our contacts with Mao Tse-tung are much promoted by Chiang Ching. Of course, she does it not without her husband's knowledge. Mao Tse-tung obviously wants us to absorb his ideas and inform Moscow accordingly. . . .

Now and then Chiang Ching invites us to meals. On such occasions political talks are taboo for us.

Yesterday Mao Tse-tung said without any connection: "Confucius stood for the sacred right to uprising if the powers-that-be go off the road of justice." He was leisurely watching me, looking into my eyes to see the impression produced by his words. This is his habit—to speak and look into your eyes.

When he speaks, even at home, all keep silent. He noisily pulls at his cigarette and deliberates in a low voice. He remains an actor even here.

September 22, 1943

The Politburo has made Jen Pi-shih a "commissioner for the opium problem." Besides, Mao Tse-tung often instructs him to make various communications for us.

It is impossible to conceal the true scale of opium production in the Special Area. Opium is one of the most important items of local trade. Jen Pi-shih tried to build an ideological basis under this "business." From a long and tedious talk it became clear that, contrary to the statements of the CCP leadership, the Special Area's economic and financial situation was critical. Inflation ravages. Fiscal operations become increasingly difficult with every day. Six million dollars have been issued! However, this has failed to improve the economic situation.

Jen Pi-shih spoke in detail about the economic difficulties. In the Special Area all people, ourselves included, feel these difficulties.

Economic difficulties were discussed by the Politburo. A rather original way out was found. The Politburo sanctioned an intensified development of the "state sector of opium production and trade." In the meantime as an immediate measure, it was decided to supply at least 1.2 million liangs of opium to the market (called the external market) of the provinces controlled by the Central Government within one year.

Opium—that is, poppy growing and processing—will be handled mostly by army units. The main suppliers are the areas of Ho Lung's 120th Infantry Division (which has long been engaged in this business).

An order has been given concerning the mass purchases of opium. Opium is not bulky. It is not difficult to bring it to Yenan or other designated points in the Special Area from where it will be sent to the provinces controlled by the Central Government and sold at exorbitant prices.

In conclusion Jen Pi-shih said that Comrade Mao Tse-tung realized that opium growing, processing, and selling were not very good. However, Comrade Mao Tse-tung said that in the obtaining situation opium was to play a vanguard, revolutionary role and it would be erroneous to ignore it. The Politburo unanimously supported the viewpoint of the Chairman of the CCP Central Committee.

Jen Pi-shih tried to orientate me so that I could "correctly" understand the CCP leadership's "opium policy." Jen Pi-shih asked Soviet correspondents to understand this decision. I said I would tell this to my comrades. After that we parted.

September 23, 1943

Without centralized and disciplined leadership at every echelon there cannot be a Marxist party, which is, essentially, an instrument of class struggle. This, however, does not mean that the party is a silent and humble executor of the will of its leaders.

The will of the leader should be a concentrated expression of the will of the party. In its turn, the will of the party is formed through democratic centralism.

Without democratic centralism a Marxist party cannot become a real force and will inevitably turn into a group of talkers and rowdies—

an easy prey for the well-organized state machinery of the bourgeoisie.

In the CCP, democratic centralism is replaced by suppression of anyone who disagrees with "Chairman Mao" and degenerates into the slavery by conviction ridiculed by Marx. . . .

Mao Tse-tung knows old Chinese literature, which largely explains why his compatriots look at him with awe. He has a poor knowledge of Western philosophy, and his ideas of Marxism are vulgar.

None of us saw translations of Shakespeare, Stendhal, Chekhov, Balzac, or Tolstoi at his place. . . .

Mao Tse-tung scorns everything that is not Chinese. For him the Chinese is the acme of world culture, the ultimate truth, so to speak. . . .

His constant companions are a selection of Chinese encyclopedic dictionaries, ancient philosophical treatises, and old novels. . . .

Moscow is recalling Yuzhin, Aleyev, and Dolmatov. A plane will take them away late in October. By agreement with the CCP Central Committee leadership, Orlov, Rimmar, and myself will remain in Yenan till the end of the war.

In this connection Mao Tse-tung has had a long talk with me, sounding out my sentiments in every way.

September 24, 1943

During our routine meeting today Kang Sheng began to speak of Wang Ming in a highly significant way. He said in Hankow that Wang Ming had not behaved as a party member should. There Wang Ming and his associates had allegedly put together something like another Central Committee of the party and neglected the instructions of Comrade Mao Tse-tung. Practically, Wang Ming had ignored the entire Yenan leadership headed by the Chairman of the CCP Central Committee. There was proof that Wang Ming had disobeyed Comrade Mao Tse-tung's instructions and even refused to reprint a number of his very important articles.

Kang Sheng further said that, as the CCP representative at the Kuomintang, Wang Ming violated the instructions he had received. Wang Ming had entered into direct correspondence with Chiang Kai-shek without Comrade Mao Tse-tung's permission. Conducted without the knowledge of the Chairman of the CCP Central Committee, this correspondence is alarming, since nothing is known yet about these documents addressed to Chiang Kai-shek. . . .

Kang Sheng obviously wants to discredit Wang Ming in every respect. The facts he cited cannot be regarded as something serious. And he knows it perfectly well. In some cases, when the situation demanded, Wang Ming departed from the usual routine and, acting on the directives of the Communist International's Executive Committee, adopted corresponding decisions. In this respect the doubts cast on this aspect of Wang Ming's activities—on some unknown part of his correspondence with Chiang Kai-shek—are plainly provocative. This is nonsense, but nonsense in which all will believe soon. This is another charge against Wang Ming. . . .

After that Kang Sheng said that the Politburo had taken this matter up in September 1941. As a result, sharp disagreements had emerged. The relations between the Chairman of the CCP Central Committee and Wang Ming have been very tense ever since. (As far as I know, Mao Tse-tung had tried to control the legitimacy of the decisions of the Executive Committee of the Communist International, that is, to rise above this working body of the Comintern.)

The Ching-pao-chu chief also said that as a result of the discussion of Chou En-lai's report and of a number of "related questions" by the Politburo, all those concerned admitted their mistakes in one way or another except Wang Ming, who "sets himself in opposition to the party" (Mao Tse-tung wanted to drive Wang Ming precisely into such a position).

Kang Sheng said that speaking in connection with their mistakes, some comrades were not frank and sincere, that their "confessions are obviously formal."

"We have no doubts on this score. It's not so simple to fool us!" Kang Sheng summed up.

Kang thinks, by naïveté or stupidity, that I am inclined to take his view. Talking with me, he sometimes does not conceal facts which clearly compromise himself and the Chairman of the CCP Central Committee. Well, although this state of things will hardly last for long, at present I am learning much that is really valuable and interesting and that was carefully hidden from us before.

Maybe this is Mao's tactic? Maybe he wants thus to neutralize me and turn me into his mouthpiece? . . . In any case, Chiang Ching's attitude to us shows this. She is simple and affable and tries to be in our company more often. Sometimes her importunity seems almost indecent and contradicting national traditions which set very strict limits on female behavior. . . .

September 29, 1943

Chiang Ching is much more well read than her husband. In any case, she is familiar with world classics.

Mao Tse-tung is indifferent to his sons, who study in the Soviet Union. None of us can recall his mentioning them or inquiring about their health. Incidentally, he shows little concern for his young daughter as well, and if he does, it is only thanks to his wife, who does her best to revive his paternal feelings. She has a very strong influence on him.

Chiang Ching looks after his health, daily work, clothes, and food. She is his most trusted secretary.

The Chairman of the CCP Central Committee has disunited his ideological opponents. Using a carrot-and-stick policy, he won them over to his side, then set them against one another. . . . He settled his accounts even with Wang Ming and Po Ku through their former associates and friends. . . .

October 1943

October 3, 1943

Any struggle for power reflects the laws of economic and social processes. Seizing power, Mao Tse-tung and his close associates promote, objectively, the interests of China's petty-bourgeoisie and nationalist elements. Petty-bourgeois trends assume different ideological manifestations, depending on specific historical conditions. However, proponents of petty-ownership philosophy always unwittingly reveal its reactionary essence by opposing it to the revolutionary ideology of the proletariat.

I feel satisfied. Our presence has prevented the murder of Wang Ming, the leader of the internationalist trend in the CCP.

———

Apparently, our knowledge of the Yenan affairs has also prevented the murder of other Chinese comrades and restrains terror to some extent.

I am confident that the campaign of exposures of Kuomintang and Japanese "spies" was meant to be followed by an undiscriminated physical destruction of all "dogmatists," particularly those called the Moscow group. . . .

———

At night somebody wrecked the antenna feeder of our radio station. Dolmatov had to use the stand-by radio station while Rimmar was engaged in repairs. . . .

October 7, 1943

Shortly before his death Yang Sung spoke of Kang Sheng's hatred for him.

On October 5 *Liberation Daily* published Mao Tse-tung's article on Kuomintang developments in Chungking.

The Chairman of the CCP Central Committee alleges that except for his Eighth Route and New Fourth armies nobody fights against the Japanese, that the leadership of the Special Area promotes, rather than frustrates, Chungking's military efforts.

Mao Tse-tung cites Chiang Kai-shek's statement at the latest plenary meeting of the Kuomintang Central Executive Committee:

". . . It should be stated in all clarity that the Kuomintang Central Executive Committee does not make any other demand but only hopes the Communist Party will give up its idea of the armed alienation of territories. . . ."

Mao Tse-tung has something of a provocateur about him. He writes:

". . . Properly speaking, the Kuomintang people's intention was to let the Soviet Union fight Hitler singlehandedly and, by provoking the Japanese bandits' attack on the Soviet Union, to bring about the downfall, or weakening, of the socialist power. . . ."

Indeed, God's way past finding out! Didn't Mao Tse-tung's policy in respect to the Soviet Union in these years mean the same? Didn't Chiang Kai-shek and Mao Tse-tung jointly pursue the same aim—a war between the Soviet Union and Japan! . . .

October 10, 1943

The Chiao-yuan is the residence of Mao Tse-tung. In Yenan nobody knows what it looks like. A few steps from the orchard, in a mountain slope, is the house of the Chairman of the CCP Central Committee, a reliable bomb shelter with numerous secret galleries leading to desolate nearby gorges.

Not far from the little Yang River, in the shadow of peach trees, behind the loess wall, under the protection of Mauser-armed guards, Chairman Mao enjoys his leisure hours. . . .

Even his closest associates do not come to the Chiao-yuan as they wish. People are summoned to it. Nobody may disturb Chairman Mao without his consent.

Fulfilling Mao Tse-tung's will and adding his own zeal, Liu Shao-chi lords it over in Yang-chia-lin. No longer a modest military commissar of the New Fourth Army, he is now the party's number-two man, endowed with tremendous powers!

Artillery salutes thunder in Moscow nearly every day! The Red Army is freeing one city after another. . . .

Although the Kwantung Army is still deployed near our frontier, the war threat for the Soviet Union in the Far East has disappeared. . . .

But how many Soviet divisions this position of Japan has distracted and how it has helped the Germans fulfill their military tasks! And how many lives have been lost to compensate for these dozens of full-strength regular Soviet divisions not being at the front! . . .

October 19, 1943

One thought, possibly heretical, does not leave me. I don't see much difference between Mao Tse-tung and his supporters, on the one hand, and Kuomintang leaders, on the other.

Listening to Japanese radio, I heard the following words about Chiang Kai-shek: ". . . Persistent, merciless, and highly ambitious. Married for the fourth time. . . ." Isn't this characteristic of Mao Tse-tung, too?! Things coincide even in intimate details. . . .

Two nationalists, although they act from different positions, are obsessed with the desire to lay their hands on power.

However, if one does it openly in Chungking, at least resisting foreign occupation, the other has forgotten the honor and sufferings of his country, deceives his party and destroys its honored leaders. . . .

It's sad to look at my comrades packing. I am longing for my family and Russia, and I am dead tired of the cruel Yenan reality. . . .

Although nobody accuses Peng Teh-huai of the failure of the Hundred Regiments Campaign, such an implication does exist. And this gives Mao Tse-tung ground to consider the military leadership, including Chu Teh, incompetent. This allows Mao Tse-tung to wind up steadily the combat operations of the Eighth Route Army. He is the supreme military authority here. Nobody dares to say that in the past Mao Tse-tung, too, had a hand in the direction of all major operations of the CCP troops. The failure of the Hundred Regiments Campaign makes commanding officers even more dependent on Mao.

October 24, 1943

A TB-3 has gone as a smoke in the sky. There are three of us now, Orlov, Rimmar, and myself.

Tomorrow I move to our house near the Chiao-yuan. Farewell to cave life. . . .

My greatest concern is how long my health will last. I must get to the root of many things here, since very important events are taking place in the humble Yenan. Despite all difficulties, I endlessly tell myself: Hold out, hold out, hold out! . . .

October 28, 1943

I have read a batch of letters. Maria and kids are all right. . . .

In actions near Kursk, Dmitri [a brother of Maria Danilovna Vladimirova's] was killed, and the twenty-year-old nurse Nadya [a niece of Peter Vladimirov's], together with the wounded in an ambulance, was shot dead by a German plane.

Of Maria's three brothers, two have already lost their lives.

The situation in Yenan is depressing. The latest events have made people shun friendships, avoid contacts outside business, and distrust one another. The behavior of people betrays tension and fear.

People have no desire to defend the truth and their slandered comrades, or receive explanations on one question or another. Everybody struggles for his own life. Needless to say, how many rascals make their way up playing on their "devotion to Mao." For such things professional knowledge, services, and experience are not obligatory—what is important is to show oneself a devoted supporter of Mao Tse-tung, shout much about this, and fling dirt at one's comrades.

Party principles are replaced by self-seeking, undisguised toadyism, and self-humiliation. Self-humiliation is becoming characteristic of Yenan life in general. People seem to go mad, striving at any cost to survive, preserve their jobs, and, maybe, make a career. Honor, dignity, comradeship, everything has been forgotten. . . . Instead of giving their opinion, people cite statements and articles of Chairman Mao. And all this smells of anti-Sovietism, distrust in our party and the policy of the Soviet Government.

In these circumstances Wang Ming cannot expect understanding or even objective criticism in accordance with the generally recognized party standards. He is in an exceedingly bad state. The disease and base insinuations have broken him down physically and morally.

Wang Ming is accused of every sin conceivable. He, it is alleged, rubbed shoulders with enemies of the people, traitors, and Chiang Kaishek. He "exposed" himself by trying to impose the capitulationist line upon the party (that is by upholding the Comintern line). He "wallowed in opportunism" (also because he was supporting the Comintern line and friendship with the AUCP(B)).

Kang Sheng has done his best. Literally all meetings, rallies, and other undertakings are organized by his people. All kinds of discrediting, dirty arguments against the internationalists and "dogmatists" came from his office. He got cheng-feng into high gear. While Liu Shao-chi is cheng-feng's theoretician, Kang Sheng is its practical organizer. As to the Chairman of the CCP Central Committee, he is the godfather of all campaigns.

Kang Sheng was especially hard on Wang Ming. Besides everything else, he has a strong personal dislike for Wang Ming. He has his political foe in his death grip (way back in Moscow Kang bore Wang Ming a grudge for his insincerity in a number of questions). When talking to him, I mention Wang Ming, the Fall Minister's face changes, he breathes hatred. What continuously whips Kang Sheng's hatred is the inability to simply kill Wang Ming, as well as the difficulty of political struggle with Wang Ming, who has highly placed adherents in the party and who, until recently, represented the course of a powerful international working-class organization. He speaks of Wang Ming in a plainly disdainful manner. . . .

The anti-Comintern campaign presumes Comrade Wang Ming's expulsion from the party. From Kang Sheng's tone I felt that Wang Ming is under threat of expulsion and that it is practically planned by Mao's entourage.

Wang Ming's position is desperate. He cannot believe he is being destroyed politically for his devotion to the Comintern, the policy worked out by the Comintern, and his contacts with outstanding workers of this international proletarian organization. He is convinced that the Comintern's political guidelines are just and correct. For him the anti-Japanese front is the shortest way to rout militarist Japan, liberate his country, and strengthen the CCP. It is impossible to meet Wang Ming, as the Fall Minister took every precaution to isolate him. I managed to receive Mao Tse-tung's permission for Orlov to visit Wang Ming. It is imperative to control the work of Kang Sheng's doctors since Kang may stop at nothing. . . .

When Orlov came, Wang Ming was with his wife. On seeing Andrei Yakovlevich, Wang Ming burst into tears. . . .

Wang Ming has lost considerable weight; he is very weak and still unable to walk. During a medical check-up Wang Ming asked Andrei Yakovlevich to send a telegram to Comrade Dimitrov.

Andrei Yakovlevich said he considered his duty to fulfill this request. Wang Ming dictated the text. Orlov promised to send the telegram immediately via our radio station. Wang Ming asked him not to tell anyone about the telegram, since this would not be forgiven him.

Wang Ming looked exhausted and depressed. He could be understood, as the matter is not so much in his illness as in his exceptionally difficult position. Wang Ming's friends abandoned him, nobody comes to see him. He is all alone in the full sense of the word. And what is more, he doesn't know all that is taking place around him. His wife conceals from him the real scale of the anti-Comintern campaign (which is also, in a way, the anti-Wang Ming campaign). He doesn't know of his forthcoming expulsion from the party, of party functionaries' unanimous dislike for him, and of many other facts. He is disowned by all who used to work with him and who believed that the Comintern's political guidance was correct. He doesn't know that the great majority of his adherents turn away from him and even come out against him, add fresh accusations against him (to the delight of the Chairman of the CCP Central Committee), and denigrate his name before the party. . . .

Kang Sheng has surpassed himself. At present he is organizing the harassment of Wang Ming's wife.

Kang's plan boils down to killing Wang Ming with persecution, if not with poison. He is not left without "attention" for a single day. . . .

I immediately radioed Wang Ming's telegram. Wang Ming asked former Comintern leaders to tell the CCP leadership that he had followed the Comintern's guidelines, complied with its decisions, and that this had been his task and duty. He insisted that Mao Tse-tung's new line contradicted the interests of struggle against fascism and was, to all intents and purposes, a splitting one. . . .

The decisions of the December 1937 conference and partly of the sixth plenary meeting have already been recognized as opportunist. This is another blow at the CCP's internationalist wing.

Indicatively, pressure was exerted on public opinion in the absence of Peng Teh-huai and Chou En-lai. . . . Both of them participated in that plenary meeting. Since the plenum's ideas were distorted, it was the easiest way to discredit them in their absence.

The entire history of the CCP, even its recent history, is being hastily revised. . . .

November 1943

November 1, 1943

Yeh Chien-ying, chief of staff of the Eighth Route Army, has been virtually relieved of his duties, just like Chu Teh, for being a member of Wang Ming's group. At present he is processing information pertaining to the Japanese and Kuomintang armies. He is a clever diplomat, and they often appoint him for talks with Kuomintang representatives. A close friend of Chu Teh's. Hates Kang Sheng.

Both Yeh Chien-ying and Chu Teh live in Wan-chia-ping.

Liu Po-cheng is commander of the 129th Infantry Division. He is a tall, stocky man with a big head. Is unassuming with people under him. Was seriously injured several times. Has good command of military science. He has always acted in the Japanese rear and arrived at Yenan together with Peng Teh-huai. He and Yeh Chien-ying are awaiting punishment for belonging to the Wang Ming group.

Nieh Jung-chen, commander of the armed forces in the Shansi-Hopeh-Chahar region, has arrived from his field headquarters. He is accused of "dogmatism" and "empiricism" as Wang Ming's supporter. . . .

The greater the successes of the Red Army, the more enthusiastic the CCP leaders in asserting their friendship with the Soviet Union. Every day I'm congratulated by those who only yesterday jeered at our misfortunes. Even Kang Sheng has abandoned the surveillance under which he had put me. . . .

November 5, 1943

The Informburo has reported on the results of the Red Army summer campaign (July 5–November 5). One hundred and forty-four enemy divisions have been smashed, 900,000 Hitlerites were killed and 98,000 taken prisoner.

Officially Peng Teh-huai is Chu Teh's deputy. He arrived at Yenan from the Eighth Route Army field headquarters this autumn. A member of the Wang Ming group, he is an empiricist by Mao's definition. The CCP Chairman bends every effort to win him over to his side.

Peng Teh-huai is well versed in military matters and is popular with the Army.

Even by Yenan standards Peng Teh-huai dresses very simply. Modesty is his outstanding feature. His voice is low and a little husky, and his ways are unhurried.

His sense of dignity is rare. He respects Mao Tse-tung as the leader of the CCP.

From now on all the reporter's work is solely my responsibility, too. I saddle my mare and in the course of the day go to all kinds of places and meet many people. More and more often I sit over my papers till dawn. Kolya lends a helping hand. He draws up detailed reports of radio newscasts. . . .

November 6, 1943

Mao Tse-tung's telegram on the occasion of the twenty-sixth anniversary of the October Revolution:

> To Comrade Stalin, the Central Committee of the AUCP(B), the Red Army, and the peoples of the Soviet Union.
> As I represent the Chinese Communist Party and the Chinese people I warmly welcome and congratulate you on the occasion of

the twenty-sixth anniversary of the October Revolution and the great victories of the Red Army in the antifascist war. . . .

Inspired by your victories over the past twenty-six years, the people of China will always march forward united and hand in hand with you, and will work as one for the final victory in the anti-Japanese national liberation war. . . .

My day at Yenan begins at dawn.

The Chiao-yuan comes to life by noon when Mao Tse-tung wakes up. He holds meetings and calls people in to his place. . . .

I must not miss a single fact of any importance. I am trying to clarify the party leaders' view on this or that question and to dig up the real meaning of events.

Later at home I analyze and check my impressions and translate documents. I snatch a few hours' sleep and resume work. . . .

November 10, 1943

. . . Very important documents came into my possession.

The first document is the Letter from the Central Front Committee to the Assistance Committee, of December 5, 1930.

The second—Emergency Circular Message of the Provincial Executive Committee No. 9, of December 15, 1930.

The third—Letter to the CCP Central Committee from Liu Ti, commissar of the 172nd Regiment, XX Corps, of January 11, 1931.

After translating the documents and their careful analysis I made the following conclusions:

In 1930 Mao Tse-tung was in the office of the chairman of the Central Front Committee. (Apparently this is where he "borrowed" his post of "chairman" for the CCP.) In the autumn of the same year Mao Tse-tung was sharply criticized for extremes in military and agrarian construction at a plenary meeting of the Western Kiangsi Party Committee. The same meeting expelled Liu Shao-chi, his associate, from the party.

Informed of the decisions of the Western Kiangsi Party Committee, the CCP Central Committee in Shanghai resolved to recall Mao Tse-tung and appointed Comrade Hsiang Chung-fa to replace him.

Mao Tse-tung concealed the CCP Central Committee decision from the Front Committee, deluded its members by accusing the Western

Kiangsi Party Committee of alliance with kulaks and landlords, and on his own initiative set up the Assistance Committee with the intention of destroying the party cadres of Western Kiangsi. On December 5, 1930, he began to act. . . .

Letter to the Assistance Committee from the Central Front Committee:

> To Comrade Liu Shao-chi to be referred to the provincial Assistance Committee.
>
> The extremely serious uprising of landlords and kulaks who have penetrated the party has already spread far. You must suppress it with determination.
>
> You must look for the address in a different way, not like you did the last time, when the Special Committee was destroyed. Otherwise our leadership will be killed off soon.
>
> According to Lung Chao-ching, the chairman of the Provincial Komsomol Committee Tuan Lien-pi, chief of the Agitation and Propaganda Department Yuan Chao-huan, and chief of the Organizational Department Chiang Ko-huang are now in Tung-tien. They should all be immediately arrested and thoroughly interrogated.
>
> Li Po-fang is an even more dangerous criminal!
>
> We hope that you have already arrested them!
>
> Besides, use them to discover even more important criminals!
>
> Two Red Army men were sent in the evening with a letter informing of the interrogation of Ting Shu-chi, an important criminal. He hasn't given a sincere testimony yet.
>
> You must not limit yourself to following the instructions of this letter. Tomorrow more of the prisoners will be interrogated.
>
> Let the two Red Army men who will deliver the letter stay with you so as to send them back with the post in two or three days' time. If you are in need of delivering an emergency report, send it with the postman. Have him put the papers in an inside pocket with an ordinary letter on top so that the AB group [a reactionary organization of kulaks and landlords] is not able to read your reports.
>
> Emergency Circular Message of the Provincial Executive Committee No. 9.
>
> Central Front Committee
> Huai-po. December 15, 1930

In an atmosphere of the turbulent revolutionary upsurge the

dominant classes, anxious to save themselves, are patching up their internal conflicts for the time being. This is an inevitable reaction of the dominant classes to the revolutionary upswing and fully proves that if we are victorious in one or several provinces, the Chinese Revolution will score an all-round victory extraordinarily fast. However, the situation being what it is, the complete victory of the revolution will require co-ordinated work of all the Communists of the country, with its activization primarily in one or several most important provinces.

Therefore it is necessary to answer the enemy onslaught by a decisive class struggle and to launch an offensive against the enemy throughout the country; to destroy him once the dominant classes are suppressed; and above all, to seize power in Kiangsi to be followed by the creation of Soviet China.

An outbreak of such struggle and its outcome will doubtlessly bring about an early victory of the revolution and defeat of the dominant classes. This is why the enemy has launched a large-scale offensive in all directions. The moment for resolute struggle and destruction of the enemy has come. We shall gain victory only through active offensive and revolutionary self-sacrifice in battle.

Naturally, the right-wing elements in the party are vacillating on the eve of the outbreak of fierce class battles; they are retreating and becoming renegades of the Bolshevik Party and class enemies. For example, giving in to his right-winger sentiments in the course of the mounting class struggle, Mao Tse-tung has worked out a treacherous plan of extermination of his comrades in the party. Making a signboard of his tactics of alluring the enemy in order to allegedly destroy him afterward, Mao Tse-tung actually curtailed the struggle and laid ground for desertion. Thus, when the enemy was already moving into the heart of the Soviet regions, Mao was still advocating retreat and was not fighting the enemy.

In the Third Army the Provincial Executive Committee had submitted its considerations. But he personally resorted to . . . [illegible in text], without calling a meeting. Such vacillations on the part of Mao Tse-tung led to him becoming a 100 per cent right opportunist and criminal in present-day class struggle. Hence Mao Tse-tung's intention to attain his right-opportunist and deserter's ends and to accomplish other dirty and shameless deeds.

Thus Mao Tse-tung has long since nurtured his plan against the Bolshevik organization of Kiangsi. He is seeking to destroy all responsible workers and, acting in accord with his right-opportunist line, to liquidate the revolutionary struggle and then, his dreams come true, to become the emperor of the party. Such are the reasons behind the developments in Futien.

1. Mao Tse-tung as a person.

As everyone knows, Mao Tse-tung is a very sly and treacherous man with an extreme sense of individualism. His head is full of vain thoughts. His way of influencing his comrades is through orders and threats and a system of repressions. When he takes a decision on party questions, he seldom discusses them at meetings and is always concerned with obtaining approval just of his own views.

Mao Tse-tung is particularly weak when it comes to an action. He adopts a right-opportunist line and tends to anarchism and "khvostism." He doubts every operation and is very unstable, especially in connection with the present stage of the bitter class struggle, which he tries to avoid and run away from, sparing no effort to extinguish it.

Mao Tse-tung has long been against the Central Committee. He sabotaged instructions of the previous committee many times when he chose to, using insignificant practical difficulties as a pretext. He read and distributed among the lower party organizations only a few of the Central Committee instructions. He did not reckon with the workers sent down from the center and raised every obstacle in their way. For example, the Central Committee had sent Tsai Shen-hsi to the IV Corps to rectify the mistakes of the fallacious guerrilla tactics. Later Tsai Shen-hsi was supposed to have assumed the post of commander of the III Corps.

Mao Tse-tung not only ignored the Central Committee's advice but even organized baiting of Comrade Tsai Shen-hsi and prevented him from taking the post of corps commander.

The Central Committee has repeatedly sent in letters demanding that Mao Tse-tung be transferred to another post, but he pays no heed to anybody.

Shunning no political trick, Mao Tse-tung constantly attacked his comrades.

In his work with the cadres he wholly relied on factional methods and, using relations of companionship and personal ties, was raising a group which served him as an obedient political instrument.

Mao Tse-tung has not proved himself as a revolutionary leader in any of his past activities, and not even as a rank-and-file proletarian Bolshevik and fighter.

From head to toe Mao Tse-tung is a right opportunist, carrier of vain ideas, and enemy of the party organization. He is an embodiment of the idea of evasion of battle and liquidation of the revolutionary class struggle. He is an out-and-out renegade of the Communist Party. The party of Bolsheviks will not hesitate and will expel him from its ranks.

2. Details of the developments of December 7.

A few days before the events, Mao Tse-tung detailed Liu Shao-chi with a company of men of the XII Corps from Hua-nien-po. The conspirators set out for Futien in a hurry and arrived there at noon on December 7, 1930.

At 3 P.M. in Futien Liu Shao-chi stationed his men at the entrance to the building of the Provincial Committee, announcing that he was looking for a place to spend the night.

Liu Shao-chi went to the Executive Committee and asked for Tseng Shan and Chen Chen-jen. At that time comrades Jen Hsin-ta and Pai Fang were talking.

Traitor Liu Shao-chi saw that his accomplices Tseng Shan and Chen Chen-jen had left the room and immediately followed them. By that time Comrade Tuan Lien-pi had returned.

Then the traitor Liu broke into the building of the Provincial Executive Committee with some ten soldiers and tied Tuan Lien-pi and Pai Fang first of all. Comrade Liu Wen-ching and Comrade Jen Hsin-ta were arrested right there. A little later comrades Hsieh Han-chang, Chi Wen-pang, Ma Ming, and others were arrested. When they asked what the matter was, Liu Shao-chi and his accomplices Tseng Shan and Chen Chen-jen only threatened them with revolvers.

The traitor Liu commanded the soldiers and did the searching. Tseng and Chen helped him.

Then the traitors ordered the company to surround the building.

The soldiers started an over-all search. All documents were destroyed and the valuables appropriated. This lasted for several hours.

By night another nine people, operators of the communications system of the Provincial Executive Committee, had been arrested.

At night the comrades were put to horrible torture. They were cruelly beaten right before Liu Shao-chi, Tseng Shan, and Chen

Chen-jen, who were asking such questions as: "Do you admit your membership in the AB alliance? When did you enter it? How is it organized and what are its tactics? Who are its responsible workers? Tell us the whole truth!"

The comrades denied the charges. They were tortured with burning kerosene wicks. Then the interrogation was resumed.

If the prisoners were stubborn, the torture became diversified.

They had no choice but to plead guilty. Their nails were broken and their bodies were covered with burns. They could neither stir nor speak. Such was the situation on the first day.

On the second day, December 8, the traitor Liu Shao-chi and the others, on the basis of verbal admissions wrenched from the tortured comrades, arrested another ten people from the provincial government, the political guards, the Finance Department, youth organizations, and the Provincial Executive Committee. They were also tortured with burning kerosene-dipped wicks. And they all "admitted" their guilt—not to do so would mean death from torture. Liu, Tseng, and Chen supervised the interrogations. The screams of the prisoners never stopped. The most monstrous tortures were devised.

The wives of comrades Pai Fang, Ma Ming, and Chou Mien were arrested at the same time. They were undressed and beaten up, their hands were pierced with a sharp tool, their bodies and private parts were burned with the flaming wicks, their breasts were cut away with pen knives. The butchers went to such extremes, mere mention of which curdles the blood.

The prisoners, both those who had been interrogated and those who had not been, were kept separately, tied hand and foot. They dared not speak or move. The guards were standing over them with bayoneted rifles at the ready. The second a voice was heard, the bayonets would go into action.

The prisoners were fed on offal. Such was the situation on the second day.

On the third day another punitive platoon arrived. Wang Huai and many other comrades from the Executive Committee of Western Kiangsi were arrested.

After breakfast the soldiers marched away twenty-five people to be executed, many of whom had not even been questioned.

The traitor Liu Shao-chi set out for Tungku with the prisoners of the XX Corps, including Hsieh Han-chang. The rest of the prisoners were taken away to the mountains where torturing continued in the villages. Such was the situation on the third day.

In Tungku the prisoners were tortured again. The comrades were tied with ropes. Only once were they given food.

Savage tortures were applied at those interrogations. First a name would be given and they would demand that the particular person be acknowledged as a "counterrevolutionary" and the prisoners' "accomplice." In this way all the provincial officials were named. . . .

Each one of the prisoners would be tortured for two or three hours before the questioning even started.

The executioners were going to leave the following morning. So they executed a large group of comrades in the evening.

However, at this point the 174th Regiment of our XX Corps arrived unexpectedly. The men surrounded the building and released the prisoners.

The XX Corps exposed the members of the punitive expedition in Tungku and launched an uprising. The traitor Liu Shao-chi was seized.

The officials of the XX Corps and Hsieh Han-chang were also released. They were the ones to have related the happenings in Futien.

The men of the 174th Regiment were enraged when they learned the story. Comrade Liu Ti led them to Futien.

In Futien they surrounded the building where the prisoners were kept, disarmed the punitive detachment, and seized the principal reactionaries. The traitor Tseng Shan fled.

Such was the situation on the fourth day.

We have told only briefly about the events of a few days. Other monstrous, indescribable facts are numerous.

3. Until we get the Central Committee's sanction we do not allow openly proclaiming the slogans of overthrowing Mao Tse-tung.

Obviously, Mao Tse-tung is a bad man, a criminal in the class struggle, an enemy of the Bolshevik Party. It is necessary to mobilize all party members to overthrow him without ceremony.

But it is not only the question of Mao Tse-tung's personality. It is a vital question bearing on the prospects of the Chinese Revolution and concerned with the international revolutionary movement. That is why we must be very careful before making any decision. The crime must not be left unpunished. The Kiangsi party organization must launch a determined struggle against Mao Tse-tung from Bolshevik positions.

However, the party organization in Kiangsi must not settle the question on its own. It is our duty to inform the Central Committee of Mao Tse-tung's scheme to destroy the leading cadres of Kiangsi and its party organization, and it is up to the Central Committee to pass its decision.

Therefore, until we receive sanctions from the Central Committee we have no right to proclaim slogans to overthrow Mao Tse-tung among the masses; we act this way in the name of the Chinese Revolution! Openly to call for the overthrow of Mao Tse-tung will mean that his political activity will end for good. The masses will lose their trust in him. Suspicion and misunderstanding of the meaning of events may prevail among the masses.

As far as the case of Mao Tse-tung is concerned, we are intensifying our explanatory work in the party and the Youth League. We are explaining the meaning of his criminal actions, particularly in the light of the December 7 events.

We expose Mao Tse-tung's plot before the party and the Youth League of the country to mobilize them against him so that he is not allowed to crush the party organization in Kiangsi, make the party his own group, himself emperor of the party, to ruin the Chinese Revolution.

We have put forward the slogans of overthrowing Mao Tse-tung in the past. Now we have distributed letters in order to organize a struggle against him in the spirit of this document.

On December 7 the Bolshevik organization of Kiangsi was hanging by a thread. That was a crucial moment for the Chinese Revolution. Had not Mao Tse-tung's black conspiracy been frustrated, not only the Kiangsi party organization but the whole of the Chinese Revolution would have been harmed.

Comrades, this is a question in which we must firmly adhere to the Bolshevik platform, raise obstacles in the way of Mao Tse-tung's efforts, and at the same time continue fighting the AB alliance!

Kiangsi Provincial Committee
Yunnan. December 15, 1930

Letter from Liu Ti, commissar of the 172nd Regiment, XX Corps, to the CCP Central Committee.

. . . Liu Ti entered the corps headquarters, and Liu Shao-chi went into the inner apartments to have a talk with corps commander Liu Tieh-chao.

After a while he sat down beside me, looking very strange, and said, "Liu Ti, you're in grave danger."

"What is the danger?" I asked.

He replied, "Very many testify against you."

I asked, "What is their evidence?"

"They say that you are a member of the AB group."

I looked at him and asked him, laughing, "And what do you think, do I look like a member of the AB group?"

I knew that terrible tortures were practiced with regard to members of the AB group, and said quite frankly, "If I'm being discredited by the AB group members, I can't help it. I'll only ask the party to be just and clarify all the circumstances of the case. I'm not afraid to die, but the tortures are unbearable."

Feigning concern, Liu Shao-chi replied, "This will never happen. This is not a question of the AB group but a political issue. If you admit your mistakes and follow instructions, then, of course, things will not go as far as beating up and execution."

Since Liu Shao-chi said that it wasn't a question of the AB group but was a political issue, I felt there was some trap somewhere.

I always knew that Liu Shao-chi was not a person of ideological integrity, that he lacked proletarian awareness, and that he was always up to some dirty tricks that ended in squabbles. . . .

Liu Shao-chi said that the Second Congress of the Southwestern Kiangsi had been arranged by the AB group. But I knew perfectly well that the Second Congress just fulfilled the Central Committee instruction to fight peasant psychology and the ideas of fragmentation of guerrilla actions and to pay special attention to work in towns. I had already heard that the Central Committee criticized Mao Tse-tung for his peasant psychology. Mao Tse-tung had never been a big authority with me. He had written a letter to Lin Piao in which he criticized the Central Committee and which he openly published in *Red Flag*.

On August 1 the Central Committee sent in a letter announcing Comrade Hsiang Chung-fa chairman of the Provisional Workers' and Peasants' Government. But Mao Tse-tung continued to publish orders bearing his signature of chairman of the Chinese Workers' and Peasants' Revolutionary Committee just as before.

After Tsian had been seized extreme anxiety and disillusionment began to be felt among the army cadres who had at least an elementary training. I also saw that the Bolshevik spirit was dying down in the party day by day. Such was the reaction to the methods of building a system dominated by one man.

Before the ninth offensive on Tsian, I met Mao Tse-tung. He asked me about the Second Congress of the Southwestern Kiangsi.

I told him what I knew. Mao Tse-tung remarked then: "The credit for the egalitarian distribution of land and offensive on Kiangsi goes to Liu Shao-chi!"

I asked him about Liu Shao-chi, and Mao Tse-tung replied, "He is chief of the Secretariat of the Central Political Department. Comrade Liu is very capable."

I never believed Mao Tse-tung to be able to lead us; as for Liu, he is a dirty and mean person. . . .

I realized that the goings on had nothing to do with fighting the AB group, but that simply Mao had sent down the hound Liu to destroy the party cadres in southwestern Kiangsi.

I also realized that should I stick to the party stand, I was as good as dead. So I adopted a different attitude and began to sing the song of Changsha: "I'm your old servant, my political level is very low, I will follow your political instructions and will admit my mistakes. I'm sure that Mao Tse-tung is not a member of the AB group, no more than you or the corps commander. I will follow you three anywhere. What am I by myself?"

After that Liu's and the corps commander's attitude to me changed immediately. They began to console me and advised me not to get panicky. And since they had to question people, I was asked to wait in a small guarded room.

I heard Liu Shao-chi questioning Shang Chi-lung, chief of the political sciences sector of the Political Department. He was beating him up so brutally that the sky itself heard the screams and the earth shuddered. . . .

"What change has taken place in the political situation," I asked Liu Shao-chi and the corps commander.

The reply was, "You are an intelligent person, so why all this nonsense? It is quite plain who belongs to the AB group and who has lately been in error. We do not know yet if we shall be able to transfer the 175th Regiment or whether Li Shao Ta-peng from the 172nd Regiment is sufficiently reliable. You see your regiment is the only, in fact the main, force of the XX Army Corps. You must crush the AB group in your regiment by whatever means."

After that they had the orderly take me to the battalion headquarters. When I came there, Comrade Chang Hsing (battalion commander) and Liang Hsueh-tai (political representative) were surprised but obviously pleased at my arrival. In those days many party comrades were aware of the fact that all Communists lived in fear, expecting all sorts of contingencies, and were given to panic.

Comrade Chang Hsing said: "I don't believe that all these men belong to the AB group."

I also wanted to stay out of danger, but my heart was aching for the party.

The more I thought, the more I became convinced that there was nobody around whom I could turn to for advice.

On December 12 I got up very early. I felt sick at heart.

After breakfast Chang Hsing, Liang Hsueh-tai, and I opened an emergency meeting at the premises reserved for classified material. At first I informed on the current affairs and made a brief analysis. The other comrades agreed that the events were part of some dark scheme. Acting in line with the Bolshevik principles, we decided to send Liu Shao-chi an invitation to join our conference, and then to arrest him. Should he guess that something was up, we should call in troops (by that time already three battalions of the 174th Regiment had been sent to arrest the commander and the political representative of the 175th Regiment) and release the comrades in trouble.

At the end of the conference Comrade Chang Hsing remarked that apparently Chiang Ping-chun and the others had been accused of complicity with the AB group for no reason at all.

Therefore, I went to the corps headquarters and asked Liu Shao-chi and corps commander Liu Tieh-chao about this matter. But they began to put questions to me and I arrested them. After that I drew up the troops fast and decided to go all the way; that is, I surrounded the corps headquarters, tied up Liu Tieh-chao, and released Comrade Hsieh Han-chang and the others.

The same day in the afternoon we arrived at the Futien school and released a whole group of other prisoners. . . .

That was how the turnover in Tungku occurred. From an organizational point of view this action is absolutely impermissible. It is all the more said that the turnover took place at a turning point in the class struggle. But I risked it in that particular situation, on the basis of Bolshevik principles and also for the sake of saving the party. I had no instructions from higher bodies. Liu Ti has always fought under the Bolshevik guidance of the Central Committee and the Provincial Committee. He pledges never to betray this principle. He is asking the Central Committee to punish him for faulty actions.

Long live the victory of Bolshevism!

Liu Ti
January 11, 1931, Yenan

November 15, 1943

Wang Ming has been named among the Trotskyites who, according to former statements of the Chairman of the CCP Central Committee, have been working to undermine the unity of the anti-Japanese front.

It turns out that Wang Ming, who is now under the lash for loyalty to the Comintern, loyalty to the united anti-Japanese front, is a Trotskyite!

Some statements by the Chairman of the CCP Central Committee, and even rather recent ones, are well known. Here are a few of them literally:

". . . The frontier areas are a part of China and are subject to the Central Government just like the other provinces of China. . . ."

"In this way our policy . . . should be (1) resolute conduct of armed resistance, (2) consolidation of the united anti-Japanese national front, (3) conduct of a protracted war. . . ."

"The major task of the Communist Party after victory in the defensive war will be . . . the creation of a free and independent democratic republic. A single democratic government will be set up in China, a single parliament representing the will of the whole people, and a single constitution representing the interests of the people. All nationalities living in China will enjoy equal rights, and on that principle the union of all the peoples of China will be shaped. Industry, agriculture, and trade will develop rapidly. The people and the state will together carry out economic construction, an eight-hour working day will be established, the peasants will receive land, a single progressive tax will be introduced, peace and trade agreements will be concluded with foreign states, as well as agreements of mutual assistance. The people will be ensured freedom of speech and assembly, organization and religion; every citizen will be able to develop his abilities, the general cultural standard of the people will rise, sciences will develop, and illiteracy among the population will be fully liquidated. The relations between the Army and the people will be that of friendship."

"Will China be able to come out of the difficult situation in which it is right now? Of course it will. The united front will play a decisive role in it."

"Is the anti-Japanese national front limited to co-operation between the Kuomintang and the CCP? No, it is not. It should be a national united front. Undoubtedly, the Kuomintang and the Communist Party are the leading forces of the united front, but still they are only a part of it. The anti-Japanese national front should be a united front of all the parties and organizations . . . a united front of all the Chinese who love their country."

"The struggle against Japan requires mobilization of the whole people and its involvement in the united front. . . ."

"The development of the united anti-Japanese front and the fulfillment of the tasks facing us will lead China onto the glorious, great road of national liberation."

The number of such statements is just countless!

Facts convince me that the words of the Chairman of the CCP Central Committee should be treated with utmost caution. For him the only important thing is to move ahead to his goal. The rest is of no significance.

From the very beginning he was against the tactics of a united anti-Japanese front, but the patriotic sentiment that surged through the country in the year this front was being created forced him to maneuver. Hence, the statements like the above. . . .

One must know this man's intentions before drawing any conclusions from what he says. Too often he says something directly opposite to what he is going to do. . . .

November 28, 1943

Our troops are already somewhere near Gomel, between the Dnieper and Berzina, in the regions of Cherkassy and Kremenchug. . . .

With the departure of Dolmatov, Yuzhin, and Aleyev my cave living sank into oblivion. Now I live in the left wing of the house, and Kolya is in the right wing where the radio room is.

The house is empty, hollow, and lonely.

It seems Moscow is inclined to share my opinion. I can judge by the short replies to my reports. To my last report Comrade Dimitrov replied that Mao Tse-tung should not be identified with the CCP, that the Chinese Revolution is anti-imperialist in character and brings liberation to the five-hundred-million population, and that in itself is a great victory of the progressive forces. . . .

November 29, 1943

While Wang Ming is bedridden and isolated completely from the external world through the efforts of Kang Sheng, the developments are becoming ever more grim for the entire political course that he headed.

One sitting of the Politburo is followed by another. At present one of such enlarged sittings is analyzing the mistakes of the "Moscow group."

Wang Ming is accused of all mortal sins. It is his blame that "opportunist tendencies" have taken root in the CCP. It is he (together with Po Ku, Chou En-lai, Lo Fu, and some others), they allege, who paralyzes the development of the national liberation movement with his conciliatory attitude to the Kuomintang. It is at the sittings of the Politburo and not just any place that he is labeled "Kuomintang accomplice and counterrevolutionary."

They use the meanest pretext to prove Wang Ming's "counterrevolutionism"—he was arrested in Shanghai and then released, there is something fishy about it, and for that reason it proves "treason." . . .

Besides, Wang Ming is being accused of instilling various antiparty views based on disregard for the national conditions of the struggle of the Communist Party. Those who have been reprimanded by the CCP Central Committee for faulty actions during the time Wang Ming was one of its leaders are the most vicious in branding him.

The statements by Yeh Chien-ying, Lo Fu, and Chou En-lai, who unhesitatingly admitted that their views were harmful and profoundly faulty, has confirmed the bankruptcy of the "line of Wang Ming."

To consolidate the results of the struggle, the CCP Central Committee has published urgently, on Mao Tse-tung's instructions, the book entitled *Two Lines*. Even a superficial glance at it is enough to see that it is wholly devoted to Chairman Mao's struggle against the "pernicious" policy ("opportunism") of Wang Ming.

Po Ku also commands special attention as a former leader of the Communist Party. Pressed by Mao Tse-tung, he had to speak up three times to explain his views and every time to admit his mistakes.

Po Ku was bitter when he was telling me about it. But his humiliation did not end there. Yesterday the Chairman of the CCP Central Committee and Kang Sheng suggested that he should prepare thoroughly and speak on all points in greater detail.

The leading workers of the Central Committee are in a funereal mood. They try to sit it out at home and are afraid of each other. They prefer to talk without witnesses and avoid contact under various pretexts. The mood is oppressive and grim everywhere and in everything. . . .

I am still astonished at the attitude to the Soviet Union on the part of the leading officials of the CCP Central Committee. A concealed dissatisfaction with the Soviet Union is always present because it does not supply to the Special Area arms, equipment, and simply various goods. . . . Either they cannot or would not understand here that our people are waging the bitterest war of their history, that the Soviet people are bleeding, that the Soviet economy has suffered colossal damage. . . .

They automatically ascribe their ideas about America to the Soviet Union. But on American soil not a single bomb has exploded, towns have not burned, and the enemy has not occupied whole industrial regions. Its people have not been exterminated ruthlessly and in a planned manner.

Although the United States is fighting, its economy is developing in extremely favorable conditions. Hence its opportunity to render vast assistance on lend-lease to the countries of the anti-Hitler coalition.

Any assistance on the part of the Soviet Union means overexertion of the economy, which is strained as it is. They view the Soviet Union here like a horn of plenty from which it is possible and necessary to draw all kinds of means. But even during these difficult years our state has rendered assistance to the CCP by way of big sums of currency. That was assistance almost beyond the last strength.

I myself witnessed such transactions. And Mao Tse-tung knows perfectly well about it. He got these very substantial sums personally. . . .

December 1943

December 7, 1943

A conference of the allied powers—the Soviet Union, the United States, and Britain—was held in Tehran. The declaration of the three powers showed their resolve to do away with the Hitlerite regime.

The avalanche of Red Army victories compels Chinese party leaders to do an about-face in their attitude: The Soviet Union is winning the war—line up with the Soviet Union!

I think that tonight I will complete my translation of the collection *The Two Roads*. I have three more pages to do.

The collection consists of three sections: (1) the period of the great revolution, (2) the period of the Civil War, (3) the period of the anti-Japanese war.

The collection contains documents of the Central Committee and the Politburo, speeches of Mao Tse-tung and Wang Ming.

The collection is intended for high- and middle-ranking political workers. Its main line is to laud Mao Tse-tung's policy and fiercely denounce Wang Ming's "sedition." . . .

December 14, 1943

Of Wang Ming the Chairman said: "A regular kingling in the party!" How he hates Wang Ming!

A feeling of loneliness sometimes sweeps over me. I am surrounded by many people, but I am alone. Everything here seems improbable, and it is then that I particularly regret that I am not at the front. . . .

December 19, 1943

Despite the blockade the Special Area is carrying on a lively trade with the Kuomintang provinces and even with areas under Japanese occupation.

From the Area come deliveries of salt, wool, and cattle, and, of late, opium in ever increasing amounts.

Starting this year the authorities of the Special Area are conducting a policy of regulating labor power by bringing down land rent. Particular attention is devoted to crediting and encouraging the best households as a measure against the growing dislocation and the fleeing of peasants from the Special Area.

According to Kang Sheng's data, peasants and settlers received credits to the sum of 4 million local dollars in 1942, and to the sum of 30 million local dollars this year. The plan for the development of new lands has been overfulfilled by 350,000 mus. The land under irrigation is steadily growing.

Military units, educational establishments, and Soviet institutions have been drawn into production.

Chu Teh bears himself as a man who knows his own value. Always even, calm, and friendly. To my knowledge, he does not indulge in denunciation ("criticism"). Accepts Mao Tse-tung's authority but does not curry favor.

Besides, here he is ranked with Mao Tse-tung as the founder of the Red Army. These names are frequently used together. . . .

December 22, 1943

Yeh Chien-ying was born in 1897. Member of the CCP from 1924. A professional military man. Participant of the Nanchang uprising in 1927. Has a close personal relationship with Chou En-lai. Studied in Moscow and Paris. Received military training in Germany. Helped Mao Tse-tung in Tsunyi and during collision with Chang Kuo-tao in 1935. A talented staff officer. Displays little initiative.

December 23, 1943

The movement for the "rectification of the three styles of work" brings its bitter fruits.

The enlarged meeting of the Politburo of the CCP Central Committee sums up the results of the exposure of the "capitulatory Menshevik" line of Po Ku, Wang Ming, Lo Fu, Yang Shang-kun, and other members of the "Moscow opposition." Their policy is branded as antiparty. The "dogmatists" guided ideologically by the "Muscovites" are stigmatized as traitors of revolutionary interests, who "grovel before the Kuomintang" and promote the penetration of "Western Marxist dogmas" into the ideology of the Chinese Revolution.

Now the entire party has been informed of the party struggle that rent only the upper crust of the CCP. Thus a new torrent of slime was gushed into cheng-feng whose task is "to help young Communists of petty-bourgeois stock to take up more staunchly the stance of the working class."

In party organizations, biased by the trustworthy executors of Mao Tse-tung's and Kang Sheng's will, a most detailed discussion of the "deviative and opportunist" course of Wang Ming and the course of the Chairman of the CCP Central Committee was launched.

The first stage of cheng-feng was concerned only with indoctrinating the public. The struggle inside the CCP leadership was concealed from the party rank-and-file members. Suppression concerned "dogmatists" in general. The names of Wang Ming and others were only vaguely mentioned at one time or another. But Wang Ming himself was kept in strict isolation.

Now Lo Fu, Po Ku, and Chou En-lai in a series of statements at the sittings of the Politburo of the Central Committee have admitted to having erroneous views. Mao Tse-tung has "covered" Wang Ming with different "proofs" of his guilt before the party.

Lo Fu, Po Ku, and Chou En-lai have admitted their "harmful and erroneous views" in specially written documents addressed to the Chairman of the Central Committee.

Cheng-feng assumes a qualitatively new state. Now each internationalist in the CCP leadership is discredited personally, as is consequently the entire "procapitulatory course of the Comintern" and "Soviet dogmatism" in general. . . .

Now it is a practical campaign which has become concretized in names.

It has become impossible to keep Wang Ming in ignorance. Rosa Vladimirovna told her husband the whole truth. Wang Ming was confronted with the glaring truth in all its magnitude. . . .

But Mao Tse-tung's aim is not only to smear Wang Ming. He is set on breaking his spirit. It is important to make Wang Ming admit the "correctness of his course" by word of mouth.

Work on Wang Ming has begun. Li Fu-chun, an official from the CCP Central Committee, has been selected for talks with Wang Ming.

When Rosa Vladimirovna told her husband the entire truth about what was going on, he realized that in effect he had found himself isolated ideologically. He was not even aware of all the lies that had been piled up against him in this period by Mao Tse-tung and Kang Sheng.

December 24, 1943

I called on Wang Ming.

The other day the Chairman of the CCP Central Committee paid him a visit and had a long talk with him on the plea that he had responded to his requests and promised to single out a group of party workers to hear him out.

Wang Ming is depressed physically and morally. He has agreed to capitulate before Mao Tse-tung. He considers his address to Comrade Dimitrov, which we transmitted to Moscow on his request, as erroneous and unbefitting a party member. In his opinion relations with former Comintern workers are liable to wreck his reconciliation with Mao Tse-tung, which is beginning to take shape. . . .

December 26, 1943

Nearly 2 million men are drafted yearly into the Chinese Army. Yet its numerical strength is approximately the same—3.5 million.

The losses in battles with the Japanese are insignificant as compared with desertion and mortality from diseases and undernourishment.

Corruption, bribery, and depravity reign among the Kuomintang officers.

On the eve of the Tehran Conference Chiang Kai-shek had a meeting with Roosevelt and Churchill. It seems that the present and future of China were among the problems discussed in Tehran. It is difficult to foresee its prospects for the next few years. But one thing is clear: The land question and the rule of foreign capital promote and will continue to promote the development of the antifeudal and anti-imperialist revolution. Mao Tse-tung takes into account the inevitability of this process. War, in his opinion, favors seizure of power, for it weakens and shatters the power of the Chungking Government. According to the situation, one can build up one's power by jeopardizing the armies of the Central Government and avoiding active struggle against the Japanese. Of course, the passive character of actions undertaken by the CCP troops against the invaders does not exclude combat operations, but their scope was and is clearly out of tune with the actual possibilities of the Eighth Route Army, being of a limited and forced retaliatory nature. Data on the actions of the Eighth Route Army and New Fourth Army which are intended for the outer world are deliberately exaggerated. In this way preparations for a civil war are camouflaged.

Sooner or later the Allies will rout Japan. This is the starting point of Mao Tse-tung's entire policy. However, he cannot ignore the anti-Japanese sentiments of the people and the character of the common struggle of the world progressive forces against fascism. That is the reason why CCP troops take part in the war. However, all their actions are marked by the ideological conceptions of Chairman Mao.

1944

January 1944

Kang Sheng's data:

Strength of the Eighth Route Army: 387,245 troops.

Armaments: rifles, 190,000; machine guns, 3,187; heavy machine guns, 360; artillery pieces, 232.

The area of dislocation, activities, and influence of the Eighth Route Army: 350,000 sq. km. in northern China, i.e., 40 per cent of its territory with a population of 34.5 million.

This territory is divided into the following four military-administrative districts:

1. Shansi-Hopeh-Chahar frontier district (the strongest base of the Eighth Route Army).

Acting here are Hsiao Ko, Chung [Chi-kuang(?)], and Nieh Jung-chen. Operationally, the troops are subordinated to Nieh Jung-chen.

2. The frontier district of the northwestern part of Shansi province.

Area, 40,000 sq. km.; population, 1.75 million. Troops, numbering 65,000, are commanded by Ho Lung. His deputies are Hsu Fang-ting and Commissar Kuang Hsiang-ying.

3. Shansi-Hopeh-Honan frontier district.

Area, 225,000 sq. km.; population, 13.5 million. This is the least militarily important area where active are Liu Po-cheng's 129th Infantry Division and other troops, totaling 95,000.

4. Shantung frontier district.

Population, 40 million. The main combat unit is Lin Piao's 115th Infantry Division which co-ordinates operations with Chang Ching-wu's 85,000-strong Shantung column.

By agreement between the Central Government and the CCP leadership, the Eighth Route Army is limited to three divisions (the 115th, 120th, and 129th). That is why every division has assumed the proportions of an army.

Mao Tse-tung has apparently received a telegram from Dimitrov. Nobody is received in the Chiao-yuan. . . .

January 3, 1944

Po Ku confirmed my guess: A telegram from Moscow has come.

In his telegram Dimitrov expresses concern over the relations with the Kuomintang, the CCP leadership's policy in respect to the "Moscow group," and gives his evaluation of Kang Sheng's heinous role in the Yenan affairs. . . .

Referring to the cheng-feng in the Special Area, Po Ku said with a sad grin: "He who was there, he knows. He who will be, he will know."

January 4, 1944

Unexpectedly, I received Mao Tse-tung's invitation to spend an evening with him, listening to an old Chinese opera.

I had come earlier, since we had to go to Yang-chia-lin. Mao and Chiang Ching were already waiting for me. After the exchange of compliments we started for Yang-chia-lin.

Mao behaved simply. He knows, when he needs it, how to behave simply, disarmingly simply. He knows how to be amiable.

Without spending time on formalities, he immediately began speaking of his respect for the Soviet Union, the Soviet Communist Party, and I. V. Stalin. Chiang Ching was walking in silence.

Mao said he sincerely respected the Chinese comrades who had received education or worked in the Soviet Union.

This was the main subject of our talk. To be more exact, it was a monologue, as Mao did all the talking. He spoke of the Soviet Union's significance for the existence of the Special Area, the importance of the united anti-Japanese front, and the political role which the former Comintern played for the CCP.

His jacket sleeves were somewhat long. He used them as a muff to warm his hands. His long hair came out from under his conelike cap on his temples. He put it back absent-mindedly, but it came out again. . . .

There was nobody around with the exception of guards walking at a distance.

During the performance Mao was distracted but polite. He didn't say a word about what occupied him.

Chiang Ching told me at length about the theater and actors. Mao was looking into the hall, his eyes narrowed. He had a habit of narrowing his eyes, but I felt he was anxious and he needed me.

After the performance Mao told me he wanted to have a detailed talk with me.

I said I was ready.

When nobody was around, Mao said he had received Comrade Dimitrov's telegram concerning the Comintern policy. He thought at length over the telegram, which excited him, and he took its apprehensions and concerns close to heart. He understood Comrade Dimitrov's profound and sincere desire to help the CCP leadership and he appreciated his assistance, which had always been wise.

Parting, Mao Tse-tung said he would meet me without fail to discuss the questions raised in the telegram.

January 6, 1944

January was destined to become a month of surprises. Unexpectedly, Andrei Yakovlevich, Kolya, and myself received an invitation to have dinner with the Chairman of the CCP Central Committee. Present at the dinner were CCP leaders. Everything was ceremonious, friendly and . . . servile.

The aim of the invitation was quite clear—to convince us that cheng-feng has nothing to do with the struggle against the "dogmatists" and the "Moscow opposition," that no actions were taken to undermine the united anti-Japanese front, that anti-Comintern propaganda did not exist. They were simply catching spies, only spies. . . .

We were to persuade Moscow that everything was all right in Yenan —that's what Mao's aim was.

The behavior of Liu Shao-chi, Chou En-lai (he has changed rapidly to suit Mao and now is one of the most fervent supporters of Mao Tse-tung), and Kang Sheng has confirmed my surmises. They have changed beyond recognition. Besides flattering me, unexpectedly, they fawned upon Kolya, whom they knew only slightly. This show was masterminded by Mao Tse-tung.

Upon receiving the telegram from the Comintern's former head, the Chairman of the CCP Central Committee hastily distributed roles, pointing out who was to say what, how to treat us, and what to get out of us.

Mao has shown once again that he knows how to handle people. He knows how to treat and win people over and talk about the most abstract things in an easy manner. If Chou and Liu felt ill at ease, Mao spoke almost without interruption and was gay and pleasant. It was clear he was playing. This play was to win our confidence.

We saw a smile on Mao's full lips and kind-heartedness of a hospitable host in his squinted eyes. He only smoked more than usually. . . .

He didn't leave me without his attention for a moment. Liu and Chou actively "worked on" Andrei Yakovlevich. Kang portioned out his attention among all of us.

Chou differs outwardly from all. He is neat. His clothes are not bulky.

January 8, 1944

Mao Tse-tung suddenly came to us at nine o'clock yesterday. He was without guards and Kang Sheng, Liu Shao-chi, Chou, and Jen Pi-shih, who were usually present at our talks.

The visit of the Chairman of the CCP Central Committee was like a bolt from the blue. And not only because he never comes to us in such a simple manner but because he usually sleeps at this time . . .

I invited him to the parlor. Kolya hastily made tea and brought spirit and snacks. But Mao Tse-tung waved the food aside and got down to business without beating around the bush. He began to explain energetically the essence of the CCP leadership's line on inner party and foreign-policy questions.

I understood that Kolya embarrassed him, and I asked the radio operator to leave us. Mao was very pleased.

The Chairman of the CCP Central Committee said that he regarded the united anti-Japanese front as a great force capable of withstanding Japanese aggression, that he was a sincere supporter of the unity of all national forces, and that he was doing all he could to strengthen and develop the anti-Japanese bloc. However, he considered a firm hand was necessary to restrain the aggressiveness of the Kuomintang. This would neutralize the enemies of the Special Area.

After nearly every phrase the Chairman of the CCP Central Committee repeated how deeply he respected the experience of comrades Stalin and Dimitrov.

All of a sudden the Chairman of the CCP Central Committee began to speak of Wang Ming—in an entirely different, almost friendly, tone! At first I didn't realize he was speaking of Wang Ming. . . .

It was a long talk. Mao finished one pack of cigarettes and began another. He looked worried and his eyelids were red. Now and then he would stand up heavily to noiselessly pace the room in his felt shoes. His long hair fell and covered his eyes. He would often throw it back and look around absent-mindedly. . . .

The visit ended in a quite unexpected way. The Chairman of the CCP Central Committee asked for a few sheets of paper. He sat down at the desk and wrote a telegram to Comrade Dimitrov. He asked me to "tick it out" to Moscow without delay. Mao looked perturbed, his gestures betraying tension and nervousness.

Parting, the Chairman of the CCP Central Committee said he and other Chinese workers had given us insufficient aid. He promised to make up for this.

He looked extremely tired, as if he hadn't a moment's sleep that night.

I saw him off. . . .

In his telegram to Dimitrov, as the former head of the Comintern, Mao Tse-tung asked him to understand correctly the inner party policy of the CCP leadership. He asked Comrade Dimitrov not to worry, to calm down since he understood Comrade Dimitrov's feelings and took them close to heart. The essence of his and Dimitrov's concern was the same because they had the same thoughts.

Mao Tse-tung wrote that apart from the telegram dispatched to Moscow on January 2 he would like to point out once again the basic principled questions for which the leadership of the CCP was struggling.

The January 2 telegram explained his viewpoint of these questions, but it was necessary to determine the essence of the tasks and policy once more. Mao Tse-tung thanked the Comintern's former head for his assistance and warning against the inadmissibility of the split of the united anti-Japanese front and the inadmissibility of the anti-Kuomintang policy in the prevailing conditions. Mao Tse-tung assured the Comintern's former head of his sincere respect.

He wrote that since July 1943 and up to that day energetic measures were being taken to strengthen the unity of the party. As a result, the situation in the party had improved drastically. The essence of this inner party policy is unity and cohesion. As for Wang Ming, he is treated proceeding from the selfsame main provisions of the inner party policy: unity and cohesion.

The policy toward the Kuomintang had remained unchanged. It proceeded from the necessity of the united anti-Japanese front, and the CCP leadership had always strictly adhered to it. The essence of this policy was co-operation with the Kuomintang, the necessity of this co-operation. In the current year improvements should be expected in the relations between the CCP and the Kuomintang. Mao Tse-tung stressed he counted on this.

Well, he gave me food for thought. Mao certainly grasped my attitude to political events in the Special Area. The aim of his visit was not only to convince Moscow of the CCP leadership's friendliness but also to show how I should interpret his, Mao's, policy. This was an attempt to shake me, if not lead me astray. This means that Mao will act in the same spirit and that he tries, well in advance, to secure the freedom for such actions for himself, actions which are essentially anti-Soviet.

January 9, 1944

Wang Ming doesn't know of Dimitrov's telegram. It is not possible to tell him of it. In the changed circumstances Mao Tse-tung is trying to use pressure brought to bear upon Wang Ming in order not only fully to discredit his political opponent but also to prove, to some degree, the ungroundedness of Dimitrov's telegram. . . .

Wang Ming gave in and says his political line is erroneous. Preserving Wang Ming's isolation, Mao Tse-tung began to maneuver in an attempt to wrest away confessions from him in the spirit necessary to answer Dimitrov's telegram. Indeed, if Wang Ming himself considers his policy fallacious, what doubts can there be as regards the correctness of the CCP leadership's actions? . . .

On January 6 Mao Tse-tung had a long talk with Wang Ming. Judging by what Mao said himself, in this talk he kept to a rather soft position, which differed sharply from his previous irreconcilability. . . . Moreover, Mao intimated reconciliation was possible, as was joint work in the future in case Wang Ming improved, confessed, etc.

This had its effect. Unaware of Dimitrov's telegram and regarding the change in the behavior of the Chairman of the CCP Central Committee as a desire to put an end to the conflict, Wang Ming became firm in his opinion and began giving up his positions. Wang Ming takes Mao's curvets for sincerity, same as he takes the change in their relations at its face value. Mao is rapidly moving toward his aim. . . .

It was a clever move on Mao's part to send the telegram via our radio station. Besides everything else, this will show that the Chairman of the CCP Central Committee and the Soviet group "live in concord," that there are no, nor were there, attacks on the Soviet Union, on the "dogmatists" who studied in the Soviet Union and all others who have sympathies for my motherland.

The telegram of the Chairman of the CCP Central Committee also pursued another aim—to retain, at any cost, Kang Sheng in the CCP leadership, who has completely exposed himself as an enemy of our party and people. Mao Tse-tung decided on a double deal: to preserve Kang Sheng in the CCP leadership, for himself, so to speak, and, simultaneously, to leave Wang Ming in peace, as a proof of his devotion to the Soviet Union and the AUCP(B). The Chairman of the CCP Central Committee wants to use Wang Ming to cover up, without delay, his actions which have unexpectedly become known not only outside the Special Area and China . . .

Mao acts not so much skillfully as resolutely and brazenly.

Doubtless, Mao has guessed how the cheng-feng and the struggle with Wang Ming were understood in Moscow and what role I played in this.

January 10, 1944

The Fourth Army was set up by agreement between the Central Government and the CCP in 1937. It includes regular troops as well as guerrilla units from the central and southeastern provinces of China.

In January 1941, violating the agreement, Kuomintang troops inflicted a heavy defeat on the Fourth Army. By Chiang Kai-shek's order of January 17 of the same year the Fourth Army was disbanded, but the January 20 decision of the CCP Central Committee restored it, to include seven divisions, under the name of the New Fourth Army.

Chen Yi is commander in chief of the New Fourth Army. Chang Yung-i is deputy commander in chief. Liu Shao-chi is commissar.

The area of the Army's operations covers the Nanking-Shanghai and the Shanghai-Hangchow railways and the southern section of the Tientsin-Pukow Railway.

The Army has some 99,000 troops.

Guard units, numbering 40,000 troops, are billeted in the Special Area. Ho Lung's 120th Infantry Division is being transferred there.

———

Mao's desire is to leave party members with a meager selection of slogans and theses.

People here continue to learn "The Twenty-two Documents" by heart, criticize the "dogmatists," disavow Wang Ming, etc. The documents are learned zealously, as if they were the Gospel. People believe, sincerely and otherwise, that "before honor is humility. . . ."

January 13, 1944

The CCP leadership's attitude to our group is emphatically "cordial." They receive me at my first request and talk willingly. . . .

Having realized that Moscow knows the state of affairs in the CCP to the minutest detail, Mao Tse-tung and his supporters are changing their ways. They understand they will not pull through without Soviet assistance. They replace brazenness with a special care for the camouflage of their sectarian policy.

A conclusion I sent to the center is that Mao Tse-tung and his supporters would never give up the policy for which they have been fighting for so many years and which had crystallized and triumphed.

Mao Tse-tung's telegrams are a tribute of politeness. The flirt with me and obligingness are just a mask! . . .

I am watching an incessant tragicomedy. . . .

January 21, 1944

Had another meeting with Mao Tse-tung. What was peculiar about the talk was his attitude to the United States. Though he said it in passing, his words sounded quite meaningful: "For China the American policy is a question of paramount importance."

Mao "explained" the essence of the CCP-Kuomintang relations to me once again. "The Kuomintang does not admit Communists to the government. However, in due time we shall raise this question before Chiang Kai-shek," Mao said. After that he began to scold Chiang Kai-shek and the Central Government.

No doubt, Chiang Kai-shek's government is reactionary in its nature and it cannot be otherwise. However, if one proceeds from this in one's relations with Chungking, the united anti-Japanese front will become simply impossible. It should be recalled that China's political weakness was used by the imperialists and is being used by fascist Japan at present.

Mao, for one, thinks that the war will be long ("many, many years"). He has curtailed, and does not intensify, military operations against the Japanese. Who will fight against the invaders? The reactionary Chiang Kai-shek? The Allies? . . .

As usual, we met at night when the Chairman of the CCP Central Committee was working. It was cold in his spacious cave-flat. Mao looked unwell. He smoked much. Treated me to tea.

His desk was all covered with papers. Orderlies were bringing telegrams. He put them aside without reading. Stooping, he was pacing the room. He has a hollow chest. His speech is simple and even coarse. . . .

I was returning after midnight. I responded to sentries' calls. When I came close up, they smiled at me. Guards already knew me. A snowstorm was whirling and it was very cold. A real Siberian frost was in the air. . . .

January 23, 1944

My relations with the CCP leadership develop under the influence of Comrade Dimitrov's telegram. As the telegram contains Kang Sheng's frank political evaluation, the Ching-pao-chu chief tries to show me (and Moscow through me) his loyalty. He is always very discreet to me. The last time we met he suddenly began to speak about Wang Ming, although this subject had been taboo before. Although nobody was prohibited from speaking about Wang Ming, not a single person dared do so. I also avoided this subject.

Kang Sheng told me, with malicious joy, about the mistakes Wang Ming had admitted in the presence of the Chairman of the CCP Central Committee. He said Wang Ming asked Mao Tse-tung not to accentuate his, Wang Ming's, mistakes at the forthcoming Seventh Congress of the party or, at least, to mollify the discussion of his errors.

The main thing, Kang Sheng said, was that Wang Ming had admitted his political mistakes and that was why the Chairman of the CCP Central Committee assured him he would take every precaution to prevent an anti-Wang Ming conflict at the forthcoming congress.

Cringing to me, Kang Sheng could not, at the same time, conceal his triumph. He tried to impress on me that we were all comrades, if not friends, and that there was no—nor could there be any—misunderstanding between us.

Kang Sheng said that Wang Ming was much better, that the danger was over, and therefore there was no reason to worry about him. "Wang Ming is much stronger than Wang Chia-hsiang," Kang said.

I asked why he was so sure.

Kang Sheng explained. It turned out that during the New Year holidays the Chairman of the CCP Central Committee had twice visited Wang Ming, had long talks with him, and became convinced that Wang Ming was in decent shape. However, this was not all. Following Mao Tse-tung's visits, Chou came to see Wang Ming. They had a talk which lasted for about five hours.

Kang Sheng said this was the most convincing proof of Wang Ming's strong health.

"He is almost well!" Kang said.

This was especially important for Kang, as he was suspected of Wang Ming's premeditated poisoning. Following Dimitrov's telegram, which showed that Moscow knew everything, he needed proof to remove all suspicions. Now it was simple: Wang Ming was just ill! Why should people speak about this any longer? . . .

The situation in Yenan continues to be cheng-feng-wise. Wherever you go, you see anti-Kuomintang slogans, cheng-feng slogans. The rocks, wherever possible, are all covered with characters.

January 25, 1944

I was again summoned by the Chairman of the CCP Central Committee. Again candlelight, orderlies, calls of sentries, and Mao's persuasive speech. . . .

Everything is done to win me over and convince me of the correctness of Yenan's present-day policy. And, in this way, to soothe Moscow.

Mao was noiselessly pacing the room and talking without end. . . . Now and then he would sit beside me. He drank piping-hot tea and joked.

The jokes and manifestations of a sincerity conceal the mind which works unhesitatingly, leaving no room for doubt. . . .

Mao was trying to convince me that Chiang Kai-shek had to give Communists posts in the government, that the Special Area needed big amounts of arms to fight against the Japanese. . . . However, not a word was said that combat operations against the Japanese were being curtailed. This is an indisputable fact. Mao recognizes the united anti-Japanese front only in words. All his thoughts are there, in Chungking. There, there are people who must be put out of the way, crushed and deprived of power—and that is the main thing.

The revelations of the Chairman of the CCP Central Committee and Kang Sheng are not accidental. On the one hand, the Soviet Union has defeated, acting practically all alone, fascist Germany, and the victory is not far off, and, on the other, Moscow has learned of anti-Sovietism in the Special Area and repressions against the internaionalists.

The telegram was a shock for Mao. He thought that, relying on the Soviet Union's support, it was also possible, at the same time, to defame the Soviet Union and . . . cause harm to its interests! His behavior, as well as that of Kang Sheng, is the continuation of the self-same pitiful cancan they are perplexedly dancing before us after Comrade Dimitrov's unexpected telegram.

January 27, 1944

The Japanese use against the Eighth Route Army five infantry divisions, eight infantry brigades, and one cavalry brigade, totaling 140,000 officers and men and 650 artillery pieces.

In the area of operations the Japanese control supply routes and river crossings. The main bases of the Eighth Route Army have been skillfully broken by the invaders into small fragments.

Against the New Fourth Army the samurai have two infantry divisions and two infantry brigades—60,000 officers and men and 240 artillery pieces. This is according to Kang Sheng. . . .

February 1944

February 3, 1944

Soviet troops are attacking in the direction of Narva.

The Americans have landed on the Marshall Islands.

Now on the near and distant approaches to the Special Area the Kuomintang has over forty infantry divisions (Kang Sheng reported forty-two), that is, about 440,000 soldiers and officers.

Simultaneously large military forces of Chungking are blocking the militarists.

Chiang Kai-shek is forced to hold 100,000 soldiers under arms in the direction of Tibet and Sinkiang. And another 120,000 against the Szechwan militarists. Besides, considerable military forces are blocking the smaller militarists scattered all over the country. All these military forces of the Central Government do not take part in combat actions against the Japanese.

Among Chinese party functionaries there are no people who could correctly and competently interpret the policy of the Soviet Union. They judge our country primarily by British and American reports.

The libraries have little (practically no) Marxist literature, particularly literature from the Soviet Union and on the Soviet Union. Even the Chairman of the CCP Central Committee has a very meager collection of Marxist literature. . . .

Mao Tse-tung recently remarked to me that Chu Teh was rather old for real work. . . .

Andrei Yakovlevich performs difficult operations day after day. He works with inspiration and virtuosity. More often than not he whiles nights away at the bedside of the seriously ill. In Yenan he really is the only highly skilled surgeon. Mao Tse-tung is his diligent patient. Last summer Andrei Yakovlevich operated on Chiang Ching. . . . I feel lonesome when I do not see Orlov for a long time. . . .

At a traditional Chinese theatrical performance one may be deafened by the percussion instruments. But later you begin to catch in all that a rhythm, a deep link with the plastic body movements and facial expressions. . . .

What I cannot get accustomed to is the walking in the hall, the talking and laughing during performances. . . .

February 12, 1944

Cramming "The Twenty-two Documents" goes on and on! . . .

The Chinese people associate their hopes for a new life with the Communist Party and its leader. Life without poverty, national humiliation, and feudal and capitalist plunder.

The objective historical necessity makes the CCP one of the leading political forces in China.

Enslaved peoples turn to nationalism as a protest, as self-assertion, as a force that spontaneously unites a country. But there's only a step to make—and "protesting" nationalism becomes chauvinism and racialism!

Millions of people voted for the Communist Party in Germany in the early thirties. The chauvinism implanted by Hitler reversed it all—those millions, among whom workers and peasants make up the absolute majority, are now fighting against their class brothers. Fighting supposedly for their fatherland! . . .

For Krupp, Schacht, and company—this is, of course, a "war for the fatherland"! Only which fatherland?! . . .

People have come to Yenan dreaming of socialist China. Though they are illiterate, though they have been defamed, they are prepared to fight for their country. Playing on the ideals of fatherland dear to every man provides for Mao Tse-tung an excellent weapon against the internationalist essence of Marxism-Leninism. Nationalism is being imperceptibly substituted for patriotism in the CCP.

Historical lies and forgeries—that's the method of Mao Tse-tung for the seizure of power.

The overwhelming majority of the Yenan party cadres are honest people, but maimed precisely by this nationalistic and anarchistic propaganda. Their lack of culture and their isolation not only from the world at large but also from their own country make them receptive to "spiritual purification." The Ching-pao-chu boss deals with the unreceptive. . . .

In behalf of socialism Mao betrays socialism, in behalf of the Communist Party he destroys the Communist Party, in behalf of democracy he imposes terror. . . .

February 22, 1944

One of the purposes of cheng-feng is the "spiritual purification" of delegates to the future Seventh Congress of the CCP.

The delegates are to approve and justify before the party and the entire world the political course of Mao Tse-tung.

The delegates have been in Yenan for quite some time. For several years they have been "spiritually purified" with great zeal. Doubtlessly, the congress will not be held until Mao Tse-tung becomes fully confident of the "spiritual purification" of all the delegates and, consequently, the absolute triumph of his policy. . . .

———

Orlov described his colleagues—foreign doctors.

Ma Hai-te received medical education in Switzerland (he himself told Orlov so). Ma Hai-te says he is a dermatologist, although he undertakes to treat any disease. He speaks English, French, Hebrew, Chinese, and Arabic.

Dr. Fray. Orlov has great doubts about his medical education. If Ma Hai-te is a not bad dermatologist, Fray is quite an ignoramus. He gives himself out to be a therapeutist, but in fact he is just a bad doctor's assistant. He claims that he studied at a medical institute in Vienna. He has been in China since 1939. He writes and speaks German, English, and Chinese.

Dr. Mueller. A German Jew from Düsseldorf. A therapeutist. He says he fled Hitler's Germany. He is unsociable and keeps aloof.

Dr. Bi Meitis. Son of a Malayan and a Chinese woman. He graduated from a medical institute in Berlin and fought in Spain against Franco. He speaks German, English, and Chinese.

These people are accepted guests in the families of Chinese Communist Party and military leaders and are on good terms with many of them. It seems to me that the actual activity of these "volunteers," naturally except Bi Meitis, is a far cry from medical work. There is too much affectation in their behavior, too much medical incompetence, and too much importunateness in contacts with highly placed patients. The gathering of political and military information—that's what, in my opinion, they are interested in.

February 25, 1944

Before the war, China underwent the rapid formation of a progressive intelligentsia, which came out for the creation of genuinely revolutionary art. At the head of this intelligentsia was Lu Hsun. It was a young intelligentsia, traditionally linked with the past, but forward-looking.

Nieh Erh is my favorite Chinese composer.

From each business trip to China I brought back records of his remarkable music. In it ancient folk tunes blended with modern rhythms. Nieh Erh is an entirely new phenomenon in Chinese music. The truly unique Nieh Erh! . . .

Nieh Erh means the rhythms of life, sunshine, victory. . . .

The man in charge of work with Japanese war prisoners is Okano. He is of a gentle disposition, but strong-willed. The results of his work cannot be called impressive. The Japanese military has reared the youth in fanatical reverence of the Emperor, the "descendant of the goddess Amaterasu," and disregard for other peoples. The mission of a soldier is to die for his Emperor. A soldier is to despise death ("death is lighter than down").

However, there is already a group of activists from among the war prisoners who are taking part in propaganda against the Japanese expeditionary forces in China.

Okano was in America. He has an excellent command of English.

February 28, 1944

In the Special Area they are actively preparing for the Seventh Congress. After a telegram from Dimitrov, Lenin's works "Two Tactics" and " 'Left-wing' Communism—an Infantile Disorder" have been urgently included in the list of precongress materials being "studied." . . .

During conversations Mao Tse-tung often refers to examples from Chinese history.

Not infrequently he wanders from the subject of conversation to some other, and then still another, and then again returns to the previous topic, and suddenly skips to a new subject and again returns to the old one, as though he were talking with himself.

Sometimes he unexpectedly asks your opinion, but prefers a brief answer. If an interlocutor starts to develop his thought, he at first listens attentively and does not contradict, but soon cuts the conversation short. . . . He several times complained to me that after "talkative interlocutors" he is tired and feels poorly, particularly when the interlocutor was an unfamiliar one.

I was destined to be an eyewitness of what was, perhaps, the most dramatic and sad event in the history of the CCP.

The Chairman of the CCP Central Committee would hardly have ventured to sabotage the military efforts of the Soviet Union, fight against the Comintern, and suppress the friends of the Soviet Union and the AUCP(B) in the CCP, were it not for the favorable circumstances that arose during the World War for his personal plans.

First, the isolation of the Special Area had sharply increased as, consequently, did the possibility of camouflaging extensively his political and terrorist actions.

Second, along with the disunity of the international working-class movement due to wartime conditions, there also took place the inevitable weakening of the role of the Comintern, which, in addition, declared its self-dissolution.

Third, the brunt of the struggle against fascism fell to the lot of the Soviet Union. Practically the entire economic potential of Europe had been mobilized by fascist Germany against my country. Particularly critical for her were the first years of the war. The facts leave no doubt: Mao decided that that was the end of us. It was then that he declared cheng-feng to be the main political task of the CCP. Using pseudo-revolutionary phrases as a cover of his true aims, not stinting all kinds of demonstrations disguising the sinister purpose of cheng-feng, Mao began speedily implanting in the CCP ideas foreign to Marxism-Leninism. . . .

There are also other causes that induced Mao to resort to cheng-feng precisely in 1942. For example, the impossibility of covertly carrying on his opportunist and splitting course without the suppression of the healthy forces of the party, etc. But the main reason why Mao ventured cheng-feng was, as it seems to me, the extremely arduous conditions of the World War, with each state fighting for its survival. This fight has absorbed all the military, economic, political, and diplomatic resources of states.

Act as promptly and resolutely as possible, stopping at nothing—these are the conclusions which I think Mao arrived at in the summer of 1941 and in whose correctness he became convinced in the summer of 1942. The defeat of the Soviet Union seemed to him predetermined. Hence even the imprudence, the hastiness, and the crudeness in the forms and methods of carrying out cheng-feng, as well as in its very direction. (For Mao this was not so important.) It seemed to Mao Tse-tung that the situation for the complete seizure of power in the party by pursuing his own opportunist course had never been more favorable: The world was preoccupied with the war, the world was choking in its own blood, the world was disunited by the war. . . .

But something unexpected has happened. The Soviet Union has held out and is winning. The military and political situation in the world has changed abruptly. One has to adapt. The new situation leaves no time for such campaigns. Besides, cheng-feng has done its job, and it would now be inexpedient to attract attention by unseemly behavior. The attention of the Chairman of the CCP Central Committee is engrossed by the future alignment of forces in China and by the forces which may influence this alignment.

For Mao there begins a new round of the political game. Many facts, even though insignificant as yet, convince me of my conjectures. . . .

March 1944

March 3, 1944

The "rectification of the three styles of work"—a political campaign. Its aim is the ideological "rectification" of the Communist Party, that is, the struggle against petty-bourgeois corruption in the party, for its Marxist-Leninist purity.

The Chinese Communist Party lives and works chiefly in rural areas. It is constantly under the influence of the petty-bourgeois environment, with its inherent ideological tendencies.

V. I. Lenin wrote that the petty-bourgeois democracy is not a haphazard political establishment, which emerged by chance, but an inevitable product of capitalism, and that it is made up of not only old, precapitalist, economically reactionary middle peasantry.

In China it is precisely the "old, precapitalist, economically reactionary middle peasantry" that constitutes the backbone of society. . . .

Cheng-feng began with Mao Tse-tung's talks on art, that is, on the relationship between proletarian and nonproletarian cultures. Proletarian culture continuously undergoes the influence of hostile cultures.

Lenin writes in his article "The Achievements and Difficulties of the Soviet Government": "I say again that the task of combining the victorious proletarian revolution with bourgeois culture, with bourgeois science and technology, which up to now has been available to few people, is a difficult one. Here, everything depends on the organization and discipline of the advanced sections of the working people. If, in

Peter Vladimirov.

A. Y. Orlov.

N. N. Rimmar.

Peter Vladimirov shortly after his arrival in Yenan on May 11, 1942.

Landscape in northern Shensi.

Yenan in the autumn of 1942.

The new urban community outside Yenan's city wall.

The house of Soviet military correspondents in Yenan.

Russia, the millions of downtrodden and ignorant peasants who are totally incapable of independent development, who were oppressed by the landowners for centuries, did not have at their head, and by their side, an advanced section of the urban workers whom they understood, with whom they were intimate, who enjoyed their confidence, whom they believed as fellow-workers, if there were not this organization which is capable of rallying the masses of the working people, of influencing them, of explaining to them and convincing them of the importance of the task of taking over the entire bourgeois culture, the cause of communism would be hopeless.

"I say this not from the abstract point of view, but from the point of view of a whole year's daily experience. . . ."

That such a section of workers is absent in the present sphere of action of the Chinese Communist Party is a fact.

To corrupting influences one can and must add also the influence of the intelligentsia, on which Lenin remarked: "We've always known you were weak and flabby. But we don't deny we need you, for you are the only educated group."

Cheng-feng has a correct premise at its foundation. It is indeed the question of the attitude of the proletariat (including the proletarian party) to the petty-bourgeois democrats. And, of course, it is no secondary question. I shall not dwell upon the theoretical propositions of Marxism as regards the solution of this question.

Take the facts of cheng-feng.

The practices of this campaign convince me that in the Chinese Communist Party the Marxist-Leninist principles are being replaced by the principles of petty-bourgeois revolutionariness, and that this party has long since been working without being in touch with the working class and has been enlarged by the admittance of nonproletarian elements.

Outwardly the content of cheng-feng (including ideological premises) agrees with the principles of Marxism-Leninism, but the inner process provides evidence of a distortion of the Leninist ideas by "Marxism in reality." This petty-bourgeois revolutionariness of "Marxism in reality" drills and reforms the party in its own style and spirit. And this is not even the "Left idiocy" of the Bukharin style, of which Lenin wrote. It is a pretty good petty-bourgeois program enunciated by Mao Tse-tung and reflecting the real relationship of social forces in China. With the dissolution of the Comintern, these processes have become impetuous and irreversible. The defeat of the "Moscow opposition" has proved the direction of this process and is evidence of the final wreck of the Bolshevik principles in the CCP.

It is not for nothing that Mao Tse-tung has been destroying the class content of patriotism, reducing it to a purely nationalistic feeling, a tribe instinct. . . .

March 13, 1944

The commander of the border region of Shansi-Hopeh-Chahar is Nieh Jung-chen.

Nieh Jung-chen was born in 1899 in Szechwan province. He studied in France and Belgium. For several years he worked at the Renault car plant in France. In 1923 he joined the CCP. Later he studied in Moscow. A participant in the Northern Expedition and the Long March and a delegate to the forthcoming Seventh Congress of the CCP.

In the border region which Nieh Jung-chen is in charge of, there operates the army group of Hsiao Ko.

Hsiao Ko was born in Hunan in 1907. He comes from the same province as Mao Tse-tung. He joined the CCP in 1927 and has been in the Chinese Red Army since its inception. Participated in the Long March. For some time served as Ho Lung's deputy.

The commander of the Shansi-Hopeh-Hengyang border region is Liu Po-cheng.

Like Nieh Jung-chen, Liu Po-cheng hails from Szechwan. He is fifty-two. Received military education in the Soviet Union. Was the chief of the general staff of the Chinese Red Army. Led the advance detachments of the Red Army in the Long March.

———

I came round to Mao Tse-tung at the appointed hour. He was pacing the room, glancing from time to time at a number of sheets of paper fastened to the wall. This is his way of thinking over an article or a speech. He first writes it down and then hangs up the written pages and, during a day or two, he studies them and makes changes in the text. . . .

March 14, 1944

About cheng-feng.

Mao Tse-tung fairly often repeats the thesis about the nonpartisanship and class ambiguity of the intelligentsia.

On the basis of this thesis he physically and morally destroys the intelligentsia, replacing it with his own dogmatists and his own brand of dogmatism. Moreover, this policy is being applied to the intellectuals who have joined the revolution on principle.

In my opinion, he has a very vague idea of the fact that it was the intelligentsia—the bourgeois intelligentsia at that—that gave impetus to the great emancipation movement of the proletariat of the world, including China.

Lenin writes:

"We have said that there could not have been Social Democratic consciousness among the workers. It would have to be brought to them from without. The history of all countries shows that the working class, exclusively by its own effort, is able to develop only trade-union consciousness. . . . The theory of socialism, however, grew out of the philosophic, historical, and economic theories elaborated by educated representatives of the properties classes, by intellectuals."

Instead of businesslike co-operation with the intelligentsia Mao Tse-tung actually fosters a suspicious and offensive attitude toward it.

March 15, 1944

Here is another unofficial version of the biography of Chu Teh.

He comes from a well-to-do family. A native of Szechwan. In the revolution since 1924. Before that he had served in the militarist army of Tsai O (a Yunnan general-militarist), reaching an officer's rank. For some time he was a small militarist himself.

In 1922 he left for Germany, where he joined the Communist Party.

In 1928 Chu Teh expressed his disagreement with Mao Tse-tung on a number of questions and broke with him. However, he soon recognized Mao Tse-tung's political supremacy in his troops. He shared the views of Wang Ming and stood for an active war against the Japanese invaders. As a punishment he has actually been removed from the leadership of the Communist troops, although formally he has been their commander in chief since 1939.

Chu Teh is for strict discipline, for the study of the combat experience of the Soviet Army. But he is inert as regards everything that is beyond military matters. . . .

People in Yenan treat him respectfully. They certainly know that he is one of the creators of the Chinese Red Army.

March 17, 1944

The idea that Mao Tse-tung is one of the continuers of the Marxist-Leninist philosophy is being propagated here in every way possible. His name is ever more frequently being ranked with the classics of scientific communism.

The invalidity of such claims can be proved without going into the essence of Mao Tse-tung's theoretical investigations.

Marx, Engels, and Lenin were men of great culture, who possessed an enormous knowledge virtually in all branches of the humanities and natural sciences. They knew many ancient and modern languages and read the works of geniuses of mankind in the original. They studied the development of society in all its stages, being outstanding scholars in such fields of learning as history, philosophy, sociology, theoretical economics, and aesthetics.

Lenin pointed out: "But it would mean falling into a grave error for you to try to draw the conclusion that one can become a Communist without assimilating the wealth of knowledge amassed by mankind. It would be mistaken to think it sufficient to learn communist slogans and the conclusions of communist science, without acquiring that sum of knowledge of which communism itself is a result."

How can one be a continuer of what one does not know properly? Up to now most of the works of Marx, Engels, and Lenin have not been translated into Chinese. Mao Tse-tung did not find it necessary to learn any European language.

In this connection the following words of Lenin assume a special meaning:

"Marxism is the system of Marx's views and teachings. Marx was the genius who continued and consummated the three main ideological currents of the nineteenth century, as represented by the three most advanced countries of mankind: classical German philosophy, classical English political economy, and French socialism. . . ."

March 26, 1944

In the Special Area there are many experienced, seasoned fighters of the revolution. The life story of each of them is a story of the ordeals of the Civil War, of the loss of relatives and friends, of the trials of the first years of the active struggle against the Japanese invaders. There are people on whose body there are more wounds and scars than birth-marks. For them the Red Army (now the Eighth Route Army and the New Fourth Army) and the Communist Party are their family, their home, their purpose of life. They just don't have anything else. They are utterly devoted to the revolution. For its sake they are ready to undergo any new trials, any ordeals. They are incapable of separating themselves from the revolution. For them the purpose of life lies in the struggle for a new China.

And the Communist Party, which is led by Mao Tse-tung, is for them the banner of the revolution. . . .

March 27, 1944

The intellectuals were hardest hit by cheng-feng. A special zeal was shown to purify them "spiritually." Most, even really gifted people, were charged to learn from semiliterate agitators. Strong recommendations were made for physical re-education measures to develop a correct class consciousness in them. This kind of indoctrination was partly due to the scornful attitude to scientific knowledge and education in general. The value of the intellectuals was proclaimed only in words. In practice they were subjected to a most severe "spiritual purification." As an educational measure, they were forced to do manual work, often useless and insulting (like the obligatory sock-knitting). The scarce cadre of party intellectuals were reduced to the role of technical executors like clerks, messengers, unskilled workers, officer's attendants, etc.

Mao Tse-tung is hewing out the forest of millennial trees of one of the greatest national cultures of the world. His sermons on proletarian culture are a distortion of Marxist principles. Here culture is far from being enriched with revolutionary élan. The ancient opera loved by Mao Tse-tung has been flourishing in Yenan for ten years now, while not a single good novel has been produced here, nor a collection of short stories, nor songs of the kind of our famous songs of the Civil War period.

In Yenan they do not even speak of a culture lofty, multiform, and morally pure: They won't understand and won't take it seriously. Although it was Mao Tse-tung who started cheng-feng from the "analysis of proletarian art."

Hostility to living thought clearly shows in the Chairman of the

CCP Central Committee. This already presupposes a cultural stagnation. The words about the value of the intellectuals for the revolution are only words. In reality the true intellectuals are being replaced by uneducated people crammed with dogmas. The severe conditions of the revolutionary and later anti-Japanese struggle are no justification for such a policy.

This unjustifiably offensive attitude toward the intellectuals engenders difficulties in the management of the economy, as well as weakens the struggle against bourgeois ideology. The cheng-feng policy is already a norm of party life and does harm to the party. This harm ever more perceptibly makes for the vulgarization of Marxism.

The highly educated party intellectuals bear the responsibility for the training of cadres. With years, as a result of cheng-feng, this part of the intellectuals has been either ousted or itself turned into dogmatists.

Even the learned secretaries of the Chairman of the Central Committee have an education which clearly falls short of their duties and responsibilities.

Thus, disregard for the cultural legacy of the world's past and the sum total of philosophical knowledge leads to a scantiness of knowledge and disregard for, and the primitivity of, the teaching process (studies in the so-called higher institutions of learning in Yenan are conducted, at most, five to six hours a week).

Party dogmatism becomes a testimony to political maturity and loyalty. "Marxism in reality" assumes the disguise of omniscience, dogmatism, and scorn for genuine knowledge and culture.

By culture they gradually begin to understand the small amount of the required reading of historical novels, amateur plays with a political content, simple poems, which again are a primitive rehash of political slogans, and, of course, the selection of writings included in the list of "The Twenty-two Documents."

By his utterances on proletarian culture the Chairman of the Central Committee proclaimed cheng-feng (Mao's talks in 1942). The party is being deprived of Marxism for the sake of "Marxism in reality," which is nothing but a dogma subject to learning by rote. Henceforth art is fettered to the cheng-feng ideas. It has become a rule of political life that everything outside the ideas of cheng-feng (Mao Tse-tung's "Marxism in reality") is to be subjected to "purification."

March 28, 1944

At the request of Mao Tse-tung, I sent a telegram to Moscow, to his son An-ying.

He informs his son that he has received all his letters and that he is very pleased by his successful study.

Mao Tse-tung asks his son to convey his sincere greetings to the command and instructional personnel of the academy, to the Chinese youth receiving education in the Soviet Union, and to An-ying's brother—An-ching. He asks his son not to worry about his health. He feels well. Mao Tse-tung informs his son of the course of the Sino-Japanese War. Military operations are being conducted in extremely difficult conditions, but the Chinese people cannot be broken, because they are stubborn, hardy, and brave. The Communist Party of the country constitutes an impressive force of 900,000. Of this number, not less than 100,000 are in the Kuomintang-controlled provinces and in the Special Area. The remaining 800,000 Communists are fighting at the various fronts against the Japanese fascists.

Mao Tse-tung asks An-ying, if the latter sees comrades Manuilsky or Dimitrov, to convey without fail his warm greetings to them. And adds: Comrades Manuilsky and Dimitrov have assisted and continue to assist the Chinese Revolution. It is to them that Chinese comrades and their children owe their education in the institutions of learning of the Soviet Union, their upbringing and maintenance.

March 29, 1944

The CCP leadership is probing for contacts with the Americans. To begin with, it is out to lay the groundwork for the arrival of a group of foreign correspondents. But it tries to present the whole matter so as to give the impression that foreign correspondents are seeking this visit themselves.

Meanwhile Kang Sheng assiduously supplies the embassy and military administration of the Americans with various information. . . .

Chiang Ching is somewhat too amiable with me and finds many excuses for meetings. Gay, sometimes cautious, witty, but, perhaps, too amiable. This makes me avoid her company. . . .

Kang Sheng has a sparse little mustache on the upper lip, thin and restless lips, and high fair eyebrows. . . .

April 1944

April 3, 1944

Yenan is excited in connection with the forthcoming arrival of foreign correspondents.

The Chairman of the CCP Central Committee understands that the attitude to the unity of the anti-Japanese front is a key point to gauge the sincerity of the CCP leadership's policy. In this respect Chungking has very many complaints and facts of all sorts. It is important for Mao Tse-tung to convince correspondents of his loyalty to the cause of the joint struggle against Japan, fidelity to Chiang Kai-shek as the head of the national defense government, and disperse suspicions, that is, to present his aggressiveness in respect to Chungking as peaceableness and show Chiang Kai-shek as the culprit of "all misunderstanding." That is why the program of the meeting has been elaborated in every detail.

In Yenan the Chairman of the CCP Central Committee prohibited any more or less sharp references to, or attacks on, the Kuomintang and its political leaders, especially on Chiang Kai-shek. However, "spontaneous" outbursts of discontent with the Central Government's policy will be organized in the areas to be visited by the foreign newsmen. The CCP leadership named the villages and army units where such sentiments would be demonstrated. Local authorities are being instructed accordingly.

The Special Area bears the imprint of all the stages of the anti-

Kuomintang campaign. Anti-Kuomintang slogans can be seen on the walls of mud huts, city ruins, and even on rocks. That is why Mao Tse-tung ordered the removal of all traces of such slogans. Since they are everywhere, a big army unit was detailed for the purpose. Its troops engage in removing slogans all over the Special Area. The anti-Kuomintang slogans are immediately replaced with new ones: "Strengthen the United Anti-Japanese Front!" "Co-operate with Commander in Chief Chiang Kai-shek till the Final Victory over Japan!" "Defeat Fascist Japan!" "Long Live the CCP-Kuomintang Alliance!" "All Efforts for the Struggle Against Fascist Japan!" etc.

To win the sympathies of the foreign press and consequently to exert pressure on the governments of the United States and Britain, the foreign correspondents will have the full freedom of movement and communication with people in the localities they will visit. Model villages are being hastily tidied up and talks are rehearsed with people. In a word, this freedom of "communication" is to follow a preconceived plan. Everything here confirms the old truth—a lie causes another lie to be confirmed. . . .

April 4, 1944

Our armies broke through to the Prut River—the state frontier of the Soviet Union—and entered Romania.

Troops of Zhukov's First Ukrainian Front came to the foothills of the Carpathians by cutting the German front in two.

———

Liu Shao-chi and Mao Tse-tung come from one place. Liu is forty-six at present. He joined the CCP in Moscow in 1921.

Liu's indisputable asset is his closeness to the working-class movement. Since 1922 he has been active in trade unions. Participated in all major strikes, demonstrations, and armed actions of the working class. In 1941 he was appointed military commissar of the New Fourth Army.

After Dimitrov's telegram Mao Tse-tung invites me, from time to time, to Chinese opera. We always sit together. Chiang Ching knows how to make an atmosphere unconstrained. When I find it hard to understand sophisticated comparisons or libretto idioms, she readily provides explanations. . . .

April 7, 1944

Wang Cheng's 359th Brigade distinguished itself in fighting the Japanese in 1938–39. This is a veteran combat unit of the Chinese Red Army. In those years the Eighth Route Army and guerrillas were inflicting substantial losses on the Japanese. Later Mao Tse-tung decided to curtail combat operations and have the activity of the Eighth Route and the New Fourth armies reduced sharply.

Wang Cheng is a capable commander. He is inquisitive and disciplined. His brigade is the best in the Special Area, and not only there, for that matter.

Before army Wang was a worker. He is about forty now. Very thin, he looks like a teen-ager. It's hard to believe he has been fighting for nearly fifteen years now. His brigade will be shown to the foreign newsmen.

April 13, 1944

The Yenan press was suddenly flooded with bombastic reports from the fronts about CCP troops' fictional major battles against the Japanese and their puppets, the recapture of cities and villages, POWs, and captured matériel.

The government was ordered to prepare information about the democratic character of the system in the Special Area. Model villages are being set up along these lines.

A series of newspaper articles will feature CCP units' heroic efforts to save American pilots. Facts have already been selected.

The CCP leadership thus wants to convince the foreign correspondents, now regarded as nonofficial representatives of their countries, that the Special Area is the only democratic and military force in China.

April 20, 1944

In its foreign policy the CCP leadership counts on the Americans' interest in the armed forces of the Special Area.

The CCP leadership knows the Americans are looking for soldiers for decisive fighting against the Japanese. Mao Tse-tung is prepared to lend the CCP armed forces for future offensive operations against the

Japanese. However, Mao wants to do this on certain terms, the crucial ones for him. . . .

Politically, this presupposes American reorientation on the CCP as the main force of the present-day and future China. Materially, this means extensive American assistance with combat equipment, munitions, and arms.

My suppositions were confirmed by Po Ku and, partly, by Jen Pi-shih. Mao Tse-tung is developing contacts with the Americans. His goals remain immutable: to use the anti-Japanese bloc to capture key positions in national government (the concentration of the CCP's efforts and energy for solving this task) and, eventually, unleash a civil war. In the plans of the Chairman of the CCP Central Committee active struggle with Japan features only as a point of the reciprocal agreement with the United States.

The CCP armies are Mao's main trump card in his game with the Americans.

Should I say that Mao conceals all this from me? His intentions are far divorced from the statements he makes to me and Moscow.

Practically, the activities of the Chairman of the CCP Central Committee boil down to the intensive preparation of a civil war and bringing the country to the brink of this war, a war when the aggressor is ruining the country.

April 22, 1944

The CCP leadership's fidelity to commitments under alliance needs proof. That is why in Sian negotiations began between a CCP representative and the chairman of the Special Area's government, on the one hand, and Wang Shih-chieh and Chang Chih-chung, who act for the Kuomintang and the Central Government, on the other.

Lin Tsu-han is Lin Po-chu's alias. Not to attract attention to such a well-known man as Liu Po-tsui, he was sent to the negotiations under the name of Lin Tsu-han, his old party pseudonym. In all official reports on the negotiations he is mentioned as Lin Tsu-han. A vain precaution, as everybody knows he heads the government of the Special Area.

General Chang Chih-chung is the former head of the Political Department of the Central Government's armed forces. Born in 1891, he is a leader of the "blue shirts," the profascist elements in the Kuomintang. He is for suppressing the CCP by armed force.

In 1933 General Chang commanded the Fourth Army in Hunan, which was suppressing the resistance of the Chinese Red Army. Later, at Chiang Kai-shek's order, he led punitive expeditions against CCP troops. For a year and a half he was chief of Chiang Kai-shek's office. . . .

Wang Shi-chieh, a member of the Central Government, is professor of law. He exerts noticeable influence on the Kuomintang's international policy. . . .

April 28, 1944

In the foreign correspondents' forthcoming visit Mao sees an opportunity to establish official contacts with the leading capitalist states of the anti-Hitler coalition. Journalists will shape opinion, and politicians will get down to business, he reasons.

Yet, here the CCP leadership came to face an unforeseen difficulty. The Special Area specializes in opium production, and this means that vast stretches of land are sown to poppy. A very unpleasant and shameful fact.

How can one cover it up if the sowing is in progress, hundreds of hectares have already been sown, and poppies, not innocent garden flowers, will be in full bloom. . . .

The famous 359th Brigade was sent to destroy poppy plots along the roads connecting the brigade with Yenan and its winter quarters. The same job is also being done by the 1st Brigade.

April 29, 1944

The overthrow of the monarchy in 1911, the May Fourth Movement in 1919, and the subsequent revolutionary events vastly influenced the Chinese art which is fettered by feudal classic patterns and canons.

A group of progressive poets, writers, musicians, and journalists emerged in the thirties. Lu Hsun, Nieh Erh, Chang Tien-i, Emi Siao, Mao Tun, and others became known in China and elsewhere. . . .

Enjoying the cunning stories of Lu Hsun, "The Surprising Stories of Our Time," "Tang and Sung Tales," novels by Shih Nai-an and Lo Kuan-chung (it's impossible to enumerate them all), I read with pleasure works written in an expressive contemporary language. And how many new authors there are now! Ting Ling, Yeh Sheng-tao, Tien Han, Pa Chin, Lao She, Yao Peng-tzu, Kung Lo-sung, Ping Hsin . . .

They declared a war on the religious dogmas, foreign and feudal oppression which hinder the country's progress. Chang Tien-i aptly said, referring to the old Four Books:

"In the primary school I studied the Four Books and I was to learn texts by heart. I often startled in my sleep, recalling this horrible cramming."

How fine his tale "The Big Ling and the Little Ling" is!

It is only too natural to love the history and culture of one's country. However, to speak of the correlation of cultures one should know not only old classics. How can one analyze the tasks, aims, and achievements of the proletarian art without having any idea of it? Talks with Mao Tse-tung made me convinced he doesn't know the new, young literature (progressive literature of the twenties and thirties). The only exception in this respect is, perhaps, works by Lu Hsun.

The Chairman of the CCP Central Committee knows the names, not works, of a number of writers and journalists. Possibly, they are studied by his learned secretaries, but the learned secretaries' opinion cannot, of course, become a programmatic party document for speeches on this question. None of the more or less known writers or philologists took part in preparing this document on the party's attitude to the art and the progressive intelligentsia.

May 1944

In April the CCP and the Kuomintang began negotiations. They have run into an impasse and have been terminated at present.

———————

Tan Cheng was born in Hunan. During the "Chingkangshan sitting" (the late twenties) he was Mao Tse-tung's private secretary.

The Chairman of the CCP Central Committee is true to himself. In time people from his entourage usually receive high posts in the Army. At present Tan Cheng is the chief of the Political Department of the Special Area's Joint Forces. A very influential figure.

It seems that Mao Tse-tung purposefully tries to implant his people in the Army. Precisely in the Army, which Mao regards as his main support. It is not accidental that all former private secretaries of Chairman Mao hold commanding posts. In various places they control, as it were, the loyalty of army cadres.

Chang Ching-wu is the chief of staff of the Special Area's Joint Forces. He was also born in Hunan. A career army officer, he is one of Ho Lung's pets. . . .

Tsai Chang is one of the few women who conduct party work. She was in a group of CCP future leaders who studied in France. In 1923 she became the wife of Li Fu-chun. She was in the Soviet Union on several occasions. Participated in the Long March.

She heads the Women's Department of the CCP Central Committee.

May 5, 1944

The first tide of arrests dates back to the autumn of 1942. These repressions accompanied the "spiritual purification."

The "cadre screening" campaign was energetically conducted in the winter of 1942–43.

The second tide of arrests swept the country in the spring of 1943 and was connected with the possible arrival of Chiang Kai-shek's representatives in Yenan.

The third tide of arrests broke out in June 1943 in consequence of the conflict with the Kuomintang. This campaign became known as the "exposure of Japanese and Kuomintang agents in the Special Area."

None of the campaigns have been completed as yet. They have fused into cheng-feng, a massive campaign of repressions.

Various smaller-scale repressive campaigns are continuously building up the cheng-feng. The Kang Sheng Commission for the Review of Party Cadres and Nonparty Personnel began its work in 1941. This means the repressions have been under way for a longer period than it may seem.

The formidable wave of violence rolls and maims Mao Tse-tung's opponents. The task of cheng-feng is to secure Mao's undisputed victory at the forthcoming congress. Not having confidence in the victory, Mao will not convene the congress.

May 25, 1944

Mao Tse-tung is stepping up the establishment of contacts with the Allies. In any delay he sees a risk.

He does his best to convince the Americans, through his Chungking mission, that the Communist Party and its Army is the only force that has prospects in China. It appears the Allies have joined the game. . . .

Kang Sheng treats me as his friend. During our meetings he does not spare assurances of his friendship.

I am worn out by dysentery. My stomach aches and I have a high temperature, but there is no time to stay in bed. . . .

May 30, 1944

In Hupeh the samurai are advancing along the Canton-Hankow railway and highway. In Hunan Kuomintang armies are attacking General Hsueh Yueh.

Exploiting the great success in Hengyang, the Japanese command spares no effort to establish a single front extending from Indochina to northern China.

In western Yunnan Chinese troops are moving toward the Ma-mien Pass.

U.S. Vice-president Henry Wallace said in an interview that his visit to China did not pursue narrow party election aims. This was a political step of great importance.

The Vice-president emphasized the seriousness of the military situation in China and added that this, however, should not cause disappointment in the American people. . . .

June 1944

June 14, 1944

The Allies are successfully expanding their beach head in France. General Dwight D. Eisenhower is in command of the allied forces.

The samurai have almost reached their purpose—the seizure of the entire Trans-Chinese Railway Line. The Kuomintang armies are unable to rebuff the onslaught of the Japanese divisions. China is facing the threat of defeat in the war.

As a rule, dances are given in Wan-chia-ping on Saturdays. Chiang Ching and the jovial Yeh Chien-ying are the soul of the parties. Chu Teh is the first dancer.

June 19, 1944

The Soviet troops are mounting their offensive in the Karelian Isthmus. They have broken the third Finnish defense line, the famous Mannerheim line.

The Allies landed in Cotentin Peninsula. They lost about 16,000 men in France, including 12,600 wounded. Eighty-five hundred Germans were taken prisoners.

A battle on Saipan Island has been raging for three days now. The Allies are stubbornly landing more and more troops. The Japanese are violently resisting. The functioning India-China air route is called the hump by the Allies. Several hundred tons of cargo are transported over this route every month.

The Japanese are attacking the railway junction of Chu-chou (south of Changsha and Ling-ling), obviously aiming their blow at Kweilin, an important American air base in China. Battles are fought at the distant approaches to these cities.

Japan's military gains in China largely compensate the losses they suffered on the islands of the Pacific and Indian oceans. The seizure of the Trans-Chinese Railway Line gives Japan an opportunity to export the most valuable industrial raw materials and foodstuffs from continental Asia without any hindrance.

Trains loaded with loot will be able to cross the whole territory of China, Manchuria, and Korea. It is only some two hundred to three hundred kilometers from the Korean port of Pusan to Japan. The Japanese can defend this sea communication with their weakened Navy and Air Force. The seizure of the Trans-Chinese Railway Line and the military defeat of China secure for Japan all the necessary material resources for continuing war.

Japanese war potential largely depends on the normal function of these communications.

In the dusk that lasts so long in June goatsuckers are gliding noiselessly over the pasture beyond my village.

I am standing there, knee-deep in the grass—the summer is rainy and they have not started mowing yet. Flowers cannot be seen in the twilight, but in the daytime the meadows are strewn with them.

Wherever I go this milky twilight, goatsuckers' dances, the high vibrant voice of a little bird coming from the orchard that formerly belonged to the landlord, and the angry buzz of night beetles always follow me.

June 22, 1944

Three years of the war! Radio Moscow reported on the military and political results of these years. The German Nazi Army lost millions of soldiers, in dead or wounded, and scores of thousands of tanks, planes, and guns at the Soviet-German front.

On June 20 Wallace arrived in Chungking.

Chou En-lai always follows international developments. He knows the top of Kuomintang very well. Enjoying the respect of Chinese intellectuals, he has wide connections in the most different strata of society (the military, bourgeoisie, and the Chinese émigrées). He speaks English and Japanese and some French. He lards his speech with French mots and proverbs. Chou is hard-working and efficient. He makes quick and precise decisions, but always abides by Mao Tse-tung's instructions. He is well read and follows the developments in the world cultural life as regularly as he can. He is well informed about the Soviet events. He is rather expansive and hot-tempered.

June 27, 1944

The Central Government's military defeat is the best present for the CCP leadership. Mao Tse-tung's chances in his political gamble with the United States have unexpectedly highly improved—the Americans are feverishly looking for the military support in Asia. Reciprocal probing can any moment end in business contacts.

———

A former Japanese POW, and now one of the most active Okano assistants, showed me some captured photographs. These are the blood-chilling pictures of the Japanese atrocities. I asked him to give me some of the photographs.

It is hard even to imagine that such things were possible!

The photographs show peasants' bodies stripped naked and crucified on the walls of their houses.

Here is a disemboweled corpse, and then more and more such corpses.

The Okano worker explained to me that it was the Japanese soldiers' custom to disembowel their victims. They do it to most of the Chinese war prisoners and to almost every male. But they don't stop at it. According to the medieval belief, liver is the symbol of courage and valor; that's why in many cases the Japanese soldiers not only disembowel their victims but also cut out their liver and eat it. I would take it for madman's ravings unless I had such a photograph right before my eyes.

Here are the photographs of massacres. They show the victims in the most terrifying poses. The Japanese do not shoot their victims, and not at all because they save their bullets. They herd together children, women, and old people and then stab them with bayonets like dummies for exercise. Here is one such photograph. It shows the shortish soldiers in kepi working hard with their bayonets and sabers amid the frantic crowd. . . .

Photo after photo show heaps of flesh that once were human beings. And in each photo officers and soldiers pose.

Here is a photograph showing several dozen women with their skirts up and their pants pulled down to their knees, and the Japanese soldiers squatting in front of them. I wish it were the only photo of this kind!

Most of the photos depict scenes of rape and humiliation. Here and there tortured women and the soldiery.

Another typical photograph. It shows the traditional decapitation of the victims. It can be seen even in the photographs that the Japanese regard it as a sport, a competition in skill.

The soldiers' faces are shockingly calm, indifferent, and even sleepy.

Fascism is the most inhuman, brazen form of violence born of capitalism.

June 30, 1944

Last time I had a talk with Mao Tse-tung he said: "It was not necessary to know Marxism-Leninism to lead China! The main thing is to know China, her needs and customs. . . ."

The CCP Central Committee Chairman calls all those who visited the Soviet Union "dogmatists," even if he does not know them personally.

Mao Tse-tung and Chiang Ching have a five-year-old daughter. I saw her only a couple of times. They rarely take her home from her kindergarten.

July 1944

July 1, 1944

The question of the American delegation's arrival in Yenan has been settled at last. The preceding events took a dramatic turn.

At first Chiang Kai-shek was against the Americans' coming in Yenan. On three occasions the allied military leadership in China asked for Chiang Kai-shek's consent to the trip and every time he refused.

By that time U.S. Vice-president Wallace had come to Chungking, and American officials requested the Vice-president's assistance. He immediately contacted the White House.

The White House reacted promptly. Four hours later President Roosevelt sent a telegram to Chiang Kai-shek. He demanded, in the form of an ultimatum, that the Central Government permit the arrival of the American plenipotentiary delegation. Having seen no way out, Chiang Kai-shek was compelled to sanction the trip.

The delegation will be led by the American military attaché. The date of the delegation's arrival has not yet been established. This important delegation will include ten persons.

Agitation in Chiao-yuan . . .

July 2, 1944

The Chairman of the CCP Central Committee convened a special meeting on June 29. This meeting (with only a few persons attending) discussed the forthcoming visit of the American military delegation. . . .

Mao Tse-tung demanded the alteration of all information on the New Fourth and the Eighth Route armies as well as on the puppet and field Japanese armies (figures are being currently juggled with in the most unscrupulous manner).

Mao Tse-tung described in detail the mapped-up Communist Party leadership's stand at forthcoming negotiations with American plenipotentiary representatives. The primary thing was to obtain arms from the Americans and, as the first step, to secure weapons for four full-fledged infantry divisions. As a guarantee, Mao Tse-tung was ready to promise to co-operate with the Americans during the war and after the victory, and offer them the use of the Special Area's resources (military and economic).

July 7, 1944

Today marks the seventh anniversary of the beginning of China's war against Japan, although practically the war started much earlier, with the alienation of Manchuria. What suffering and grief has this slaughter brought to the Chinese people!

For half a year now I have been studying Japanese. I shall hardly learn to speak, but can already read fairly well. Japanese hieroglyphs are based on Chinese characters. This facilitates my studies. . . .

July 13, 1944

Vice-president Wallace made big efforts to create prerequisites for liquidating the split in the national unity. Judging by press reports, this was the main aim of his visit.

In May, Lin Tsu-han came from the Special Area to Sian to resume the CCP's talks with the Kuomintang.

China's public opinion sets great hopes on the beginning of the talks which have practically not been conducted for the past few years.

Foreign radio broadcasts emphasize the great importance of these talks since, as a result of the seven-year war, the increased CCP-Kuomintang split has worsened the situation in China. Indeed, the country is experiencing tremendous financial and economic difficulties. The entire economy has been disorganized. Most of the industrial enterprises have been ruined or are in the occupied areas.

The resumption of talks in May has also given rise to optimism as regards overcoming the split, which is the reason behind the successful Japanese offensive.

July 15, 1944

Had a long night talk with Mao.

He looked tired, and he stooped more than usually; dropped cigarette ash on his knees and papers. Now and then he stood up and paced the room, hands behind his back. All Mao's jackets have sleeves which are a bit long. This is his peculiar style. All his jackets have big sewed-on pockets.

Highly indicative were Mao's words to the effect that from that moment the Communist Party's general line would be fully independent and opposed to the Kuomintang. From his remarks I gathered the situation that was taking shape in the country was a pleasant surprise for the CCP leadership. Chiang Kai-shek's Chungking regime was on the brink of crisis and collapse. That was why the method of talks with the Kuomintang had outlived itself. Talks were not needed any longer; they were a bygone stage. . . .

"America's position is of tremendous importance for our future," said the Chairman of the CCP Central Committee.

He and his supporters are convinced of the inevitable rapprochement between America and Britain, on one hand, and the Special Area, on the other. The Eighth Route and New Fourth armies are the forces needed by the White House. Besides, the Allies cannot but be attracted by the cohesion and strength of the Yenan authorities. The Allies have no choice but to recognize the Special Area (of China and other Soviet areas after that) as the only real force in China.

Mao didn't say a word about the Soviet Union or its interest in the solution of the Far Eastern problem, although the Soviet Far Eastern frontier had been more than once an area of military tension and bloodshed.

In his book *On New Democracy,* put out by the Yenan Liberation Publishers in 1940, Mao Tse-tung had written (at least he can be interpreted in this way) that without the Soviet Union China would not be able to triumph over fascist Japan. He has now come to the opposite conclusion and intends to associate himself mostly with the United States and Britain.

I think behind all this there are some other things, too, of which the

Chairman of the CCP Central Committee prefers not to speak. He banks on America's and Great Britain's apprehension connected with the Soviet Union. This apprehension should, in his opinion, push these states to the slow but sure rapprochement with the Special Area.

Mao Tse-tung and his supporters clearly want to blackmail the Allies using the myth of the Soviet Union's aggressiveness and its alleged eagerness to swallow China (especially Manchuria). In future relations with the Allies, they believe, this bogey Soviet threat will be a key argument in favor of the United States' and Great Britain's rapprochement with Yenan.

Yet this is not all either. The Chairman of the CCP Central Committee not only wants to receive weapons and oust Chiang Kai-shek. He plans to use recognition of the Special Area by the United States and Britain to preclude any effective participation of the Soviet Union in the solution of the Far Eastern problem. In general, he wants to neutralize all Soviet diplomatic efforts.

With the aid of the United States and Great Britain Mao plans to receive the force which will help him to establish control all over China and conduct the policy serving his own interests.

Of course, the Chairman of the CCP Central Committee did not tell me of this, but preparations for the meeting with the American mission proceed precisely in this direction. Simultaneously, he increases correspondence with Moscow in an attempt to cover up the true motives of future negotiations. Talks with me are meant to dissipate my doubts.

This runs counter to what Mao told Moscow but recently. Although he continues to send his "friendly telegrams," he considers the Soviet leaders' opinion burdensome. With the Central Government troops being defeated, Mao Tse-tung counts on the Americans' unavoidable agreement with his main proposals. Outwardly everything looks quite respectable: Arms are needed to throw the Japanese from the sacred land of China!

Our talks look strange. Mao does most of the talking. Sometimes he speaks for an hour or two and even more. I am to play the role of a listener. He is very displeased when I disagree. When I manage to express my disagreement, he sharply changes the subject (in similar situations he treats others in an insulting manner) or becomes absorbed in nervous chain smoking. At such moments I feel how difficult it is for him to tolerate me, how unpleasant I am to him, and how far he actually is from us. . . . All this interchanges with cordiality, invitations to meals, and rather crude jokes. . . .

Peter Vladimirov in Yenan, 1943.

Peter Vladimirov with the wife and son of one of the commanders of the Eighth Route Army, 1944.

Homes built in loess caves outside Yenan. The dark slits serve as the entrance.

Casings for homemade hand grenades were made in such kilns.

This is how
coal was
mined in the
Special Area.

When we parted today, Mao gave me, as a gift, his book *On New Democracy* marked with the seal of the private library of the Chairman of the CCP.

July 16, 1944

That the Soviet Union is the leading force of the anti-Hitler coalition is recognized by Mao Tse-tung only in words which are meant for articles and telegrams of congratulations to Moscow. However, this recognition also shows his lack of confidence in his position as regards Chiang Kai-shek. What if tomorrow a military conflict breaks out? Who helped him before and will help him this time? That is why Moscow is invariably served with a selection of slogans, assurances, and statements of "good will."

Wang Ming is never mentioned. The struggle against the "Moscow group" is a thing of the past for Mao Tse-tung—the stage which has been passed, although not very smoothly. . . .

Now that I know Mao Tse-tung well enough, I see another motive (of course not as important and significant as the main one) of his clash with Wang Ming. Before the World War, Wang Ming had been regarded as one of the noted theoreticians of the Chinese Communist Party. Mao could not put up with this situation. Of course, this is not the main point, but this is characteristic of Mao. . . .

Night, deep silence. When I look through my papers, the flame of the candle grows and dances. Reports, newspapers, and endless translations. The concluding words from the latest translation: "Mao Tse-tung is the militant leader of our party and people." This is how things develop, and there is no getting away from it.

My contacts with Mao convince me that he is truthful only when this is in his interest. Moral standards are not for him. If you have strength or possibility to achieve something (even through the most unseemly means), do! Justification will be found later!

Lenin said that the policy is not shaped to suit the psychology and actions of an individual, that it is made for the good of millions. However, neither any individual nor millions are of interest to Mao. What is important is to move power. Little does he care what sacrifices will be required, whether this or that step is adventurist or whether more can be achieved with smaller losses. It would be right to say that he doesn't care about all this at all. For him the people are just a tool to implement his plans. I see something Messiah-like in his talks sometimes. He stands above humanity, laws, morals, and suffering. Carried away by the talk, sometimes Mao speaks precisely in this tone. He is absolutely callous. For him the good and the evil turn into the things of personal expediency. Excited, he becomes eloquent and talks without end. . . . At such moments no trace of his usual inertness is left.

July 19, 1944

The Chairman of the CCP Central Committee sent, through me, another telegram to Moscow.

The telegram describes in detail the reasons for the defeat of Chiang Kai-shek's armies. In the Hengyang (Hunan) operations the Central Government's troops either evaded fighting or scampered about at the first contact with the enemy. Officers were demoralized. The population did not support the Army. The CCP-Kuomintang negotiations have not produced any results, although the CCP leadership maintains a cautious course. The talks will be continued.

There is a great difference between the CCP troops' combat operations in the rear of the Japanese and the Kuomintang troops' operations at the front. And this difference is increasing. The CCP troops are advancing, steadily strengthening, while the Kuomintang armed forces are being increasingly affected by crisis. Chiang Kai-shek troops are retreating in panic. They are disintegrating. If the enemy continues the offensive, the difference between the armed forces of the Communist Party and the Kuomintang will become ever more evident.

The Communist Party has been conducting successful operations, particularly in the past few months, in the enemy rear. The population of the main bases has increased, constituting not 70 million (as was reported previously), but nearly 86 million. On different fronts in China the CCP troops have put out of action large numbers of puppet army men and enemy officers and men. On the southern, central, and northern fronts several areas have been recaptured, as have many towns, including twenty-four district centers.

I added the following to Mao Tse-tung's telegram:

—Mao Tse-tung's point of view as regards the principal issues does not coincide with the real situation. The Chairman of the CCP Central Committee evaluates the relations between the CCP and the Kuomintang and their participation in the war against Japan lopsidedly and not objectively enough.

—The figures given in the telegram were taken by Mao Tse-tung from the materials prepared, specially and tendentiously, for the arrival of a group of foreign correspondents to Yenan.

July 20, 1944

The Domei Tsusin News Agency reported the resignation of the Todzio Cabinet.

Tass correspondent Protsenko is among the foreign newsmen now in Yenan. He is accredited in Chungking. He tells me a lot of interesting things about the political backstage of China's provisional capital. . . .

During negotiations with the Americans CCP leaders want to secure diplomatic ties, independent of Chungking, with the United States and Britain. They will offer the Allies to open consulates in the Special Area.

Mao Tse-tung told me: "No matter what form the contacts with the Americans will take, our revolution will eventually turn against the imperialists. . . ."

July 22, 1944

A day of supreme triumph for Mao Tse-tung! The first nine officials of the American mission have come to Yenan.

The day was quiet and cloudless. All CCP leaders came to the airport. Mao Tse-tung and Chu Teh, wearing new *tan-i*s, meant to show the unity of the party and the Army.

Mao looked impressive.

Military music. Brave-looking soldiers demonstrated the high morale of the CCP armed forces. The impatient crowd. My humble self with a Leica, and Protsenko . . .

During the landing the Douglas went off the runway. A cloud of dust, the propeller fell off with a crash, and the cockpit was dented. Happily, there were no casualties. The plane was piloted by Captain Robert Champion.

Mao Tse-tung was very much excited. After all, it did not matter whether or not the Americans would recognize the CCP as China's leading force (that was Mao's thought before their arrival); the main thing was to get weapons, the greatest possible amount of weapons! As for the handling of weapons, the Chairman of the CCP Central Committee has always known that power is seized by force. . . .

The occupation of the country by Japanese, connivance at aggression, the treachery of the interests of the Soviet Union struggling against fascism in the name of all revolutionary forces of the world—all this was for Mao just "tactical conventionalities," and nothing more. . . .

Following the official ceremony, the Americans and Chinese concertedly pulled, using ropes, the Douglas back to the runway.

Judging by the visitors' talks, the mission would stay here about four months.

The Americans wear crumpled uniforms with badges of rank on the collar. Compared with Chinese, they seem very tall, talk freely, and like jokes.

Like Colonel Barrett, many of them have, on the left shoulder, the emblems of American military advisers of the Chinese Army—a little flag, the upper part of which shows the multi-ray Kuomintang star next to the American one, and the lower part is covered with blue and white vertical stripes.

Colonel Barrett is the head of the mission. He is a stoutish short man in an exotic cork helmet.

Barrett arrived from Kunming, where he had come from the hell of the Burmese jungle. . . .

An amusing sight: peasants and townsfolk in broad-brimmed straw hats and in the center a group of American military specialists carefully protected by guards from the crowd. The guards saw that the Americans should not be pushed, that their toes should not be trodden upon. I with my Leica was pushed aside. . . .

July 23, 1944

Chiang Kai-shek set the final number of the U. S. Army Observer Group at eighteen persons. Nine came yesterday. The others would visit Yenan whenever necessary. Part of the mission will stay here permanently. . . .

The Americans look sure of themselves. They all wear much-used uniforms. Often click their Kodaks and Leicas. An army doctor is among them. . . .

Chiang Ching complained to me that for some time her husband had been suffering from insomnia and taking sleeping pills. . . .

Mao Tse-tung easily catches cold. He likes wadded clothes and avoids warm quarters.

The more I learn of him, the clearer I see how narrow-minded he is. By the local yardstick, he is a rather educated man, but not by ours.

Mao Tse-tung is extremely pleased when military successes are put on his account, and he doesn't even try to refer them to the Central Committee or the army command.

July 24, 1944

On July 22 arrived Colonel David D. Barrett, Majors Ray Cromley and Melvin A. Casberg, Captains John C. Colling, Charles G. Stelle, and Paul C. Domke, First Lieutenant Henry S. Whittlesey, and Staff Sergeant Anton H. Remeneh. They were accompanied by John Stuart Service, second secretary of the American embassy in Chungking.

July 29, 1944

Chu Teh knows the Army well, but he is kept away from it. Military leadership is fully concentrated in the hands of Mao Tse-tung. However, Chu Teh untiringly tries to be in the know of all affairs on Chinese fronts. He has long talks with front-line officers and men.

Despite all "spiritual purges," Chu Teh is invariably friendly with us.

August 1944

Most of the Army Observer Group members are officers of the
Chungking apparatus of the American military attaché or officers of
General Joseph W. Stilwell's staff. These are specialists in intelligence,
politics, communications, artillery, and infantry arms. A new and quite
numerous group of officers is to join the team.

There are specialists in Japanese affairs among the team officers.

My earlier contacts with regular American servicemen convinced
me that they have deep-rooted anti-Soviet feelings, which in many
cases grow into frank Russophobia. Regular intelligence men and political officers of this team are no exception in this respect, though outwardly they are perfectly genteel. Anti-Sovietism is a necessary quality
for each regular officer in the United States and, especially, for the intelligence officer.

Chou is the CCP leadership chief expert at the negotiations with the
Americans. There has not been a single talk without his participation.
All these days he never parts with Mao Tse-tung. It would not be an
exaggeration to say that in the course of many months Chou was
preparing and pushing through all the negotiations and measures connected with the organization of the Observer Group visit. He is the
soul of this meeting. His entire Chungking apparatus worked hard to
overcome the difficulties that were in the way of this meeting.

Chen Chia-kang is the chief interpreter at the negotiations with the

Americans. He is one of Chou En-lai's close assistants. He specializes in contacts with the Americans. Such contacts are established directly with the American military attaché's staff.

Ma Hai-te immediately assumed the role of an interpreter for the American delegation. Americans call him Dr. Ma.

August 3, 1944

The Chinese front is crumbling up. There is, practically, no front at some sections, and the Japanese are occupying Honan without encountering any resistance.

The CCP leadership rejoices at the news of the defeat suffered by Chiang Kai-shek's troops in Honan and Hunan. It is a gift from heaven for Mao Tse-tung. His chances in the bargain with the Americans are growing quickly. His future enemy in a civil war is being weakened.

His calculations are simple—whenever Chiang Kai-shek suffers a defeat, the Special Area benefits from it.

The Americans have brought the samples of weapons to Yenan so that the most suitable ones could be jointly selected.

August 5, 1944

Lin Tsu-han's negotiations with the Kuomintang representatives have been transferred from Sian to Chungking and recently ended in failure.

Defeats suffered by the Chinese troops in Hunan placed Lin Tsu-han, the Special Area representative, in a fundamentally new position. Formerly the CCP leadership feared the Kuomintang's reciprocal sanctions for its policy of sabotaging the united national front and reducing the war waged by the regular CCP army units against the Japanese to local skirmishes (guerrilla war).

The reasons the negotiations reached a deadlock became generally known.

By that time the Communists brought up the numerical strength of their troops to 477,000 soldiers, and the people's volunteer force to 220,000, according to the Chungking and foreign press reports.

Foreign newspapers began to report that the Communists organized in the Japanese rear base areas with their own organs of power, which do not obey the Central Government orders. Naturally, the attitude of the government in Chungking to these areas is full of suspicion. The

Communists also demanded that their power be established in Shansi, Hopeh, and Shantung.

During the last weeks of negotiations Lin Tsu-han demanded that the CCP be granted its lawful place in the government. Then, in Chungking, Lin Tsu-han laid down new conditions (twenty points this time).

Chiang Kai-shek resolutely rejected them. The head of the Central Government hopes to reach a compromise by the organization of the coalition government.

August 7, 1944

The other members of the U. S. Army Observer Group have arrived today. They were Lieutenant Colonel Reginald Foss, Major Wilbur J. Peterkin, Major Charles E. Dole, Captain Brooke Dolan, Lieutenant Simon H. Hitch, First Lieutenant Louis M. Jones, Sergeant Walter Gress, and Technician Fourth Class George I. Nakamura.

Raymond Ludden, the second secretary of the American embassy in Chungking, has also arrived.

The welcoming ceremony was the exact replica of the one that took place on July 22. Mao Tse-tung, Chu Teh, and Chou En-lai were present throughout the entire ceremony.

The Americans were also met by foreign correspondents, among whom were Epstein, Votaw, and others. Ma Hai-te was also present. . . .

August 8, 1944

Until the Hunan-Honan developments the political situation in the Special Area was tense. Chiang Kai-shek was feared despite the anti-Kuomintang propaganda. Besides, the Kuomintang divisions at the Special Area southern border also presented a threat. Now the attitude is changing sharply.

Americans visited the hospital, went sight-seeing in Yenan, etc. Ma Hai-te is like one of their own men.

Receptions and all kinds of theatrical performances are given in honor of the Americans.

Chu Teh gave me the Eighth Route Army commander badge—a round medal with the number 249. It must symbolize the unity of the anti-Japanese front, the unification of all the national forces in the struggle against the invaders.

There is a blue circle with a twelve-pointed star of white metal in the center of the badge. The characters on the red rim of the badge certify that the bearer belongs to the Eighth Route Army personnel. Well, it will be a memory of Yenan, of the years of war for me.

August 12, 1944

Today Mao Tse-tung summoned me and said: "We've been thinking of renaming our party, of calling it not 'Communist,' but something else. Then the situation for the Special Area will be more favorable, especially with the Americans. . . ."

The documentation on the Eighth Route and New Fourth armies, as well as on the Japanese Army, has been made available to the Americans. They were acquainted with the course of military operations conducted by the CCP forces in the past few years. There is no need to say how tendentiously it was all presented.

August 13, 1944

The rout of the government troops in Honan and Hunan and the arrival of the United States correspondents and military observers have changed considerably the military situation in the Special Area. Developments are more favorable for the CCP leadership than they ever have been. They surpassed even the most optimistic forecasts.

The general political course of the CCP has not changed; it is still sharply anti-Chiang Kai-shek, only the latest events have created more favorable conditions for its realization.

The authority of the CCP Central Committee Chairman is growing still greater—after all, he had always been against the united anti-Japanese front and for the civil war against the Kuomintang. And now the rout of Chiang Kai-shek seems to confirm the righteousness of all his splitting activities and the "Marxist profundity" of his historical analysis.

The CCP leadership and the Americans are having their honeymoon. They are zealously courting each other.

It is impossible to learn anything of Mao Tse-tung's biography except the official, varnished version. He never shares the memories of his youth or speaks of his loves or friends. This topic is taboo. There is his official biography which everyone must study in order "to fortify the revolutionary spirit."

August 16, 1944

Despite the racket in the press and other forms of anti-Kuomintang campaign, Chiang Kai-shek was feared. Fear and uncertainty were felt in the anti-Kuomintang campaign. Every day, every hour, they feared reciprocal repressions from Chungking—a sudden and general invasion by its troops as a cover and a kind of a guarantee. The CCP leadership decided to send Lin Po-chu to conduct negotiations once again. The Kuomintang leaders were informed about it, and the bureaucratic machine started working. I am sure (it was Mao's behavior that convinced me first of all) that the Communist Party leadership would certainly make concessions if not this sudden change in the situation at the front.

Anti-Kuomintang propaganda and cheng-feng created an oppressive, suffocating atmosphere in the party. People in the party organizations were afraid of tomorrow, they abandoned any initiative, mechanically crammed the instructions handed down by the CCP Central Committee, crammed "The Twenty-two Documents" to redeem themselves from their nonexistent sins and for greater loyalty. The lack of confidence was clearly felt. The slogans they shouted and oaths of loyalty they gave to Mao Tse-tung, the "militant leader of the party and the people," only covered confusion, loss of comradeship, fear, and even frustration.

As for unity it was absent in the party from bottom to top, the unity for which the CCP Central Committee Chairman has allegedly fought and is still fighting. In his talks with me he likes to say over and over again that cheng-feng is, actually, the "struggle for the party unity," without mentioning the details of this campaign, of course. Here again, I agree with him—it is the struggle for the unity in subordination to Mao Tse-tung, for the unity in recognizing him as the leader, for the unity in sharing his and only his opinion by all the party members.

Such was the situation within the party and leadership (and, to some extent, it still is).

The majority of the leadership—Liu Po-cheng, Yeh Chien-ying, Po Ku, Chou En-lai, Peng Teh-huai, and a number of other leading comrades—were deliberately opposed (at Mao's instructions, of course) to the minority made up of Liu Shao-chi, Ho Lung, Peng Chen, and Kang Sheng, of course.

At first this majority of the Communist Party leadership "repented their convictions" to some or other extent and sided with the pernicious Kang Sheng's handful, and then after the ideological "bone-crushing" of 1943, they became the implicit followers of the CCP Central Committee Chairman.

However, the relations between the two parts of the leadership were tense, distrustful, and full of suspicion and in a number of cases frankly hostile, though outwardly they shared the same views.

The Hunan-Honan catastrophe, the foreign press representatives' trip in the Special Area, the arrival of the Observer Group, the Soviet Army victories, and the growing authority and might of the Soviet Union strongly affected the situation in Yenan and the atmosphere in the Communist Party. The possibility of repressions on the part of the Central Government was precluded, at least temporarily—a load was taken off everybody's shoulders. The situation in other base areas improved correspondingly.

It seemed that the fresh wind blew through the party organizations. As if everything woke up after a nightmare in the stale Yenan atmosphere. It had an immediate effect on the CCP leadership. Slowly but steadily the life is changing from petty intrigues against each other, the police ways, and fear to realistic activity. Real work that everybody longed for heals the wounds inflicted by the "spiritual purges," and transforms people. Life is coming back to normal, not without difficulty, of course.

But Mao Tse-tung pretends that everything is going on according to his plans. After all, he was preparing the party and the Special Area for the conflict with Chiang Kai-shek, he fanned the anti-Kuomintang passions, or take the Hunan-Honan events—did not he foretell them?

In some way or other Mao interprets all these facts in his favor, to confirm the rightness of his policy. And, of course, there are more than enough yes-men and toadies. . . .

August 19, 1944

Today I have met two soldiers pushing a cart on the road. The portraits of Stalin, Churchill, Roosevelt, and King George VI were piled up on top of the rolls of cloth with slogans in this cart. The portrait of King George was much bigger than the other portraits. I don't know where and for what purpose they had to deliver these portraits. Most likely the preparations for the reception of a new group of foreign correspondents are going on and, judging by the size of the portraits, the British correspondents are expected.

August 20, 1944

Fighting is going on in Burma for the overland route to China. Mitkin is the transshipping point where the overland India-China route begins.

Roosevelt announced that Donald Marr Nelson and Patrick Jay Hurley would visit China as his personal representatives.

Nelson is head of the U. S. War Production Board. General Hurley is the former American Secretary of War.

The CCP Central Committee Chairman is getting adjusted to the new situation. The former "empiricists," "dogmatists," and "Muscovites" are drawn into work. Mao Tse-tung badly needs experienced and efficient cadres, who can by no means be replaced by those promoted by Kang Sheng's department. Speaking of the leading workers, Mao more and more willingly employs the services of Chu Teh, Peng Teh-huai, Po Ku, Chou En-lai, Nieh Jung-chen, and Yeh Chien-ying. Gradually they are becoming his chief associates. All this is not so much the CCP Central Committee Chairman's good will, as a forced necessity.

It leads inevitably to the loss of authority of the formerly powerful Kang Sheng's minority. Life pushes them into the background. There are obvious signs of the weakening of the Ching-pao-chu chief's power.

Yenan is awakening slowly and painfully.

The party is gradually doing away with idle talk, self-destruction, fear of repressions, and is getting down to life, active work, independently of the efforts of its Central Committee Chairman.

Everything here is full of the joy of this awakening. The 1943 actions would be simply impossible in the party organizations today. Communists wouldn't accept them. Kang feels it. And Mao also feels it, as well as all the others.

Not to accept the new situation would mean to lose control over the future developments. That's why Mao adapts himself to it in order to use the change in the situation for his own benefit.

The main events—the final rout of Germany, the rout of Japan, and the political destiny of China—are still ahead. But the breath of these major events is awakening Yenan. It is most important to have a united, mighty party in such conditions, and Mao does everything to draw into work and to rehabilitate (if only unofficially, only by placing his "trust" in them) the party and Soviet cadres.

The party members are rejoicing. It seems to them that the repressions of 1942 and 1943 were aberrations and the full blame must be laid on Kang and his associates.

Mao does nothing to prevent the development of such an attitude. It is a kind of tactic. He remains clean, wise, and impeccable. He is blameless. Cheng-feng is the campaign necessary for the CCP but, regrettably, distorted by its "technical executors." This is how the CCP Central Committee Chairman's attitude can be interpreted.

August 21, 1944

The American President declared that he was sending Hurley and Nelson to China with an urgent and strictly confidential mission.

Donald Marr Nelson is, practically, the most important Washington administrator. Nelson is in charge of the entire United States defense production program, or, in other words, of the militarization of the United States industry. He actually holds the key positions in the management of the entire American economy. The very fact that such a person goes to Chungking testifies to the exclusive importance attached to the Chinese problems by the White House. This, undoubtedly, is the visit with far-reaching consequences and of paramount importance for the development of the American policy.

Fierce battles are fought in the Hengyang area again, Stilwell and Chiang Kai-shek making desperate efforts to repulse the Japanese offensive.

The Kuomintang troops are trying to break through to Yicheng.

The 1944 campaign promises to be a triumph for the Japanese, but only China, of course. In the Pacific basin they yield one position after another to the Allies. The Americans are full masters in the ocean and in the air.

It should be noted that the Japanese are putting up a truly desperate military resistance. They lost about 45,000 soldiers killed in action on the islands of Saipan and Tinian. Only 100 soldiers and officers out of this number were taken prisoner.

Kolya and I live under the same roof, but we don't see much of each other. On some days we only exchange a couple of words. I am roaming Yenan from morning till night, and then write my reports in a hurry. Kolya transmits them while I am sleeping.

August 24, 1944

Today the Americans inspected the 359th Brigade under Wang Cheng. Among chief experts were David Barrett, Reginald Foss, and Brooke Dolan. Raymond Ludden also took an active part.

To Nanniwan, where the brigade was stationed, the Americans and correspondents were brought in a car.

I didn't deny myself the pleasure of taking part in the inspection tour.

The Americans were introduced to the commanding officers of the brigade, which showed off its armaments and gave an account of its military record. Everything seemed to have been rehearsed to impress the visitors.

On Chu Teh's command some of the soldiers in the back rows shouted: "Down with the Kuomintang!" One more demonstration of the spontaneous mood of the people and the Army . . .

Colonel Barrett treated the soldiers to a speech.

The Americans are evidently keen on finding the shortest route to Tokyo through the Special Area. . . .

August 26, 1944

I don't know for sure anything about the negotiations with the Americans. These negotiations are in full swing. . . .

Many foreign journalists visited the Special Area, and now new journalists arrive from time to time. Everybody is eager to know what will come out of these contacts.

Protsenko knows almost all the Chungking journalists. He tells me a lot about the specific situation in the provisional capital of China.

The events are developing in purely Mao Tse-tung style. Now the CCP Central Committee Chairman is inclined to lay the whole blame for the "aberrations" of cheng-feng on Kang Sheng and to keep his own conscience clear. There are plenty of facts testifying to it.

For example, the CCP Central Committee Chairman sends all the articles written by the chief of Ching-pao-chu to Po Ku(!) to be corrected. Po Ku is one of the most bitter enemies of Kang Sheng. Po Ku never made up with Kang and always let him feel what a nonentity he was.

Such gestures by Mao Tse-tung need no comment. He seems to dissociate himself from the punitive actions of cheng-feng pointing his finger at the one who is really responsible for them. It is a cruel kick in the ribs for Kang Sheng.

Distributing reports to be delivered at the forthcoming Seventh CCP Congress, Mao Tse-tung "forgot" about the chief of Ching-pao-chu. Kang Sheng is left without any report. Another kick in the ribs!

Mao Tse-tung complains of the aberrations of cheng-feng, alleging that everything was planned in a clean and just way, but, and it should be admitted, the methods of the party cadres' purge campaign were wrong, harmful, and even arbitrary to some extent. Another kick!

Kang looks lost. He did not expect anything like this from his worshiped patron.

Mao Tse-tung said the same to me, too: Kang exceeded his authority, distorted the valuable undertaking, and "made havoc of things" in the cadres' policy.

I would like to know what will happen to Kang. Will it come to the public condemnation and investigation? That's exactly how the party members feel about it.

August 29, 1944

Not to yield his positions on the major issue, the necessity of struggle against the "Moscow group," headed by Wang Ming, the CCP Central Committee Chairman gave instructions to write a play condemning Wang Ming. But still it is not like poisoning him with a mercury preparation or isolating him in a cave without any qualified medical aid. It is quite an acceptable variant of the condemnation of the "Muscovites" in the new conditions. It is not merely the condemnation but the continuation of struggle, too! Mao Tse-tung is true to himself. His hatred for the "Muscovites" has taken a new form which is in the spirit of the times, and outwardly is perfectly harmless.

The play has already been concocted. It is entitled *Comrade, You*

Follow the Wrong Road. The play condemns the party members who made the co-operation with Kuomintang and Chiang Kai-shek possible.

It is impossible for Kang to make up with those whom he "lashed" (literally and figuratively). They hate him and now they give vent to their hatred.

Peng Chen and the workers of lower ranks openly desert their chief. They fear condemnation and isolation, and they do their best to establish contacts with those whom they "lashed," and especially with the CCP Central Committee Chairman's new associates. These associates are gaining authority and influence by leaps and bounds.

Mao Tse-tung's authority (as questionable as it is in the CCP) is growing still greater. He has managed to present crime as merit! That's exactly the case. Now he has the reputation of a "prophet," and "the one who punishes for unjustice." People are grateful to him for letting them work again, for respect, and for justice.

August 30, 1944

Favorable changes in the military situation (for the Special Area only), foreign correspondents' visits, and the stay of the Army Observer Group forced Mao Tse-tung to curtail cheng-feng. At least all the outward manifestations of cheng-feng are absent. . . .

September 1944

September 1, 1944

There is an undercurrent of discontent among the Communists over the "spiritual purification" and the reprisals of the previous years. The sharply changed political situation in the world and in China herself has caused Mao Tse-tung to make sharp verbal pronouncements against the past activities of Kang Sheng's Commission for the Review of Party Cadres and Nonparty Personnel, as well as against the personal activities of Kang Sheng as the instigator of punitive operations and various political campaigns ("rectification of styles," "apprehension of spies," "confessions," etc.).

Mao Tse-tung is not against the ideological implications of the cheng-feng and the party purges. He only repeats reluctantly that Kang Sheng has gone a bit too far and has committed "certain distortions." . . .

The American mission to the Special Area is headed by Colonel Barrett, assistant military attaché in Chungking. The most active members of the American delegation are Service and Ludden.

John Stuart Service and Raymond Ludden are political advisers at the Stilwell headquarters.

Barrett has informed the CCP leaders that he will gladly serve as a liaison between Yenan and the American administration.

Chou En-lai behaves as if he were an old pal of the Americans.

September 3, 1944

Donald Nelson and Major General Hurley have left Moscow by plane for China.

————

It is getting increasingly clear that politically the balance of forces within the CCP leadership has changed very much against the Ching-pao-chu chief. It would not be inaccurate to say that, with the rise of the new influential group close to the Chairman of the CCP Central Committee, Kang Sheng is getting more and more isolated.

Kang Sheng's bloc is falling apart. He is being abandoned even by those who until recently supported him, curried favor with and toadied to him. One of them is Chen Yi, commander of the New Fourth Army. This man who but yesterday was Kang Sheng's devoted supporter has not only disavowed any personal associations with him, but in private conversations makes critical and highly disrespectful remarks about him.

A reverse process is under way. All those who have stained their reputation with participation in the cheng-feng campaign are trying to save their bacon by heaping accusations on Kang Sheng. All this has not yet graduated into the open censure of Kang and his close associates. Their criticism still stays at the level of private discussions, hints, and the ostentatious refusal to maintain any relations with Kang. For example, Chen Yi has allowed himself the liberty of making disparaging remarks about the Ching-pao-chu chief in talks with Chu Teh and Yeh Chien-ying. He did not dare to say more. . . . Even in a talk with me Chen Yi could not resist the temptation of making caustic remarks about Kang.

Kang could never have expected that things would take such a turn.

Chen Yi was born in 1901, in the family of an imperial official in Szechwan. He studied at Shanghai University and later at Peking University, where he majored in law and commerce. In 1919 he came to France. A member of the CCP since 1923, he joined the Red Army of China on the day of its inception and has been there since. Before 1941 he held down various military and party posts. After the Fourth Army had been routed by the Kuomintang and its commander, Yeh Ting, had been taken prisoner, the Politburo of the CCP Central Committee appointed Chen Yi commander of the New Fourth Army.

September 4, 1944

Barrett is personally concerned with equipping, arming, and manning the Eighth Route Army and the New Fourth Army.

He has no trouble getting various documents, maps, and tables.

The nights are rather cool in September; it's easier to breathe, too. The climate here is so odd. Dust storms which can drive one crazy. Hot rain in summer. In fact, whole torrents come tumbling down when the heat is well-nigh bearable—straight powerful streams, fast and very hot. . . .

September 6, 1944

It is hardly likely that someone will dare criticize Kang Sheng openly without knowing how the Chairman of the CCP Central Committee feels about it. It is important for Mao Tse-tung not only to come out of this dirty business unstained but also to revivify the party, which has been strangled by the cheng-feng campaign. For him this is a matter of top priority, for he needs party cadres. In the new conditions this need is highly acute and will be still more acute tomorrow. The ardor and enthusiasm of the Communists are responsible for the outcome of the collision with the Kuomintang. The "spiritual purification" has paralyzed the cadres, has debilitated them, and instilled in them the fear of being independent.

This is why at the last meeting of the Secretariat of the CCP Central Committee Chou suddenly cracked down on the cheng-feng campaign.

Chou, who had up to now been zealously carrying out all the cheng-feng precepts, and who now made humiliating avowals not to make these "mistakes" in the future, suddenly demanded condemnation of the forms and methods of cheng-feng! Chou is tacitly backed by the Chairman of the CCP Central Committee. It is he who, using Chou as his mouthpiece, addressed an appeal to the party cadres: "You have suffered in vain! You are innocent! Let's work! Don't be afraid of work!" Being certain that his words had gone down with his audience, Chou En-lai demanded not so much that cheng-feng as such be condemned as that its technical prepetrators be called to account.

The new mood in the party has given rise to a spontaneous protest against the mind-boggling and humiliating practices of cheng-feng.

Nevertheless, Mao Tse-tung holds the reins of power firmly in his hands and directs all those "scheduled protests" the way that suits him best. In this case it was necessary to denounce the technical perpetrators of cheng-feng and to alert the party cadres and make them "combat-ready." Nobody here would have dared to open his mouth if they did not know Mao's opinion on the matter, for political independence can be enjoyed only within the limits set by Mao himself.

Chou En-lai's speech was spearheaded against Kang Sheng, who seems to be universally disliked here. The only exception to the prevailing fear and distrust among the CCP leaders is their unreserved recognition of Mao Tse-tung's authority and their unanimous hatred of Kang Sheng. Friendly feelings are a rarity. All this comes from the political and ideological aberrations born of the cruel struggle for power.

But there is another side to Chou En-lai's speech. He apparently sought to separate Kang Sheng from Mao Tse-tung and range him against the Chairman of the CCP Central Committee. In doing so he pursued a multiple aim. In the first place he is doing his utmost not to hurt Mao Tse-tung, to show in clear-cut terms who is to blame for the reprisals, to whitewash Mao and in this way to get in favor with him. In the second place, he is seeking to undercut the prestige of the Ching-pao-chu chief. This would give satisfaction not only to Chou but to all those who have suffered from Kang Sheng's punitive power. His loss of influence would at the same time seal his inability to retaliate.

Chou's speech aroused great excitement among the leading members of the party. Now Mao's concern is to see to it that the new course does not develop into a runaway process.

In his speech Chou En-lai praised Mao's wisdom and then said that Kang Sheng had grossly violated the rules of the cheng-feng campaign drawn up by Mao Tse-tung.

"The Chairman of the CCP Central Committee has formulated nine conditions for the verification of the party cadres," said Chou En-lai. "Kang Sheng has arbitrarily ignored these conditions, violated these conditions, neglected these conditions. . . ."

September 7, 1944

Large contingents of the Japanese Army are pushing on to Kweiyang. Kang Sheng has said that these are only a few divisions, unattached regiments and brigades.

The attitude of the Chairman of the CCP Central Committee to the idea of a united anti-Japanese front can be justified by neither tactical nor political arguments. Whatever has been said about collaboration with the Kuomintang has nothing to do with the consolidation of the united anti-Japanese front. This sabotage has taken different forms: public anti-Kuomintang campaigns, refusal to negotiate, unrealistic demands advanced allegedly for preventing the split. This policy facilitates the victories of the Japanese, which, however, does not throw off Mao Tse-tung, who regards Kuomintang's defeats as one of the main ways of weakening it.

Mao is taking advantage of the specific geographical position of the Special Area, most of which lies in out-of-the-way and almost inaccessible mountain provinces, with hardly any industry in them. Moreover, Mao Tse-tung has ordered scattered fighting, instead of sweeping planned operations against the Japanese, and has thus directed the bulk of his troops to nibble at the Kuomintang positions. In addition to this the CCP is now able to concentrate sizable contingents in the border area with a view of fighting the Central Government.

Mao Tse-tung is looking for his victories in the victories of the Japanese, in the collapse of the fronts of war, in gratuitous speculations over Chiang Kai-shek's defeats. At the same time he is trying to hallow his tactics with the "Marxism of reality," a theorized speculation of an inveterate enemy of the national front, a product of rankling, pent-up enmity not only for Chiang Kai-shek but also for joint actions against the Japanese. Back in 1938–40 this hostility was manifested in Mao's clashes with Wang Ming. At that time Mao Tse-tung voted for the united front but was doing all he could to bring about its disintegration. In fact, he conspired to achieve his objectives in defiance of the Comintern's tactics.

Mao Tse-tung is no less responsible for the split in the national resistance forces than the most reactionary elements of the right-wing section of the Kuomintang.

It could well be assumed that all these years Mao Tse-tung's policies have made it much easier for the Japanese to choose directions of their military operations.

The Japanese have been continually on the offensive but have at the same time drawn practical conclusions from the passive tactics of the CCP troops.

The military command of the Central Government held a conference in Hung-shan under the chairmanship of Chiang Kai-shek. Taking part in the work of the conference were China's allies.

The CCP leaders received this news with avid interest. Chu Teh and Chou En-lai immediately demanded an explanation from Colonel Barrett.

The head of the Army Observer Group did not deny the reports from Hung-shan.

The Eighth Route Army and the New Fourth Army have actually folded up military operations since 1941. The last major operation against the Japanese took place in 1940 (known as the Hundred Regiments Campaign). That operation was aimed at disrupting the Japanese communications in northern China. The Japanese repulsed the offensive and inflicted heavy losses on the CCP troops. Resistance to the Japanese was greatly weakened by the conflict with the Fourth Army, which broke the latter's backbone.

These events tallied beautifully with Mao Tse-tung's intention to start an inner party struggle. Mao Tse-tung used these facts to bear out the correctness of his views which had taken shape long before these events and some of which had been set forth in his work *On New Democracy*. Mao considered that the participation of the CCP in the anti-Japanese resistance front was a mistake. The folding up of the military operations was part of the plan for unleashing a civil war. The inner party struggle (the struggle for the "Marxism of reality") has brought forth cheng-feng.

September 10, 1944

The most active member of the Observer Group is Service. At the last meeting with the Chairman of the CCP Central Committee he raised a number of questions. Service believes that no further talks have any substance without having these questions answered.

In actual fact the Americans queried Mao Tse-tung: If you reply, we will know what your faith is.

Service also asked Mao Tse-tung on what political and economic grounds American capital investment was possible in China, and what he thought about Americans being at the head of (or being allowed to take part in the control of) large industrial complexes.

Service showed a good deal of interest in the employment of American personnel (engineers, technical experts, etc.) in China.

He asked Mao Tse-tung point-blank about what he thought the future state organization of China would be (both in form and in substance) and about how the CCP leadership was planning to achieve power in the country.

Service stated apropos the views of the Americans about this future organization.

"What is your economic program?" Service asked. "What is its essence, and what are its stages? Will you follow in the footsteps of the Soviet Union in this respect and build an industrial basis? Will you build up your industry notwithstanding the low standard of living? Will you do it at the cost of the standard of living?"

Service is young, full of bounce, and has a good, retentive memory. Mao answered his questions in detail and even gave advice to him, then trailed off into a long lecture, as he is wont to do. Service listened patiently, then asked more questions—well formulated and to the point. When Mao declined to give a straightforward answer, Service pressed his point home by asking additional questions and in this way received all the information he wanted. He also told the Chairman of the CCP Central Committee that an important dispatch had been received from Washington. The American embassy had been given to understand that a reorganization of the Chungking Government was desirable. This meant that pressure would be brought to bear upon Chiang Kai-shek. Public opinion in China (central newspapers, social groupings, political leaders, etc.) would thus also come under pressure. Service announced that the White House deemed it expedient to set up a new government in China—a coalition government. This government would have to include representatives of all the influential political organizations, groupings, parties, and, of course, the Communist Party.

American policy in China has thus entered a new stage. Washington has rushed into the fray to obtain the key positions in the country and to put the Special Area under its control. The Roosevelt Administration believes that it will not be thwarted in its efforts to set up a pro-American grouping in the Special Area.

On the American side all political questions are handled by Ludden and Service. It is clear that they would not have dared to make such contacts without authorization from Washington. I do not doubt the existence of such authorization.

Barrett is in charge of military strategy.

At the meeting with the Chairman of the CCP Central Committee Mr. Service solicited the views of the CCP leaders about the role the Soviet Union might play in the industrialization of China and about foreign investment in general.

Service is conducting talks in such a way that the participants are left in no doubt about the nature of China's future political make-up. The question is about building a People's China in which the CCP will be the leading force, although Service made no outright comment on this point.

Service is clearly the most important member of the American group. The first few weeks in Yenan he refrained from discussing politics. On a number of occasions when the Chinese comrades raised some political problems with him, he said evasively that he, as well as all the other members of the Observer Group, was concerned only about the military aspects of the situation. But now Service has gone whole hog into political discussions, acting as a plenipotentiary representative of the United States. There is no doubt that he reports the results of his talks to Chungking and from there they are passed on to Washington. It is clear that the United States and the policy of the CCP leadership are being dovetailed as regards common objectives, the permanence of their alliance and its advantages to both sides. The phantom of the Soviet Union is invariably present at these talks, having a visible effect on their participants. On the whole the atmosphere at the talks is not free from nervous haste, understatement, and mistrust. . . .

Over the past four weeks, Service has ranged over the same problems as he did with the Chairman of the CCP Central Committee and with many ranking CCP officials. The American met with Yeh Chien-ying, Po Ku, Chou En-lai, and others. I have been receiving very scanty information which is very often at variance with what has actually happened. Po Ku helps me to see my way through these intrigues.

Ludden is not a very voluble type. He usually accompanies Barrett or Service. The Americans feel very much at home in Yenan.

The arrival of representatives of the Kuomintang Military Command for talks in Yenan.

Soldiers of the Eighth Route Army.

Chen Yi (left), commander of the New Fourth Army; Liu Po-cheng, commander of the 129th Infantry Division; and Nieh Jung-chen, commander of the Shansi-Hopeh-Chahar border area.

Mao Tse-tung and Peng Teh-huai (standing), Chen Yun (left), and Wang Chia-hsiang (sitting).

In the foreground: Ho Lung (left), commander of the United Forces of the Special Area and commander of the 120th Infantry Division; Chang Ching-wu, chief of staff of the United Forces of the Special Area; and Chu Teh, commander of the Armed Forces of the CCP.

September 11, 1944

Service, Ludden, and Barrett met Chou En-lai and Yeh Chien-ying to discuss in detail the results of the Hung-shan Conference. At this conference the generals had drawn up a plan of military operations against the Japanese (counteroffensive plan). However, the American representatives confronted Chiang Kai-shek with terms of their own. The point is that the Kuomintang divisions have lost much of their fighting efficiency. That is why it was necessary to fit out new full-strength divisions trained in special training centers by American military instructors (such divisions are now being formed by Major General Albert C. Wedemeyer). About fifty thousand American officers are expected to arrive as instructors and advisers. It is clear, however, that the United States will by no means allow the new armed forces to be used against the Communists (civil war).

Also at Hung-shan the Americans warned the Chinese generals against planning a counteroffensive based on the striking power of General C. L. Chennault's air force (based in India and used only for supporting operations) or on American landing troops. The United States is unable to send any sizable number of its infantry into China.

September 12, 1944

The results of the Hung-shan Conference were discussed in detail by the leaders of the Chinese Communist Party, who accordingly made appropriate decisions.

The nature of these decisions can be understood in the light of the demands presented by Chu Teh and Yeh Chien-ying to the Observer Group. The CCP leaders demanded that the distribution of American weapons in the future be supervised, because Chiang Kai-shek might appropriate most of the weapons and the best of them (there is no doubt that the Americans will supply the Special Area with weapons). As for the amount of weapons, the Communist Party has laid claim to 50 per cent of the entire amount, 30 per cent at the very least.

The Americans have given the Chinese comrades to understand that Donald Nelson and Patrick Hurley are aware of the planned counteroffensive and are negotiating with Chiang Kai-shek and Ho Ying-chin to this end.

Barrett has said that Hurley and Nelson are keenly interested in the

Special Area, which looms large in American policy. That is why Nelson and Hurley will come at the earliest opportunity to the Special Area and will meet Mao Tse-tung. Service spoke in the same vein.

On the express order of the Chairman of the CCP Central Committee a letter of invitation was written and sent to Chungking.

Nelson and Hurley are the figures on the American political scene who are especially welcome here.

In a reply to the demands of Yeh Chien-ying and Chu Teh, the head of the American team said that he appreciated the fears of the CCP leaders but that an official document was necessary which would formulate their viewpoint. "I will then send this document to my military command," said Barrett.

Should this CCP request be granted (about the amount of weapons to be sent in), the Special Area would undoubtedly be crammed full with American advisers and all sorts of specialists.

In case the request is turned down the Americans will try to dispatch their personnel to the Special Area anyway. This has been repeatedly mentioned by the members of the Observer Group.

When he learned of Barrett's request, the Chairman of the CCP Central Committee ordered that a document to this effect be drafted immediately. This document has by now been signed and forwarded to the head of the American group.

Whatever the American observers might say, Washington will not separate the question of arms shipment from the political future of China. The United States Government is not so sure that Mao Tse-tung will not get out of hand after he has received the weapons. It is precisely for the study of the situation in connection with the supply of arms for the Eighth Route and the New Fourth armies that the American team has come here.

It is quite possible that the Americans might have different opinions on this score. So far, however, none of them have prevailed. The more conservative of the American politicians are afraid of entering into an alliance with the Chinese Communist Party led by Mao and insist that the Chiang Kai-shek regime be strengthened still further. Another body of American political opinion (Service being undoubtedly its spokesman) is aware of the fact that the whole of China is in revolutionary ferment and that it was much too risky to be committed to Chiang Kai-shek alone. It was necessary to look for acceptable political decisions and for new allies within this "national(!) force." According to them (Service proved this conclusively), the Communist

Party leadership can make a suitable partner, easy to deal with. Central to these decisions is the attitude of the Mao Tse-tung leadership to the Soviet Union and the All-Union Communist Party (Bolsheviks). By his very behavior Service seems to be trying to convince his colleagues that one need not fear the "terrible revolutionary phraseology" or the events that cannot be avoided anyway (the revolutionary enthusiasm of the masses).

These are my conclusions drawn from weighty facts. Still, I wonder which of these two American political opinions will take the upper hand!

September 13, 1944

Another American has arrived in Yenan. He is Mr. McFisher, who is chief of the U. S. Office of War Information in China.

Judging by the mood prevailing among the Americans, the United States is not intending to keep permanently its diplomats in Yenan lest this might displease Chiang Kai-shek. After all, Service and Ludden are officials at the American embassy in Chungking, and their sojourn in Yenan can easily be regarded as de facto recognition of Yenan, which Chiang Kai-shek, the principal protégé of the Allies, cannot allow to happen.

It is for this reason that Service keeps deathlike silence about the repeated proposal of the Chinese comrades to open a permanent office of the United States in Yenan. It looks like he has received strict instructions to this effect, although he seems to disagree with them.

Mr. Service's recent announcement of Washington's new move (demand that Chiang Kai-shek agree to set up a coalition government) made a deep impression on the CCP leaders. The Chairman of the CCP Central Committee has ordered its representatives in Chungking to mount opposition to the Kuomintang Government.

The CCP is represented in Chungking by Tung Pi-wu (one of the founding fathers of the Communist Party) and Lin Po-chu. The Chairman of the CCP Central Committee has sent a second cable to them demanding that they start organized action of all those who are in opposition to the government. This action is planned in the form of articles in the press as well as in the form of obstructionist tactics at the current session of the National Political Council. Mao demands that all the forces of society make over-all criticism of the government.

The military setbacks and the economic crisis stimulate the mood of opposition in Chinese society. Mao is urging his men to exercise the utmost of skill in taking advantage of the favorable situation.

Facts show that the representatives of the Communist Party have launched an all-out attack on Chiang Kai-shek and the right wing of the Kuomintang.

One such fact was the surprise visit of Hu Chen-chih, a prominent journalist and politician, to the office of Tung and Lin, official CCP representatives in the Kuomintang. He said that the Communist Party would surely be successful in its efforts. He cracked down on Chiang Kai-shek's methods, criticized the government, and praised the Communist Party. He said that the Communist Party enjoyed the support of the Chinese people and, not unimportantly, of foreigners.

Hu Chen-chih is chief editor of *Ta Kung-pao* [Great Bulletin], one of the most liberal newspapers in Chungking. It is popular mostly among the intelligentsia. The Chiang Kai-shek government imposed all sorts of penalties on this newspaper, including termination of its publication.

September 14, 1944

In his talks with the CCP leaders McFisher promoted the idea of setting up in Yenan a military information office, a branch of the central bureau. On the whole McFisher is not a zealous type.

Barrett is the head of the U. S. Army Observer Group. The first several weeks the American colonel was rather cautious, avoided discussing important problems, made no promises, and kept his opinion to himself. Lately he has suddenly changed his style of work. Just like Service, he is now vociferously criticizing the Chiang Kai-shek regime, the ineptness of the Central Government and its inability to keep the situation under control. He is also criticizing the Kuomintang armies as undependable. The colonel strongly disapproves of Chiang Kai-shek for his opposition to the Communist Party and emphasizes his friendly feeling for the Special Area and the policy of the CCP!

On his part McFisher insists that the CCP leaders allow his subordinates to work in the Special Area. The question is being aired of the arrival in the Special Area of a large group of American intelligence men, experts in psychological warfare. This group, according to McFisher, will be put to disintegrating enemy fighting units and disrupting the enemy rear. The American experts are expected to have their headquarters in Yenan.

Mao's chief assistant at the talks with the Allies is Chou En-lai. Acting in close contact with Chou is Yeh Chien-ying. Liu Shao-chi is busy with preparations for the forthcoming congress and with other party affairs.

At every opportunity Kolya tells me about his wife, Lida, and his little son, Sergei. I understand his need to get it off his chest, but every time he starts telling me about his family, my heart gives me a twinge. How are Maria and the children?

September 15, 1944

David Barrett runs to fat. He is about forty-five or fifty. His knowledge of the Peiping dialect is impeccable. His manners are simple and unobtrusive. As a rule, the cuffs of his uniform tunic are unbuttoned and folded back a little. His necktie is tucked under his shirt. His military boots show signs of long wear. Amiable, despite the sullen expression of his face.

The Chairman of the CCP Central Committee has no friends. Only people he needs, but not friends. He appreciates only those whom he needs at the moment. All that is not useful to him personally is worthless and even harmful. Besides, he lumps together what he considers useful to himself and to "his" revolution. Nothing exists beyond his own interests, nothing makes sense, even the revolution itself.

This is a special kind of vanity, a vanity which is indifferent to the comforts of life. Power is his only dream and ambition. The only path of truth and virtue is the path leading to supreme power. His whole style of life, wrought in his appearance, breathes contempt for everything that limits power. All is dust—all but power. It is at this angle that he views the deeds of all great men of history.

It is for their unlimited power that the giants of the past hold fascination for him. According to Mao Tse-tung, power is the only thing worth living for. This is a justification for everything, this is triumph, this is everything, everything. . . .

The party and the people are just a figment of imagination (some sort of abstract notions), which serve his objectives.

Mao meets many people, but for all that he is singularly unsociable and even lonely. This loneliness is somehow final and cruel to the point of being dangerous.

His power is in his intuition. He does not so much understand as he feels the invincibility of Marxism in the revolutionary upheavals of our century. He skillfully combines his own brand of Marxism (the Marxism of reality) with his aspirations for supreme power. He is moving into power in the eye of the revolutionary storm. He mangles Marxism every time the philosophy of this doctrine clashes with his personal views. Using demagogy as a shield, he goes on distorting and distorting. . . .

His entire activity can be summed up as anguished manipulation of tactics that best suit his ends in this bid for power. In his eyes, principles are nothing but a collection of commitments made by others to the cause of the revolution. A very convenient formula! This is how he bends others to his will. Principles bind millions of people hand and foot; he is acting in the name of principles, while feeling free from them. . . .

The "Marxism of reality" is his, Mao's, philosophy, a philosophy of moral poverty and hypertrophied ambition.

September 16, 1944

A rather curious editorial has appeared in the local Yenan newspaper. The American team was informed of its content ahead of time, although the concluding part of this article came as a big surprise to the Americans.

This move was clearly aimed at making the Americans distribute the weapons according to the principle of equality in order to equalize the amount of armament to be shipped to the Central Government and to the Special Area—a tall order as far as American weapons are concerned.

Another aim is to press on with the talks in order to achieve practical results.

Still another aim is to weaken Chiang Kai-shek and to curtail the amount of American aid to him.

The editorial provides details about the nature of American aid to China, about the distribution of ammunition, weapons, and foodstuffs.

As for the Hung-shan Conference, it served as a pretext for finalizing the issue of arms shipment to the Special Area. This time the question was put to the Americans point-blank.

September 17, 1944

After his inspection tour of one of the brigades Colonel Barrett summed up his conclusions on the involvement of the Eighth Route Army and the New Fourth Army in the future allied operations against the Japanese.

The head of the Observer Group sent the main conclusions set forth in his report to the military and political leaders of the Communist Party. This report was the first result of the almost two months' stay of the Americans in the Special Area.

The head of the American team sent the report to his military command in Chungking.

One thought often keeps me awake at night: The Ching-pao-chu chief can easily do away with me, for I know too much about his own and his protectors' doings.

Exhausting contagious diseases, steep mountain paths, and many other "accidents" can help him get rid of me. . . .

On the other hand, they cannot go as far as that. Moscow looms very large in their plans. . . . They might be glad to remove me, but they just cannot afford it now.

September 22, 1944

Mao Tse-tung spent two solid hours talking to me. This in brief is what he said:

The Americans cannot solve a single Chinese problem, much less the whole complex of Far Eastern questions. This means that Moscow will inevitably have to step in at the most crucial moment. By doing so and by settling the vital issues on the eastern borders of the Soviet Union, it will also "untie the Chinese knot." Chiang Kai-shek is clearly against such a move on Moscow's part.

Considering the tremendous losses sustained by the Soviet Union and the present shortage of military personnel, the Chinese are ready to provide the necessary assistance. The CCP leadership would select more than ten thousand commanders and would send them to Siberia for retraining. This commanding personnel would stand at the head of the huge Chinese Army, which could help the Soviet troops in Manchuria and other Japanese-occupied areas.

When the Soviet Far East was in danger, the CCP detailed two of its best regiments without a murmur. A similar move would be made in the future but on a much broader scale.

The obvious purport of those statements needs no comment.

In the evening Barrett, Chu Teh, and Yeh Chien-ying met for talks.

Chu Teh and Yeh Chien-ying said:

"If the government and the Supreme Command of Chiang Kai-shek is reorganized, and if the CCP does not receive arms, munitions, and other aid from the Americans, the future counteroffensive and especially the victory over the Japanese will inevitably lead to a long civil war.

"The United States is interested in trade, in capital investments, and in stable markets. A civil war would badly hurt the American economic interests. . . ."

It was the Chairman of the CCP Central Committee who had briefed Chu Teh and Yeh Chien-ying. I have learned that from Yeh Chien-ying himself.

The CCP leaders have made preparations for a serious political move in the event of collapse of their plans.

Mao Tse-tung is intending to set up a joint government of the Special Area and all of its base areas scattered in the enemy rear (in Shansi, Hopeh, Shantung, Kiangsu, Honan, Hunan, etc.).

This means that China will have a second government. The CCP leaders not only are not even trying to conceal this plan but, on the contrary, are zealously informing the Allies of all its details.

The Americans have nothing against it in principle, but suggest that this government be called something like the "joint democratic committee of the liberated areas of China."

For their part the CCP leaders are inclined to agree with this suggestion, since a name like this will not scare their American allies.

Mao Tse-tung is putting all the screws on the Americans and, through them, on Chiang Kai-shek.

September 23, 1944

In its sharply worded editorial a local newspaper once again demanded that the government and the Supreme Command be reorganized and the defeatist and fascist elements be removed from the state apparatus.

Several more articles are awaiting publication. One of these articles severely criticizes the Chiang Kai-shek system and praises the economy of the Special Area.

Conferences and meetings are being held on instructions from Mao Tse-tung. The speakers are blasting the Kuomintang and the Chungking Government: "Down with the one-party dictatorship!"

Whereas before the CCP leaders checked out their actions on this point with the Americans, today they are showing signs of growing independence, the sweeping offensive of the Japanese on Kweilin playing no small part in this. . . .

September 24, 1944

Stilwell's forthcoming visit has raised great hopes in Yenan. He is being very much awaited here. Mao believes that at a personal meeting with a high-ranking military general he will be able to solve all these questions. Besides, it is this particular general who is in charge of American war-goods deliveries to China. And this will surely help avoid the red tape of the intermediate channels.

The general's proposed visit is kept strictly secret.

Meanwhile the Observer Group is still probing for possible cooperation. The Americans are negotiating for setting up a joint intelligence network spearheaded against the Japanese. The CCP leadership is airing this question with the Americans, but all this is not what Mao Tse-tung wants most of all. So far he has not received the arms and ammunition he is so anxious to have.

With the shipment of arms, ammunition, and equipment, all the other questions will fall into place. This is what the CCP leaders believe, and this is what they give the Americans to understand.

The Americans are expecting to man the proposed intelligence network in Yenan with their own specialists, supply it with necessary equipment and money.

But without the main problem solved, that of arms delivery, no practical solution of all the other questions is possible. . . .

September 25, 1944

Mao Tse-tung did not misjudge the importance of the visit (now visits) of foreign correspondents. Against the background of Chiang Kai-shek's military setbacks, the corruption of the leadership and administration of the Kuomintang, and the bribe-taking of its officers, the Special Area looks rather attractive.

Enduring no pressure from the Japanese for a number of years, the Special Area has strengthened its positions. The CCP leadership has put it in fairly good order, which looks perfect compared with economically dislodged and poverty-stricken provinces controlled by the Kuomintang. All this is being shown off by the CCP leadership and is being skillfully played up. . . .

The foreign press has had some praise for the Special Area and the Mao Tse-tung leadership. All such reports are carefully collected here, and its authors can expect excellent reception in the future (there have been such cases already).

One can conclude from the brief remarks and comments made by the members of the Observer Group that they have a favorable view of the Special Area.

Now the improved general situation and the military might of the Special Area have enabled Mao to start his game. He has set a bait and is now expecting the Americans to rise to it. If they do, Mao will receive weapons and will possibly enjoy Washington's political protection. Such protection would enable him to solve some of the inner political problems in the country. . . .

Now the only open question is whether the White House will disown its protégé in Chungking. This part of the negotiations is being carefully camouflaged. All the facts that have come to my knowledge go to show that Mao is clearly offering himself as a partner of the Americans. . . .

September 26, 1944

Chou En-lai is especially active in the talks with the Americans. But, as I've had a chance to see, all his activities boil down to a desire to stay in power. Besides, the twists and turns of the political situation are of no importance to him. More than that, he changes his principles with ease, if the situation so requires.

Chou En-lai's activities never transcend the political views of Mao Tse-tung and assume a degree of independence only in his personal rivalry with his colleagues in the party, especially with Liu Shao-chi.

Chou has a flair for practical work, rather than for theorizing. He is sanguine of nature, is a fast talker.

Jen Pi-shih, though a former political worker in the Army, is very inert. He is a kind of trusted man of Mao Tse-tung, his mild-mannered personal executive. He is very meticulous in his ways and follows the letter of his patron's instructions.

The pleasant exception in this crew is Chu Teh, who, after all those clashes and disputes and quarrels, has retained his optimistic and benevolent disposition. . . .

Mao has of late been short and businesslike in an apprehensive sort of way.

September 27, 1944

To Mao Tse-tung the lure of power is more important than any party interests. Acting behind the back of the Soviet Union, he is trying to solve the Far Eastern question in his own way.

Speculating on the military defeats of Chiang Kai-shek, the Chairman of the CCP Central Committee is anxious to strengthen his positions with American aid in order to become the leading force in China, possibly against their will. For this reason he is willing not only to change the name of the party but also to sell the interests of the Soviet Union.

Mao Tse-tung considers the Soviet Union too much drained of blood by the struggle against Nazi Germany and therefore unable to start early and effective military operations in the Far East. And if so, there is no point in wasting the time. . . . For him, the Americans' chances of success in China are far more important, and that's why he is bidding for their partnership.

Mao is certain that the fate of the Far East and China is at stake. Only the United States can serve as the chief arbiter!

September 28, 1944

Mao Tse-tung wants to know how much the Americans are interested in the armed forces of the CCP. I think he is beginning to guess that the Americans will hardly break with Chiang Kai-shek and reorient their policy toward Yenan. And this is exactly what he is dreaming about and what he considers the ideal result of the present contacts with the Americans.

The Allies want to put the CCP armed forces under their control, without changing the correlation of their political forces in the country. Chiang Kai-shek is their man. They are afraid of the Communist Party as a possible ally.

Chiang Kai-shek can be depended on. He is a "tried-and-true force against Bolshevism." As for Mao, he has the Communist Party to back him. This fact prevents the Americans from knowing how shaky the position of its leaders is. How will Mao behave in the future? For them this is a harrowing question, the main source of all their doubts. They cannot trust his words alone. They are afraid of believing him, although they want it very much. Therefore, the Americans are trying to democratize the Kuomintang system at least on the surface and to give it the credence of being progressive.

There is much talk going on in Yenan about the future reorganization of the Chungking Government. The Chairman of the CCP Central Committee will hardly lose his chance this time. Evidence of this is a new anti-Chiang Kai-shek campaign in the local press. Despite its intensity this campaign obviously allows for a possible change in the situation. An illustration of this is the recent speech made by Lin Po-chu at a session of the National Political Council. Lin Po-chu strongly demanded that the government be reorganized.

It is remarkable that all the details of Lin Po-chu's speech had been co-ordinated with the American officials in Chungking. Mao is trying hard to convince the Americans that co-operation is possible, that he is loyal to them, thereby prodding them to still closer contacts with him.

I can imagine how upset and mad Chiang Kai-shek must be! . . .

September 29, 1944

According to Churchill, Russia's contribution to the routing of Nazism is a "service that knows no measure."

"Russia has pinned down and is thrashing much larger forces than those which oppose the Allies in the west. . . . Over long years Russia, at the price of tremendous sacrifice, has been carrying the burden of fighting on land. . . ."

In China the Japanese have seized a number of important airports and have thus created difficulties for Chennault's air force. Ten Japanese divisions have been thrown back into Burma after trying unsuccessfully to invade India.

Churchill feels affronted by a comparison between Hitler and Napoleon. For him Hitler is nothing but a mere butcher. . . .

Endeared by the trust of the Americans and their exaggerated benevolence, the Chairman of the CCP Central Committee has revealed his entire political essence. Even I (who have seen lots of things here) am surprised to see him go so far, promising, guaranteeing, assuring, and making statements which border on outright betrayal.

Softened up by the benevolence of the Allies, he makes no secret of his true feelings for Moscow. Comrade Po Ku provided me with details about this ignoble behavior of Mao Tse-tung.

October 1944

October 2, 1944

The White House announced the resignation of Donald Nelson.

Nelson considers he has fulfilled his duties of the chairman of the U. S. War Production Board. His trip to China convinced him that American commitments to China had been successfully fulfilled.

Nelson's resignation was accepted. He will receive a post in the U. S. Government.

Henri Pétain, that traitor of France, fled to Germany. . . .

Speaking at the third session of China's National Political Council, Lin Tsu-han, the representative of Yenan, demanded that the blockade of the Special Area be lifted, the CCP legalized, and armed forces united for the struggle against the common enemy.

David Barrett is well familiar with the customs and mores of China. He has broad connections in society. He is even more popular than Colonel De Pass, his chief. Before 1937 he had been repeatedly in China. Since 1937 he has been on the staff of the American military attaché in Chungking and frequently went to Chengtu.

Cordial, hospitable, and likable. An interesting interlocutor. Outwardly loyal to the Soviet Union. However, for all his courtesy, he is careful and won't say an uncautious word.

Exhausted with angina, temperature about 40° C., short breath, hoarse voice. Looked in the mirror—hollowed eyes and a chalk-white face . . .

October 6, 1944

Another group of American military specialists has come to Yenan.

Among yesterday's arrivals, who had informed the CCP leadership of their coming, were Colonel Morris De Pass, American military attaché in China; Colonel George Armstrong, of the U. S. Intelligence Service (officially known as surgeon), Colonel Edward McNally, and two sergeants. The group is led by Brigadier General William Bergin.

Mao Tse-tung hurried to the airport where he was waiting for a Douglas with the guests for a fairly long time. The Mao who never waits for anybody. . . .

The Chairman of the CCP Central Committee was accompanied by Chu Teh, Yeh Chien-ying, Chou En-lai, and others.

Mao persistently seeks contact with top rankers from the American military command or the government. It seems he wants them to change their minds, to convince them of the possibility and necessity of America's alliance with the Special Area. I think Mao doesn't want to make his innermost thoughts known to petty go-betweens from the American administration and that is why he is striving for a direct meeting with American political bosses. I am sure that here, at the talks, Mao is not frank to the end because he is afraid things may come out and compromise him before Moscow. He would choose to keep silent rather than reveal his true aims and feelings. He needs talks but not with colonels or embassy secretaries. . . .

An experienced intelligence officer, De Pass had been to China on many occasions. He has a perfect command of the Chinese language. Simple with his subordinates, unsociable, doesn't talk much.

He is a thick-set, short, baldish man of about fifty. Has a characteristic Anglo-Saxon bluntish strong chin. . . .

Chou En-lai does not usually reveal his attitude to events. Mao Tse-tung uses the strained relations between Chou and Kang Sheng, bestowing favors now upon one, then upon the other.

Chou is Mao Tse-tung's main assistant in tackling major party and military questions.

Chou has exceedingly good health. He has never complained of being unwell. He always works much and often at night. His wife is Teng Ying-chao. They have no children of their own. They have an adopted daughter.

October 7, 1944

Nieh Jung-chen, Tsai Chang, Li Fu-chun, Li Li-san, Chou En-lai, Teng Ying-chao, Fu Chung, Lo Mei, Hsu Teh-li, Chen Yi, Wang Jo-fei, Hsiang Ching-yu, and some other senior CCP functionaries studied in France (Chu Teh and Yeh Chien-ying in Germany). Their education was paid for by a bourgeois enlightenment organization by agreement with a related society in France. Special courses were organized in Peiping before the departure of the would-be students of Paris and Lyons universities.

Under the influence of the October Revolution in Russia, Europe was experiencing an upswing in the revolutionary movement. Parties, societies, organizations, and groups of every trend and shade were mushrooming.

That is why the education in France of politically immature young people had its negative aspects for many of them. Along with Marxist ideas they apparently absorbed the concepts of various leftist parties of Europe. In their revolutionary extremism many of them negated Marxism, the leading role of the Comintern, and the experience of the October Revolution. They were strongly influenced by the anarchists, who later played a highly regrettable role in the civil war in Spain. Trade-union-oriented parties, left-wing terrorist organizations, etc., were also becoming increasingly active at that time.

It was in Europe that Li Li-san accepted anarchist-putschist philosophy which emphasized the putsch and the "special ways of the Chinese Revolution." After a thorough analysis the Comintern flatly rejected this philosophy. Li Li-san's views were largely assimilated by Mao Tse-tung. . . .

Studies at Sun Yat-sen University in Moscow failed to overcome the West European petty-bourgeois background of most of the present-day party leaders. Judging by cheng-feng, a range of Marxist political and economic subjects was learned by them perfunctorily. At present Marxism is openly called "dogmatism" and the "Western classical revolutionary philosophy and practice unacceptable for the CCP" (Mao Tse-tung's words).

Highly indicative are the relations between Li Li-san and Mao Tse-tung. Angrily condemning Li Li-san's views, Mao Tse-tung, nevertheless, preserved fairly good relations with him.

Lo Mei (Politburo member of the CCP Central Committee in 1927) is a close friend of Li Li-san's. Jointly with Chou En-lai and others organized the Paris section of the CCP. In the twenties Lo Mei (his real name is Li Wei-han) lived in Mao Tse-tung's house for some time. . . .

Li Li-san was born in 1896. He and Mao came from the same province. At one time they were on friendly terms. Following his studies in France, Li Li-san conducted active revolutionary work in China. His relations with Mao Tse-tung had been friendly until the Futien incident behind which was the struggle for control over the party. For his left-wing opportunist deviations Li Li-san was removed from the leadership by the Comintern.

The Chairman of the CCP Central Committee condemns Li Li-san only in words. This is a means in the struggle against the "Moscow opposition" and "dogmatism." As Li Li-san was stigmatized by the Comintern and discredited himself by his leftist actions, it is very convenient to use his name to destroy one's enemies! This Hunan man [Mao Tse-tung] does not have a genuine dislike for Li Li-san. His public condemnation is just a political trick.

Brigadier General William Bergin decorated Colonel Barrett with the service medal. The CCP leadership gave an open-air feast in honor of the recipient. A big table was laid. The Americans filed to the table, with Barrett leading the way. The brand-new medal shone on Barrett's breast. He was met with flowers and greetings. Those present huddled around the Americans.

Mao Tse-tung and Chu Teh congratulated Barrett cordially. Then Mao Tse-tung joined the Americans and obviously enjoyed posing for reporters.

The guests were invited to the table. Yeh Chien-ying made a speech in Barrett's honor.

He said that the medal received by Colonel Barrett was also an award for Chinese Communists, who fruitfully collaborated with the Observer Group. . . .

Ma Hai-te translated the speech.

Brooks Atkinson, the New York *Times* correspondent, will give an account of this ceremony, I think. He took an active part in the celebration.

October 8, 1944

Roosevelt said it was difficult to aid China, as the coastal sea routes were fully controlled by the Japanese and Burma had not been liberated yet.

The President said at present Chungking was receiving over twenty thousand tons of cargoes a month as against some three thousand tons a year and a half ago. The "air bridge" cannot yet carry more, as super-heavy B-29s devour too much fuel.

Mao knows well how to use a fiery revolutionary phrase. That is why party members regard him as an expert on Marxism. His judgments and the way of thinking seem to be correct, seem to follow the principles of Marxism-Leninism. However (with the outwardly logically correct scheme), he makes arbitrary interpretations which look innocent at first sight. . . .

This explains why in his conclusions you sometimes find ones which seem to be written from the programs of petty-bourgeois parties. Such points can be met mostly in the secret resolutions of the Secretariat and Politburo of the CCP Central Committee. They are lost in the verbiage of the "stating parts of documents," in the enumeration of correct conclusions and thoughts. However, it is only later that you begin to understand that a document was adopted for the sake of this unobtrusive conclusion lost in verbiage. . . .

It has become Mao Tse-tung's style to hide behind the heaps of CCP documents, formulations concerning the cheng-feng, distrust in the Comintern, and anti-Sovietism presented as the struggle against "dogmatism." This is the selfsame "Marxism in practical life" of which Mao first spoke early in 1942.

Theoretical ambiguity, unsteadiness, and forced amiability toward the Soviet Union are dangerous symptoms in Mao's activities. The political situation either lays them bare, makes them more evident, or dulls them. Mao has a good nose for changes in the political situation. He sizes up the situation well in advance, but, being not outstandingly clever, he often makes mistakes. The Soviet Union did not lose the war, as he thought it would. If he had foreseen this, he would not have acted so rashly in some cases. . . .

The revolutionary struggle will probably put the Chairman of the CCP Central Committee in the position of not being able to act otherwise than in the spirit of Marxism-Leninism. Even the latest events, the criticism and condemnation by party members of the cadres screening the commission's activities, show Mao Tse-tung has to consider facts. And these facts are confidently putting the Communist Party on the road of struggle for a socialist China. This onward movement may eventually overcome the opportunism of some leaders. In any case, Mao Tse-tung has constantly to take into consideration and adapt himself to the revolutionary sentiments of the masses, the popularity of Marxism, the prestige of the Soviet Union.

During our latest talk Mao Tse-tung persistently advised me not to frown upon Oriental cunning and learn to be cunning from the Chinese.

The New Fourth Army conducts operations, having bases in Kiangsu and partly in Hupeh.

The Chairman of the CCP Central Committee was very much irritated by the visit of General Bergin. He expected the Americans to make very important proposals and enter into contact with top-ranking American politicians. However, General Bergin limited himself to the solemn presentation of a combat award to Colonel Barrett. On this occasion the Americans organized a big stag party with plenty to drink. I dare say Barrett received his order not for nothing—he is one of the outstanding and most experienced American intelligence officers in the East. This baldish, thick-set man of forty-five behaves with confidence and dignity. He is emphatically friendly and smiles often. Plays a simple, openhearted man. Mao does his best to win him over to his side. . . .

That neither De Pass nor Bergin conducted talks with the CCP leadership made Mao Tse-tung restless, as he had already prepared lists of the necessary matériel, various proposals, etc.

I think the Americans decided to check their mission's field work and discuss some very important questions. In any case, Chinese comrades were clearly disappointed.

Service is the most meticulous among the Americans. Acting on his own or fulfilling an order, he told the CCP leadership the visit of these military top rankers to Yenan was a demonstration meant for the Chungking Government. In any case, he sugared the pill for Mao. . . .

The Japanese continue the successful offensive. They occupied Sinning (Hunan province) on October 1 and Pao-ching on October 3.

October 10, 1944

Winston Churchill and Anthony Eden are in Moscow. The British Prime Minister said at the airport the Russian armies were the first to smash the spirit and the military machinery of the German Army. . . .

A radio station reported that "Gandhi has suffered a defeat in his attempts to unite India and, with a group of his followers, indulged in prayers. . . ." What a mockery of a man who devoted his life to the liberation of his country!

The main aim of Donald Nelson's visit to China is to sound out prospects for American investments. Although the Japanese have not yet lost the war, businessmen are already thinking of how to make the most of the Chinese man power and cheap raw materials. . . .

Lin Po-chu had been sent to conduct talks with Chiang Kai-shek in Chungking before the Hunan-Honan catastrophe. At that time the anti-Kuomintang propaganda in the Special Area had again generated the danger of invasion. All had thought Yenan's defeat was inevitable.

The unexpected failure of the Central Government's troops in Hunan and Honan had turned the CCP representative in Chungking from a beggar into a self-confident and wrathful accuser!

Striking transformations!

October 14, 1944

The country's split is the main reason behind the Japanese success. It is not a matter of the fighting efficiency of the Chinese Army. In the enemy's success Mao Tse-tung sees a factor which undermines the power of Chiang Kai-shek. Neither military catastrophes nor considerations of the struggle against fascism can make the Chairman of the CCP give up his divisive policy. The split is a sinister reality in China. And this split is clearly in the interests of the Japanese militarists. Mao Tse-tung's policy to disrupt the united national resistance was tantamount to dozens of extra Japanese divisions fighting in China.

Mao Tse-tung sees a threat to his policy in Chiang Kai-shek's possible success at the front. Chiang Kai-shek must be weakened by any means. This is the essence of the policy of the CCP leadership. And let the Japanese seize Chinese land and burn towns! . . .

Mao Tse-tung calls himself a Communist. But can a Communist promote the occupation of his country and the plunder of its national wealth?! He has no illusions in respect to the close-knit anti-Japanese bloc. He knows perfectly well that this is an effective force, but prefers to leave Chiang Kai-shek face to face with the Japanese and their puppets. His own resistance is limited to guerrilla warfare.

October 18–October 20, 1944

The Central Government appointed the militarist Yen Hsi-shan commander in chief of the military area which had long been under his actual command.

Chiang Kai-shek did this to prevent Yen Hsi-shan's troops going over to the Japanese. He often met with him and summoned him to his headquarters.

Yen Hsi-shan did not desert to the Japanese; he maintained secret commercial ties with them, preserving his independence of the Chungking administration.

Using Chiang Kai-shek's military failures, the Special Area's troops defeated Yen Hsi-shan with the only aim to expand the territory under their control. Yen Hsi-shan did not represent a threat to the Special Area because of his weakness and formal affiliation with the united anti-Japanese front. . . .

Chungking is alarmed with growing understanding between the CCP leadership and the Observer Group. . . .

Americans believe conditions are ripe for troop landing in China, since this will be the most effective rebuff to the successful Japanese advance. Americans are deeply convinced that in some maritime provinces CCP troops are ready to prepare (or are preparing) strongholds for allied landing parties.

October 22, 1944

Chou En-lai is actually setting up his own intelligence apparatus group not subordinated to the Ching-pao-chu. The main figures in the apparatus are Liu Shao-wen (alias Chang Ming) and Chen Chia-kang. Making him independent of Kang, the apparatus ensures Chou secret political contacts with other countries, which is especially valuable for Mao Tse-tung.

He constantly seeks the counsel of Chou, who has his own information on practically every political question and who knows things people prefer to keep secret. Chou shows much care for his staff. Doubtless, Chou is an exception among the top rankers. He has a big apparatus of his own people competent in economics and politics. Of special value are his strong and varied contacts with the Americans and the British. He has even greater sympathies with the British. The evenings I spent at Mao Tse-tung's place, where people drank much, joked, and laughed, enabled me to learn something on this score.

It wouldn't be an exaggeration to say Chou has, in a sense, his own organization connected not only by official but also by personal relations within the party and state machinery of the CCP.

October 24, 1944

Ma Hai-te persistently tries to become Yeh Chien-ying's doctor. Chief of Staff Yeh Chien-ying is informed of all plans of the CCP leadership.

Ma Hai-te does his utmost (and succeeds) to accompany Yeh Chien-ying when the latter goes hunting. . . .

Ma Hai-te spends evenings in the company of his American colleagues.

October 28, 1944

The Americans report fierce fighting with the Japanese in the Philippines. The Japanese Navy has suffered a crushing defeat off the Philippines. . . .

Churchill spoke in the House of Commons yesterday. His subject was Poland.

The four-star general got a knockout from the two-star general. Stilwell has the highest rank in the American Army. He is a full general. The American armed forces now have only six full generals.

The four-star general wound up his business and left for the United States. Well done, Hurley! Here is a go-between for you! . . .

Using America's political recognition of the Special Area, Mao wants to set two Great Powers at loggerheads and to profit at their expense. This is his clear-cut tactic. . . .

The CCP leadership is firmly convinced it is impossible to conquer Japan without liberating northern China. Northern China is covered with a network of CCP bases. That is why, it is believed in Yenan, cooperation with CCP troops is unavoidable. . . .

During my rare meetings with Americans (we avoid political talks) I learned something of William Bullitt (cannot forget his pogromlike speech against the Soviet Union). An offspring of a rich family, he is a fairly well known politician and diplomat of Roosevelt's New Deal. He was the American ambassador to Moscow and Paris. Connected with Roosevelt by close friendship and is said to be one of the President's foreign affairs aides. It is noteworthy that such a rabid anti-Sovietist can still be found among the American political bosses! . . .

I think the aim of Bullitt's statement is to convince Roosevelt to review his policy in respect to the Soviet Union.

David Barrett is a balanced and prudent politician. Even if he talks much, he reveals nothing important. Likes jokes and is good-natured. . . . Apparently, one of the principles of his work is the more acquaintances you have, the better. Chinese comrades said Barrett told them of his dream—a big house in Florida, a magnificent orchard, and fruit trade. . . .

November 1944

November 1, 1944

A truce has been concluded in Moscow between the Soviet Union and Bulgaria.

On October 27 the Japanese launched a new large-scale offensive. Its aims are obvious: to seize a railway, destroy General Chennault's air fleet's bases, prevent the joining of allied forces in China's coastal areas, and undermine the power of the Central Government.

Chiang Kai-shek has appointed American Major General Albert C. Wedemeyer chief of his staff. Major General Wedemeyer commanded troops in Burma.

General Shunroku Hata is the commander in chief of the Japanese expeditionary army in China. His headquarters is at Nanking.

———

Chiang Kai-shek has taken a decision to send a special mission to Moscow. It will be led by Chiang Ching-kuo, son of the head of the state.

Chiang is a sophisticated and dangerous politician. He understands very well that the solution of the Far East problem depends not only on Chungking, Yenan, and Washington and makes quite a logical move. . . .

The choice of young Chiang Ching-kuo is not only due to the feelings of kinship. Back in 1924, when the Kuomintang co-operated with

Okano (Nosaka) at a press conference with foreign journalists in Yenan.

Foreign correspondents inspecting the hospital in Yenan. A. Y. Orlov is in the center, George Hatem (Ma Hai-te) on extreme right.

July 22, 1944. The arrival in Yenan of an American air force plane with members of the U. S. Army Observer Group.

In the center: Colonel David Barrett, head of the team.

The welcoming ceremony for the members of the Observer Group at the airport.

The American plane, which was damaged at landing, is being hauled to the runway.

the CCP, Chiang Kai-shek's son went to the Soviet Union to study. In Moscow he successively completed a secondary school and the Frunze Military Academy.

On April 12, 1927, in Shanghai, Chiang Kai-shek carried out a counterrevolutionary coup.

The coup marked the final departure of the Kuomintang from the principles of Sun Yat-sen and led to a protracted struggle between the Kuomintang and the CCP.

In the same year, 1927, Chiang Ching-kuo condemned his father's counterrevolutionary actions and broke with him.

In 1937 the Civil War concluded with the creation of the anti-Japanese united front (the events in Sian). Chiang Ching-kuo entered into correspondence with his father.

In his reply to his son, Chiang Kai-shek wrote that at the moment it was not worth going into the analysis of the events that had led to the family quarrel; the important thing now was to decide to return to the country, and as for the future—let us make no guesses, we should see what we should see; youth has a peculiar children's disease of its own, and it was fancy . . .

Chiang Kai-shek proved correct. His son gradually betrayed his political ideals and became a loyal assistant to his father.

Chiang Kai-shek, deciding on young Chiang Ching-kuo's mission to Moscow, took into account, first and foremost, his son's knowledge of Soviet society. It is to be assumed that Chiang Ching-kuo carries with him convincing evidence on the state of affairs in the united resistance movement against the Japanese aggressor.

November 3, 1944

Everything has been gathered in from the fields: buckwheat, kaoliang, millet. Everything to a single ear. Threshing is now in full swing at the small peasant farmsteads, and the wind is scattering the dust from threshing around. A good harvest . . .

In the morning hoarfrost decorated the bushes, the rocks, and the scanty grass. The first snow can be expected in two or three weeks' time. . . .

And in Moscow snow will have fallen by then, and snowstorms will be swirling around. . . .

Attempts to check the Japanese advance have been unsuccessful.

On October 30 the Japanese took the town of Pai-yang, and yesterday they captured Kuei-hsien.

The news about the special mission of Chiang Kai-shek's son alarmed the Chairman of the CCP Central Committee and served as a cause for several meetings with me.

I once more saw for myself how hospitable this man could be when he needed you. In general Mao behaves with me as though he has no secrets to hide from me and as though we are people of like mind and old comrades-in-arms. All conventions have long since been cast away, and Chiang Ching behaves simply and with ease. Quite often Mao has discussed urgent matters in my presence, and sometimes even consulted me. More than once I have been a participant of friendly parties.

However, I know very well that after Moscow's intervention in the Wang Ming affair and a number of other circumstances, Mao regards me, if not as an enemy, then as a serious hindrance. His tactic consists in leading Moscow into error through me. So, in this sense, I am even valuable and suitable for him. . . .

At Mao Tse-tung's request I sent a telegram to Moscow.

In this message the Chairman of the CCP Central Committee reports that the fighting efficiency of the Eighth Route and the New Fourth armies has markedly increased. These armies now have more successful combat operations to their credit. A part of the troops and political, party, and military specialists are now being transferred to Hunan, Chekiang, and Honan.

The Chairman of the CCP Central Committee reports about the enhanced military and propaganda and agitation work in industrial-economic and other major centers and on the main supply routes in the rear of the Japanese fascists. The forthcoming winter will be used for the active field training of regular units of the Eighth Route and the New Fourth armies and of People's Corps and self-defense detachments. In this way the bases will be strengthened and losses inflicted upon the Japanese.

The power and prestige of the Communist Party steadily and irresistibly increase. The policy of the party remains invariable. It consists in strengthening, improving, and enlarging its forces and, besides, in continuing political co-operation with the Kuomintang. The strength of the Eighth Route and the New Fourth armies has sharply increased during the last few months. Its total strength in the bases and in the Japanese rear now amounts to about 570,000, not 470,000. In the

People's Corps there are now 2.2 million men, not 2 million as before.

Then the Chairman of the CCP Central Committee writes about the Kuomintang's being reactionary, rotten, and doomed, but that this will not affect the Communist Party's policy, which throughout the anti-Japanese resistance period has been and will remain invariable.

Mao Tse-tung complains that all the attempts to come to terms with Chiang Kai-shek have failed. The armed forces of the Kuomintang are suffering defeats and do not want to fight against the Japanese invaders. General Hurley, the personal envoy of President Roosevelt, approves of the CCP's policy and supports all its proposals. Of the same view also is the foreign press, whose representatives have in the main already visited Yenan and comment most favorably on the CCP policy and the state of affairs in the Special Area. The aim of Chiang Ching-kuo's special mission is to probe the Soviet Union's attitude to the Special Area. It is not without meaning that Chiang Kai-shek sends the one of his sons who has received education in the Soviet Union. . . .

I added my comment to the telegram.

First, the figures are far-fetched. The actual strength of the CCP's armed forces is by far less. To give overstated personnel numbers for the armies and the People's Corps is now advantageous to the CCP leaders.

Secondly, Mao Tse-tung is afraid of being exposed as insincere. Chiang Kai-shek has available evidence of the actual attitude of the CCP leadership to the anti-Japanese united front.

And thirdly, the mission of Chiang Ching-kuo may in general bring to light a number of unfavorable aspects in the policy of the CCP leadership. Mao Tse-tung tries to defend himself in advance.

November 4, 1944

The Japanese offensive is successfully developing in the direction of Kweilin-Liuchow along the West River. The Japanese forces are estimated at 350,000 men.

In the middle of this year Yeh Chien-ying delivered a report before a group of foreign and Chinese newsmen. In October, as a follow-up on this report, there came out the book *A General Survey of the Anti-Japanese Democratic Bases of China* (Yenan: Liberation Publishers, 1944).

I am completing the translation of this book. Here is the list of the anti-Japanese democratic bases in China (liberated areas):

I. The Special Border Region of Shensi-Kansu-Ningsia
II. *North China:*
  1. The border region of Shansi-Chahar-Hopeh
  2. The border region of Hopeh-Jehol-Liaoning
  3. The Shantung base
  4. The border region of Shansi-Hopeh-Shantung-Honan
  5. Western Honan
  6. Shansi-Honan
  7. The Shansi-Sui-yuan base
III. *Central China:*
  1. Northern Kiangsu
  2. Central Kiangsu
  3. Southern Kiangsu
  4. The border region of Hupeh-Honan-Anhwei
  5. Huai-pei (north of the Huai River in Anhwei province)
  6. The border region of Anhwei-Kiangsi
  7. Eastern Chekiang
  8. The border region of Kiangsu-Chekiang
IV. *South China:*
  1. The border region of Chekiang-Kiangsi
  2. The border region of Hunan-Hupeh
  3. Hainan Island
  4. The Tung kiang region (the basin of the Tung River, near Canton)

A fairly brisk traffic is going on along the air bridge Yenan-Chungking, and Yenan has been pretty busy receiving visitors. Not a day goes by without a Douglas appearing over the valley on a landing approach. . . . This time the visitors are John Paton Davies, a political adviser to Wedemeyer's staff, and a certain White.

Mao would have me believe that talks with the Americans are an attempt, if not to fool them, then in any case to blackmail Chiang Kai-shek. In this vein he comments on all the proposals of the CCP and the Americans which become known to me.

John Davies would waste no time. He has already had meetings with Po Ku, Yeh Chien-ying, Chou En-lai, Chu Teh, and a number of other responsible Chinese comrades. Barrett is also very active and is everywhere received as a dear and welcome guest.

The CCP leaders associate this new wave of activity from the American group of observers with the developments in relations with Chungking. Chiang Kai-shek has refused to yield to the pressure from the Americans anymore and taken an uncompromising stand toward Yenan. The Americans' chief man on the Chinese scene—General Stilwell—has been recalled to the United States. Barrett has been interested in knowing how these developments will tell upon the policy of the CCP.

From conversations with the political adviser to Wedemeyer's staff the following has become clear, too.

The United States is worried by the possibility of the growth of ties between the Special Area and the Soviet Union. It is particularly worried at the prospect of these ties developing into a close economic and political alliance.

If after the end of World War II "the Soviet Union limits her domination" (so said Davies, and the Chinese comrades calmly listened to that) to the northern latitudes of the Pacific Ocean, there is nothing terrible in that for the United States. The difficulty is that the Soviet Union may push beyond these limits and do so precisely via the Special Area. The United States is most of all alarmed by the prospect of the spread of Soviet influence to the entire Asian continent (so far as I know, none of the Chinese comrades tried to dispute this statement of Davies', either).

The United States is prepared to co-operate with the Special Area but fears that the Soviet Union will simply avail herself of the fruits of the American policy of strengthening the economy and armed forces of the CCP.

Davies in every way made it clear that there were no other reasons for restricting the United States' alliance with the Special Area, and, if there are any, they were unimportant.

Davies explained that the Americans' aims were always the same— to trade. They were totally unconcerned as to who they would have to trade with after the war. It might be the Special Area alone or two separate parts of China. What mattered in the given situation was the independence of the Special Area as an economic and political structure from the Soviet Union. Only if the Special Area had complete state independence would the United States be able to be a partner of the CCP and would not fear the consequences of this rapprochement.

Davies stated plainly that he had expressed not his own personal opinion, but the quite definite views of the American leaders, although they were not on record for understandable reasons.

Circumstances of which I had not known came to light during these talks. The Americans have no doubts about the acceptability of a firm alliance with Mao Tse-tung. They are not even disturbed by the Communist Party as the leading force of the Special Area and possibly of the China of the future. For them it is extremely important that the CCP should be "sovereign and independent of Moscow." This already presupposes certain nationalistic aspects in the policy of the CCP. In a word, "nationalistic socialism" in the Special Area or in China suits Washington. This amounts to an open recognition of the nationalistic tendencies in the policy of the CCP leadership.

However, the circumstances are much more complex than Davies and Mao presume. There is the Communist Party, with which Mao has to reckon despite everything, and there is the force of objective historical factors. . . .

In the Americans' actions there is a desire to drive a wedge between the CCP and the Soviet Communist Party, between the Soviet Union and the Special Area. It is characteristic that such desires receive no rebuff here. A haggle is taking place, and the price is the biggest issue. . . .

Colonel Barrett and adviser Davies handed the CCP military command their own draft plan for a landing operation. This operation is being planned in the Lienyunkang area.

The draft is verbose and incoherent. The use of airborne and amphibious troops is envisaged. During the operation the Americans would supply CCP forces with ammunition and weapons for fifty thousand men. A part of the weapons and ammunition would be dropped from planes. For the remainder CCP troops would need to go to the area of landing of the American force.

Barrett and Davies are pressing the Chinese comrades for an answer. It is important for them to know to what extent CCP troops are ready to take part in carrying out the given operation. The draft plan is being finalized at joint meetings of American and Chinese representatives in an atmosphere of deep secrecy.

In all these circumstances Mao clearly discerns a happy opportunity for a push for power. The ending of the World War, national enthusiasm, the American interest, and Chiang Kai-shek's setbacks—the situation becomes as favorable as can be. I never saw him so elated. . . .

He regards the tragedies of his people with a light heart, if they do not have an adverse effect on his personal plans.

It should be acknowledged that they drink quite a lot at Mao's evening parties. Not every stout-headed fellow can hold so much. . . .

John Davies is the second secretary at the American embassy in Chungking. I have the impression that he is more experienced than Service and has a deeper insight into problems.

He is very energetic and has a perfect command of Chinese.

A lean person with a long face and a little too broad mouth. Brown-haired.

November 5, 1944

Donald Nelson will again visit China as Roosevelt's personal representative. Nelson will be accompanied by eminent economists and industrialists. . . .

White has arrived in Yenan by plane together with Davies. Maybe he is Theodore White—the Far Eastern commentator for major American magazines? . . .

Theodore White's stories were always distinguished by a good knowledge of the Chungking political kitchen.

If that's the selfsame White, then I am translating one of his surveys at this moment.

White writes about the myths created in the American or European conception of China.

One of the myths has been created by seamen and tourists who never went beyond the port haunts of Hong Kong or Canton. These people believe that the Chinese are "beasts" and that "the right thing to do is to keep them always within the gunboat firing range." Such "China experts" say: "East is East, and West is West, and thank God for it."

Another myth is that offered by Madame Chiang Kai-shek. She would have us believe that the Chinese are courteous, subtle, etc. And that there is nothing bad about China altogether. No division, no corruption, no famine. The morale of the people is very high.

And, finally, the point of view of the Special Area. According to this point of view, the Chungking Government is a band that becomes fascistlike. There is no democracy, nor can there be. It's all a fiction. Chungking is rotten all through, and the Army does not want to fight against the Japanese.

But this point of view is not the full truth. . . .

White writes further about the three most important forces of China.

1. Chiang Kai-shek and the Kuomintang. Chiang Kai-shek strives to reconcile national traditions with the West and unite China.

2. The feudal militarists, whose domination is based on the oppressed and rightless peasantry.

3. The Communists, whose influence so far is not as great as the Kuomintang's. The Communists believe that China is backward, that it is necessary to rebuild her, and that then she will become a powerful state. In this their program coincides with that of the Kuomintang. However, the Communists ask the question: "But who is to raise China for this great cause?" And answer: "The peasantry and working class!"

The Communists do not rule out their co-operation with the Kuomintang within the framework of a coalition government. . . .

In making up my reports it is important, at all costs, to cover the substance of events, be able to record them on paper, and then, after hasty editing, transmit the reports to Moscow! . . .

And I heap rough, unpolished phrases into the endless lines of my reports.

November 7, 1944

And here is Hurley himself! He arrived without notice, suddenly.

The Chairman of the CCP Central Committee hastily went to the airfield in his antiquated ambulance car.

Hurley waited for him near the plane.

They drove back together. Rattling on the pits and bumps, in a cloud of dust, the car rolled past me. . . .

Hurley started talks without delay. Already in the evening he met with Mao Tse-tung, Chu Teh, Chou En-lai, and Yeh Chien-ying, who specialize in negotiations with the Americans. Patrick Hurley's interpreter was the leader of the U. S. Army Observer Group. . . .

Hurley handed Mao Tse-tung a list of questions to be discussed (and his own suggestions on the solution of each of them). The CCP leadership would study this draft and express their opinion tomorrow.

General Hurley informed those present that he had been sent to China on a mission by President Roosevelt with the consent of the head of the Central Government. "But my aim," stated the envoy of the White House, "has nothing to do with the establishment of relations between the United States and the Chinese Communist Party. And we shall not discuss this subject at these talks. Now of paramount importance for the successful conclusion of the World War is the unity of China, and, consequently, the settlement of disputes between the two main political groups: the Communist Party and the Kuomintang."

Toward midnight the CCP leadership gave a splendid banquet in honor of the twenty-seventh anniversary of the October Revolution. Hurley was a dear guest of honor. In fact, it was a reception in his honor. . . .

November 8, 1944

Hurley's talks with the CCP leaders.

Major General Patrick Hurley is a former Secretary of War, a millionaire lawyer from Oklahoma.

At yesterday's banquet he, obviously to seem more important, remarked inadvertently that a while ago he had been offered the post of ambassador to Russia. . . . Hurley had attended the Tehran Conference. He is one of Roosevelt's confidential persons. . . .

Outwardly Hurley is good-natured, impetuous, and impatient, probably a little less than 180 cm. tall. He is lean, with thick graying hair. Well groomed and self-confident with slightly eccentric manners . . .

In my opinion the most unhappy person in Yenan is the driver of Mao Tse-tung's antiquated car. The Chairman of the CCP Central Committee highly values this possibility of meeting guests in a car.

God knows how much the driver is pottering with this vehicle, but Mao needs it very much for his prestige. And indeed how can one possibly imagine him jolting along on horseback. . . .

November 10, 1944

Roosevelt re-elected President of the United States.

Over 24 million votes were cast for Roosevelt, and over 21 million for the profascist and anti-Soviet Dewey! . . .

In all languages of the world the radio speaks of the flight of fascists from Germany by secret routes via neutral states. . . .

Mao Tse-tung presented me with a copy of Chiang Kai-shek's book *China's Destiny*. Handing it to me, he called the author a dirty name, which does not lend itself to translation.

Mao Tse-tung told me with irritation that China's historical past could not be distorted by Chiang Kai-shek.

"An old rascal!" Mao Tse-tung said about Chiang Kai-shek and remarked angrily: "It was Wang Ming who preached that Chiang Kai-shek was the leader of the Chinese resistance movement!"

The present interpretation by the Chairman of the CCP Central Committee of the cheng-feng and the intraparty struggle of 1940–43 (the "Moscow group," the "dogmatists," the anti-Sovietism, and the anti-Comintern actions) is curious.

"Wang Ming is a renegade, a Communist who went back on Marxism-Leninism."

"By criticism and exposures we waged an active struggle to keep the party free from careerists and alien elements, from petty-bourgeois rubbish, and to prevent departures from the party line. We reorganized our ranks for the purpose of waging a successful struggle against the Japanese invaders and the aggressiveness of Chiang Kai-shek. We fought relentlessly against the capitulationist ideology of making concessions to the reactionary Kuomintang. Those people (internationalists, 'dogmatists') believed the Kuomintang (and not a word about the anti-Japanese united front, the vital need for joint rebuff to the invaders!). We brought them to heel! We frankly told the party that we should not be afraid of expanding the liberated areas at the expense of the territories held by the Japanese (everything is distorted, altered, and fitted into 'theory'!). We are waging a struggle against the exclusive leadership of the war by the Kuomintang."

It is obvious that all these questions have arisen in view of the preparations for the next party congress. . . .

Yesterday a draft agreement between the Communist Party and the Kuomintang was considered. At the insistence of General Hurley, the agreement will be given the character of an official treaty between the Communist Party and the Kuomintang. Patrick Hurley assumed the task of mediation.

It is assumed that the treaty will be sealed by the signatures of Mao Tse-tung and Chiang Kai-shek.

The treaty envisages the unification of all the anti-Japanese parties and political organizations, including nonparty organizations. This government must guarantee the right of free and open existence to all anti-Japanese patriotic forces, as well as to the Communist Party and the Kuomintang.

Under the treaty, the Military Council is to be reorganized into a Joint Council. All the major anti-Japanese armed groups will be represented in this Joint Council. The council must strictly observe the principle of proportional distribution of arms and ammunition supplied by the Allies among the anti-Japanese armed groups.

A joint national government of China, to be formed mainly from representatives of the Communist Party and the Kuomintang, will see its supreme goal in rallying all the patriotic forces of the country (armed forces, above all) for defeating the Japanese invaders. After victory this government is to start developing the country on the basis of the principles of Dr. Sun Yat-sen.

All the anti-Japanese patriotic armed groups must unquestioningly obey the decrees of the Joint National Government. The highest executive military organ will be the Joint Military Council, whose orders will be binding on all the anti-Japanese armed forces.

It is assumed that the third signature under the treaty will be that of General Hurley as the representative of the President of the United States.

On the night of November 9 in Yenan a meeting of the Central Committee was called which approved the draft agreement between the Communist Party and the Kuomintang. The document was sealed by General Hurley and the Chairman of the CCP Central Committee with their signatures.

In the evening on November 10 Patrick Hurley left for Chungking. Together with the envoy of President Roosevelt flew Colonel Barrett and member of the Politburo of the CCP Central Committee Chou En-lai. . . .

November 11, 1944

The Chairman of the CCP Central Committee is very pleased by the meeting with General Hurley. Mao Tse-tung invited me to come round to brief me on the outcome of the talks. He was in a cheerful and jesting mood.

Mao Tse-tung asked me to wire a number of telegrams to Moscow. He certainly understands that I have heard sufficiently much of the talks held between the CCP leadership and the personal representative of the American President. He hastens to forestall my reports to Moscow. . . .

November 12, 1944

Apart from intelligence work in the Special Area, the Observer Group has been taking steps to weaken the links between the CCP and Moscow. From the outset the Americans appear to have harbored no illusions—they have been cautious about giving arms to the Communists. Chiang Kai-shek has suited and continues to suit them. The CCP leaders gave themselves fully away, however. They had forgotten about everything, even about the concealment of their squalid actions —so anxious they were to get military equipment.

The purpose of Hurley's mission was not only to induce the Special Area to vigorous action against the Japanese, but to drive a wedge between the CCP leadership and Moscow.

However, the CCP leaders managed to get around the personal representative of the President and included in the draft treaty their own clauses, which Chiang Kai-shek is sure to refuse to accept.

An excessively self-confident man, Patrick Hurley, not understanding the contradictions between the Kuomintang and the CCP and basing himself on his enormous powers, affixed his signatures to four copies of the draft treaty. One was left in Yenan, two went to Chiang Kai-shek and Roosevelt, and the fourth I believe Hurley reserved for himself as a keepsake. . . . A poor souvenir for Hurley and American diplomacy.

November 13, 1944

In regard to the peasantry in the liberated areas of China the Communist Party is pursuing a policy of lowering rent and reducing usurious interest (the landlords seek to live by rent).

In 1931–34, in the opinion of the Chairman of the CCP Central Committee, the party pursued a leftist policy in the countryside: a policy of giving no land to the landlords and only poor land to the kulaks.

Mao Tse-tung says that the party cannot at the moment carry out the whole of reforms to solve the peasant question, but that the time will come when each land tiller will have his own plot of land.

November 14, 1944

On the morning of November 10 General Hurley by a personal letter informed the Chairman of the CCP Central Committee of his deep satisfaction over the results of the talks.

Hurley expressed the hope that the brilliant spirit of co-operation that marked the negotiations would also be kept up after the victory over Japan and serve to promote peace and a democratic future for China. In this the American President's envoy sees the noble aim of his mission.

He thanks Mao Tse-tung for his brilliant co-operation. Honest leadership by the Chairman of the CCP Central Committee resulted in the draft agreement between the CCP and the Kuomintang. This draft is above all the result of personal participation by Mao Tse-tung and has been confirmed by a concrete decision of the Communist Party.

The President's envoy thanks Mao Tse-tung for the confidence displayed. It greatly touched the general, who begs to believe him that he is well aware of how much sincere feeling and understanding was shown by Mao Tse-tung. A most difficult problem was solved. The draft agreement between the CCP and the Kuomintang was passed on to Chairman Chiang Kai-shek without delay.

The President's envoy expresses gratitude for the wise letter which the Chairman of the CCP Central Committee wrote to the President of the United States and which he (Hurley) was asked to hand over to President Roosevelt personally.

The general writes that the activity of the Chairman of the CCP Central Committee contributes to the cause of a united and democratic China and the victorious conclusion of the war.

In his letter to the American President Mao Tse-tung speaks of the traditional friendship between the two nations. This friendship has deep historical roots.

The Chairman of the CCP Central Committee wishes the President good health and expresses his most cherished hope that after the victorious end of the war the two great nations (Chinese and American) will march forward shoulder to shoulder in building up world peace. This path of joint construction of a new world is possible if the President wishes to follow it.

The Chairman of the Central Committee informs the President that he received the President's envoy in a proper manner. For three days he and General Hurley discussed important questions. These were the united resistance by the Chinese people to the aggressor, the political unification of anti-Japanese forces within the framework of the national government, and the democratization of China.

The Chairman of the Central Committee writes that the Communist Party has always striven for a firm agreement with Chiang Kai-shek. Such an agreement would express the hopes of the Chinese people and help promote their happiness and their best interests.

General Hurley's visit met our hopes. We received a sudden opportunity to achieve our aims. As a result of the three-day talks, a draft agreement was adopted. This draft embodies the aims for which the Communist Party has been waging a persistent struggle. This struggle has been going on for eight years now. The base for this struggle is the anti-Japanese united front.

The Central Committee of our party unanimously endorsed this treaty.

Mao Tse-tung writes further that he is grateful to General Hurley for the sympathies the latter showed for the Chinese nation and in general was extremely glad to see General Hurley and deeply appreciated his outstanding abilities.

The Communist Party will do everything in its power to get the principles of the treaty implemented. The Central Committee of the party authorized me (Mao Tse-tung) to sign the accord between the CCP and the Kuomintang. The accord was signed in the presence of your representative.

Mao Tse-tung reports that at his request General Hurley promised to hand over a copy of the treaty to the American President.

Mao Tse-tung thanks the American President for his assistance in the anti-Japanese struggle, his support in uniting the country, and his sincere concern for democracy. He expresses this gratitude on behalf of the Chinese people, the Communist Party, and its armed forces.

The letter was written following a suggestion by General Hurley, who assured the Chairman of the CCP Central Committee that he would personally hand it over to President Roosevelt.

November 15, 1944

Acting U. S. Secretary of State Edward R. Stettinius has declared that U. S. Ambassador to China Clarence Gauss has been recalled, but that a new ambassador has not yet been named by the President. So far Gauss is in Chungking.

The head of the puppet Nanking Government, Wang Ching-wei, has passed away. Opportunely so, as he would not have escaped a trial by the Chinese people.

Patrick Jay Hurley is sixty-one. He is a lawyer by profession and holds a doctor's degree in law. A veteran of World War I, at the end of which he reached the rank of colonel. He was heavily wounded in the battle on the Marne. . . . In 1943 he became the personal representative of President Roosevelt in the Middle East, India, and China. Now, with the rank of major general, he is the President's personal representative in China. . . .

Mao is lazy. A sofa and an armchair are about all he needs for leisure. He has a weakness for delicious food, and he eats a lot. He receives special supplies of fruit and nuts, which are of the best quality.

Lately, however, Mao has abstained from midnight parties. He has narrowed his circle of guests. Only a select few can now be seen at his table.

Chiang Ching has an air of independence about her and is quick to find her way to unfamiliar questions. She is inquisitive and ambitious, but ably conceals it. She places her own interests above everything else.

Mao Tse-tung is fully under her influence. He can't stand even a short absence of his wife. Orlov told me that without Chiang Ching he would become capricious and sometimes even refuses to have his temperature taken or to take his medicines.

Chiang Ching dexterously and unobtrusively pushes on her husband to solving the most diverse questions, which are far from being family matters. . . .

November 16, 1944

If the Chairman of the CCP Central Committee engages in his iniquitous deeds, he uses me as a screen. I am to wire his telegrams to Moscow.

Mao Tse-tung is well aware that the Special Area is not yet so independent a political and military force as to be able to discard the support of the Soviet Union. Therefore, Mao Tse-tung hastens to inform Moscow, so to speak, "at first hand." This mode of action pursues another aim, too. After a telegram from the Chairman of the CCP

Central Committee I would be in an awkward position to offer a different opinion.

In addition to the telegrams sent, the Chairman of the CCP Central Committee also asked me to wire to Moscow the message of thanks from General Hurley. . . .

After the prescription affair and Moscow's intervention, Mao Tsetung is always on his guard with me, although he tries carefully to conceal it. I am an eyewitness, in fact the only eyewitness who is beyond his will and power. Mao tries to "neutralize" me by his feigned confidence and his invitations to intimate evenings at his house (Mao, his wife, myself, and often no one else).

November 18, 1944

The Japanese are rapidly advancing along the railway west of Kweilin toward Kweichow province. They are already somewhere near Lucheng and Hsin-cheng. The Chinese command has evacuated a large air base in Liuchow (Kwangsi province). The Americans employed all their transport means available to rescue valuable equipment.

Donald Nelson has arrived in Chungking.

Chinese Finance Minister Kung Hsien-hsi has paid a visit to the White House.

Roosevelt has announced that he has chosen an American ambassador to China but has refused so far to name him.

The United States has set all its political, diplomatic, and military resources in motion to achieve the promptest solution of the Far East problem in her own interests. . . .

When the "lifeline" (or "Stilwell ways") becomes operational, the Americans promise to increase sharply their supply of trucks, artillery, ammunition, and other weapons and munitions on a lend-lease basis. In the eighth year of the war China lacks even the simplest arms.

The Chinese Communist Party is far from being a mass party for a people numbering over 500 million. The rottenness of the Kuomintang regime is not yet the strength of the Communist Party, but rather a favorable factor which it is necessary to use extensively for the purpose of the creation and cohesion of new party units. This factor is extremely advantageous for the qualitative and quantitative strengthening of the CCP.

The present policy of the CCP leadership deliberately ignores these favorable conditions and is aimed at sharpening relations with the Kuomintang. Such a policy hampers propaganda and organizational work to promote Communist Party interests in the country, strengthens the occupationists' and traitors' positions, and adds to the country's economic difficulties. Essentially this policy again presupposes assistance from the Soviet Union. . . .

What is most surprising is that the CCP has no clearly defined and consistent action program, apart from its leadership's persistent striving for the seizure of power in the country. The situation calls in the first place for thorough and painstaking work to win over the majority of the working class and indeed the whole people of China, as well as for fostering the workers' political consciousness. So far the Chinese Communist Party clearly yields to the Kuomintang in numbers and influence and represents a party with a conspicuously immature and putschist program.

There's a smoldering adventurist desire in the CCP leadership for civil war without regard for the objective factors, and there's the risky game of playing with the destinies of the revolution instead of revolutionary work and a program of action. The lives of hundreds of thousands of Chinese Communists have already become expendable in this game.

November 19, 1944

No doubt, the need to maintain relations with Moscow irritates Mao. He is prepared to break off all his ties with us if only . . . And so these ifs keep him from doing it and make him dissemble and maneuver. Everything international, of which the Comintern was an embodiment and which helped develop the socialist movement in China, was for Mao only fetters or tactical conventions. Now Moscow has become that.

But these damned ifs! What if the Kuomintang unleashes an armed conflict with the CCP? What if a civil war breaks out, with the CCP unprepared for it, with no arms.

And how many such ifs! And the resolution of most of the ifs practically depends on the attitude of the Soviet Union. This Mao Tse-tung understands and therefore, while relying upon support from Moscow, keeps denigrating the Soviet Communist Party's policy in an underhand way. He fears that this enforced (for him) contact will foster in the party and the people sympathies for the Soviet Union.

The very nature of the Communist movement also noticeably influences Mao Tse-tung's conduct. The Communists wholeheartedly believe in the cause of their country's liberation from the fascist invaders. They believe in her socialist future and, in general, understand that it is the policy of the Soviet Union that restricts the class aggressiveness of Chiang Kai-shek. The Chairman of the CCP Central Committee has to reckon with this. In a number of moments he is powerless to change the nature of the processes that are taking place. But how well he adapts himself to them! . . .

At parties held by the Americans whiskey, brandy, rum, gin . . . and, of course, dancing are a great hit.

The Gramophone will surely stick in my memory of Yenan! . . . And the crowding at parties, the hoarse guttural voices, the wheezing of worn-out records, the shuffling of feet, the hot sweaty faces. . . .

November 20, 1944

By juggling with facts the Chairman of the CCP Central Committee pursues very important aims.

The Communist Party leans upon a considerable military force, which exists also in the shape of a people's corps. Only recently the strength of the People's Corps was estimated at 2 million men. Now in the documents it is arbitrarily increased by 200,000 men. This new figure, 2.2 million, has been reported to both Moscow and the Americans (in regard to us Mao has no scruples either). The lie has been palmed with a definite aim in mind—to convince both Moscow and the Americans that the armed power of the CCP and that of the Kuomintang practically do not differ. This numerical relationship does not reflect the real political situation and leads to an incorrect appraisal of the alignment of forces.

I know quite definitely that the figure of 2 million is false, too. Only recently a far smaller figure was in circulation! Even by a confidential estimate given by Yeh Chien-ying it can by no means exceed 1 million men. But even the chief of staff of the Eighth Route Army also deliberately exaggerates it. By the way, overstatement is the modus operandi of all the responsible army and party workers without exception. One cannot hope to hear the truth here. With Mao's blessing lying becomes a tactic. . . .

In the Americans' military plans the use of amphibious troops occupies the central place. The CCP leadership has also changed its plans accordingly. Now these plans are based on close co-operation with the Americans' operations and envisage the seacoast as battle areas.

Pursuing his tactic of invented figures, Mao Tse-tung has officially reported to Moscow the new strength of the regular CCP army units as being 558,747 men. But this figure includes the strength of large guerrilla groups, too. Thus, the regular Army is actually much smaller. At best, it accounts for 50 per cent of the total figure.

As far as I can see, the leaders themselves do not know the exact number of their troops. In this particular case the CCP leadership had made a differentiated approach to us and the Allies. A figure of 630,000 men was reported to the Americans.

The joint operations of the Americans and the CCP Army, as presumed by Mao Tse-tung, are possible sometime next spring.

On all these questions Mao limited himself to a brief conversation with me. He was standing at the table quickly jotting down columns of characters. A cigarette was smoldering in his mouth. Quietly and in a somewhat slack manner he explained to me the substance of the telegram to be wired to Moscow. It was important for him that there be no disagreement between us. The lies he tried carefully to buttress by the talk of popular upsurge.

Mao was pale and absent-minded. He breathed loudly and heavily. Later, seeing me to the door and glancing at the pure starry sky, he said suddenly that he loved clear frosty nights. He winced at someone's loud voice, and after a moment's silence said: "We've been here for almost ten years now. . . ."

November 23, 1944

Despite the unscrupulous publicizing of their "implacable struggle against Japanese fascism," the Communist Party leaders' actual attitude to this struggle remains invariable.

The latest instructions issued by the Chairman of the CCP Central Committee to division commanders are a testimony to this.

Mao Tse-tung has declared that the paramount task is to deprive Chiang Kai-shek's troops of the possibility of advancing to the seacoast. "The most important task for the CCP forces is to block the areas of our future joint operations with the Allies. Do not let Chiang Kai-shek's troops in pursuit of the Japanese liberate territories."

Mao Tse-tung gave strict orders that large-scale operations should by no means be engaged in against the Japanese. In combat actions the troops must continue to limit themselves to small-scale clashes.

I was told about these instructions of the Chairman of the CCP Central Committee by Chu Teh.

November 25, 1944

The Japanese offensive has assumed the character of a military catastrophe for China. Kweilin was abandoned. The American air force base in Liuchow—the biggest American base in East China—was blown up. Valuable equipment worth tens of millions of dollars was destroyed. With the fall of the air force bases in Kweilin and Liuchow the road is open to the last allied air bases in Chengtu, Chungking, and Kweiyang. Chennault's squadrons are desperately attacking the Japanese assault columns. . . .

The CCP leaders conclude treaties for the sake of deception, without even pretense at fulfilling them.

Mao Tse-tung is doing everything in his power to hinder the Kuomintang from advancing to the west, in order that, under the guise of assistance to the American landing operations, he himself may get the arms and ammunition.

After they are equipped with this matériel, the CCP forces will begin to act according to their own plans, to capture large cities, strategic centers, while at the same time building up the resistance to Chiang Kai-shek. Thus, the "trouble" of driving out the invaders from his country Mao Tse-tung graciously leaves to the Allies, and in future, perhaps, to the Soviet Union, as well. He himself prefers to fight with Chiang Kai-shek for personal rule over the country.

If, for some reason or other, the variant with American landing operations does not work out, the CCP leaders will all the same persist in carrying out their plan, relying only on their own resources and the expected assistance from the Soviet Union which they have never fully ruled out.

There is no talk of North China among Mao Tse-tung's entourage. It is the citadel of the CCP, and they all regard it as their private preserve. In North China, should the plans for capturing the country fail, Mao Tse-tung intends to build his own sovereign and independent state. For it Mao Tse-tung will fight to the last man.

In case of the failure of the "American" and other variants, the CCP leaders keep the Soviet Union "laid aside." They set hopes on the support of the "fraternal Communist Party." Mao Tse-tung has broadly hinted that support is inevitable, since the Soviet Union is not indifferent to the situation in this area.

My working days seem already to be strained to the breaking point. Yet I have to pack more work into them. There's hardly any time left for sleep. . . .

I am looking into my metal mirror—and see that being just forty I look as though I were a full fifty years old. The eyes red, the face wrinkled, and the temples gray . . .

December 1944

December 1, 1944

Stettinius is the new American Secretary of State. Cordell Hull has resigned due to illness.

Charles de Gaulle has arrived in the Soviet Union.

Donald Nelson, Roosevelt's personal representative in Chungking, has supposedly taken up a post as economic adviser to the Chinese Government. This fact by itself shows the place that is being allotted to China in American policy. The United States is evidently out to take the place of Britain and Japan in China and at the same time to set up a new *cordon sanitaire* against the Soviet Union with the hands of the Chinese politicos.

————

With the routing of fascist Germany the economic and military potential of the allied powers will be concentrated on crushing the Japanese aggression. Mao is perfectly aware of this.

The Chairman of the CCP Central Committee is eager to gain a strong foothold at the expense of the United States so as to immediately pounce upon Chiang Kai-shek. The Americans know of Mao Tse-tung's actual intentions. They are hardly likely to give him arms. However, all these Hurleys and Wedemeyers would not mind neutralizing the ideological influence of the Soviet Union on the CCP and becoming the political bandmasters in the Special Area and in all of China.

Mao weighs the prospects of both sides like a huckster and concludes that the Soviet Union, being bled white by the war, will be late for the outcome of the war in the Far East. Besides, by playing with the U. S. Army Observer Group he has the opportunity to exert pressure on the Kuomintang and ensure the safety of his armies and bases. Any possible disagreements with the Americans are only concerned with their attitude to the Kuomintang.

December 5, 1944

Hurley brought a draft agreement to Chungking, which was unacceptable to Chiang Kai-shek. To consent to the agreement for Chiang Kai-shek meant to give up power of his own accord. Hurley realized his mistake after talking with him, but Mao Tse-tung and Roosevelt had already exchanged telegrams of greetings. Hurley seeks a way out of this ticklish situation. Should he brush aside the CCP? No, the Americans are attracted by the idea of using the Communists' armed bases.

Washington is in a hurry to solve the Far Eastern question while the Soviet Union is tied down by the war in the west. All this has rolled up into a tangle of the most controversial desires, which both sides are vainly trying to unwind.

December 6, 1944

Continuing their successful operations, the Japanese are moving large military forces. Numerous troop trains are running along the Tientsin-Tsukow and Peiping-Hankow lines. The CCP leadership always observes these transportations with marked interest. Troop trains move southward from the north. . . .

The Japanese will evidently increase pressure against the armies of the Central Government.

Protsenko has brought over a volume of Lu Hsun in Russian. This is a prewar edition with a preface by Wang Ming. A very clear and convincing preface.

Speaking of the necessity of establishing a single anti-Japanese front, Lu Hsun said: "Let us turn our rifles against the external enemy —this is what counts at present. . . ." It is this struggle that Lu Hsun regarded first of all as the struggle for the existence of the Chinese people.

Lu Hsun had interesting views on the necessity of carrying out a Chinese language reform.

It is from Wang Ming's article that I learned that Lu Hsun was a fervent adherent of the *ta Chung-yu* movement which advocated that the wealth of all the Chinese language groups should be made use of on the basis of a new and simpler alphabet.

Lu Hsun wrote: "These square symbols—the characters—are veritably a political weapon for fooling the people. . . ."

According to Lu Hsun, "Chinese characters are one of the malignant growths on the body of the Chinese people," for knowledge of characters requires up to fifteen years to study even among the well-to-do sections of the population, and even this is not enough to consider oneself literate.

To my mind, Confucianism and the complexity of the written language, besides other factors, are responsible for China's backwardness.

The necessity of knowing how to read and write a definite number of characters—the basis of literacy—hinders the dissemination of all the aspects of knowledge, which becomes the privilege of the elect. This accounts to a certain extent for the primitive education of the personnel. This among other reasons has evidently contributed to China's isolation and the dogmatization of millennium-old canons. In this case I disregard the socioeconomic factors governing historical processes. . . .

Wang Ming corresponded with Lu Hsun and made a special study of problems of culture.

Lu Hsun's article "Shanghai Impressions of 1935" leaves a deep impression.

December 8, 1944

Trains carrying units of Japanese divisions are running only after nightfall and are concentrated on the Siaokan-Hsinyang section of the railway.

December 10, 1944

The CCP Central Committee Chairman closely watches the advances of Soviet troops in the west. He often speaks to me on military topics (he wants to know approximately when the war will be over).

August 7, 1944. Mao Tse-tung and Chu Teh at Yenan Airport expecting a plane with the second team of the Observer Group on board. Seen in the background are members of the first observers' group.

From left to right: Peng Teh-huai, Colonel Barrett, Chu Teh, and John Service.

During the talks between the CCP leadership and the members of the Observer Group. In the foreground: John Service and Chou En-lai.

Nanniwan, August 24, 1944. The Americans inspecting the 359th Brigade of the Eighth Route Army.

At the Central Military Hospital. Ma Hai-te is seen on the left.

Mao Tse-tung talking with Captain Paul Domke, a member of the U.S. Army Observer Group. Chou En-lai is sitting (center).

It goes without saying that of late the CCP leadership has been particularly nice to me and my comrades.

The business deal with the Americans is a certain flop. . . .

Barrett is once again in Chungking. Yesterday he had a long meeting with the Chairman.

General Wedemeyer insisted that Chiang Kai-shek agree to the formation of a coalition government. The general made a special statement to this effect. Chiang Kai-shek has been warned that if he refuses to reorganize the government, the United States will settle this matter without his consent. Washington will establish independent relations with Yenan. These relations will include the supplying of the Special Area with arms, munitions, equipment, etc.

The Americans are spurred on by the fact that the war is nearing its end in the west. They are feverishly striving to establish control over all of China. They want to rule Chungking and Yenan and, finally, to block the Soviet Union in the Far East. And in this respect Mao is playing into their hands. . . .

December 11, 1944

The American President has given orders to speed up the agreement with the Special Area. Major General Wedemeyer has received orders from the White House to meet the CCP leadership. Obviously in the next few days Albert Wedemeyer will appear in Yenan.

Air cargoes will be sent to Yenan as the first measures in keeping with Roosevelt's orders. Several dozen Douglas planes have been singled out for this purpose. I know nothing of the character of the cargoes or their weight.

Generals Wedemeyer and Hurley have made this known to Chou En-lai. Chou has confirmed that the American President has actually given orders to this effect.

December 12, 1944

Life here is full of snares. I may say that I am in a state of constant stress. Attempts to fool or compromise me, attempts to make me drunk, to find out Moscow's true attitude to the events in Yenan; torrents of seemingly naïve but tricky questions; trying to lure me through obliging girls; seeking to make me believe their fabrications, and, last of all, to win my trust are undertaken not so much to get rid of me as to convert me to their way of thinking. No, not to win over to their side, but to make me "one of them" in the full sense of the words. To convince me and force me to believe in everything that Mao advocates, so that in my reports to Moscow I would present Mao's policy as infallible and defend his interests. That's what they're after here!

They already seem to believe that I have adopted their way of thinking. That is why the Chairman "unbosoms himself" so frequently in my presence. But these are not confidential talks with one's comrade— Mao Tse-tung is one of those who weighs every word and action. . . .

I enjoy his "confidence." This is playing at confidence. . . .

There is one thing in which I do yield to Mao, and that is hospitality. He often invites me. And business talks are by no means the reason. . . . Here I utterly abandon my "principled stand." It is silly and absurd to refuse the invitations.

I sleep badly. Very little, and my sleep is restless. If only for a day I could free myself of the tension. Only for a single day!

Fear of the Communist Party gets the upper hand—the Americans refuse to supply it with arms.

This causes Mao Tse-tung to have fits of irritation. Up till now things have been getting no further than making declarations.

The Chairman is losing interest in the Observer Group. The CCP leadership has received a new draft agreement between the Kuomintang and the CCP from Chungking. This is a counterproposition to the draft signed in Yenan by General Hurley and the Chairman. In Chungking they have no intention of sharing power and even less so of giving it up of their own accord. The draft evidently runs counter to Mao's plans.

December 13, 1944

Mao Tse-tung talks of the immediate need for a congress.

Important events are approaching. It is necessary to orient the party, to consolidate the gains of *cheng-ping,* to staff the higher party organs. . . .

After discussing Chiang Kai-shek's counterproposition the CCP leadership began to wonder whether it was reasonable to carry on such negotiations. After heated debates the Chairman ordered that no reaction be shown to Chiang Kai-shek's draft of the contemplated agreement between the CCP and the Kuomintang.

As a retaliatory measure which would place the head of the Central Government in a ticklish situation (for Americans were putting pressure upon him in keeping with Roosevelt's orders), Mao decided to immediately withdraw his representatives to the Kuomintang from Chungking.

Neither Tung Pi-wu nor Chou should return to Chungking—this is also an explicit order of the Chairman.

A clever move. But I am already used to the zigzags of the Yenan diplomacy.

Only a month ago the Chairman wrote to the American President of his constant endeavors to achieve the signing of an agreement with President Chiang Kai-shek. According to Mao Tse-tung, the agreement would bring happiness to the Chinese people. . . .

The departure of Tung Pi-wu and Chou from Chungking will be explained by the need of their regular reporting to their leadership.

December 14, 1944

This is how Mao Tse-tung explained to me the meaning of the foreign policy conducted by the CCP leadership:

1. Every assistance to the development of progressive forces in the country.

2. Isolation of reactionaries and conservatives by means of propaganda and agitation work.

3. Expansion of the liberated areas at the expense of the lands won over from the Japanese.

It is along these lines specifically that the expediency of contacts with the Americans was stressed. Counting on the military assistance of the CCP troops, they would make a number of concessions and exert pressure on Chiang Kai-shek. Naturally nothing was said of the actual aims.

As facts show, contacts with the Americans resulted in failure. The prudent, distrustful course of the more conservative American politicians is gaining the upper hand. The Allies prefer to link the future struggle for political predominance in China with Chiang Kai-shek's system of government for good. Testimony to this effect is the factual refusal of the Allies to equip the Eighth Route and the New Fourth armies with weapons. Evidently the White House has vetoed the prospects of using the Eighth Route and the New Fourth armies as a shock force for routing the Japanese in China. Perhaps the Americans take into account Mao Tse-tung's secret intention of seizing in the course of the struggle new vast areas of the country. Thus negotiations between Yenan and Washington are coming to a deadlock. American politicians take no risk of staking on Mao Tse-tung. The Chungking regime seems more reliable to them from every point of view. However, the growth of the liberation movement will continuously narrow this base. And herein lies their class miscalculation.

The fact that the Americans do not understand the actual state of affairs irritates Mao Tse-tung beyond measure. He has done everything to prove to them rightful character and the necessity of an alliance. He has been frank enough in his views on China's present and future and the role of the CCP at all the stages of the struggle for power.

There is sense, of course, in the stand taken by the Americans (from their point of view). They are well aware of Mao's desire to make use of the moment to snatch a prize. This element is certainly present in Mao's policy. This is a favorite method with him to avail oneself of the situation to grab wherever possible (accompanying this with lavish promises and without tying oneself down with principles). For Mao it is necessary to grab in order to gain in force. As for how to use this force, he needs no advice on this account. Force is his aim! Force by means of *cheng-ping* repressions, American armaments, demagogical gambling on the liberation sentiments of the Eastern peoples, on Marxism and alleged international friendship with the All-Union Communist Party (Bolsheviks).

Force is the main point of his policy. By means of force he wants to acquire the right to discard all principles.

However, the November negotiations in Yenan between General Hurley and the Chairman have given rise to several unforeseen (by the Americans) prerequisites which are bound to influence the relations between the CCP and the Kuomintang. At the present stage they are apt to aggravate and even sharply deteriorate these relations; this is most certain. And there is nobody to blame for this except General Hurley. It was his mediation that gave Mao Tse-tung the trumps in the political game with Chungking.

Mao Tse-tung has a formal reason for independent political action. For none other than an envoy of the United States, here in Yenan, has approved the platform for a political settlement between the CCP and the Kuomintang. Now, under pressure from Chiang Kai-shek, this platform has been declared unacceptable.

At the future party congress Mao Tse-tung intends to adopt a decision on the formation of a so-called Joint Committee of the Liberated Areas of China. This is also the result of the clumsy mediation of Hurley, who himself cleared the way to this effect by admitting at the Yenan negotiations the necessity of such a body of supreme power for China. And if nothing extraordinary happens, Mao Tse-tung will set up such a committee.

Meanwhile there is only the draft, of which the Americans have been accordingly informed. Mao will use the draft as a bugbear to win them over to his side and consequently to make them give him arms. If the Americans refuse to co-operate in this case as well, Mao intends to split the country and set the stage for a civil war.

In Yenan nobody is worried by the fact that all these intrigues are woven against the background of Japanese gunfire and cries of *"Banzai!"* in the occupied lands of China.

Juggling with Hurley's blunders, the Yenan leadership steps up preparation for the Seventh Congress of the CCP. There is no doubt that it will be held in the next few months. Hurley's rejection of the draft agreement signed in Yenan equips Mao with a whole range of weighty arguments, the chief one being that the alliance between the Communist Party and the Kuomintang is impossible. This argument gives rise to far-reaching conclusions. It is an antedated justification of all of Mao's policy during 1941 to 1944 (the rejection of active struggle against the Japanese invaders, the tactics of breaking up the united anti-Japanese front, the campaign to expose Kuomintang "agents," to unleash a civil war in the atmosphere of Japanese intervention, etc.); that is, it justifies all his sectarian activities.

Now Mao bluntly states that alliance with the reactionary Chiang Kai-shek is out of the question. And he deliberately misinterprets the aims of such an alliance. He alleges that this is a perverted alliance with a class enemy (alliance with the bourgeoisie and imperialists) and refrains from showing the qualitative distinctions of such an alliance for opposition to the aggressor. All over the world the national forces of each country have pooled their strength to rout fascism. But Mao says nothing of this. He speaks again and again of the absurdity of alliance with Chiang Kai-shek as a class enemy, and the shortsightedness of Wang Ming's group which advocated "conciliation" with Kuomintang. He represents the Comintern's tactics as "procapitulation" (tactics for a united anti-Japanese front).

Mao likes to make a show of his class approach to events, but wherever this analysis comes into contradiction with his aims, he winds up with flagrant demagogy. Yet this demagogy, too, follows a specific pattern. It is based on nationalist principles which are handed out under the guise of either patriotism, China's historical peculiarities, or "Marxism of reality." . . .

Mao will certainly tell the whole world that the Joint Committee is not the Chinese Government, that he cannot set up such a government for fear of splitting the united anti-Japanese front. Demagogy once again! Here, in Yenan, they have concocted their own explanation. The Joint Committee is claimed to be merely an effective means of democratizing the country, which will promote the common victory over Japan. Truth and falsehood are blended in these words. . . .

The Joint Committee will turn out to be none other than the second Chinese Government (disregarding, of course, the Japanese puppet government in Nanking). And its formation will result in a most drastic split of China. A split during the war. A split redoubling the people's disaster. . . .

On the other hand, Mao's cherished dream will come true: He will become head of the government and take a most resolute step to unleash a civil war. . . .

Fun is made of Hurley in Yenan. But regardless of anything contacts are maintained with the Americans. Just in case.

December 15, 1944

One cannot help seeing the difference in the sentiments of the CCP leadership and those of rank-and-file party workers. I have noticed that the latter are often dissatisfied with the attempts of the leadership of the Special Area to solve the nationalities problem with the help of the Americans. These Communists regard the political advances of the world's mightiest capitalist power with distrust.

One can often hear the following opinion: "The Americans cannot be interested in a just settlement of the Chinese question. To Communists, they are enemies who have temporarily become allies. Deceiving the Russians, these allies opened up a second front at the end of the war when Germany was already routed by the Red Army. . . ."

December 16, 1944

Mao Tse-tung has made the following statement on the peasant question: In the villages reliance should be made on the poor with a firm alliance with the middle peasant.

He has once again reproached the CCP leadership of the 1931–34 period for their leftist policy in the village. These reproaches are addressed to Po Ku, Lo Fu, and others. . . .

Mao's typical gesture: Screwing up his eyes, he rubs his forehead with the tips of his fingers. . . .

December 17, 1944

Moscow has congratulated me with the awarding of the medal "For the Defense of Moscow."

Whatever Mao does, his entire policy takes into account the assistance of the Soviet Union. In any critical situation this policy envisages the invariable support of the Soviet Union. The surmounting of any political crisis contemplates the decisive interference of the Soviet Union in favor of Yenan.

In his gamble with the Americans Mao was a welcome figure, chiefly in view of the strength of the Eighth Route and the New Fourth armies. But he was backed by the Soviet Union, and this fact made it a particularly tempting game for the Americans. The United States was out to weaken Moscow's position by opposing the CCP to it (and is keeping up this policy; the Army Observer Group has no intention of closing up). Alliance with Mao Tse-tung gives the Americans the opportunity to make a dash for the Soviet Far Eastern frontiers through the CCP bases and bring into life the notorious *"cordon sanitaire* against bolshevism."

The White House decided that the risk was much too great and did not venture to bind itself with an alliance with the CCP.

Why am I so sure of this? December 16 the head of the Observer Group asked to see Yeh Chien-ying and Chu Teh. Barrett replied that unfortunately the leadership of the allied forces in China had no opportunity to equip the Eighth Route and the New Fourth armies with arms.

Barrett stressed that this was the direct result of the obstinacy displayed by the CCP leadership which rejected the draft agreement proposed by the head of the Central Government. "We cannot deliver arms on these terms," said Barrett.

Mao Tse-tung would have made concessions but not where power is concerned. This is a blow to him. For he had intended to profit at least in some way from the Americans.

Parting with Chu Teh and Yeh Chien-ying, Barrett said that the time would probably come when aid would become possible, one only had to have patience.

So the White House decided to collect profits from guaranteed investments. Chiang Kai-shek can celebrate a victory. . . .

December 18, 1944

The Americans and British are retreating in the Ardennes. German tank divisions have delivered a blow from the Aachen-Luxembourg area and broken up the front.

The Tenth Army of the U. S. Air Force under Lieutenant General George Stratemeyer is stationed in India. Some of its units take part in anti-Japanese warfare in China.

The Fourteenth Air Force under Major General C. L. Chennault is wholly based in China. Even before Japan declared war on the United States Chennault was head of the American volunteer pilots in China.

Davies is once again in Yenan.

The Americans indulge in various parties with heavy drinking, urging Chinese comrades to join them.

A certain Berd has arrived with Davies. His insignia show him to be an army major. Berd is a representative of American military intelligence.

All these visits, new figures in the Observer Group, show that the game is in progress. Meanwhile the Americans are lying low, weighing the pros and cons. Energetic military and political reconnoitering of the CCP armed forces and the CCP leadership is going on in the Special Area.

No one is able to foresee the exact developments in the Far East. In this situation both sides prefer to maintain communications.

Berd also takes part in Barrett's meetings with the Yenan leadership.

The Chairman has sent one of his regular telegrams through me to Moscow. He reminds me of a card player playing a game of chance at two tables.

In this telegram the Chairman declares that the Communist Party is now playing a key role in the destiny of China. It is the chief force capable of saving the country and a decisive factor in vanquishing Japanese imperialism. All this is the result of the changes that have shaken China in the last eight months.

The course of events is such that the extent of Kuomintang's and the Communist Party's influence on the country's political life will be redistributed. The degree of the Communist Party's influence will soon surpass that of Kuomintang. Up to this moment it had been different. At any rate this influence is in a state of progress which is in no way of advantage to Kuomintang.

Mao Tse-tung goes on with his numerical manipulations. He says that the number of regular troops has reached 650,000. And notes that in the new year this number has every chance of reaching 1 million.

The new reorientation toward Moscow becomes a fact. Talk is rife among the party leaders on the role of the Soviet Union in defending the interests of the Chinese Communist Party, on the "common spirit of the fraternal parties," etc.

Mao Tse-tung has personal communications with Moscow (powerful radio station, personal codes), but he stubbornly keeps on sending his telegrams through me.

December 21, 1944

Mao Tse-tung shows a morbid interest in the events in Greece. The executions of Greek patriots by the British interventionists set him thinking of the possibility of doing the same in China. Besides, the Americans have refused him arms. At any rate there is food for thought. . . .

In the changed situation there is a heightened interest in the article published by *Izvestia* on December 2. . . .

My notes are extremely extensive! It is a funny thing, but even I myself can hardly believe that I have written all this by myself. But this is a fact, an indisputable fact. . . . I am obsessed by facts. Facts are the main thing in one's work. Facts, first of all, and only then, conclusions and emotions. One's memory can fail, but not this chronicle of events. . . .

December 22, 1944

The Chairman conversed with me for more than eight hours, having given strict orders not to be disturbed.

Contrary to the usual state of things, Mao Tse-tung seated himself at the table. On his right is the map of China. Three or four volumes of the Chinese encyclopedia are stacked on the edge of the table. Across from him stands a white enamel cup with a lid, a bottle of India ink, a brush, and a glass holding a pencil and a plain school pen. Sheets of blank paper lie underhand. His head inclined to his right shoulder, full of enthusiasm, Mao talked on and on. . . .

The Chairman set himself the task of explaining to me how one should understand the united front tactics as applied to the present situation. He gave the official version of the CCP leadership (which he himself ignores in practical life).

Mao mentioned the head of the Chungking Government. To him he is a "dictator, butcher, half-wit." . . .

Mao told me along what principles the relations with Kuomintang are maintained. Then shared information on military construction. Many interesting facts, but everything is dominated by the former tactics of far-fetched numbers which expose his endeavors to present everything to me in a false light.

Mao gave particular attention to analyzing the former intraparty struggle. "Former," because in Mao's opinion unity has been achieved in the party. Without mentioning the names of Wang Ming, Lo Fu, Po Ku, and others, the Chairman said that the struggle for the "rectification of the three styles of work" has made it possible to expose persons advocating the capitulation policy of concessions to the reactionary Kuomintang, etc. This struggle has made it possible to reorganize party ranks. It has armed the party with clear-cut targets. . . .

Mao Tse-tung analyzed the course of negotiations between the CCP leadership and the Americans. In this connection he gave me a detailed account of his last meeting with the head of the Army Observer Group, playing the part of each participant, conveying the intonations and gestures of Colonel Barrett.

Mao Tse-tung pointed out to me that the first draft agreement was signed in Yenan by Hurley and thus it put the Allies "right into a trap." They had nothing to do but to demand concessions on the part of Chiang Kai-shek. And they obtained them from "their toady." Now came the time to demand concessions from the CCP. And the Americans got at the CCP leadership. . . .

Here Mao got up and began to pace the room. He would stop in front of me and mimic Barrett objecting to him.

Mao explained to me that he could not agree to concessions, for any agreement with Chiang Kai-shek meant a noose for the Communist Party. The Americans were naïvely striving for concessions which nobody intended to make. For the demands were calculated to be definitely rejected by the "bastard" Chiang Kai-shek. From the very start everything was carried out so that the "bastard" Chiang Kai-shek would reject the demands of the CCP. "We knew this, and we were right."

"Then the Americans set Barrett on me," said Mao Tse-tung, chuckling to himself.

Barrett appeared before the Chairman and started talking of concessions to Chiang Kai-shek, of the inevitability of reciprocal concessions, and prompted the approximate form of these concessions.

The Chairman took the offensive and came down with a torrent of curses against the Kuomintang and the Chungking Government. And to muddle Barrett entirely, he declared, "Mr. Hurley was here. He signed the draft agreement of his own accord. Why reject that which was approved and signed by President Roosevelt's personal representative?"

The Chairman said all this to Barrett in a highly irritated voice. He recaptured his own intonations and facial expressions for me. It looked more like wrath. Righteous wrath. Hurt feelings!

Mao Tse-tung paced the room nervously and chuckled. He found satisfaction in recollecting Hurley's blunder and in this connection the idiotic situation of the experienced agent Barrett. Again and again he savored the details of this scene. . . .

Somebody tried to enter—Mao rudely demanded to be left alone. He moved his chair up to mine and began to relate in detail how all this had alarmed Barrett and how he had raised his voice to persuade Mao not to make this mistake, for this obstinacy on the part of the Communist Party leadership would not be understood by American public opinion, and it would cost dearly. American public opinion would be against Yenan and all Chinese Communists. And then all assistance would be out of the question.

The Chairman reacted even more passionately. He said that it was foolish to intimidate the Special Area with such a thing as public opinion. That trick wouldn't work here. For many years already all the conservatives and reactionaries had been hating and campaigning against the Communist Party.

"We were abused with the dirtiest words!" said Mao. "We were criminals to all of them. And we don't give a damn for all these public condemnations!"

Barrett decided to achieve his object by threatening to aid only the Central Government in Chungking. All American aid will go only to the Kuomintang. . . .

In his answer the Chairman lost control of his voice. He shouted that after all the Special Area did not care whether it would be recognized by anyone or not. The Communist Party was waging an independent struggle and would continue to do so. The United States would not gain anything by refusing to help the Eighth Route and the New Fourth armies, for "we have been doing without such aid and will continue to do without it!" Thus, to this day Chungking alone was receiving arms. Everything was given only to the Kuomintang. If that's the way things are, then the Special Area will convene a conference to form its own government. Let Chiang Kai-shek get it hot in his Chungking! And the Special Area doesn't give a hoot whether this government is recognized by the Soviet Union(!), the United States, or Great Britain. If they are wise enough, they won't be fastidious about it. If they refuse to establish interstate relations, the CCP won't be the worse for it. Ten, twenty years will go by, a century will pass, they will finally come to an agreement and send their envoys. All of them will recognize us! Maybe a hundred years later—but they will recognize us! They won't get away from it—they will recognize us!

At the end of his talk with Colonel Barrett the Chairman said that he was always glad to receive Americans.

"If the colonel flies here," said Mao, "we will meet him, I will come to the airport myself. We do not refuse to negotiate. We are for negotiations. If you come again after that, I will meet you. . . ."

The next day Colonel Barrett hurried off to Chungking to make his report (and there was enough to report on).

Speaking of his meeting with Barrett, Mao became very excited. His hair went down over his temples and he did not brush it back; his face was flushed. He spoke in a loud and hurried voice, sprinkling his speech with coarse jokes and using expressive gestures.

The Chairman made a show of being entirely frank with me. He did not even try to conceal that all this loud talk had been deliberately staged. Yet this seeming candidness was far from real and also a part of a previously rehearsed act.

Mao Tse-tung did not ever so much as mention that there were other reasons behind the colonel's visit and that the talks were also pursuing some hidden designs. Mao evidently intended to settle the country's domestic political problems by means of power, having secured the support and aid of the United States. Of course, he did not say a word about his intentions of opposing the White House to Moscow.

With the help of the Americans Mao was out to turn his future collision with the Kuomintang into a favorable channel. Actually all these months he has been offering himself to the White House instead of Chiang Kai-shek. He was well aware of the fact that the Americans would agree to such an alliance only on definite political terms and first of all if the Soviet Union was to be isolated from Far Eastern politics.

Factually it is these endeavors of Mao that are behind this wrangle for arms. He is certainly aware of all the difficulties inherent in such a rapprochement. However, he has cherished such hopes and has not abandoned them even now. It wasn't for nothing that right before Barrett's take-off Chou handed him a new letter for Patrick Hurley. . . .

It is the Americans' preference for Chiang Kai-shek that forces Mao to seek Moscow's support without breaking off entirely with the White House. Such is the aim of the secret correspondence, the scene with Barrett that he staged for me, and other facts. At any rate Mao is playing for safety, that's a fact. Moscow figures in his plans as an emergency variant, and a worse one to him.

It was along these lines that I wrote my report to Moscow.

December 23, 1944

The interest in P. Krainov's article in *Izvestia* is so great that I asked Moscow to tell me its content.

The article testifies to the invariable proletarian solidarity and kindly feelings of the Soviet Union for the Chinese people despite the unscrupulous policy of Mao Tse-tung. Mao Tse-tung, however, has interpreted the article in his own way. To him it is proof of the Soviet Union's future activity in the Far East.

The article gives China's split as the main reason for its military setbacks. Here every Japanese soldier is outnumbered by some fifteen Chinese soldiers. In China the Japanese do not use such a mass tank force as the Nazis. The allied air forces retain supremacy in the air. And although there is a shortage of ammunition, arms, and foodstuffs, this cannot be considered the chief reason for the Japanese militarists' constant successes.

The reason for China's military setback lies in the split of its national forces.

In its resolute denouncement of the right-wing elements in the Kuomintang Moscow warns them that it will not allow them to resort to force in their relations with Chinese Communists.

The article proves that it does not identify the future of the Chinese Revolution and Chinese Communists with the line of Mao Tse-tung.

The article expresses hope that the sober-minded forces of Chinese society will gain the upper hand in the policy for a single anti-Japanese front. . . .

December 24, 1944

Recalling my last meeting with Mao, I come to the conclusion that the act with Barrett was performed by Mao strictly according to a preset plan, although Mao is somewhat alarmed by its consequences.

It wasn't for nothing that he spoke his thoughts on whether he had overdone it with Barrett, fearing the Yankees would break off with him if they took this seriously.

The Chairman has no doubts that the Allies will agree with his demands (returning to the initial draft agreement). A highly significant fact! He still has hopes. . . .

By way of a compromise Mao Tse-tung considers it possible to set up a joint staff of all of the country's armed forces. The White House is liable to come out with such a project, and Chiang Kai-shek will be forced to comply with it. The Americans will make him consent. Such a staff will comprise representatives of the armed forces of the Communist Party, the Kuomintang, and the United States. It will be headed, of course, by some American general.

Mao Tse-tung hates this project in advance. It will be something like fetters for the Communist Party. And the reason lies not only in American instructors, who will be attached to the Eighth Route and the New Fourth armies, but in dependence on the joint staff. To hell with the agents, instructors, and advisers! As for dependence on the staff—this means real fetters! Not a single step without orders. This means fighting with the Japanese instead of multiplying first of all the CCP bases. And in general this will exclude all preparations for a clash with Chiang Kai-shek, which was, is, and will be the sole aim of the Eighth Route and New Fourth armies, and which all the last years had been devoted to.

Mao cannot speak Chiang Kai-shek's name without losing his temper. He usually accompanies it with a collection of abusive words; he never tires of repeating that sooner or later he will finish off the Chungking ruler ("He shouldn't be so hopeful—I won't stop at any methods or means!").

It would be strange if the Chairman was completely frank with me. Didn't he say to his soul-mates that the idea of establishing the joint staff was worse than fetters also because if the Soviet Union denounced the Soviet-Japanese neutrality pact and started military actions against Japan in Manchuria or Inner Mongolia, the Eighth Route Army might find itself blocked by American landing forces and isolated from the military operations of the Soviet troops. This would be an inexcusable mistake, for power there must be seized by the CCP. However, in that situation the Americans would never allow this. As a result the CCP would not avail itself of the results of the Soviet victories, as all ways of penetrating into such areas would be cut off by the Allies in advance.

If it will be impossible to wriggle away from the idea of the joint staff, the Chairman intends to adopt the following measures. He will hand over to the joint staff only those units of the Eighth Route and the New Fourth armies that will have to give direct support to the landing operations of the Allies. By way of an example he will refer to the plan for co-operation between the CCP and allied troops in Lienyunkang area. In keeping with this plan the CCP leadership promised to bring into action not fewer than forty of its complete regiments. One involuntarily thinks of other examples: If only the CCP leaders had put up at least half of this force in support of the Soviet Union's position in the Far East during the 1941–42 period! At that time they did not care a bit about all our troubles! Their telegrams gave vows of friendship. And they were not sparing of words. . . .

I learned of a curious detail. It turned out that the plan of military operations in Lienyunkang was already known to the Japanese command.

Well, here's your *cheng-ping!* Catching spies, exposing them, while the plan known only to a most narrow circle of CCP officials immediately becomes known to the enemy. Of course *cheng-ping* was pursuing other aims. . . .

The other aim of the act with Barrett was also kept from me by Mao Tse-tung. He certainly wants to convince the Americans that the Communist Party has become mature enough to take independent decisions on foreign-policy tasks. No wonder he intimidated them with the prospect of setting up a second government of China.

Besides, the White House still has a sharp need for live forces which it wants to replenish with Chinese soldiers. In case of a split between the CCP and the Kuomintang these soldiers will take part in the Civil War. The White House has no wish to spill the blood of its own citizens.

Here each decision is a tangle of issues, some of which exclude one another. A venomous tangle, and in general, all this is a wrangle! A wrangle behind the back of the Soviet Union engulfed in a gory battle against fascist Germany.

The Chairman was also pursuing another aim: It was important to give the Communist Party the aura of being such an independent force with which one could do business.

And although there is already no hope of receiving arms, they do not want to lose this hope. At any rate they are still hoping. . . .

And although hatred is already brewing against the Allies, they are ingratiating themselves and imposing themselves as partners—what a circus!

Mao works a lot these months. He makes terrific efforts to turn the future events into a most profitable channel for himself. He tries to forestall the chief events (the ending of the war in the Far East) and play the part of the key political force in China. However, in his opinion, this key political force should be purely national and not connected politically with the Soviet Union. He set his hopes on the United States as a counterbalance to the Soviet Union. The way things are it certainly isn't his fault that the White House has scrapped this plan. . . .

This extra-long talk with me was no mere chance. Mao wanted to look as a supporter of international relations between the CCP and the All-Union Communist Party (Bolsheviks); he substantiated the "principled" reason for the CCP's rejection of American drafts and justified his actions by giving them a theoretical base in the spirit of "Marxism of reality." Actually Mao is covering up his traces. . . .

For eight hours at a stretch Mao Tse-tung had talked with me. Talking without end, hotly, excitedly. At times he is very effusive and knows no fatigue. . . .

But at other times, as today, for example, he is dull and peevish. He gave me a limp handshake, as if he were ill, and offered me a seat. He began to ramble about the room pacing heavily, stooping as if he were cold. He was distracted, and a long silence ensued. Then he sat down, his body slack. He placed his hands wearily upon his knees.

Once again he explained to me the line of the CCP leadership in the negotiations with the Americans, showed interest in the Soviet Union's attitude to the Soviet-Japanese neutrality pact, but factually he tried to find out Moscow's attitude to his actions. . . .

He kept casting glances at me with a tired smile on his face. The vague shadows of the window lattice played on his wadded clothes.

December 25, 1944

The Allies are in a tight spot in the Ardennes. Germans are advancing toward Antwerp.

Mao's philosophical and theoretical level is primitive materialism. He was always afraid of the democratic instincts of the masses. For Mao party polemics and contacts with the masses are first of all a matter of prestige. Hence his schooling of the party's rank-and-file by means of *cheng-ping,* so as to make each of his words an indisputable truth.

Blind obedience is the ideal of party relations according to Mao Tse-tung.

The Chairman's democratism is confined to his wearing the plain *tan-i,* to which on special occasions patches are sewed on in abundance.

Mao suppresses everyone by his fervent striving for power. All his "theorizing" is but a cover for his obsession with this idea.

Mao does not and cannot have any attachments. He can form habits, but his all-absorbing passion is for power alone! This passion does not leave room for affection. It spoils Mao Tse-tung, turning him into a dangerous, aggressive person, devoid of natural human emotions. Nothing makes sense to him if it is not in keeping with his plans.

Nothing that is alien to the consolidation of personal power is alien to the CCP—such is the final political credo of Mao Tse-tung.

December 28, 1944

There are some fifty officials in the Chungking apparatus of the CCP. It is headed by Chou En-lai and Tung Pi-wu.

Chen Chia-kang is one of the key officials. A native of Kwangsi. Has a university education. For the last year has been performing the duties of Chou En-lai's secretary. Has a perfect command of English. Is well acquainted with all the military personnel in Chungking. He is their frequent guest. In Yenan the Americans received him as a good friend of theirs.

Liu Shao-wen is nearly forty. He comes from the same place as Mao Tse-tung.

However, Liu's biography has an interesting detail. In his time he had supported Chu Teh in backing up Chang Kuo-tao, who had then had a deathly clash with Mao Tse-tung over the question of leadership of the Red Army. . . . But this is a matter of the distant past.

Liu plays a special role in the Chungking apparatus. There he has charge of numerous agents. He is highly valued by Li Ko-nung.

Now Liu Shao-wen is wholly Li Ko-nung's man. If I'm not mistaken, Li Ko-nung and Kang Sheng are jealous of each other, and the Chairman uses this to his own advantage.

December 30, 1944

It becomes clear that Hitler's Germany is surviving its last days. Hence the time is near when the Soviet Union can take measures to protect its frontiers in the Far East. This accounts for the whole series of meetings held by the CCP leadership.

With a rush Mao switches over to a gamble with the Soviet Union, using this to blackmail the Americans and Chiang Kai-shek.

Yesterday I reported the following to Moscow:

"The latest events show that Mao Tse-tung and his soul-mates are rapidly realigning and protracting their dishonest game with the Soviet Union. Their aim is to squeeze as much as possible out of the Soviet Union's activities in the Far East in their own mercenary interests. . . ."

1945

January 1945

January 5, 1945

Speaking with me, the Chairman of the CCP Central Committee emphasized once again that the knowledge of Marxism-Leninism was not necessary for the revolutionary transformation of China. What is important is to know China, its needs, customs, history. . . .

Mao Tse-tung avoids even mentioning the All-Union Communist Party. He does not show the least interest in our Bolshevik Party's experience (although he likes to refer to it).

Following the irreversible consolidation of his unchallenged power, Mao has begun to show an increased desire to be an indisputable authority on all party and state matters. . . .

Mao has worked out the manner of behavior to suit his position. His listeners have to be very attentive, as his voice is hardly perceptible. He moves about slowly. He spends hours in his chair almost motionless.

He takes Chinese psychology into account in all he does and says. He is quick, very quick to take offense. . . .

January 7, 1945

Went to see Mao Tse-tung.

He was preparing documents for the congress. Looked tired. Spoke slowly, making frequent pauses and thinking over something which was on his mind. From time to time he would stand up to pace the room, stooping. His hair fell on his cheeks, but he didn't throw it back. He would stop at the desk, looking through papers and sipping tea.

Mao's gestures and behavior show the quiet confidence of a man who does not doubt that people would wait for him by all means. Usually talkative, but sometimes, "keeping up his role," he is sparing of words. . . .

Mao complained of a bout of weakness.

Tall and strong, Mao, however, does not endure physical work. He avoids strolls, sunshine, movement. . . .

Mao complained of his age. "Old age is not far off," he remarked sadly. He was smoking especially slovenly. His trousers and jacket were soiled with ash. He scattered cigarette stubs about and spat much, which was a disgusting sight.

It is surprising how failures or the slightest discomfort immediately turn him into an old man.

January 11, 1945

Hurley makes further attempts to reconcile the Kuomintang and the Communist Party under American control. Colonel De Pass, the American military attaché in China; Whitemeyer, the adviser on Japan; Major Edward, from the Wedemeyer staff; and some other officials came from Chungking to Yenan yesterday.

Now the American ambassador, Hurley, has forwarded through De Pass his message to the CCP leadership.

Hurley's message says that at present all conditions exist for the successful completion of the talks between the Special Area and the Kuomintang. He asks Mao Tse-tung and Chou En-lai for permission to visit Yenan together with T. V. Soong, the Chinese Minister for Foreign Affairs; Wang Shih-chieh, the Minister of Propaganda; and Chang Chih-chung, chief of the Chinese Army's Political Department.

De Pass talked with Mao Tse-tung, Chou En-lai, Chu Teh, and Yeh Chien-ying. All of them showed very great restraint and coldness toward the American military attaché.

Today De Pass and other Americans flew to Chungking with a refusal of Mao Tse-tung and Chou En-lai to begin talks. De Pass was given a letter in which Mao Tse-tung demands, on behalf of the CCP, an urgent convocation of a National Democratic Assembly and full freedom for *Hsin-hua Jih-pao* [New China Daily], the Communist newspaper in Chungking. Mao Tse-tung insists on a country-wide discussion of all questions pertaining to China's democratic transformation.

The uncompromising, firm position of the Communist Party leadership has as its aim isolation of the Kuomintang internationally, if not rupture of the alliance with it. Mao Tse-tung takes into account the conditions which have arisen as a result of the continual Japanese offensive. The Kuomintang is attacked by the press of practically all the countries of the anti-Japanese coalition.

The Chairman of the CCP Central Committee continues to play on the blunder made by Hurley, who signed the draft Yenan treaty between the CCP and the Kuomintang on November 10 last year. Mao Tse-tung realizes that the American ambassador has found himself in an awkward position and will be compelled to mediate in the negotiations between the Special Area and Chungking to see that the aggravation of tensions between them will not lead to an armed clash. That is why with every day Mao Tse-tung increases the list of his demands, disregarding reality. For him the reality is to attract American sympathies to the Special Area by presenting Chiang as a bankrupt. . . .

Following the *Izvestia* article (December 2, 1944), the leaders of the Communist Party have sharply changed their views as regards talks with the Americans and connect all their hopes with the immutability of our political support. However, they have not thrown out their old policy from their arsenal. They continue it in a new form. Obstinacy is now their tool to blackmail the Americans. . . .

Tai Li is Chiang Kai-shek's man. He heads the counterintelligence service. Chiang Kai-shek has an unlimited trust in him. Colonel De Pass, the American military attaché, is one of the few persons who see him. Tai Li is elusive. Almost nobody in Chungking has ever seen him.

January 12, 1945

I asked the Chairman of the CCP Central Committee to free me from the necessity to receive military-political information from the Ching-pao-chu chief. . . .

First, dependence on Kang Sheng is very humiliating. Every day I am supposed to receive the news which he deigns to tell me. In such circumstances I must not only patiently acquaint myself with all kinds of forged reports. The Ching-pao-chu chief always tries to nose out what is on my mind. . . .

Second, as a rule I must do the back-breaking work to remove misinformation from all these materials. . . .

Third, he constantly conceals from me the facts of the Yenan policy affecting the Soviet Union's interests.

Fourth, he hates me. He can't forgive me my interference when he wanted to finish off with Wang Ming. He also hates me because I told Moscow he was a traitor of Marxism-Leninism and a butcher of the Chinese Communists who held internationalist views. . . .

Fifth, I am still under surveillance. Risking his neck, a man from the Ching-pao-chu chief's office told me of new forms and methods used to keep me under surveillance. . . .

Sixth, Kang selects facts to compromise me and make me dependent on Mao by discrediting all my previous reports to the center.

Naturally enough, I didn't say this to Mao Tse-tung. In support of my request I told him that the situation in the Far East was becoming extremely complicated. In such circumstances Kang Sheng is unable to supply me with the information I need. There are neither foreign newspapers nor a press center in Yenan. Consequently I did not receive timely information on important events. In the prevailing circumstances Kang Sheng was not able (I, of course, didn't say he simply did not want to) to evaluate developments objectively. I am deprived of reliable and timely information and this does harm to the common cause.

Although it was difficult for the Chairman of the CCP Central Committee to object, he nevertheless said that unfortunately he did not see the other way out because Kang Sheng was the most informed person in the Special Area ("if not in the whole of China," Mao joked).

I said that I saw the way out. Comrade Yeh Chien-ying showed himself a clever diplomat, possessed the necessary information thanks to his position, and was capable of giving effective evaluations of events. Most important, this would make work more efficient (which will undoubtedly raise the value of information). Comrade Yeh Chien-ying's knowledge was a guarantee that his reports and surveys would be up to the mark.

A mere two years ago the Chairman of the CCP Central Committee would not have even discussed this matter with me. At that time all the radio stations of the world had counted hours left for Hitler to triumph fully over the Soviet Union. . . .

That is why Mao reluctantly agreed to make Yeh Chien-ying a "press attaché." It wasn't that he gave in to weakness. He simply

Yenan, October 1944. Ceremony marking the decoration of Colonel
Barrett with an American military award. From right to left: Colonel
Barrett in uniform with the new medal on his chest, Captain Robert
Champion, Lieutenant Simon Hitch, Captain Domke, and First Lieutenant
Henry Whittlesey.

At a ceremony held in honor of Colonel Barrett. On the right is Mao Tse-tung; on the extreme left is Raymond Ludden, second secretary of the American legation in Chungking.

Mao Tse-tung forges ahead to become the virtual ruler of the CCP, now that the "Moscow opposition" is crushed.

On the eve of his departure from Yenan Peter Vladimirov was presented with this photograph by Mao Tse-tung and his wife, Chiang Ching. The inscription reads:

> To Comrade Sung Ping.
> Mao Tse-tung, Chiang Ching.
> Yenan, November 14, 1945.

began a serious game with Moscow, and I was assigned a certain place in his plans. Was it worth irritating me?

Parting, Mao Tse-tung said with a smile that the point was not from whom I would receive information; the main thing was for this information to serve the "common cause."

January 14, 1945

Mao went out with me.

Yeh Chien-ying came up. Mao took out a cigarette and lit it. He can wait and be silent.

Yeh Chien-ying said the Americans showed an interest in the Russians in Yenan.

"Your press office interests them very much, Sung Ping," Yeh Chien-ying said in conclusion.

"It was of interest to the reporters as well," Mao Tse-tung added.

Mao referred to the last year's visits of foreign correspondents to the Special Area. Of course, both the U. S. Army Observer Group and inquisitive reporters could not but be interested in sounding out "Moscow's position" here. . . . All were surprised to find only three Soviet men here—myself, Orlov, and Rimmar (Protsenko doesn't count, as he turns up in Yenan occasionally), whereas the Americans were represented in the Special Area by a big mission, which numbered, at times, several dozen officers. As sportsmen say, in this respect the score was clearly in the Americans' favor. . . .

I think the Americans know a lot about the cheng-feng. (Thanks to whom: Fray, Ma Hai-te?) Even if they do not know all the intricacies of party disagreements, they have grasped the main thing—Mao Tsetung's desire to substantiate his nationalistic "Marxism of reality." They interpret this "Marxism" as anti-Sovietism. And they don't need anything more.

Of course, not all the observers evaluated the meaning of chengfeng in this way. But such persons as Davies, Service, Ludden (and partially Stilwell) apparently realized, in time, the opportunities offered by such views of Mao Tse-tung. With such a party leader, they don't think much about the CCP economic platform. The basis for alliance with him is here at hand—his striving for political isolation, the striving behind which one can discern anti-Sovietism. Messrs. Observers unmistakably sensed the smell of anti-Sovietism in the sentiments of the CCP leadership.

Stilwell, Davies, Service, and Ludden are the most dangerous variety of "allies." They see further, much further, than their colleagues who didn't believe Mao's anti-Soviet trumps and who decided that the Chairman was bluffing. Other American army officers exactly followed their instructions and nothing else, whereas Mao's behavior did not fit in any instructions which said that Mao Tse-tung was "Communist No. 1"—what kind of advances could be spoken about in such circumstances! . . . Messrs. Officers decided that the "Communist No. 1" was simply bluffing. . . .

Stilwell's group (Davies, Service, and Ludden) understands that the United States alliance with the Special Area opens up much more important prospects than the traditional orientation on Chiang Kai-shek or the limited use of CCP army units. . . .

Joseph Stilwell understands the situation perfectly well. It is not accidental that such people grouped around this general. Indisputably, Stilwell is an expert on China. In his youth he spent a long period with the American military mission in China. That is why with the beginning of the war in the Pacific President Roosevelt appointed him commander in chief of the American armed forces in the Chinese-Burmese Theater of Operations (to act also as Chiang Kai-shek's chief of staff).

January 16, 1945

Relations with the Americans have entered a new stage. The Communist Party leadership realizes that the chances for a success in the talks with the Americans are gradually coming to nothing. The hopes to solve domestic-policy problems with American assistance are collapsing. At the worst, Mao wanted to neutralize Chiang Kai-shek by the American interest in the cohesion of the anti-Japanese bloc. In case of his coming to power he guaranteed American monopolies quite substantial profits from their investments in the Chinese economy.

That the Americans wouldn't allow the national liberation war to assume revolutionary character does not trouble Mao. It was important to use their assistance to gain strength, push the old Chiang to the background, frighten the White House with the rottenness of the Chungking system, the inevitability of its downfall, and the unreliability of this system from the viewpoint of economic prospects. Mao behaved as a merchant trying to prove that his commodity was the best. . . .

So the Americans are overcome by their mortal fear of the Communist Party. They are ready to believe the CCP leaders, but not the force they are heading. They are not bold enough, although they are trying, to demarcate clearly the Communist Party leaders' petty politicking and the growing revolutionary movement. The White House thinks the risk is too great. Its emissaries keep traveling from Washington to Chungking and Yenan. The temptation is great, but the fear is even greater. The Americans think that Moscow is behind the back of the Chairman of the CCP Central Committee. Mao Tse-tung realizes it full well! It is not for nothing that this Hunan man tried to convince the Americans of the full national independence of the CCP(!) and gave them to understand in every way that the Soviet Union's isolation in the Far East met not only the American interests. Washington did not treat his advances seriously. Washington decided that Mao just wanted to profit at its expense. . . .

Increasingly angry with the Americans, Mao has now decided to use their interest in the CCP troops to wrest another important advantage from them—to hold Chiang Kai-shek under constant control and pressure with their aid. Although the Americans were stingy with weapons, they do not preclude aid to the Eighth Route and the New Fourth armies. Who will fight against the Japanese here? Let them bind Chiang Kai-shek with all kinds of demands which will be prompted by Yenan. . . .

January 18, 1945

Mao continues to intensively feed the Americans and myself with the same figures. I wonder what Barrett thinks of all this?

As before, the White House is eager to lay its hands on the CCP armed forces. The Americans are trying to bring about a political settlement between the CCP and the Kuomintang. This means Barrett is swallowing the bait. The Americans shuttle between Yenan and Chungking and coax, alternatively, Chiang, Mao, and Chou. However, it is possibly not only the matter of the Eighth Route and the New Fourth armies. The Americans want to control political developments in China; they dream of directing this political process and have all events under their control.

The other day I dispatched a significant telegram. Usually when I receive telegrams from the hands of the Chairman of the CCP Central Committee, it provides a pretext for our meetings. He has finally chosen me his transmission link in his correspondence with Moscow. He has come to believe in this tactic. . . .

Here is the essence of the telegram.

The Chairman of the CCP Central Committee is preoccupied with the World Trade Union Congress in London. In the congress he sees another instrument to form definitely oriented public opinion. This opinion will whip up the Americans to increase pressure on Chiang Kai-shek. Consequently, participation in the congress will promote the solution of the selfsame political problems (the isolation of Chiang Kai-shek, the possible American reorientation to Yenan, the possibility of continuing the tactics of evading major operations in the war with Japan).

The telegram to the World Trade Union Congress was sent via Chungking. Mao is not sure that Chiang Kai-shek's censors will let it go. That is why he tells Moscow, confidentially, that a special messenger will be sent to India to dispatch a telegram to the organizing committee of the London congress.

In this message to Moscow the Chairman of the CCP Central Committee develops his old tactic of figure juggling. Thus, he puts the membership of the trade union organizations in the main districts of the central provinces at 200,000 (this applies to eight areas). Generally speaking, it's doubtful that such trade unions exist. China has long been living through the chaos of war and rigid wartime limitations. What trade union cells can one speak of in this situation?!

However, if such trade unions do exist, nobody counts their membership. The CCP leadership cannot even tell the precise strength of its armed forces. Every commander may report figures practically at will. The center doesn't control things. Figure inflating is practiced at every echelon. This is advantageous for everybody: It enhances the prestige of the commander, increases his merits, and simultaneously promotes the interests of the Yenan leadership.

In a talk with me Mao complained about militaristic survivals in the CCP troops. This convinced me once again that "figure juggling" was legitimate here.

The trade unions of the neighboring Shansi province's southeast districts number at least 124,000 members. God knows how they could establish the figure in a situation bordering on war.

For the Yenan area the trade union membership was more or less plausible but, I say it emphatically, more or less, as even this figure was approximated to 61,000. . . .

Mao Tse-tung told Moscow these were approximate figures, as farm hands had not been counted.

The Shansi-Sui-yuan districts account for the smallest number of trade unionists—17,000. But the Proletarian Association of Resistance to Fascist Japan and Liberation of Motherland numbers precisely 235,000 trade unionists who work in the Hopeh-Shansi district.

In the Communist Party's northern stronghold (Shantung trade union organizations) there are about 144,000 of such workers.

Mao Tse-tung wrote that the Communist Party leadership had decided to send trade union delegations to the World Congress to be convened in the capital of Great Britain.

The total strength of the trade unions was 800,000. The Communist Party leadership wanted to send a plenipotentiary delegation to London.

The Chinese character for Mao's family name was at the bottom of the telegram. . . .

A careful collation of figures and the way in which the text of the telegram to Moscow was drafted convinced me that this was a deliberate piece of misinformation. One of the many sent out in the past few years. . . .

I added my opinion to the telegram of the Chairman of the CCP Central Committee. I told Moscow that the telegram could be regarded only as a document testifying to his desire to confuse the leaders of the All-Union Communist Party.

Mao Tse-tung does not expect to receive any counsel from the All-Union Communist Party leadership. This counsel is of no interest to him, since he has long embarked upon actions without co-ordinating them with the platforms of progressive world trade unions.

The aim of the Chairman of the CCP Central Committee is to use the trade congress for another attempt to reach his domestic-policy targets which run counter to the interests of the struggle against Japan. In so doing, the Chairman of the CCP Central Committee stresses that he allegedly fights for the unity of all national forces. In reality, his efforts are designed to cause a split and a crisis of power in the country. As for the driving of the Japanese invaders out of China, he wants this to be done by foreign forces (the Soviet Union and the United States).

The strength of the trade union associations was determined arbitrarily. This telegram was prepared by Chou En-lai, Politburo member. It might be said without an exaggeration that this is a pearl of his zeal and sleepless nights. Chou En-lai is the author of most foreign-policy documents. He unreservedly supports the dishonest course of the Chairman of the CCP Central Committee in respect to Moscow. . . .

Po Ku told me that it was Chou En-lai who had inserted a point in the telegram concerning the dispatch of a special messenger to India with instructions to send a telegram to the organizing committee of the World Trade Union Congress in London. But nobody intended to send such a messenger—this is a collective lie of the CCP leadership. There is a secret resolution concerning the dispatch of a special delegate with documents containing every detail (and not only about trade union activities in the liberated areas). These documents are supposed to provoke new political complications in China, shake again the situation, unstable as it is, and, what is the main thing, compel Chiang Kai-shek to put up with the future losses of new areas. Clearly, Chiang Kai-shek won't agree to such a "unity" in resisting the aggressor. The London congress will thus be another blow at the united anti-Japanese front. And this dirty game is being conducted when the Japanese are advancing successfully. . . .

Chou also said it was necessary to take all measures, in case the delegation (or its representative) would not be able to come to London, for Kang's chain of secret agents to ensure the transfer of the documents to London.

Mao Tse-tung ordered that everything for the special political report of the liberated areas' trade unions be made known to the congress.

The data of the telegram which Mao gave me to send to Moscow differs much from the dates when the decisions on this question were taken. This shows once again that I am right. Nobody here was interested in Moscow's opinion. . . .

January 19, 1945

I felt Mao was to a certain extent discontented with me. This is certainly the result of Kang Sheng's preaching. Yeh Chien-ying intimated that the Ching-pao-chu chief was exerting pressure upon him. However, Yeh Chien-ying is firm. Besides, he is clearly satisfied. Since the cheng-feng has got into top gear, his relations with Kang have been cold politeness, to put it mildly. The time has come to win back. Yeh Chien-ying artfully harasses Kang. Kang's futile attempts to restore old relations make Yeh Chien-ying cheerful. Indeed, this is the self-same Ching-pao-chu chief who mocked at everybody and administered "justice" a mere one and a half to two years ago.

January 20, 1945

The Chairman of the CCP Central Committee suffers from attacks of emotional depression. At his request, Orlov makes him pantocrinum injections. However, even then Mao Tse-tung exercises the personal direction of party and military affairs.

Chinese colleagues envy Orlov. Andrei Yakovlevich complains to me that many of them constantly try to discredit him in one way or another.

January 21, 1945

Kang has succeeded in bringing the Chairman of the CCP Central Committee into the desired mood. Mao Tse-tung clearly regrets that he permitted me to receive information from Yeh Chien-ying.

Yeh Chien-ying intimated that this worries him little, that this has nothing to do with him. He only carries out instructions. Possibly, Yeh Chien-ying exaggerates a bit and is worried, but his contempt for Kang Sheng prevails over career considerations. . . .

The Ching-pao-chu chief has tried to exert pressure on Yeh Chien-ying so that he would voluntarily give up the role of my "press attaché." Yeh Chien-ying has an opportunity to spite Kang and prevent him from poking his nose into other people's business.

Kang is outraged. . . .

January 22, 1945

Colonel De Pass, carrying another letter from his ambassador, flew by a special plane from Chungking to Yenan on Sunday.

The White House is prepared to promote the Communist Party's representation on the Military Committee of China—a very substantial concession.

However, the Chairman of the CCP Central Committee is against Chou En-lai's trip because Chiang Kai-shek's Military Committee at the Executive Chamber (the government) is a fake designed to deceive public opinion and hinder the Communist Party's initiative. . . .

Measures have been taken to foil this move of Chungking and to further discredit Chiang Kai-shek in the eyes of the public in the country and elsewhere. . . .

The Americans show exceptional energy and nervousness. Possibly, this is connected with a forthcoming conference of the three Allied Powers and, possibly, with President Roosevelt's contemplated visit to China. One thing is indisputable—they want to boss the situation here. They want to ride two horses at the same time. But nobody has so far succeeded in doing this. . . .

But the fact remains—Mr. Hurley persistently asks Chou En-lai to come to Chungking. The American ambassador still hopes to correct his blunder and establish control over China, both the Kuomintang and the Communists.

The Americans are specially impatient with all kinds of talks because they fear the Soviet Union's inevitable actions in the Far East. Mao Tse-tung, too, takes them into consideration. The political merry-go-round is gaining speed! Every day brings new visits, press conferences, and meaningful newspaper leaders. . . .

January 25, 1945

The American ambassador's proposal was discussed for three days. For three days and nights Mao and his associates were racking their brains over possible ways to reject the Kuomintang's latest proposal without causing public discontent. For three days Colonel De Pass was patiently waiting for the answer. . . .

On Tuesday Chou En-lai and the American military attaché flew to Chungking. It seemed to me De Pass spoke less than usually. Admittedly, there were few reasons for joy. . . . At the airport he was seen off by a group of his compatriots. De Pass stood out for his well-pressed coat and shiny shoes. He is a typical career army officer. His tired aging face does not fit in with his strong broad shoulders covered with the green shoulder straps of a colonel.

The official aim of the trip is talks with Chiang Kai-shek, with Hurley acting as a go-between.

Ambassador Hurley is sure to come down in the history of American diplomacy as a "go-between ambassador." . . .

Mao Tse-tung told me confidentially that "the Communists were, in principle, against participation in Chiang Kai-shek's Military Committee."

As always, the Chairman of the CCP Central Committee was not frank to the end. Now the CCP leadership expects to gain more, at the expense of the Soviet Union, than through American mediation. That is why it agreed to the talks in order not to irritate public opinion by its sharp changes in political demands. Chou En-lai is overloaded with documents and conditions which Chungking will surely not accept. . . .

At Chungking airport Chou En-lai made the following statement:

"Last November I and General Hurley flew from Yenan to Chungking. At that time I was authorized by the CCP Central Committee to discuss concrete questions with the Kuomintang authorities bearing on the formation of a coalition government. The country's situation has become even more critical ever since.

"To mobilize and unite all the anti-Japanese forces of the Chinese people, co-ordinate our actions with the Allies for the attainment of victory over the Japanese invaders and save the situation, it is now extremely necessary to discuss concrete steps connected with the formation of a democratic coalition government with the government and other quarters.

"That is why I have come here again. As a representative of my party I'll ask the national government, the Kuomintang, and the Democratic League of China to convene a conference of all parties and political groups, which is to become a preliminary meeting before the calling of a national congress, and I'll also propose to discuss the plan of the organization and calling of a national congress and the formation of a coalition government.

"We believe this is the only way to mobilize and unite all the forces of the Chinese people, repulse the enemy offensive, co-ordinate our actions with the allied counteroffensive, the only way out to save the situation. All palliatives, used to treat disease symptoms, will not cure the disease itself, will in no way help us solve the problem.

"What the Chinese people are expecting from the national government now is the immediate abolition of the one-party dictatorship and the formation of a coalition government. We ardently hope the government will accept these proposals without delay."

February 1945

February 4, 1945

Chou En-lai had a meeting with Kuomintang representatives in the office of Foreign Minister T. V. Soong in Chungking on January 30.

On behalf of the Kuomintang Wang Shih-chieh proposed that a Democratic League representative be included in the government, but he was against calling meetings of different parties.

Chou En-lai spoke against the Kuomintang dictatorship and demanded the convening of a national assembly.

Despite Hurley's active mediation, Chou En-lai refused to make concessions. Hurley said he intended to leave for the United States. . . .

February 6, 1945

Mao Tse-tung has nothing against freezing all diplomatic activity with Chungking and Washington, but he is afraid of losing the game: What if the Soviet Union does not begin a war against Japan!

What makes the CCP leadership restless is the Soviet Union's strengthening positions in the Far East, the resulting new alignment of forces, and the inevitable consolidation of the CCP positions. On whom to bank—America or the Soviet Union? . . .

Thinking of the Yenan affairs, I involuntarily recall the words of one Frenchman who said that "delusions are like counterfeit coins:

they are made by criminals but are spread by the most honest persons. . . ."

Nationalism, canonization of the ideas of the "Marxism of reality," and unprincipledness gradually overcome CCP functionaries. Mao is worshiped as living God, sinless, wise, and omnipotent. . . .

February 7, 1945

The most indicative article from the foreign correspondents' reports about their Yenan trip which I managed to receive appeared in *Life,* December 18, 1944, by Theodore White. What is interesting about the article is that our ideological opponents emphasize some facts there. They unmistakably grasped (this is seen from Teddy White's every thought) the essence of the revision of Marxism-Leninism by the Chairman of the CCP Central Committee—his rejection of the "Western Marxist dogmas." Behind this rejection there grows, among other things, Mao Tse-tung's anti-Sovietism. This is the most important proof for *Life*'s respectable subscribers. Mao's deliberations concerning the harmfulness of the "Western Marxist dogmas" repeated by persons who are "just a Gramophone" confirm this most clearly. After cheng-feng I understand what kind of a "Gramophone" the Chairman of the CCP Central Committee had in mind—the principles upheld by the CCP's internationalist wing crushed by Mao Tse-tung and Kang Sheng.

The article also confirms that Mao Tse-tung has succeeded in confusing public opinion as regards the true character of the Eighth Route Army's war against the Japanese invaders and the figures which allegedly reflect this struggle. The efforts, made in the Special Area to misinform the foreign press, have produced their effect. Among them is the survey of the CCP armies' war against the Japanese militarists. The survey was read by Yeh Chien-ying before the foreign correspondents last year and later put out by the Liberation Publishers of Yenan. The figures from the report have become official data. They were cited not only by foreign correspondents but also by officials from the Observer Group. Mao Tse-tung wants these figures to go down in history. Judging by these falsified figures, the war is a serious victory for the Mao group. These figures are repeated by White in his article.

Our ideological opponents confirm the revision of Marxism characteristic of Mao Tse-tung's party activities. The words concerning Mao Tse-tung's "stone-hard pragmatism" express, precisely enough, the essence of his political views. Pragmatism is a variety of subjective ideal-ism erasing the difference between knowledge and faith. According to Marxist classics, pragmatism paves the way for the arbitrary falsifica-tion of science and provides the foundation for reactionary philo-sophical concepts. . . .

Articles such as White's map, as it were, a "new gold-bearing area" for the future activities of American politicians and businessmen.

The interview with White was not a thoughtless action on the part of the leaders of the CCP. The revelations they made to this young bourgeois journalist were not accidental. This was a thought-out move camouflaged by the specificities of the war in which the United States is an ally of the Soviet Union in the anti-Hitler coalition. Mao Tse-tung uses allied relations to effect his own anti-Soviet and anti-Bolshevik actions.

In *Life* the CCP leadership proclaim their political and economic program to the American business quarters. And this is not a trick that, under certain circumstances, can be brushed aside.

February 8, 1945

Mao Tse-tung received Chou En-lai's detailed telegram concerning the peripeteia of the negotiations. On several occasions Chou En-lai spoke with Hurley, T. V. Soong, Wang Shih-chieh, and Chang Chih-chung.

Chiang Kai-shek does not intend to scrap the one-party rule, al-though Hurley tried to persuade him to the contrary. Hurley admitted that the Kuomintang leaders' talk about democracy was eyewash, that he mistakably considered T. V. Soong and Wang Shih-chieh liberals. Like Chiang Kai-shek, they were sticking to the old.

Hurley proposed reorganization of the Military Council. The United States, the Kuomintang, and the Communist Party should unite their forces. An American should be appointed commander in chief (to command all CCP troops, including those operating in the Japanese rear), and his deputies would be a Communist and a Kuomintang man.

Chou En-lai said this solution was inexpedient and unjust. Hurley begged to be understood.

Hurley warned he would tell President Roosevelt about his defeat unless the question had been settled positively. But if they do come to terms, the American President might visit China to become personally convinced of the results of the agreement.

T. V. Soong told the American ambassador the Communist Party was trying to seize power in the country.

Hurley has nothing against supporting even such CCP demands, excessive from the viewpoint of senior Kuomintang functionaries, but he fears concessions and agreements will be used by the Soviet Union which allegedly wants to seize China. . . .

February 9, 1945

At the talks Chou En-lai advanced a new proposal the adoption of which would mean a drastic strengthening of the CCP's armies, at the expense of American lend-lease weapons supplies, and establishing its control over the armed forces of China. . . .

In its struggle for power during the talks in Chungking national interests were forgotten. Nobody seriously thinks of the war against Japan, which continues to capture new Chinese territories—in this respect they connect hopes with the Soviet Union and the United States. Chungking and Yenan are bargaining heatedly. . . .

When will my endless watch come to an end? Day and night in tension, I cannot take my mind off Yenan life for an hour. I work here all alone.

February 10, 1945

Had an hour's walk with Andrei Yakovlevich. Unburdened our hearts with a talk. A lot of news . . .

I told Orlov of the latest news and developments. He was silent.

One thing is gnawing the Hunan man now, I said. It's the destiny of the Soviet-Japanese neutrality pact which expires in a month and a half. Will Moscow denounce the pact or not?—this Hamlet-esque question torments your patient. If the pact is denounced, we shall begin military operations against the Japanese. In this case Mao sees entirely different opportunities for himself. Counting on Chiang, the Americans are, at the same time, exerting every effort to keep Mao under control. From his viewpoint, the further course of events will enable him to make the correct choice. . . .

"My patient is very nervous about his health," Andrei Yakovlevich said. "And Chiang Ching is no better in this respect. I am summoned several times a week. They are anxious about arrhythmia, weakness. . . . But I wish we had their health. . . ."

The Chairman of the CCP Central Committee decided to recall Chou from Chungking. The situation was developing in such a way that President Chiang Kai-shek was prepared, unexpectedly, to make concessions on a number of questions on which Yenan insisted.

A radiogram recalling Chou En-lai was sent to Chungking. It was risky to allow Chou to stay in Chungking any longer. Chiang's concessions will be made public, while the Chairman of the CCP Central Committee will continue to ignore the draft agreement between the Kuomintang and the Communist Party. This maneuvering threatens to expose the political bluff of the Yenan leaders. Indeed, while appealing for a compromise, Yenan refuses to meet it halfway.

Yenan must decide how, without antagonizing public opinion, to discredit Chiang Kai-shek and brush any concessions aside. Chou is the main consultant here. He is reputed to be Diplomat No. 1.

In reality, Yenan's obstinacy is acquiring a new quality. What is the destiny of the Soviet-Japanese pact? Is it worthwhile to make concessions if the Soviet Union, having denounced the pact, will smash the Kwantung Army? In this case wouldn't it be simpler to obtain all political, material, and military advantages at Moscow's expense?

The Chairman of the CCP Central Committee is more than just kind to me. Jen Pi-shih said to me, "Perhaps you are a more trusted person than many of us, his old comrades-in-arms." . . .

As Rousseau said, ". . . they have turned their own impotence into a merit. . . ." This aptly defines a characteristic feature of Mao Tse-tung's behavior. He does not disdain to speculate even on his own treachery.

Retuning himself to the Soviet Union, he is singing "an old song from Changsha"—I have always been a true friend of the All-Union Communist Party and the Soviet people. . . .

Mao Tse-tung has much experience in presenting his meanness as a virtue. . . .

February 11, 1945

In Mao's reception room you can usually see a guard on duty who doesn't miss a single gesture of a visitor. Mauser-armed guards are in ambush over the cave. Numerous overt and secret sentries guard the approaches to the residence. All vegetation before the residence is carefully preserved so that nothing can be seen from a plane. . . .

Yesterday, conferring with a narrow group of his associates, the Chairman of the CCP Central Committee said that, however regrettable, the compromise with Chungking was hardly avoidable. However, this should not be done before mid-April when Moscow's intentions had become clear.

"To make everything possible to prolong uncertainty in the talks with Chungking until that time" is the essence of the instructions given by the Chairman of the CCP Central Committee to his representatives at the Kuomintang.

In the past few days the Chairman of the CCP Central Committee transmitted a series of telegrams via me. He pretends to be honest and floods Moscow with figures, versions concerning his relations with Kuomintang and exposures of American intrigues. . . .

It would be wrong to assert that Mao Tse-tung knows little. He thoroughly studies materials relating to the East. He digests large numbers of accounts, reports, military reviews, and other documents. He has an exhausting knowledge of the present-day questions connected with China. In the spiritual sphere he recognizes only Chinese culture and history.

Old China's culture is the subject of his special adoration. He doesn't doubt its unchallenged superiority over any other culture. . . .

In one of his telegrams the Chairman of the CCP Central Committee said Chiang Kai-shek and Company connected all their hopes with American aid. Chungking was urging Washington to begin the transport of allied troops to China as soon as possible. Chiang Kai-shek's aim was to reorganize his armed forces with Yankee assistance, equip them with the latest weapons, mechanize his infantry, etc.

The Chairman of the CCP Central Committee wrote that Washington's aim was to lasso the Communist Party. Both Chiang Kai-shek and President Franklin Roosevelt were working for this. . . .

This part of Mao Tse-tung's telegram is indicative by itself. Both Yenan and Chungking were dreaming of alliance with the United States. Both sides tried to settle their scores with the aid of American weapons and dollars. In exchange for this, both sides offered complete control over their country to transoceanic traders. Washington chose Chiang Kai-shek, and Mao was now reminding Moscow of class solidarity: The Americans and Chiang have come to terms and this presents a threat to the Special Area.

To make Moscow angry, Mao saturated his telegram with facts concerning the "Kuomintang's political prostitution" (as Mao put it in a talk with me). Here again Mao resorts to his tested tactic of figure juggling.

He writes the Central Government's armies have about 1.5 million officers and men. This shows their strength has been considerably reduced.

The fighting capacity of Chiang Kai-shek's armies is at the lowest point since the beginning of the national liberation war. This points once again to the growing might of the Eighth Route and the New Fourth armies, which number 710,000 officers and men.

The Chairman of the CCP Central Committee writes:

Still last year the Kuomintang armed forces had indisputable superiority over all our divisions. However, the Japanese resorted to large-scale offensive operations. This resulted in the major redistribution of forces between the Eighth Route Army, the New Fourth Army, and Chiang Kai-shek's armies. Even before the catastrophes in Hunan, Honan, and on the southern fronts, the Eighth Route Army, the New Fourth Army, and guerrillas had contained at least 51 per cent of the elite Japanese formations. Already at that time the Japanese invaders had used over 49 per cent of their combat units to suppress the Chungking armies. The shameful catastrophe of the Kuomintang troops in Hunan, at the southern fronts, and Honan had compelled the Communist Party's armed forces to make up for the falling resistance of the Kuomintang armies. At present the Eighth Route Army, the New Fourth Army, and guerrillas contain 64 per cent of the enemy's strongest formations. The Eighth Route Army, the New Fourth Army, and guerrillas also conduct operations against 90 per cent of the puppet Nanking formations. The Kuomintang troops retreat before the invaders, although they are now attacked by no more than 36 per cent of the total strength of the enemy's expeditionary forces in China. This bargain has a foul smell especially now that the Japanese are turning the country into a concentration camp and ruins.

February 12, 1945

An unambiguous conclusion suggests itself from the telegrams sent by Mao Tse-tung to Moscow. The Chairman of the CCP Central Committee writes that way back last year the Kuomintang armed forces considerably surpassed the Eighth Route Army and the New Fourth Army. It was only a wholly irresponsible person that could, in July 1943, expose the Special Area to the danger of defeat by the anti-Kuomintang campaign and the withdrawal of troops of the Eighth Route Army from the front!

This was a special kind of irresponsibility! Besides everything else, it was necessary to justify the tactics of disintegrating the united anti-Japanese front. The best means for this was the anti-Kuomintang hysteria and the sabotage of combat operations against the Japanese (which suited the invaders).

The tactic of the disintegration of the anti-Japanese front can be traced nearly to the signing of the Sian agreement. Its aim is to rupture ties with the Comintern and then gradually to eliminate the party members who are connected with the Comintern and recognize its tactics and prestige. This gave rise to the cheng-feng.

In these circumstances Mao Tse-tung unhesitatingly risked the destiny of the Special Area and the Communist Party only to achieve his domestic-policy aims. But this risk was altogether reckless! The Chairman of the CCP Central Committee believed the Soviet Union would not allow the Kuomintang to put an end to the Chinese Communists. However, I saw Mao Tse-tung's panic during the July 1943 crisis. Mao suddenly became hesitant—what if the Soviet Union, engaged in the struggle against the Hitlerites, would not be able to come to his aid?! This staggered Mao Tse-tung. Then I learned that Mao suffered from chronic diarrhea sarcastically called "bear's disease" by the Russians. . . .

Mao Tse-tung knew what 1943 had meant for the Soviet Union—severe military and economic difficulties, the turning point of the war. I kept him fully informed of this. Mao disregarded this fact and took the risk of drawing the Soviet Union into the conflict in the Far East.

The Soviet Union should now, according to the opinion growing in the CCP leadership, join the war against Japan and use its forces and matériel to liberate the territories which the CCP then will turn into its base areas. As for the CCP armed forces, they are largely preserved precisely for this future division of the country in the struggle with Chiang Kai-shek. CCP troops should only promote the future operations of Soviet or allied armies which are to play the main part in routing the Japanese. And this opportunity should not be missed! It should be exploited—this is the key point of the plans hatched by the CCP leaders.

February 13, 1945

The cheng-feng character is being interpreted in a peculiar way these days. This period in the CCP history now has its theory which rests on "indisputable" conclusions made in the spirit of the "Marxism of reality." The distorted Marxism-Leninism was put at the service of Mao Tse-tung's aims—but not for the revolutionary struggle against the feudal capitalist system. Here all are being convinced, were convinced, and forced to believe that violence in the party is a necessity, part and parcel of the general struggle against the class enemy. This was used to cover up the spiritual and physical chastisement of the internationalists ("dogmatists").

The cheng-feng has become less conspicuous. It is being transformed under the cover of new pseudo-Marxist deliberations in order to uproot all that does not correspond to the views of the Chairman of the CCP Central Committee and does not fit in with his "Marxism of reality." In general, criticism is impermissible and simply impossible here. All were "convinced" that everything was untrue unless blessed by Mao Tse-tung. People here speak about the Leninist style of work, having no idea what it is like.

Party democracy is interpreted here as the right of all to repeat Mao Tse-tung's pronouncements, to cite them on every occasion, even a ridiculous one. Party members are allowed to display initiative only within the limits of orders and instructions.

Mao Tse-tung's guidelines have been carefully turned by Liu Shao-chi into the theses which repeat, in different forms, the idea to the effect that the cheng-feng campaign was a historical necessity, that it reformed new young party members affected by bourgeois morality and philosophy. Cheng-feng, it is alleged, reformed these petty-bourgeois elements into genuine Communists and helped them "to keep firmer to the positions of the working class." Cheng-feng allegedly exposed the opportunists whose representatives in the Communist Party's leading bodies came out against the growth of the people's struggle, against setting up new liberated areas, and opposed the qualitative and quantitative growth of the Chinese Red Army (the Eighth Route and the New Fourth armies). These opportunists, it is alleged, were against recapturing the sacred Chinese territories from the Japanese, the territories which were supposed to be under worker-peasant power. Fear of Japan "dulled the class consciousness of some party members," and "they began to yield their proletarian positions to the Kuomintang," saying it was necessary for the strengthening of the united anti-Japanese front.

Mao Tse-tung allegedly liquidated this deviation, saved the party, and indicated a clear and concrete road to victory.

Comments are not needed here.

First, this theorizing betrays the desire to adapt Marxist scientific philosophy to one's egoistic aims. The struggle against "dogmatism" actually means the discrediting of Marxism (deliberations concerning the "dogmas of Western Marxism").

Liu Shao-chi's theses, conceived by Mao Tse-tung, hold no water (although they are indisputable here!). These theses, sent to all party organizations, actually recognize the fact that the hope of the party, its new young members, are mostly nonproletarian elements.

Chiang Kai-shek told his old comrades-in-arms and senior party functionaries that under Sun Yat-sen's last will he, jointly with the Kuomintang, was to build a new China.

". . . I may transfer power only to the people," Chiang Kai-shek's actual words were, "but under no circumstances to any other party or person. Hurley is a fool! The Americans do not understand the situation in China. We'll be able to destroy the CCP." . . .

These revelations of Chiang Kai-shek were cited by Mao Tse-tung in one of his telegrams to Dimitrov.

Hardly a day passes without a meeting with Kang Sheng. Looks dejected, although tries to show that everything is all right. The Fall Minister is anxious about his future. I don't doubt his real attitude to me. He is, of course, in the know of Mao's correspondence with Dimitrov and my relation to this matter. Moscow's sharp condemnation of the behavior of the Fall Minister has made me his rabid enemy forever.

February 18, 1945

Jen Pi-shih told me didactically, "The enlarged plenum of the CCP Central Committee in Tsunyi removed left-wing opportunist elements from leadership; since January 1935 the party has been led by Comrade Mao Tse-tung, who learned the art of applying Marxist-Leninist philosophy to the practical aspects of our revolution. . . ."

Clearly, all these talks about the distant and not-too-distant past of the Communist Party are connected with preparations for the Seventh Congress.

The Communist Party leadership is engaged in feverish activities. Foreign radio reports and the official statement of the Soviet Informburo concerning the Crimean Conference of the heads of the anti-Hitler coalition (Stalin, Roosevelt, and Churchill) are the subject of thorough analyses and forecasts.

Mao Tse-tung had a long talk with me.

What interested him most of all was whether the Soviet Union would participate in the war in the Far East. I made a most detailed account of the communiqué's official text published in newspapers. . . .

It is extremely important for Mao Tse-tung to know the Soviet Union's intentions. With whom should he form a bloc? Maybe it would be better to yield to the Americans and accept Chiang Kai-shek's plan?

Briefly speaking, Yenan diplomacy is at the crossroads.

The Solomon-like judgment of Mao Tse-tung is to wait—to wait till mid-April, without taking any important political decisions, and, simultaneously, to delay the opening of the party congress.

The Soviet Union's attitude to its pact with Japan, which expires on April 13, must make everything clear for the Yenan policy, since the Americans do not want to make further concessions. . . .

Po Ku said at the meeting the Crimean Conference could not fail to have discussed the joint operations of all Allies against fascist Japan. Po Ku is confident the head of the Soviet Government signed an agreement envisaging the Soviet Union's entry into the war in the Far East.

Po Ku's position is logical. It considers the aggressive course of Japan which had for many years striven to alienate a number of Soviet areas and which was finally sobered only by the Stalingrad victory.

Po Ku was and remains an internationalist in his views. He cannot but take into consideration the fact that the Soviet entry into the war will help the enslaved peoples of China. He expressed these considerations, expecting that in my turn, too, I should be frank. With all my respect to him I could not tell anything definite.

Equally, I could not satisfy the curiosity of Lo Fu, who thinks the Soviet Union would not fight against Japan. Lo Fu's position still bears an imprint of cheng-feng sentiments.

The Chairman of the CCP Central Committee thinks much about the Soviet Union's armed participation in the war in the Far East. In Mao Tse-tung's view, the Soviet Union has been bled white, its economy disorganized, its man power exhausted.

Liu Shao-chi is preoccupied with the preparation of congress materials.

Chou is evasively affable with me. His eyes on the Chairman of the CCP Central Committee, he does not say anything definite concerning the possibility of the Soviet Union's entry into the war against Japan.

The Hunan man is also cautious because of prestige reasons. Not knowing for sure what turn the events will take, he may find himself in an awkward position (he is not supposed to and may not make mistakes!).

The Chairman of the CCP Central Committee connects new far-reaching political decisions (in respect to the Kuomintang in the first place) with the destiny of the Soviet-Japanese neutrality pact—blackmail Chiang Kai-shek, pressure him, gather forces for a civil war in the near future or come to agreement, recognize the Chungking head's correctness, and sign the draft agreement proposed by the Americans.

That is why contact is not ruptured with the Observer Group, although much anger is harbored against it.

Chu Teh, Yeh Chien-ying, and other military leaders are confident the Soviet Union will denounce the pact with Japan and join the war against Japan. Chu Teh doesn't believe the Soviets will forgive the Japanese fascists the intervention during the Civil War (the organization and support of the Kolchak movement, different White Guard governments, and the Semyonov movement), provocations in the Khasan Lake area, the bloody Khalkin-Gol fighting, and preparations for attack in 1941–42. CCP military leaders firmly count on Soviet assistance.

In a word, there are most contradicting opinions in the CCP leadership.

Flexible and taciturn, Soviet diplomacy confuses Mao. He cannot fail to see that for some time now Moscow has preferred not to keep him informed of its important decisions. Moscow's reserve depresses Mao. He cannot but see what's behind it. . . .

February 19, 1945

A big booze, with clouds of tobacco smoke, guttural shouts, jokes, and laughter, is arranged by Mao Tse-tung's entourage to celebrate every political and military success, or Chiang Kai-shek's failure.

Mao is prepossessingly friendly with me, as, incidentally, he has been since the memorable January telegram to Dimitrov . . . on behalf of the Executive Committee of the Communist International in connection with cheng-feng's anti-Marxist essence.

From time to time he would sit beside me, treat me to drinks so obtrusively that I couldn't resist, and drink himself. . . . Ate little after drinks. Smoked much.

All parties, like this one, pass as if they mark important dates in Mao's private life, his birthday, for example. People drink willingly, laugh, and gossip. However, all ears are turned to Mao to catch his mood. . . .

When he is tipsy, Mao's speech is particularly unintelligible. His monotonous inarticulate patter of a Hunan man becomes especially heavy at such moments. Now and then this monotonous mumbling is interrupted by two or three sharply accented words. Slightly drunk, Mao loses his important looks and sometimes yells in a hoarse voice like a peasant in an eating place.

Taking me by the hand, he said unexpectedly that so far there had not been, nor had he seen, a better worker from Moscow in China. On this occasion I had to gulp down another glass of some diabolical mixture. More stuff was poured into my mug without anybody taking the trouble to see whether it was empty or not. . . .

Mao also drank from his mug. His face reddened and his hair parted in the middle. His eyes glittered; he was smiling absent-mindedly. His face became lively, having lost its usual impassivity.

"I am glad that you, Sung Ping, co-operate with us precisely in this great period in the history of our party. I have a sincere respect for you, you know."

People vied with each other to drink with me. It was impossible to refuse. Each drank his glass. But there were too many toasts, for me. . . .

Incidentally, toasts are not frequent here. They just talk and drink. I wanted only that my head remain clear. I was tormented with endless questions of different kinds. I was practically showered with questions. . . .

All this intermingled with rather crude jokes which Mao liked very much. The jokes were frequently outright erotic, very frivolous.

Opinions were briefly exchanged all the time. Jeers at their comrades' slips, taunts, and bursts of laughter.

From remarks and passing observations I learned that the seventh plenary meeting of the CCP Central Committee would begin one of these days in connection with the coming congress, that there arose big "discrepancies as regards the evaluation of the party history's period since Tsunyi—that is, since Mao Tse-tung took over leadership—that attempts are made to smooth away all these 'discrepancies.' " . . .

Chou was in Moscow in the autumn of 1939. In passing, he told me of his impressions of that time. Not of all impressions, of course. Soviet weapons for the revolution in China were the aim of Chou's visit inspired by Mao Tse-tung. The question of weapons was discussed, if not point-blank, in Moscow in the autumn of 1939. I was informed of this in due time. That is why it was with pleasure that I listened to a different version of his visit. . . .

At the same time in Moscow Chou clarified the Executive Committee of the Communist International's positions which had already been known to him—a joint rebuff of China's all-national forces to Japanese aggression. In general, he was sounding out the Soviet Government's attitude to the Far Eastern problems in an attempt to determine the direction of its policy and the possibility of the Soviet Union's entry into the war against Japan with all the ensuing consequences.

I know Chou well enough. I don't doubt the main aim of his visit was the desire to learn something of the possibility of the Soviet Union's rupture with Chungking for the good of the provision of the CCP troops with all the necessary arms.

This was a complete ignoring of the military-political situation which arose at the beginning of the World War! They thought only about their plans and interests and did not care about military complications for the Soviet Union. Life has proved this. . . .

Chou asked me about our military mission in Chungking, although he was very well informed. He spoke in his usual charming manner. A polite talk and nothing more.

After drinks all felt themselves at home. They talked interrupting one another and paying no attention to gestures or words. . . .

Here they are very satisfied with the turn of events! At present all their hopes were connected with the Soviet Union. They spoke about this without beating around the bush with premeditative sincerity so that I would report everything to Moscow. The Americans were only mentioned scornfully.

Some even said the Soviet Union's war in the east was not so much in the interests of China as in the interests of the Soviet Union. . . .

Mao said that my head was turning gray but this was not a defect. In any case, this showed a man was not as naïve as in his twenties. Wisdom would be dearer than youth but for . . . And amid general laughter he specified what he meant by his "but for." . . .

February 21, 1945

It was officially decided to convene the Seventh Congress of the Chinese Communist Party this March.

This decision and a number of others were adopted at the meeting of the Communist Party's Central Committee. The meeting heard Chou En-lai, Politburo member of the CCP Central Committee; Mao Tse-tung, Chairman of the CCP Central Committee; and Chu Teh, Politburo member of the CCP Central Committee. There were no debates.

One of the important decisions was practical steps toward setting up a political and administrative center of the Special Area as well as all territories liberated by the Communists. The formation of the center was postponed until the Sixth Kuomintang Congress. The results of this Kuomintang Congress will provide the necessary arguments for justifying the formation of the "united administrative center"—one of the most important actions of the Communist Party leadership. The establishment of the united center will split the country finally and irreversibly (not counting, of course, the principalities of the puppets of different caliber).

Following the establishment of the united center, frictions with the "Chungking clique" will become unavoidable. That is why a civil war is not precluded.

This scheme was carefully elaborated in Yenan. The entire cycle, from the formation of the united center to the possible beginning of a civil war, is to take several years. This will require five or six years, possibly more, because the war against Japan will, in the opinion of the Chairman of the CCP Central Committee, continue for several years. ("China will be cleared of the Japanese in the next two or three years," Mao Tse-tung said.)

The Sixth Kuomintang Congress will inevitably pass a decision on strengthening its power.

The Chairman of the CCP Central Committee does not intend to miss this opportunity. The Kuomintang will be heavily criticized by the Yenan and liberal Chungking press, by all progressive public circles.

The plan of forming a united administrative center of all base Communist areas will be looked upon as something natural. At such a moment this step will not cause discontent either in China or in other countries, although it will certainly widen the split in the national resistance to the aggressor. In Mao's opinion this step will cause tremendous damage to the Central Government's power, undermined politically and economically as it is. Chiang Kai-shek will be regarded as the main culprit responsible for the disintegration of the united front and all other failures.

The meeting speakers emphasized that the united center should be formed only after the Kuomintang Congress.

Chou En-lai, a Politburo member of the CCP Central Committee, gave a long report on the talks between the Communist Party leadership and Kuomintang leaders. His report confirmed my surmises and some other facts.

Incidentally, practical measures to form Mao Tse-tung's future government (the united center of all Soviet areas) were decided upon. They will be effected in a matter of days.

It will take not more than a week to inform the country's territories liberated from the invaders of the establishment of an all-China trade union center. Its final name has not yet been determined by Yenan comrades. In any case, there will emerge a united trade union organ of all liberated Soviet areas, in which the leading role will be played, of course, by the smoothly functioning party and administrative machinery of the Special Area. This will be the first peal of thunder of an eventual civil war!

Chou En-lai's report did not exhaust the agenda of the meeting. Needless to say, the most important event was the Chairman of the CCP Central Committee's speech, which was much discussed over the following days. In his speech the Chairman of the CCP Central Committee clearly formulated, for the first time, his attitude to the Crimean Conference decisions (mostly bearing on the Soviet Union's participation in the war against Japan).

There should be no doubts, Mao said, that the Soviet Union will certainly take part in combat operations against Japan. This should be realized clearly!

The Chairman of the CCP Central Committee said further that the Communist Party's task was to demand that the leaders of Great Britain, the Soviet Union, and the United States interfere in the affairs of the Chungking "one-party regime." The leaders of the anti-Hitler coalition should understand Chiang Kai-shek's government must meet the main demands of the Communist Party. The probability of all members of the anti-Hitler coalition agreeing with such demands is highly doubtful, practically precluded. The following is the gist of Mao's further statements: A possible refusal of the heads of the United States, Great Britain, and the Soviet Union should not take us unawares. Be it as it may, we shall not give up our strategic plan (the establishment of the united center). We shall defend the plan to the last ditch before the leaders of the Soviet Union, United States, and Great Britain, and only extreme circumstances will force us to retreat.

The compromise may become inevitable—this is regrettable. This factor has to be counted with, and if we are compelled to agree with the compromise, we must let it become our little victory. "To persist on the main in order to retreat afterward at the highest price!" was the main idea of this part of the speech by the Chairman of the CCP Central Committee. These words of Mao Tse-tung met with the approving hum of the audience.

Here Mao Tse-tung gave himself away completely—he won't receive power from Chiang Kai-shek. It is unprecedented for the stronger to yield power voluntarily. But to force Chiang Kai-shek, using the pressure of international political forces, to share power is, perhaps, not a utopia. Not a utopia, considering the specificities of the war in China!

For this purpose, Mao declared, the Communist Party should employ all means for the anti-Hitler coalition's leaders to adopt specific decisions on China as a member of the antifascist bloc. The Chungking regime's head will certainly give in before such a force as Roosevelt, Churchill, and Stalin. It is then that he will find himself in the trap! He will have no choice but to concede, and this will be a concession in our favor! We shall try to win the support of the most powerful political forces. That is why it is not precluded that Chiang Kai-shek will reconstruct his government. And this reconstruction must be radical! In this respect the Communist Party has every chance to succeed! The "Chungking dictator" must accept the terms which hold the greatest advantage for us. The situation is most favorable for us at present.

In such circumstances any talks with the Kuomintang would be a mistake. We should wait until mid-April (the hint that the situation will become clear following the decision of the destiny of the Soviet-Japanese pact).

Immediately after that the Chairman of the CCP Central Committee recognized that practically there was little chance to form a coalition government in China! Facts should be judged realistically! If the struggle for a coalition government proves to be unfeasible, this, nevertheless, will be an effective means to change the sentiments in the country in the favor of the Communist Party. In the future, too, we shall present demands and conditions which Chungking will hardly accept! "This is our strategic political plan in relation to Chiang Kai-shek! There should be no conditions on which he could retreat before us!"

Mao Tse-tung's position is crystal clear. The main thing is "to drive Chiang desperate," that is, to unleash a civil war! The rest is public opinion handling, which is to give the Communist Party time for full mobilization.

Territorial seizures camouflaged as the struggle against the Japanese mean expanding bases for a future civil war. Besides, the tactic of conditions binds, in a way, Chiang Kai-shek, who is also beginning preparations for a clash with the Special Area. In this connection the Americans may sharply increase military aid to the Kuomintang. That is why Mao struggles to limit this aid, if not preclude it completely, and compel the Americans to consider public opinion. . . . Yenan will expose all such actions of the Allies. . . .

There is something else which troubles Mao seriously—he is not altogether sure the Soviet Union will fight against Japan. He says the Soviets will fight, but he is not sure of this. This explains the Communist Party leadership's delay of all resolute foreign- and domestic-policy actions until the latter half of April. Very typical of Mao! He does not say everything even to his comrades-in-arms.

Apart from the evaluation of the current political situation and relevant tasks, Mao laid special emphasis on the situation in northern

China. To the applause of the audience he solemnly said the situation in northern China was so good that it could be regarded, without exaggeration, as a domain of the Communist Party. Here its power, influence, and forces are strong beyond doubt. However, it would be fine to reshuffle cadres there: "Strengthen cadres! Struggle is ahead!"

". . . We should not indulge in self-delusion: It is necessary to strengthen cadres in Chahar, Sui-yuan, and Jehol as well. All inefficient Soviet and party leaders should be removed! This equally refers to Inner Mongolia and Manchuria. . . ."

After that the Chairman of the CCP Central Committee returned to the question of setting up a central committee of the trade unions of all Soviet areas.

As far as I understood Mao Tse-tung, the committee is to act as a fuse. The trade unions' preparatory committee will convene delegates. The delegates will adopt decisions not only on trade union matters. They will pass a decision concerning the necessity to establish a united administrative center of China's all-Soviet areas (in any case, they will demand its immediate formation). This will blow up "Chiang Kai-shek's regime of one-party dictatorship." . . .

Mao Tse-tung, as, incidentally, all other party leaders, did not say anything about the state of affairs in Shantung, Shansi, and Hopeh. In these provinces nobody can shake the power of the Communist Party. True, there are Kuomintang troops there, but they are being gradually destroyed and will be completely eliminated in the near future.

Although it did not preclude the compromise, Mao Tse-tung's entire speech was a call to prepare for a civil war. In this respect Mao doesn't think seriously of the situation in the country. The course toward territorial seizure by force of arms is the essence of the guideline of the Chairman of the CCP Central Committee. The political maneuvering of Chou and Mao's other assistants in Chungking is nothing but the play for time, the fooling of the public quarters and blackmail!

Chu Teh made an account of his activities at the meeting. His speech showed the unmistakable "relapses of cheng-feng." Quite unexpectedly he began to repent (repentance is in vogue here). He said he had underestimated Mao Tse-tung's military talent. That was why he had made the blunder by insisting on the transfer of the Communist Party's big army contingents to the southern and southeastern provinces. Comrade Mao Tse-tung's timely instructions had averted the danger (the erroneous choice of regions of military actions, division of forces into small units, etc.). Mao is again in the role of the Savior!

Chu Teh also said he had erred in the main political question. He had hoped for a revolutionary explosion in the whole of China, whereas it was necessary to fight for power in the country gradually.

"The faith that power can be seized in the entire country at once is my big political blunder," Chu Teh said.

In this way, the Chairman of the CCP Central Committee called, through Chu Teh, for the tactics of the seizure of the Kuomintang-controlled territories, using the specificities of the war with Japan. Simultaneously, Mao warned all that an open general clash with the Kuomintang was fraught with a defeat for the CCP! Mao all over! To capture Kuomintang-held territories, build up forces, "organize" incidents—that is, provoke Chiang Kai-shek—and, at the same time, to realize that the relation of forces was clearly not in the favor of the Communist Party, that a civil war will lead to the destruction of the Special Area.

This is not only Mao's adventurism and hope for Soviet assistance in case of serious complications, but also his ardent desire to seize power, the desire which frequently (too frequently) deprives him of common sense!

Mao Tse-tung regards the peasantry as the main force to be used in a civil war. The peasants are in the vise of a land crisis. The agrarian crisis must help him to stir the country, shake Chiang Kai-shek's power, blow up the country!

The maturity of Marxism does not turn into the maturity of the CCP. The party leadership is increasingly turning toward petty-bourgeois leftism. . . .

The thunder of the Soviet Army's victories over the fascist forces in Europe reaches Yenan. Increasing importance attaches to the fact which is already evident to Mao Tse-tung: The Americans do not wish to part with Chiang Kai-shek. Mao Tse-tung has no choice. The CCP has no other ally but the Soviet Union. Mao's promises have not dispersed the suspicions of American political leaders. The United States is strengthening Chiang Kai-shek. This fact determines the behavior of the Chairman of the CCP Central Committee.

Alliance with Moscow in the struggle against Japan may play, objectively, a positive role in normalizing the situation in the CCP, in forming a new generation of Communists-internationalists.

February 22, 1945

On February 18 *Izvestia* carried an article entitled, "Some Facts Concerning the Situation in China." The article states the Soviet Union's desire to solve the Far Eastern problem with due account for the interests of the Chinese Communists.

It is quite clear that despite Mao's political machinations our leadership in Moscow firmly maintains the course toward the support of the CCP.

The support for the CCP is the support for the Chinese Revolution and the Chinese people struggling against domestic and foreign oppressors. If the socialist revolution triumphs in China, this will be the greatest defeat for imperialism after our October Revolution. The Soviet Union will have a mighty friend in a free China, the alliance with whom will place the socialist camp in an exceptionally favorable position.

The All-Union Communist Party regards the Chinese people's struggle against Japanese fascism and feudal, capitalist, and foreign bondage as their sacred right and assistance to the Chinese people as its great internationalist mission. This is Moscow's firm position, which cannot be influenced by the political gambling of Mao's group. There is hardly another word for the entourage of the Chairman of the CCP Central Committee. Against the background of the party and the country's tremendous population running into 500 million, they really look like a handful of political intrigants. As for the great people's road, it is clear and unmistakable—the socialist revolution in the future and the peaceful construction of a new China.

February 23, 1945

Yenan is in expectation of the Communist Party congress.

Whatever the subject, Mao invariably directs the talk to his hobbyhorse—class struggle. Daily, hourly struggle . . . I have enough information, and saw for myself its manifestations, about the class struggle conducted in Mao Tse-tung's style. This is one of the main subjects in the talks of Mao, who uses it to justify the violence cheng-feng did to the party, the violence which marks all its road. . . . It was violence rather than plenums, conferences, or resolutions that decided the outcome of the struggle. . . .

Mao Tse-tung's policy seems contradictory. Today he puts forward certain demands, and a week later he would insist on entirely different ones. Yesterday he denigrated respected party workers, while today he gives them important posts. Now he is "honeymooning" with the Americans, then he is backheeling them, etc.

This is often called the mysterious Oriental diplomacy, tricky and misty. . . . However, this is a layman's idea of it. In actual fact, this policy is logical and consistent.

This logic and consistency is also typical of the policy pursued by the Chairman of the CCP Central Committee. Circumstances change, and he, adapting himself to the situation, continually changes the outward forms of struggle, not its essence. The main thing remains intact. In this case this means a full rejection of the united anti-Japanese front; anti-Sovietism; and the eradication of "dogmatism."

There is not a trace of the mysterious Oriental cunning here. Yes, he violates his promises and agreements. He denigrates and praises people, pretends to be a democrat while at home, conducts himself as an aristocrat. He puts on shows for Barrett and foreign reporters, passes on rubbish to me, deceives Moscow. . . .

Nonsense! This doesn't even smell of Oriental wisdom and cunning. All this is triteness and lies! If there does exist the so-called Oriental diplomacy here, it may be called unscrupulousness!

February 25, 1945

Mao Tse-tung's characteristic feature which has somehow escaped my attention: He is, in fact, doing everything for which Chen Tu-hsiu and Li Li-san were removed from the leadership of the Communist Party.

To some extent, Li Li-san's mistakes were predetermined not only by China's petty-bourgeois revolutionary specificities but by the general immaturity of the young Communist Party which was then making its first steps.

All his life Mao has been consciously struggling against the influence of the Comintern revising Marxism. . . . And how dodgy this Hunan man is! Here is a congratulatory telegram to Comrade Stalin. Under the text are two familiar signatures: the Chairman of the CCP Central Committee and the commander in chief of the New Fourth Army and the Eighth Route Army.

The text bears not a trace of the cynical mockery which Mao Tse-tung used to entertain his supporters in the autumn of 1941. Today the calendar shows 1945! And Mao Tse-tung flatters Stalin.

The Chairman of the CCP Central Committee writes about the spectacular victories of the Soviet armed forces! In the opinion of the Chairman of the CCP Central Committee, the Soviet Army is invincible at present. The Soviet armed forces have covered themselves with unfading glory, and he (Mao) doesn't doubt they will be glorified for many other exploits.

Now Mao Tse-tung assures Stalin that his experience of a genius makes him confident of the eventual triumph of the greatest liberation struggle. . . .

February 26, 1945

The decision to call the Seventh Congress of the Communist Party stirs up passion. Again fuss around Wang Ming, Yang Shang-kun, Wang Chia-hsiang, and Lo Fu. Again public denouncements (at meetings) and secret denouncements . . .

Wang Ming is not called otherwise than a "right-wing opportunist element." This definition is taken as a matter of fact. All have already become convinced that Mao has saved the party from Wang Ming's course toward capitulation "before the Kuomintang." People say in so many words: "Wang Ming licked Chiang Kai-shek's boots." . . .

The motto of the internationalists (Lo Fu, Po Ku, Wang Ming, and others)—"Fidelity to the united national front is fidelity to the interests of the party"—has been forgotten and slandered! The Mao Tse-tung leadership has gradually convinced all that Wang Ming "has been implanting alien elements in the party ever since 1931–34." Way back in 1931 when Wang Ming turned up in Shanghai, he, it is alleged, like a mandarin, arbitrarily decided questions crucial to the party's destiny. . . . Foolish and ridiculous, but nobody can or may object!

Cheng-feng has effectively coped with its task. Even Wang Ming's former associates have begun to discredit him again. Thus, Yang Shang-kun said Wang Ming had "conducted" the class-capitulationist line in respect to Generalissimo Chiang Kai-shek. It was said by Yang, who is more than just a former comrade of Wang Ming's.

In the Shanghai period they jointly fulfilled the instructions of the CCP Central Committee. They jointly countered the opportunist actions of Mao Tse-tung and Li Li-san. . . .

The forthcoming congress agitates the former members of the "Moscow group." They have been slandered. Party members have no sympathies for them. Cheng-feng "has exposed these capitulationist-opportunists." Cheng-feng has made everybody believe that "all here in Yenan are alive thanks to the wisdom of the Chairman of the CCP Central Committee."

At party meetings speakers repeat without end: "Comrade Mao Tse-tung is the correct way of the Chinese Revolution, the earnest of the victorious end of the liberation war!"

Verbally and in print all are impressed that "as regards Marxism, we must think proceeding from the Chinese reality, not like Western Marxists."

The most tragic aspect of this is that nationalism is presented as creative self-sufficiency in Marxism. This is the foundation of Mao Tse-tung's political platform. I become convinced of this talking with Chen Po-ta, who echoes Mao's thoughts.

I become convinced that the congress may take the road of ideological reconciliation with nationalism!

Last time I had an unusual talk with Mao Tse-tung. It passed without gin, whiskey, and guests' hubbub. We were talking of some trifles when Mao changed over, unnoticeably, to deliberations concerning death, the inevitability of death, and the cruel inexorability of one's fate. In such situations the best thing is to listen to him. If you don't, he would become introvert and, preserving amiability, would wait until you go. He likes to be listened to. Objections deeply injure him, although he doesn't show this: He would politely part with you but would remember everything!

He was meditating aloud on the fragility of life and immortality. The thought of death depresses him. Carried away by his thoughts, he cited Confucius, old writers and poets, and read stanzas from his own verses. . . .

He became tender and, at the same time, excited. Not a trace was left of his wax-figure-like solemnity. He spoke rapidly, crying out stressed syllables in a hoarse voice. He gestured away all who tried to enter the room.

He asked me questions and, without waiting for the answer, developed his thoughts. At times it seemed he had forgotten about me.

Impatiently, he rummaged in the pockets of his wadded jacket. He lit a cigarette, inhaling avidly and deeply. Smiled absent-mindedly.

When the cigarette burned to the end, he would pull out a new one. A button came off his jacket. He angrily knocked it aside.

After that he repeated his question. Unfortunately, I did not know that old saying. Waiting for the answer, Mao was looking at me. His glittering moist eyes radiated excitement and passion. . . . He didn't try to expose my ignorance. No, he was just engrossed in his own thoughts.

What could I say? I shrugged my shoulders and admitted I didn't know it but I would, since I was young enough and still had time to read something. . . .

"But," I said, "before the revolution in a village school we were taught the Holy Scripture, which says about death: 'Dust thou art . . . unto dust shalt—' "

Mao grinned and threw the cigarette to the floor.

Parting, he suddenly asked me: "Haven't you liked a single pretty woman here? Don't be shy. . . ."

I laughed the matter off.

February 27, 1945

Of all the provinces, the Japanese penetration is the deepest in Kweichow. The Japanese offensive slowed down when China's military defeat seemed to have been unavoidable. . . .

The Americans throw parties which are luxurious by the Yenan standards. . . .

Although the question of Americans leaving for home sooner or later is not touched upon yet, they are, incidentally, establishing contacts with an eye to the future. Goddamn those drinking bouts! Every other day till everyone is sick! Americans do not exert special efforts to make their guests drunk. Guests don't need to be urged. I involuntarily recall a melancholic aphorism of Chekhov, who wrote, referring to the hero of one of his stories, that although he said he was thirsty he actually wanted to become drunk. . . . Here, too, you'll find "revolutionaries" with the kind of thirst mentioned by Chekhov. But just try to talk with them. They will shower you with citations from Marx. . . .

March 1945

March 1, 1945

The CCP leaders have been avoiding Hurley's mediation but show no intent of breaking with the Americans. On the one hand, they pretend to be rejecting the "imperialists" and confidentially report about the latter's "designs" to Moscow. On the other, they will not sever contacts with the Observer Group.

Mao Tse-tung waits for the time when the treaty between the Soviet Union and Japan will expire and it will be possible to act fully sure of success. . . .

Today, quite unexpectedly for himself, Mao Tse-tung has received a telegram in reply from I. V. Stalin. The Chairman of the CCP Central Committee immediately called a conference. . . .

March 2, 1945

The congress-convening decision has electrified party life. They are holding meeting after meeting! . . .

But how to handle it all? The cheng-feng had a pronounced anti-Soviet character. "Dogmatism" is nothing but the negation of the ideological principles of the All-Union Communist Party.

At the congress all this may come to light. How to foresee what delegates will speak about? You can't check each word. The situation is delicate—and the Chairman of the CCP Central Committee is seeking a way out.

Once again CCP Central Committee instructions for the study of certain documents, the majority of which are made up of the works of Mao Tse-tung and Liu Shao-chi. Special importance is being attached to the study of Mao Tse-tung's *On New Democracy*. . . .

Even glancing over the list of the "works being studied" is enough to see that their chief purpose is to show Mao Tse-tung's works to be the legacy and extension of the ideas of the classics of Marxism.

The meaning of the work *On New Democracy* lies in conforming Marxist ideas to Mao Tse-tung's views. The correct premises and propositions of Marxism are regarded in it from a clearly petty-bourgeois standpoint.

Marxist terminology, references to the works of Marx and Lenin, and quotations from these works create the illusion of a profound knowledge of the subject. Flattery to I. V. Stalin covers up the dangerous conclusions made in the spirit of "Marxism of reality. . . ."

By the work *On New Democracy* Mao Tse-tung provided the theoretical basis for the struggle against the Comintern's ideas. In it lie the origins of the cheng-feng, of the destruction of the "Moscow group," and of nationalism.

"Marxism of reality" is really Mao Tse-tung's own views on the ways of development of the Chinese Revolution. The muddledness in the definition of the class composition of society puts one on the alert. . . .

At meetings chapters from this book are again being drummed into everybody, and the thought is being imposed (and imposition is really no longer required, since they themselves have been saying all that over and over again) that cheng-feng steeled the party!

Terror and violence—this they now call a steeling of the party. That's what cheng-feng was all about!

They are all saying in unison that the petty-bourgeois elements that had penetrated the party in the years of the upsurge in the anti-Japanese movement re-educated themselves during cheng-feng.

Well, well! . . . And what about Wang Ming, Po Ku, Lo Fu, Yang Shang-kun, Chu Teh, Wang Chia-hsiang? . . . I could continue this list, and most of the responsible party functionaries would be there. But the point is that these people have been in the party almost since the day of its foundation! What bearing did cheng-feng—this struggle against the "fresh-baked newcomers"—then have on them?!

There was only one purpose there! And it was to remold the minds of all (even the loyal subjects of the Chairman of the CCP Central Committee) so as to ensure their recognition of his absolute power over the party in the future. One and all, from top to bottom, took a beating! So to speak, a purge of party and nonparty cadres in which loyalty to Mao was the main test—"the people's welfare is the supreme law!"

It is difficult, but not impossible, to hope that also sober voices, not only cheng-feng gibberish, will be heard at the forthcoming congress. There are still healthy forces in the party. . . .

There is hope. The Italians say that time is an honest fellow. . . .
But honesty is clearly lacking here. Ordinary and simple honesty . . .

March 5, 1945

There's much gossip about the fate of the Soviet-Japanese pact. The opinion of Mao Tse-tung about the reasons for the Soviet Union's inevitable war against Japan has crystallized and comes down to the following:

—The Russians will not forgive the Japanese the intervention of the civil war period (atrocities, plunder).

—They will get even with the Japanese for the provocations near the Khasan Lake and in the Khalkin-Gol area.

—They will punish them for the continuous raids on Soviet borders by White Guard bands reared by the samurai, and for the ambiguous stand of Japan during the present war. . . .

"Well, there are attractive girls, aren't there?" the Chairman of the CCP Central Committee said to me at the end of our conversation. "And absolutely healthy. You doubt it? Or maybe you have an eye to someone? . . ."

Really, I had never thought Mao Tse-tung could be a procurer! I laughed it all away, and we parted.

But toward evening a girl appeared in our house, softly and quietly. She shyly greeted me, saying she had come to tidy up the house.

Like everybody, she wore coarse clothes, but above her quilted jacket there was a white collar, so rare here. Her waist was girded by a soldier's belt. A very slender waist. Round cheeks. Dark pure skin. A well-shaped open forehead. Black hair falling to the shoulders, with a flower instead of a hairpin. Large narrow eyes . . .

Yes, people living on the meager Yenan ration look somewhat different. . . .

I took out a stool and placed it under our only tree near the wall. She sat down, tense but smiling. Then she amiably answered my questions and was all the while waiting cautiously, her legs crossed, small slender legs in woven slippers. . . .

I took a few photographs of her and saw her off.

She was a smashing girl, indeed!

As we walked, she told me that she was a university student, just enrolled. How young she really was.

Goodness, how base and wicked it all is! How much I wish I were home! Sitting at the table, with my family around me! Will it ever happen?! Shall I really see my home?! But when, when?! . . .

And who of my friends will meet me? Who has been spared by the war?!

March 7, 1945

The Yenan newspaper in huge characters has printed the telegram sent by I. V. Stalin in reply to the greetings of Mao Tse-tung and Chu Teh.

March 13, 1945

At the end of 1944 the Kuomintang also began reducing definitely the scale of combat actions against the Japanese. They are also infected with the spirit of preparations for a civil war which, although covertly, are systematically being carried out by Yenan.

This is a retaliation to the sabotage of many years by the CCP leadership of large-scale combat actions against the Japanese. At the same time CCP troops are actively driving Kuomintang units from individual areas under the pretense of combat operations against the Japanese.

The Japanese military, engrossed as they are in the struggle against the Americans, on Pacific islands and in Southeast Asia, exercise control by insignificant forces in comparison with those of the Chinese over the occupied territories, and are even expanding them at some points.

March 15, 1945

Reorientation continues in the policy and the mood of the CCP leadership. The latest events have sharpened and crystallized their views and appraisals further still. The publication in the Soviet press of Mao Tse-tung's and Chu Teh's telegram to Stalin, and then Stalin's telegram in reply, with permission to publish it in the Yenan newspaper—for the CCP leadership this is above all an indication of the Soviet Union's forthcoming entry into the war against Japan.

On March 4 Stalin's telegram was published under a huge headline. Its text was repeatedly read out over the radio.

The *Izvestia* article has buttressed the CCP leadership in their opinion.

The CCP leaders have made for themselves two important conclusions:

1. The Soviet Union will inevitably start a war against Japan.
2. Moscow is interested in the fate of the Special Area.

The telegram from Comrade Stalin was received on March 1. On the same evening the Chairman of the CCP Central Committee held a conference with Chou En-lai, Chu Teh, Liu Shao-chi, and Jen Pi-shih.

The conference lasted till four o'clock in the morning. What they discussed is unknown. All of them keep deathlike silence. But that the meeting was linked with the telegram is beyond doubt.

The next day Mao Tse-tung declared that now it was easy to hold the congress—everything had cleared up! . . .

———

Mao may sit for hours in the armchair, expressing no emotions. According to tradition, he represents a preoccupied statesman. He is "concerned with great problems, and all that is vain and worldly cannot distract him. . . ."

I think that at the start of his activity Mao Tse-tung consciously developed these qualities in himself and that they were not his own expression. However, years of work over himself have made them a part of his character: the character, that is, to represent in the eyes of the people a true statesman of the Great Celestial Empire . . .

With me Mao Tse-tung less and less plays the dignitary. The more obvious his somewhat unpolished manners and slovenliness (even with all that looking after his simple clothes). His jests are crude, his admonitions often spiced with vulgar words.

In the private rooms of the Chairman of the CCP Central Committee Chiang Ching rules the roost (and not only here). Mao Tse-tung and his wife have never invited anybody to their living quarters. But wait—Chou! Yes, Chou is an exception. He knows how to be an exception. . . .

What strikes me in Mao Tse-tung is his conviction that cruelty is the result of justice and that, properly speaking, there is no cruelty at all! There is justice—and only justice! He never questions the justice of his own decisions. And then this conviction in cruelty turns into violence. This is his typical style of work. . . .

I never heard him express sympathy to anybody except, perhaps, in talks with such guests as foreigners or delegations from other base areas. . . . He can then talk of his sorrow for the oppressed peoples, complain of the cruelty of the Japanese, and find a word of cheer for "ordinary people." . . .

There are several Mao Tse-tungs. One, whose image is being projected by the press, one bearing the aura of a Chairman of the CCP Central Committee. The one that appears at conferences, meetings of activists, and plenary meetings . . . Here he is quick, witty, attentive.

Another for the local government, military, and party workers who more or less frequently come into contact with him in work. Here the Chairman of the CCP Central Committee is the living image of the ancient ruler, somewhat democratized by the address "comrade" and a handshake. . . .

And there is also the real Mao whom I ever more frequently see in private. . . .

This is no gossip. This particular political metamorphosis takes into account precisely all the national traditions. It is also a tribute to the times. Mao Tse-tung always appears before people in a pose that would best suit the given situation. Either simple and friendly—a true "party comrade"—or monumentally immobile, deliberately absent-minded. A kind of an armchair thinker engrossed in his thoughts, a philosopher aloof from everything mundane. . . .

In his armchair he either listens, shrouding his interlocutor in clouds of tobacco smoke, or talks himself. If in an easy and cheerful mood, then monotonously, accenting lightly the stress syllables of words; if excited, then croaking loudly, with a striking oratorical endurance.

He can speak for two, three, four hours on end! And this in a private conversation! . . .

He may also sit there thinking his own thoughts, without looking at his interlocutor and only occasionally politely nodding his head. . . .

March 17, 1945

Service again visited the Special Area. He was received with respect. A quite definite opinion has formed about him in the Special Area. Service knows China. Not only was he born in Chengtu, but he also received education in China. True, in a special Shanghai school for the rich (mainly Europeans). All his diplomatic career is linked with China, which he has traveled all over.

Chou En-lai regards him as a person of progressive views and without prejudices. Service does not act as a spy, although it is hard to believe that this is not so. He is cautious and prudent, wary of slippery ground, and unobtrusive in behavior. Simply businesslike.

It turns out that Service arrived at Yenan without the sanction of his ambassador. Patrick Hurley himself is now in Washington, and Service had seized this opportunity.

In a confidential conversation with Yeh Chien-ying and Chou En-lai, the second secretary of the American embassy told them that Hurley would hardly have let him go to Yenan.

I almost immediately learned what they had talked about. The matters discussed were so unusual that the Chinese comrades deemed it possible to initiate me into their secrets, so that they themselves might understand what had happened. The Chinese comrades were bewildered by the unusual frankness of the American diplomat.

The age of Service is not equivalent to his experience. After completing the school in Shanghai, Service in his own country (in California) received a bachelor of arts. He started his career as a member of the technical staff at the American mission in Kunming. Then he turned up in Peiping as a dragoman at the American Embassy. In Peiping he worked for several years. He apparently showed his abilities, and right from the position of a dragoman was raised to the rank of vice-consul.

In general, Service produces a very pleasant impression. Well bred, fully at home in the Chinese, able to listen, and, most important, a man of sense. This is probably why already in 1941 he became third secretary at the embassy and shortly after, second secretary [in 1943].

Service is young and has nothing of the presuming conceit of Hurley. Sensible thoughts most frequently come to precisely such people. . . . It is likely that he was highly valued by Joseph Stilwell, on whom only recently depended all major American decisions on China. It is just as likely that this played a role in the rapid promotion of John Service.

When Service is in Yenan, everybody is on the alert. His post is not high, but his knowledge is extensive. And, in general, he does not waste time and is not from among those who will never do anything beyond instructions. . . .

The second secretary of the American embassy called his ambassador a conservative. Without knowing the country, its traditions, and the present most complicated situation, Patrick Hurley undertakes to tackle all Chinese problems! This is precisely why he is the opponent of Hurley—that's what Service's statement meant. Service reported further that Hurley had his own point of view regarding the conflict between the Communist Party and the Kuomintang. A point of view of a conservative, which came in conflict with that of the former commander of the American armed forces in India and China. As a result Stilwell was compelled to leave China. The same fate befell Davies and would also befall all those who tried to find ways for new political solutions in China.

I think that in this part of the talk John Service was also truthful. I witnessed Hurley's gross political blunders. I watched the general and politician also at the banquet, where, after he had had a drop, he began to brag of his "personal links with the Kremlin." He clearly did it to impress the Chairman of the CCP Central Committee. Then Hurley, taking a goodly gulp of whiskey, declared that from November to December 1942 he was the personal representative of the American President in Moscow. After Moscow he attended the Tehran Conference as an adviser of the American delegation. And again Hurley bragged of his involvement in deciding the destinies of the world and his "links with Stalin. . . ."

The decisions of the Tehran Conference, the meeting between Roosevelt and Chiang Kai-shek in 1943—all these events had caused a morbid interest in Yenan. Hurley felt that and, slightly intoxicated, began to boast of his participation in the battles in the Philippines, his wound, and the exotic details of the life in Oklahoma. . . .

Now Hurley heads the American embassy. Neither in age nor in rank and credit can Service compete with him. Hence his desperate move—the trip without permission to the Special Area. In regard to Yenan, in Service's opinion, America in the person of Hurley makes a political mistake. Hurley has confused the already complicated relations between the two most influential political groups in China: the Kuomintang and the CCP. But well, Hurley's task was exactly the opposite—to stop the gaps in the united anti-Japanese bloc. Hurley makes mistake after mistake. He will listen to nobody. For him there is only one man whose opinion he heeds, and that man is Chiang Kai-shek. But it is absurd to try to solve the problem in this way. The opinion of only one side can hardly lead to a solution of the problem. So Hurley is removing from China all the intelligent and progressive men in the American military and diplomatic administration. And who will dare to go against him?! The selfsame Patrick Hurley who was the Secretary of War of the United States from 1929 to 1933! ("Good gracious, can anyone know more than a minister?! Even if he is a former minister"—such were the unexpressed thoughts of Service.)

Service said that he believed Hurley's policy to be harmful, both for the CCP and the Kuomintang and for the United States. Therefore, he and Ludden had sent a report to Washington criticizing the methods and the policy of the new ambassador. Whitemeyer, too, knows the contents of this report, and he also agrees with their conclusions. . . .

Service left for Chungking without delay. At present he, apart from the office of the second secretary of the American embassy, performs the functions of a "political officer" at the allied command headquarters in China. . . .

John Service discussed with Chou the prospects and the essence of the policy of the CCP at this stage. The American obviously sought to learn the concrete aims of Yenan diplomacy. He was concerned with only one question: the substance of the present policy of the Yenan leadership.

March 18, 1945

It is clear that the political and military alliance with the Americans did not come off. The White House has officially declared that the arms being supplied to the armies of the Central Government are designated only for the struggle against Japan. America will not allow these arms to be used for resolving the internal political issues in China.

A change of heart has followed rapidly in Yenan. The relations with the Observer Group are deliberately strained.

Nevertheless, Mao Tse-tung does not exclude circumstances which may cause the White House to change its attitude to the Special Area. His secret hope is that Washington may still evaluate correctly the advantages of rapprochement with Yenan. Service's visit shows that among the Americans there are people with "sober views," and it is possible that such people are also in the highest administration. . . .

Therefore the group of observers is, as before, in Yenan, although matters do not move further than a mere exchange of courtesies.

But it is clear that Mao Tse-tung fears lest such uncertainty continue too long. He fears to be left face to face with Chiang Kai-shek, behind whom is the most powerful capitalist state. This is why simultaneously a shift of policy toward Moscow is evident.

One of the expressions of this shift was the order of Chou En-lai to change the number of students in the department training Russian interpreters and translators. Recruitment was promptly carried out, and now the number of students is increased by another fifty.

Not without a secret hint at solidarity with the Soviet Union, Yenan has taken certain moves in regard to Chungking. The press of the Special Area has started writing of Chiang Kai-shek's rule in openly hostile tones. On all the clauses of the draft treaty with the Kuomintang, put forward earlier as desirable, the press now speaks out in terms which sound almost like an ultimatum. No concessions! This is also the main theme of broadcasts. . . .

The Americans in Yenan took alarm. They are here not only for intelligence work. Their mission is, besides, to inhibit Mao Tse-tung's initiative. To encourage, persuade, drop hints, and actually prevent Yenan from taking vigorous action in a number of military and political directions. But now Mao refuses to take chances! And the tone of the press is sharper, more implacable. . . .

The Americans immediately caught this change in the political course of the CCP leadership. In Chungking friction arose between the CCP representatives and the American command. Not really friction, though. The Americans had simply decided to put pressure on Mao Tse-tung, who until now had showed such readiness for understanding! . . .

But they failed to take into account the fact that Mao had his own opinion on this score. Allies who cannot be "milked" he does not need; in such a situation one does not always choose the "favorite." That's precisely how Mao behaved.

The Chairman of the CCP Central Committee gave orders to change relations with the Observer Group. Though the door to negotiations must be kept open, it must be made clear to everybody that the Special Area is not alone and they will have to reckon with it. The Soviet Union is the ally of the Special Area. . . .

Mao regards the situation in Inner Mongolia and Manchuria as very promising. In the future they will wholly fall under the CCP's control. Just as firm are its positions in North China.

March 19, 1945

It is not in the nature of Mao Tse-tung to play cheap. There has followed a sharp change of attitude by the Yenan authorities to the Observer Group, too. Its temporary head, Major Ray Cromley, immediately reported everything to Chungking.

In Chungking the atmosphere has become tenser still.

Despite everything, the Americans are seeking to bring about conciliation between the CCP and the Kuomintang (they still hope to work out an acceptable draft of the treaty).

Chiang Kai-shek struggles to keep his control over the country. By their demands the Communist Party's representatives strike precisely at the foundations of such control. The Americans try to talk Chiang into making concessions. Reluctant as he is, he does agree. But the CCP representatives take a "no compromise" stand. The Americans keep up pressure on the CCP mission in Chungking, but this immediately boomerangs against the Observer Group in Yenan.

A big row in Chungking. Hurley clearly is in an impasse.

Major Cromley visited Yeh Chien-ying and expressed his protest in due form. But Yeh Chien-ying had already been given firm instructions on this score. He plainly told Major Cromley that the worsening of relations was entirely the Americans' fault. . . . Tension is mounting from day to day. . . . Kang Sheng is clearly in isolation.

The Yenan intrigues cause disgust for politics. But politics are a reality. Life outside it is a utopia. And the harsh reality of politics is better than even a little of utopia. . . .

The atmosphere is heavy and tense in Yenan.

The fate of the congress will be decided by an enlarged plenary meeting of the CCP Central Committee. Here they "roll smooth" the reports to be made and choose the main characters for the spectacle.

March 20, 1945

The Americans are overcoming the conflict-prone situation in a rather peculiar way: Parties are being continuously held in Yenan. Their aim is not only to restore good relations, but, having found out the prevailing sentiments, to again put Mao Tse-tung "on a leash."

And that's exactly what they did before—kept Mao in leash, by tying him up with hopes "to settle somehow the question of arms supplies," etc. Perhaps against the will of the initiators of sending the group in Yenan, but this team certainly tied up the initiative of the Chairman of the CCP Central Committee. He waited and hoped. Time went by, but the cause for which he had ventured—rapprochement with the Americans—remained where it was. Mao Tse-tung patiently endured the leash, although sometimes he did get balky. . . .

This gave Andrei Yakovlevich occasion to nickname the American team in Yenan a "wait-and-see mission."

However, the situation has changed, and this has been made clear to the Americans. Mao has defined the direction of his policy. The game with the Americans appears to be nearing its end. . . .

March 22, 1945

Parties follow one after another. What a motley mixture of people! American career intelligence officers, local government and party workers, the people of Kang Sheng and Li Ko-nung, and at times visiting journalists. The unlimited alcohol supplies of the Observer Group allow them to maintain the tempo taken.

Dashing boys are in the American intelligence! With an exception or two, from the Observer Group one can safely form a quite decent football team. All hand-picked boys, strapping, confident. And, most important, they are lavish here. At banquets whiskey, beer, chocolate, bread, canned food, butter—all are in abundance! A too strong temptation for the local authorities . . .

Now in the houses of party and local government workers, I fairly often notice Black & White on the tables. Even the silhouettes of the little dogs on the labels of this whiskey have become familiar to me.

Monumental-looking are four-faceted bottles of Johnnie Walker, the most popular kind of whiskey here! Besides, people are not spoiled in these parts. . . .

Chen Yi—a gourmand! He has a special flair for entertainment. Where is whiskey and refreshments—you will always hear his laughter. . . .

High-ranking Yenan officials, as a rule, do not attend these banquets. Only the pawns of the big figures of both sides are here. And they drink, drink, drink . . . both in thirst and in the performance of their official duty, in order to loosen the other side's tongues. A harmful profession it is, being a spy: Cirrhosis is inevitable. . . .

In the CCP leadership, a fierce struggle around the future reports at the Seventh Congress of the party. . . .

March 23, 1945

Mao Tse-tung is exerting himself to the utmost. He works quite a lot, but it is not this that depresses him. He fears lest questions concerning the activity of the "Moscow group" should be raised at the congress—I was told about that by Po Ku. Mao is afraid that this may influence the stand of the Soviet Union in solving a number of important Far Eastern problems. . . .

March 24, 1945

There are also Chinese comrades who detest these parties with the Americans. They are mainly people from port cities. They are very few, but they are there. And they well remember the arrogant treatment of the Chinese by British and Americans. That dirty nickname "yellow," the quarters for whites only, the enormous opulence of the whites, and the constant humiliations of the Chinese before those "visitors" from overseas. . . .

Mao Tse-tung has acquainted me in detail with the course of the negotiations between the CCP and the Kuomintang and a number of other matters.

An obvious demonstration that he has no secrets from Moscow.

The meetings of the CCP Central Committee are continuing. They are discussing congress documents. An atmosphere of hush-hush surrounds the work of the plenum. What they are really talking about there is a carefully guarded secret. So far they think it necessary to inform me on this score.

March 25, 1945

As it was to be expected, the date for the congress has again been postponed. The congress will now be held in April, probably beginning the fifteenth. This decision of the leadership of the Communist Party directly indicates that its future decisions are contingent on the fate of the Soviet-Japanese pact. The pact expires at the beginning of April. They in Yenan are awaiting this day with great impatience.

The question of who will deliver the congress reports is a big issue. Each fights for this right.

On the military question, there was practically no dispute. Chu Teh is the commander in chief. So let him report on it.

Jen Pi-shih is a loyal operator. This was well considered by Mao Tse-tung when he entrusted him the report on the intraparty struggle. True, the report will sum up the policy of the CCP over a period of four years only (1931–35), but what years! In fact, Jen Pi-shih is charged with substantiating ideologically the incorrectness of the former course of the party and the inevitability of the coming of a new leadership, with Mao Tse-tung at the head.

Of course, the Chairman of the CCP Central Committee will be the main speaker at the congress. His political report is roughly ready. The only thing left is to dot the *i*'s, but without being certain about the fate of the Soviet-Japanese pact, this so far would be a rash action.

Nor did the Chairman of the CCP Central Committee pass over Kang Sheng. The chief of the Ching-pao-chu will report on the results of work done by the Commission for the Review of Party Cadres and Nonparty Personnel.

Significant is the following fact: The report was not planned, but cheng-feng had affected the entire party so painfully that it is impossible to hush the matter. Here, of course, Mao Tse-tung has nothing to fear before his party comrades. He is absolutely confident on this score. His authority is unshakable.

The report of Kang Sheng will make it possible to give a Mao Tse-tung-inspired account of what the intraparty struggle of 1942–44 was all about. A smooth version will appear once and for all in the party's history. The same report will also ward off the blow from Mao Tse-tung himself, as it is possible that Kang will shoulder a part of the blame. And for Mao this is a fine way out—just a case of a matter carried too far by a zealous operator of policy, no more. . . .

Kang Sheng's report will sum up the results of cheng-feng, justify them in behalf of suppressing any "dogmatism," and make them a rule of party life.

At the same time through the mouth of Kang, Mao Tse-tung intends to declare that the cheng-feng is a legitimate and necessary development and must not and cannot be condemned. And so after many talks and meetings it was decided to include this report in the agenda of the congress. The decision was adopted literally in the very last hours.

The question of the united national front of resistance to the aggressor is also a point on the agenda. The end of the war is in sight, and so ahead are battles for new bases, which so far are under Japanese control. It is important to determine the party's stand and the framework of co-operation with the Kuomintang in the future battles against the Japanese militarists. A most delicate question. Well, it is usually Chou En-lai who tackles delicate questions. So this decided the CCP leaders' choice.

Kao Kang is to make a report on questions in which he is the best versed. He will report everything about the Special Area (political work, the economy, religious problems).

A report has also been entrusted to Chen Yi. As an expert on Central China (in charge of the liberated bases and the CCP troops) he is to give an account. The main question here is the possibilities for a new expansion of the bases.

Nor has the head of the Special Service, one of Kang's zealous assistants, been passed over. Peng Chen, the most active of the exponents of cheng-feng and a convinced anti-Sovieteer. In the past Peng worked in cities, engaged in clandestine activities, and was even imprisoned in Shanghai. So, as one of the functionaries (if not the only) who are more or less familiar with the problems of revolutionary work in cities, he is charged with dealing with the appropriate subject.

Peng is a striking example of an opportunist. On the shoulders of Liu Shao-chi he got into Yenan. Joined Kang's secret service. Knows how to make a career out of provocations and unscrupulous behavior. If necessary, he will "believe" in anything. . . .

I dislike this man. Very tall, strapping, energetic. He has polished his wits in perpetual obedience. A conveniently chosen obedience. A typical product of the impeccable toadyism that flourished in the years of cheng-feng.

One of the reports to be made at the congress is the report of Peng Teh-huai. A calm, robust man, Peng Teh-huai is an old acquaintance of mine since the days of my first missions to China. Our comrades then managed to render some assistance in arming his units. A true fighter and a Communist in the full sense of this word. At that time I also made the acquaintance of Chu Teh. . . .

At the congress Peng Teh-huai will make a report on what he knows thoroughly: the course of combat actions in the northern provinces of China. The establishment and expansion of bases is the main task of the Eighth Route Army.

The report of Liu Shao-chi (a change in the rules of the Communist Party), together with the reports of Chou and the Chairman of the CCP Central Committee, will be one of the main ones. In the draft of the new rules, kept in great secrecy, there are provisions which will clearly place Mao in an exclusive position. Will Mao dare to make these provisions a part of the future party rules? In any case, this draft is kept secret, just as a number of other congress documents, which is in no way due to the fear of divulgence of economic and military secrets. . . .

The Politburo of the CCP Central Committee has officially approved the themes of the reports and the rapporteur candidates. A plenary meeting of the Central Committee of the Communist Party is to decide on the agenda of the congress and the procedure of work. The plenary meeting is scheduled for the last days of March.

Kang Sheng, for all the hostility around him, outwardly has not given in. Efficient and businesslike. Behind the spectacles the same haughtily raised eyebrows . . .

He, after all, will be given, and is already taking, a beating—but there is more to it than him. . . . Perhaps he understands it and is therefore so self-possessed. Here, in Yenan, a compromise in politics means an ability to deal the final blow to all that has survived (or, to be more precise, has not degenerated) after the spiritual purification of cheng-feng. Well, but didn't he, Kang, engage in this job? In its essence the process has not changed—all admit this. Cheng-feng is claimed to be a righteous cause. Partially, fully, or with reservations, but all recognize it! Kang understands: It is not his political reputation that has been damaged. . . . Why, he is even to deliver a report to the congress! And this speaks volumes!

Am I intolerant in describing these people? Hardly so. Simply seeing how people hang on and stick to and soil the party and then boast of revolutionary services disgusts me. Even the usual routine work of such "leaders" is being lauded as special services performed for the country. . . .

March 29, 1945

The most farsighted approach to the Yenan problem in American policy is that of Davies and Service.

As the last visit of Service showed, he correctly caught the nationalistic community between the leaders of the two largest groups in China. A realistic political calculation in behalf of the future interests of the United States—that's the reason behind the surprisingly frank conversation which he had with Chou En-lai.

Service is far from being a political idealist.

The second secretary of the American embassy in China, just as Davies, is more perspicacious than many of his eminent compatriots—it's a fact. The conversation with Chou shows that Service is the most dangerous American here. Not the one who in all cases shies from the "Bolshevik plague." He is interested not in words, but in political reality.

But the irony of fate! His protectors—Ambassador Gauss and General Stilwell—are no longer here. Davies, who shared his political views, has been removed, too.

Such people like Service usually fail in their careers. He is too independent. . . .

April 1945

April 1, 1945

Mao Tse-tung cannot allow the condemnation of Kang Sheng, for this would mean indirectly that his own course, too, was erroneous. That is why Kang Sheng's report has been removed from the agenda of the congress. Mao took this step not without much hesitation, although a report like this would be very much in order: It would sum up the results of cheng-feng.

Peng Chen's report has also been removed from the agenda for no obvious reason. Could it be that it did not contain enough material on the CCP's work in the cities? For Peng was expected to speak precisely on this question. . . .

Po Ku has also been scored off the list of speakers at the congress. The reasons are not clear either. At all events Mao does not trust Po Ku, although he could certainly find him very useful, considering the rapprochement with Moscow. Po Ku was to report at the congress on the work of the party press.

All these decisions were made on March 24.

It was no other than Mao Tse-tung himself who suggested that all those questions be taken off the agenda. The enlarged plenary meeting of the CCP Central Committee endorsed these proposals.

Also taken off the agenda is the report of Teng Fa (on the work of the trade unions). This, too, was done on Mao Tse-tung's instructions. . . .

Mao has decided to head off the blow being aimed at Kang Sheng and his supporters not because he felt so strongly for the Ching-pao-chu chief. Even a perfunctory look at cheng-feng makes it clear who stood behind the personnel review commission, and what was the ideological meaning of the 1942–44 campaigns.

Mao firmly believes that the congress must not call Moscow's attention to questions involving the integrity of the Chairman of the CCP Central Committee. . . .

Service's revelations are not accidental by any means.

He does not betray the interests of his country, as it might seem on the surface. He turns to the CCP leadership as a potential ally of his country. And this is as far as his "candor" goes. Davies and he seem to have grasped the nationalist implication of the policy of the CCP leadership. They see it as a future force which the United States can and must be friendly with if it wants to retain its position in this part of Asia. According to Davies, the nationalist line in the policy of the CCP leadership renders the CCP program harmless to the United States and will in fact help neutralize the might of the Soviet Union in the Far East. . . .

Therein lies the substance of Service's revelations, the entire meaning of the activities of Stilwell's retinue: Davies, Ludden, Service, and Whitemeyer. That is why Service seems to lose self-control and flies into a passion. Hurley shows up the cowardice and the short-sightedness of the entire Far Eastern strategy of the United States. It is for this "lack of understanding of the policy of the CCP leadership" on the part of Hurley that makes Mao Tse-tung angry.

Until recently Mao Tse-tung had been exchanging affectionate messages with Hurley, expressing his gratitude to the general for his "brilliant mediation" and his noble human qualities. . . .

April 2, 1945

Foreign Minister Gheorghe Tătărescu of Romania has said that relations with the Soviet Union must rest on lasting co-operation which will signify a new era in the history of relations with the great eastern neighbor.

Anti-Sovietism which is sprouting in the party has taken a rather peculiar form. On the surface everything is all right. The Soviet Union and the All-Union Communist Party are spoken of with respect. . . .

In this case anti-Sovietism has donned the garb of the "Marxism of reality." "The Soviet Union is our friend and brother"—words like this are being used in great profusion by newspapers and political workers.

However, the internationalist essence of Marxist philosophy has been dumped. The interests of the Mao Tse-tung group dominate over "all the other" interests of the international working-class movement. Cheng-feng has inculcated in the party the painful nationalist sentiment (reduced it to an instinct) which in certain circumstances may graduate to the denial of everything that is not Chinese. These are the elements which have given rise to the "Marxism of reality" of Mao Tse-tung.

"Wang Ming wanted to make himself a petty ruler in the party. He kowtowed to Chiang Kai-shek. He is an opportunist," etc. This is what everybody is sure of. And this means that all that Wang Ming has stood for has been discredited. What else could it be but the other side of the "Marxism of reality"?

The internationalists inside the Chinese Communist Party are vilified for trying to introduce the principles of "Western Marxism," which are allegedly alien to China. All the difficulties and troubles of the Communist Party are being blamed on the "dogmatists," for they have failed to take into consideration the national peculiarities of the country. . . .

And cheng-feng-buffed masses have absorbed these precepts, so that now Mao need not even try to convince anybody of their correctness. Mao Tse-tung has many years been working to compromise Wang Ming on political grounds.

The disdain with which Wang Ming and his supporters are treated in the Communist Party is a manifestation of nationalism in the first place: the rejection of the main principle of the Marxist doctrine—that is, the common struggle of working people throughout the world. In Yenan, by contrast, everything is being done for their own interests.

The inner party struggle of 1942–44 affected everybody. Nobody doubts the correctness of cheng-feng. On the other hand, everybody considers himself an orthodox member of the party and completely innocent.

Hence is the main danger for Mao: Everybody understands the correctness of cheng-feng, agrees with it, everybody is loyal to the Chairman of the CCP Central Committee, but at the same time considers himself unjustly hurt. On the long count all those hurts add up to a feeling of gross injustice and dissatisfaction with the campaign and its criminal practices.

The wave of wrath rising against Kang Sheng is in fact threatening the whole inner party policy of Mao Tse-tung. This arouses apprehension in Mao Tse-tung himself, a painful, anguished desire to put out the fire he has fanned up. The personal loyalty to Mao Tse-tung and the hatred for Kang Sheng, who has made almost everyone suffer unjustly, augurs trouble for the Chairman of the CCP Central Committee, trouble which nobody is aware of besides Mao himself and his close associates. Therefore the entire work of the enlarged plenary meeting of the CCP Central Committee and of the future congress will be directed to suppress this spontaneous rebellion of the congress delegates, those who sincerely identify Mao with the very conscience of the party, who wouldn't even dream of wounding anybody's pride or casting a shadow on Mao's personal authority and integrity as the leader, those who have implicit faith in him and are ready to die for him.

The wave of wrath raised against Kang Sheng is already threatening Mao Tse-tung, who is the only one to see it. Mao finds it difficult to fight against such sentiments for the simple reason that he cannot call things by their proper names. In the conditions of reorientation to the Soviet Union it is dangerous to continue the struggle against the "dogmatists" under the guise of struggle for the national character of the Communist Party. In its future actions Moscow might take into consideration these sentiments of the CCP leadership.

Mao is doing all he can to avoid the discussion of the cheng-feng or just gloss over it by endorsing it in as few words as possible, and to allow no discussion on this question. And this he does only when he feels there is no getting around it.

It looks as if Mao Tse-tung is going to hold Kang Sheng up as the sole perpetrator of the reprisals ("distortions").

In this way Mao hopes to keep the cheng-feng ideas unsullied, for cheng-feng has become a glorious landmark in the history of the Communist Party of China.

The travesty of the congress, which has been carefully rehearsed over many years, is drawing near.

April 3, 1945

The Chairman of the CCP Central Committee is trying in every way to avoid discussions on inner party problems. Otherwise such discussions might throw light on the struggle which he has inspired all this time: the suppression of the Wang Ming group, the efforts to emasculate internationalism of its meaning, covert anti-Sovietism. Therefore, Mao Tse-tung is intending to concentrate all his efforts on the solution of current problems. By doing so he will thus forestall any divergence of views at the congress which will come off in an atmosphere of unanimity. This unanimity will convince its participants of the infallibility of Mao Tse-tung's political line.

Day after day Mao is pushing through his plans, consistently and unswervingly. At last draft reports have been handed out to the members of the CCP Central Committee. Then party comrades will have to submit their views at the plenary meeting of the CCP Central Committee.

I have looked through these reports. What reports! Not a word about the substance of the processes that have taken place in the party over the past decade, and especially over the past three years!

All ticklish questions must be passed up in silence—this is what Mao considers of primary importance. Everything possible must be done to prevent the delegates from taking up inner party problems!

There is no other explanation of the fact that no names are mentioned anywhere in the reports.

April 4, 1945

At a press conference in Washington, on April 2, Patrick Hurley announced America's intentions to co-operate only with the Kuomintang and to cut off all deliveries of arms and equipment to the Special Area.

Having committed a political blunder—the signing of a draft treaty between the Communist Party and the Kuomintang on November 10, 1944—Hurley has been trying in every way to save his reputation as a "democrat" and a "China expert." This, however, did not do him any good. He stopped at nothing short of risking the expulsion of his colleagues from China. . . .

Apparently forgetful of the fact that he was no longer Secretary of War but a diplomat, Hurley, at the Washington press conference, hurled threats at the Yenan leaders. His mask of a peacemaker had vanished. . . .

Hurley's performance was largely prompted by his hurt feelings, it's true. In the first place he had failed to resolve the conflict between the CCP and the Kuomintang and had in fact exacerbated it. To cover up his failure he let go with a harangue loaded with insults for the CCP. This general-cum-politician cut a poor figure, and that's for sure. He had probably forgotten that China is not a bar counter where arguments are settled by fist-shaking and tongue-lashing.

In his talks with Patrick Hurley the Chairman of the CCP Central Committee had showed his true face. He had hoped that the Americans would understand him. So much kowtowing had gone into these talks, on which Mao staked his personal reputation, often at a grave risk.

Mao had expected that the Allies would be interested in his "iron fists," in the Eighth Route and the New Fourth armies.

Put away in the safes of the Chairman of the CCP Central Committee are the full texts of the numerous talks he had with General Hurley. Some of these documents are real gems! I doubt any of them will see the light of day in their present form. Everything in them is called by its proper name. The Chairman of the CCP Central Committee had proposed to the Americans that they form an alliance, an inviolable alliance. He had guaranteed that Yenan would be politically independent from Moscow, etc.

The exasperated Chairman burst into abuse, cursing the Americans, for the collapse of the proposed alliance was the collapse of his most radiant dreams.

In San Francisco an international conference is under way to set up a united nations organization. This is a tremendous achievement of all progressive forces of the world. After a short argument here, Wu Hsiu-chuan, Tung Pi-wu, and Chen Chia-kang were delegated to go to the conference, where they will represent the Special Area. . . .

In his draft report at the congress Mao Tse-tung has made a retrospective analysis of the relations between the Soviet Union and the Chinese people in the past. In it the Chairman of the CCP Central Committee stresses the sincerity of Soviet assistance, the readiness of the Soviet Union to protect the interests of the Chinese Communist

Party. Mao Tse-tung points out that the Pacific problem cannot and must not be discussed without the participation of the Soviet Union, which is a great Pacific nation.

The Chairman of the CCP Central Committee devotes much of his report to the mercenary character of the Kuomintang's relations with the Soviet Union, relations which are basically hostile to Moscow. The Kuomintang only camouflages its hatred of Moscow with superficial benevolence, and nothing else.

In the past Wu Hsiu-chuan shared Wang Ming's views and, as a "dogmatist," had more than his share of suffering.

He has been included in the delegation of the Special Area to the united nations conference in San Francisco because of his perfect command of the Russian language. And his knowledge of Russian is truly superb. If you shut your eyes and listen, you will never believe that this is a Chinese speaking. Not even a trace of accent! Mao Tse-tung is sending Wu Hsiu-chuan with a certain purpose in mind. In the first place Wu Hsiu-chuan knows Russian. In the second place he is listed as an internationalist, which means that he might very well be received by the Soviet delegation.

As always Mao Tse-tung is now hoping to settle the main problems of his policy in San Francisco with Soviet assistance.

Chen Chia-kang is Chou En-lai's man.

Chen has a university education. In the past he was active in the youth movement. Since the summer of the last year he has in fact been Chou En-lai's secretary.

Between 1927 and 1930 Wu Hsiu-chuan studied in Moscow. He is a highly cultured person; has specialized in political economy.

Tung Pi-wu was born in 1886 in Hunan. A veteran revolutionary. Took part in the First Congress of the Chinese Communist Party, also in the Long March. Was a liaison man between the CCP and the Kuomintang both in the period of co-operation between them (until 1927) and now at the time of the united anti-Japanese front. Took part in last year's talks between Lin Po-chu and Wang Jo-fei (for CCP) and Wang Shih-chieh, Shao Li-tzu, and Chang Chih-chung (for the Kuomintang).

Shao Li-tzu almost invariably represented the Kuomintang at the talks with the Chinese Communist Party. Former ambassador of the Central Government to Moscow (he also figures under the names of Shao Wen-tai, Shao Fen-shou, and Shao Chung-huai).

April 6, 1945

All the plans and dreams of the CCP are linked with the future participation of the Soviet Union in the solution of the Far Eastern problem,
a solution which would benefit the Special Area and which would to a
certain extent make up for the frustrated hopes placed earlier on the
United States. This has inevitably led to a realignment of the forces
within the party.

The representatives of the much hated political course—the recent
favorites of the Chairman of the CCP Central Committee—the Ching-
pao-chu chief, and Peng Chen, also functionaries who stand on a lower
rung of the local hierarchy, are losing much of their former prestige
and weight. This is easy to explain. The ideological annihilation of the
"Moscow group" has affected only some of its representatives: Wang
Ming, Po Ku, Lo Fu, and some others. As for the work of the Commission for the Review of Party Cadres and Nonparty Personnel, it has
rocked the whole party. Even the top military and party leaders
suffered from the reprisals in one way or another. . . .

The changed correlation of forces in the world, the rapidly growing
prestige of the Soviet Union, could not but affect the position of Mao
Tse-tung. Now he has been forced to look for other people he might
trust. In the diplomatic field it is Chou En-lai. Mao Tse-tung has now
been compelled to co-operate with Po Ku. Those are the people who
cannot forget the humiliation of cheng-feng. Neither can the military
leaders forget this ignominy (of course, nobody would dare apply this
term to Kang Sheng's activity). These army comrades are again in
Mao's good graces: Peng Teh-huai, Chu Teh, Nieh Jung-chen, Yeh
Chien-ying, Chen Yi. Now they are strong enough to give Kang Sheng
a kick, and they never miss the opportunity.

Jen Pi-shih was expected to give an evaluation of the political line of
the party over a period between 1931 and 1935. For some reason his
report was taken off the agenda of the congress.

Kang Sheng and Peng Chen are loathed wholeheartedly by the delegates.

Stalin's message, the article in *Izvestia,* and finally the collapse of
the talks with the Americans go to show that the reorientation to the
Soviet Union is the only correct course. This process is gaining ground.

In other words, it would be much too risky to ignore Moscow in the
present conditions. And this, in turn, means that compromise in the

party is inevitable. Therefore, Mao Tse-tung is hastily removing from the agenda two questions which in one way or another reflect his anti-Soviet policy, his struggle against the Comintern's influence and other "deeds" which may badly reflect on Mao Tse-tung.

Thus, it has been decided that Kang Sheng and Jen Pi-shih will not speak at the congress.

April 7, 1945

Mao Tse-tung has taken off the congress agenda two most important reports [Kang Sheng's and Jen Pi-shih's].

This adroit move will enable the Chairman of the CCP Central Committee to cushion the blow at Kang and his associates and, possibly, to ward it off altogether. Otherwise they would get it hot at the congress, for it was the members of the Commission for the Review of Party Cadres and Nonparty Personnel who were the inquisitors of the party.

However, it is impossible to pass up this question in silence. In the first place, cheng-feng is the favorite brain child of Mao Tse-tung. In the second place, it is ill advised to call Moscow's attention to altercations that might flare up at the congress. That is why the draft report of the Ching-pao-chu chief will be discussed at the current enlarged plenary meeting of the CCP Central Committee.

The delegates to the future congress will be busy discussing current affairs only. The reports on military and political matters will distract their attention. At the same time the "Moscow group" will be saved from criticism and vituperation (which will inevitably pull the curtain off Mao's nationalism). "Saved" is exactly the word for it! This last circumstance seems to be highly perturbing to the Chairman of the CCP Central Committee. The details of his correspondence with Dimitrov are still fresh in his mind. What would happen if the same political issues were heard on the eve of the crucial events in the Far East?

Mao is afraid of exposing himself, and not so much before the congress delegates (here Mao feels perfectly secure—he is the leader!) as before Moscow. Therefore, he suggests that the main, the most painful question be raised and discussed at the plenary meeting and not at the congress. In the first place, the plenum is not the congress. Besides, it is much easier to control the plenum which, by the way, will not draw so much attention from outside.

The current political questions, just like the military ones, cannot arouse controversy—this point is central in Mao's plan. In this case the congress will demonstrate to the whole world (and especially to Moscow) the monolithic unity and cohesion of China's Communist Party.

This, too, is meant to cover up yet another dishonest move in Mao's political game. Since no questions of inner party policy will be discussed at the congress, this will be automatically interpreted as the unanimous agreement of the delegates, and consequently of the party, with this policy as some sort of axiomatic truth. In other words, Mao Tse-tung's general course will be given unqualified approval without discussion or debates!

April 10, 1945

Patrick Hurley's press conference in Washington made a depressing impression. The CCP leaders regard the statement made by the American ambassador as a serious political blow at the positions of the Communist Party in China and outside its borders.

Mao Tse-tung is talking irritably about "the United States new policy toward China in general and toward the Communist Party in particular." Now that all his hopes for American assistance have collapsed he is vociferously calling Hurley an "imperialist." And a mere five months ago Mao Tse-tung admired the "outstanding talents of the envoy of the American President" and thanked General Hurley "for his warm feelings for the Chinese people." And how many tender words were said at the banquet; how cheerful was Mao Tse-tung then and how delighted he was with the energy of this "sober-minded American politician"!

What a change of heart! Just like in that Russian saying: "Was adored and then abhorred. . . ."

The news report about the statement of the American ambassador was received on April 3, and on the next day the CCP leaders held an unofficial conference at which two proposals were made:

1. To make a reply statement:

—The Kuomintang is also an armed political party which, besides, has taken power by force of arms.

—To render assistance to the Kuomintang would mean to strengthen its aggressive, reactionary core, which might eventually lead to a new civil war.

—To reply to Hurley: Chiang Kai-shek is a fascist!

—To repudiate Hurley's statement that the Communist Party had requested the United States to provide it with arms and military equipment.

2. To address a message of protest to Patrick Hurley personally.

At their meeting on April 6, however, the top five decided to desist from this action.

Hurley is universally resented here. It looks like nobody is going to forgive him for what he has done. Evidence of this is Mao Tse-tung's order to make a photocopy of the treaty between the Communist Party and the Kuomintang drafted on the night of November 9 last year, and signed by Hurley and the Chairman of the CCP Central Committee.

The photostat was given to Tung Pi-wu, who shortly afterward left by plane for the San Francisco conference. In an appropriate situation the photostat will be given to the press for publication. Hurley will then be unable to deny that a draft of this treaty did exist. If the newspapers question the authenticity of this document (after all, the treaty was supposed to be a secret), Tung Pi-wu will present the authentic copy of the treaty and will thus compromise Hurley, because it bears his signature.

The CCP leaders are very much perturbed by Hurley's visit to London and by his talks with Churchill as well as by his forthcoming trip to Moscow for a meeting with Stalin, at which he is expected to forward President Roosevelt's personal message to the Soviet leader. It is widely speculated that Hurley's activities have a direct bearing on the problems of the Far East and primarily on the problems of China.

April 12, 1945

The draft reports of Jen Pi-shih and Kang Sheng are being discussed at the current plenary meeting of the CCP Central Committee. The congress is supposed to have begun its work, but the passions raging over these reports have turned into violent altercations. Debates are raging with particular intensity at the meetings of the delegates who represent the party organizations of the Special Area. This group of delegates is headed by Kao Kang. It is easy to understand the delegates: The cheng-feng has hit the Special Area the hardest of all. It is impossible to calm the delegates. The entire history of the Communist Party of China has come under review. Chen Tu-hsiu, Li Li-san, Po Ku, Wang Ming, the "Moscow group," and also Kang Sheng with his crew—all have come under heavy fire.

Mao Tse-tung is taking all possible measures to put an end to this undesirable turn of events. Delegates are taken aside one by one for private conversations.

The political report made by the Chairman of the CCP Central Committee was approved unanimously. Some remarks were made on military reports which were then duly altered.

The draft report of Liu Shao-chi on changes in the party rules was endorsed, albeit without the clauses which would raise Mao Tse-tung above the party and above criticism.

Thus, the enlarged plenary meeting of the Central Committee of the Communist Party has practically exhausted its agenda. However, the long-drawn-out debates on Jen Pi-shih's and Kang Sheng's reports will force the CCP leadership to postpone the opening of the congress by a week or so.

As could be expected, Jen Pi-shih's report "On the Political Line of the Party Between 1931 and 1935" sparked off a hot debate. It was certainly clever of Mao Tse-tung to move this report from the congress agenda to the plenary meeting. He, of all others, knew, of course, what could have happened if he had not.

April 14, 1945

On April 12 the President of the United States, Franklin Delano Roosevelt, suddenly died.

Roosevelt's death is a great loss not only for the United States. Roosevelt was a sober and farsighted political leader.

He died while posing for an artist.

Vice-president Harry Truman has taken over as President.

Chiang Kai-shek's confidential letter to his generals:

—The Communist Party is tightening its control over the Japanese-occupied territories and is now busy spreading its influence in the central part of Hunan province, in the northern part of Anhwei province, and along the Yangtze River.

—The Communist Party is spreading propaganda which is detrimental to the national liberation war.

—The Communist Party is carrying out all its measures in order to hold back the counteroffensive of the Chinese Army and to foment disturbances in the country, for which purpose it is seeking foreign assistance.

Chiang Kai-shek calls upon the soldiers, officers, and generals of his army to improve discipline. He points out the fact that his general staff is ridden with corruption, that the generals are deceiving the military command. . . .

All the Kuomintang is dreaming about is to drive the Japanese out with its own forces. This would help them keep control over the occupied territories.

American radio commentators are sounding alarm about the future relations between the United States and China. The Americans say: "Our relations with China after the war mean the question of war and peace for the United States."

The Americans are very hypocritical about the relations between Chungking and Yenan, saying that this is China's internal business. The great powers must not get involved in this old dispute. It would be interesting to compare these words with what is actually happening here. . . .

———————

The maneuver of the Chairman of the CCP Central Committee aimed at dampening the fire of disagreement by transferring the reports of Jen Pi-shih and Kang Sheng to the plenary meeting has come off well, and the current debates on these documents are evidence of this. Most of the delegates are still smarting from the memories of the Commission for the Review of Party Cadres and Nonparty Personnel and from the reprisals of cheng-feng. It is easy to imagine what the debates would be like at the congress itself, judging from the fact that at one of the sittings of the plenum the white-haired and venerable Lin Po-chu was literally driven to tears during debates on Jen Pi-shih's report.

Lin Po-chu is one of the delegates from the Special Area, member of the Communist Party since its very inception.

The passions raging over the reports may draw attention to the entire ten-year political course of the Chairman of the CCP Central Committee. That's why he is so keenly interested in temporizing the sharp tone of the debates (or better still to wind up the discussions altogether). Mao Tse-tung is holding regular meetings with the heads of delegations who represent the party at the current plenum. At the last briefing the Chairman of the CCP Central Committee accused the leaders of the delegations of "being too soft on those who have rotten and backward sentiments" and called for greater firmness, that is, for putting an end to the debates on Jen Pi-shih's report.

Kao Kang has apparently found it beyond his power to change the prevailing mood of the delegates. The Chairman of the CCP Central Committee then announced that he would speak before each individual delegation which had been worst affected by the practice known as "dragging the tail." This applies in the first place to the delegation of the Special Area.

The Chairman of the CCP Central Committee is anxious to see Jen Pi-shih's report through in order to cut short the debates which have suddenly brought to light the dangerous symptoms of disagreement and discontent. Mao Tse-tung intends to indoctrinate the delegates, using his unchallenged authority in the party (to make the situation "healthier"). He wants to direct these sentiments into the right channel so that everything will come off well at the congress and nobody will so much as squeak about "Comrade Kang Sheng's distortions."

The activities of the Ching-pao-chu chief were directed by the Chairman of the CCP Central Committee. This means that any criticism of the activities of this commission will in one way or another put the correctness of Mao's policy in doubt.

Mao Tse-tung has reduced Wang Ming into a pawn in his political game. The election of a former member of the Executive Committee of the Comintern to the CCP Central Committee will dispel Moscow's incredulity (the reprisals against the "dogmatists," the attempts to kill Wang Ming with Dr. Ching's medication, Dimitrov's exposing telegrams, certain aspects of Mao's talks with the Americans). Mao Tse-tung is already putting pressure on the delegates, trying to make them believe that the election of Wang Ming at the forthcoming congress to the new Central Committee of the party will be a necessary move.

The long campaigns of slander and the pressure put on public opinion have made Wang Ming an unpopular figure among the delegates. This, too, is another reason for the postponement of the opening of the congress. The re-election of Wang Ming to the Central Committee of the CCP is a clever dodge which might bring many political gains. That's why Mao Tse-tung is not in a hurry. . . .

All these years Mao Tse-tung has been fanning up passions over the "Moscow group" and the "dogmatists," attacking the internationalists. In other words, he has been fanning up the flames of the inner party struggle, or rather a conflagration which was supposed to wipe out his political opponents. But now he is trying to dampen its flames in order to serve his tactical aims. Mao's perseverance is amazing. . . .

April 16–19, 1945

Taking Jen Pi-shih's and Kang Sheng's reports off the agenda of the congress, the Chairman of the CCP Central Committee had little worry about his personal prestige. He has long since crushed all opposition. Nobody will even dare to say that Mao Tse-tung "is not right" in this or that case. For ten years Mao Tse-tung has been trying to project the importance of his policy for the party. He has been doing it in every way possible. His main expedient proved quite correct: to make use of nationalist instincts. At all stages of the struggle (at times the situation was very complicated) Mao Tse-tung resorted to this tried-and-true stratagem. He has even put it on a philosophical basis: the "Marxism of reality." Just orthodox Marxism which takes into consideration the realities of the situation.

Mao feels easy about his prestige. All that hubbub at the plenary meeting was caused by the fear of being discredited in the eyes of Moscow. Mao is clearly aware of the fact that the cheng-feng reprisals, the persecution of Wang Ming, and the attempts to come to terms with the Americans behind the back of the Soviet Union may influence the attitude of the Soviet Union to Yenan.

What is now going on at the plenary meeting is a desperate attempt to hide and blur the essence of his anti-Soviet and anti-Comintern activity. The Chairman of the CCP Central Committee is now leaning over backward to enlist Soviet support. He is even prepared to sacrifice Kang Sheng, to blame him for all the "distortions" in order to secure Moscow's backing. The latest press conference of Patrick Hurley has now fully convinced him of the reality of a coalition between the Kuomintang and the United States. To his dismay Mao Tse-tung has suddenly realized that he is now standing on the edge of a precipice.

Mao is now bending his skillful politicking to the solution of the main problem: to win Moscow's trust, to prove his right to this trust so that he could use it as a crutch. The debates that followed each report centered on wordy passages about the traditional friendship between the All-Union Communist Party and the Chinese Communist Party. The trouble is that the delegates, and the party itself to be sure (save for very few of its members), see no distinction between Mao's policy and his true aims. In his report Mao Tse-tung laid down the line of behavior in relation to the Soviet Union now and in the near future, at the congress.

Now all the speeches and all the reports are being modeled on the pattern of Mao's political report: "The Soviet Union—the friend, brother, and hope of all oppressed nations!"

Nevertheless the "Marxism of reality" remains the basic philosophical doctrine of the Chinese Communist Party, although this point is carefully passed up in silence. It is clear, though, that here Mao will not yield an inch. He would rather disavow Kang Sheng and Peng Chen but will not give up the main thing for which he has been fighting all his life. . . .

The Chairman of the CCP Central Committee has made his choice for several years to come. He has been forced to do this; he knows that he will not be able to stand up to Chiang Kai-shek, who is supported by the whole power of the United States. To look up to the Soviet Union is all he has left to do. It is in this way that the entire pattern of the CCP's work is being revamped.

Mao's derisive cancan performed for Moscow's benefit suddenly changed to a low respectful bow down to the ground and a flow of orthodox Marxist phrases.

Mao is now staking everything on the internationalist principles of the All-Union Communist Party. This he is doing coolly and calculatedly. . . . The rank-and-file party members take all this at its face value. They are rejoicing in the Soviet victories. The press, radio, and speeches of politicians have created an atmosphere of exaggerated benevolence for the Soviet Union.

Mao is holding firmly in his hand the strings of this puppet show. He is anxious to make his mark without giving himself away. To make his mark without yielding an inch on his principles, the principles of the "Marxism of reality." To sacrifice his loyal comrades, if necessary, in order to retain his ideological positions. Mao is well aware of the fact that the outcome of his game depends on his political sleight of hand.

Mao is all tensed up. He is afraid that the delegates might break out of the framework of the endorsed texts of carefully tailored speeches. He does not spare himself in this new role of theatrical prompter. The anguish and groans of the internal party struggle of this most terrible decade in the history of the Chinese Communist Party must not break out into the open!

Yenan is abuzz with the dialects of all the provinces of China. Crowds of people can be seen everywhere—delegates, Soviet representatives, busy-looking patrolmen. . . .

The precongress tension, the pent-up energy of the coming great event, are felt in practically everything.

The Soviet Government has denounced the neutrality pact with Japan. This is evidence of the fact that we shall not stand aside from the developments in the Pacific area.

Loud cheers have gone up in Yenan. Mao Tse-tung has been excited all these days. The Soviet Government's decision enhances the prestige of the Communist Party of China. Everybody understands here that the Kuomintang will soon seek agreement with the Communist Party.

It is widely speculated in Yenan that contacts between the Soviet armies and the troops of the CCP in a future war with Japan are inevitable.

The favorite occupation of the leading Chinese comrades now is singing hosannas for the Soviet Union and for Stalin.

Everybody in Yenan—from a rank-and-file party member to a top-rung party worker—now takes it for granted that the Soviet armed forces will solve all the problems which Yenan cannot solve alone. They will liberate Inner Mongolia for the CCP, they will rout the Kwantung Army in Manchuria, while the laurels of this victory will also go to the CCP. Mao obviously hopes to turn the Special Area into a vast territory which the Soviet Union will win for him.

They are particularly vociferous about the Soviet Government's decision following General Hurley's press conference in Washington.

April 20, 1945

Mao Tse-tung is always alone in his living quarters. Dead silence reigns in this subterranean labyrinth where everybody walks in soft-felt shoes (there is no other kind in Yenan). But here, deep underground, this silence gives an impression of complete isolation from the outside world. And his servants look like some sort of shadows or ghosts. . . .

Mao is very sensitive to gossip.

He cannot listen and in fact does not like to.

Carried away by his performance he can speak for hours. His words and speech sharpen him up. In a way Mao's whole life is in his own words. When he speaks, he changes and becomes a new man, oblivious of his audience. . . .

When he speaks before a crowd, the Chairman of the CCP Central Committee is quite different, though. Now his speech is a passionate harangue, contrasting sharply with the dull tone of his voice, richly interlaced with quotations. Now it is an easy peasant banter and crudish jokes which draw laughter from the audience. Now it is the imperturbable and dispassionate muttering of a desk-bound thinker. . . .

April 21, 1945

So the enlarged plenary meeting of the CCP Central Committee is a thing of the past. Using pressure, flattery, and promises, Mao has got what he wanted. The speeches made at the plenary meeting were endorsed and the passions allayed. Discipline and obedience reign among the delegates.

This was achieved only thanks to the personal interference of the Chairman of the CCP Central Committee. The report "On the Political Line of the Party Between 1931 and 1935" brought its author to the verge of physical exhaustion. In the heat of argument he was hauled over the coals: "He failed to consider," "He distorted," "He did not say the truth," etc. That was a harrowing experience for Jen Pi-shih's delicate health, and Andrei Yakovlevich's assistance was called for.

The Chairman of the CCP Central Committee has pulled this historical report from the bog in which it had sunk. Mao Tse-tung made long speeches before delegates in an effort to smooth down the troubled situation. It was only his personal authority and outright pressure that brought the brooding storm under control. Even I did not expect that the delegates would react so violently!

On Jen Pi-shih's report the plenum passed a decision called "On Some Questions of the History of Our Party." Much of this document was devoted to the defamation of Po Ku and Wang Ming, and especially of the concepts of the Communist International.

It has been announced that the congress will be officially opened in a few days.

———

The following words of Lu Hsun may be applied to describe Mao Tse-tung's behavior in the present situation: "In a dark corner he prepared a different face and a different banner so as to come upon the stage set for the new situation. You think that this is the gate of a temple, but instead you see the maw of a monkey. . . ."

I feel I can be frank enough with my own diary. Years of life at Mao's side failed to make me respect him, to put it mildly.

This man, who would not hesitate to destroy tens and even hundreds of thousands of lives, if the situation and his personal interests warranted it, is noted for his cowardice. I saw him "funk" many times when things took a serious turn.

He puts his own health above everything else. Hardly a week goes by when Andrei Yakovlevich is not called to him, although the complaints are very minor. . . . At the same time he is indifferent and cruel to the sickness and even death of others, even his relatives. . . .

Once I told Mao about the threat of civil war in Hegel's words that the truth paves the way for itself when its time has come, and not earlier. Mao vouchsafed no reply. I don't think he wanted to make me feel humiliated. He simply has other ideas on this score. History must submit to his temperament. This is the conclusion I made after many years of knowing him so well. . . . Mao is one of those men who think they are immortal.

As for Hegel's works he is not familiar with them. I asked him about Hegel not out of sheer curiosity. After all, Mao is a "leader" and Hegel is not a Shanghai ricksha whose name can be dismissed as unimportant.

———

I have summed up all my notes and reports over the years and have come to the following conclusions:

1. Mao Tse-tung's contacts with the Americans were aimed at receiving arms from them. This point requires no elaboration.

2. The political demands to Chungking were aimed at isolating the regime of the Central Government. The Chairman of the CCP Central Committee was completely oblivious of the fact that his actions might create a split. The war is merely a convenient expedient for achieving his personal objectives.

The demands were unrealistic. His aim was to paint Chiang Kai-shek as an obdurate blockhead who is sabotaging the cause of joint resistance to the Japanese occupationists; to win the Americans over to the idea of signing an agreement with the Special Area. His main trump card was the interest the Allies took in the Eighth Route Army and the New Fourth Army.

3. The draft treaty signed in Yenan and endorsed by Hurley was couched in terms making its realization impossible. Chiang Kai-shek would never agree to turn all political power over to the Communist Party. This intention was inherent in the articles of this treaty. Hurley has fallen into a trap and still cannot get out of it. The United States has in a way been also discredited by the blunder made by one of its leading politicians who, besides, is close to the White House.

4. Mao Tse-tung tried to achieve his political objectives by sheer force, regardless of the military and political situation in the country (using the Sian agreement as a cover, he captured whole areas controlled by the Central Government ostensibly for the purpose of setting up new bases there).

5. Mao Tse-tung sought to bring the United States into an alliance with the Communist Party. In the course of these transactions Mao Tse-tung presented the CCP as a force America must rely on. Despite the fact that he had very slim hopes of success, the Chairman of the CCP Central Committee tried to convince the important American political officials he negotiated with that he could be depended on as an ally.

6. By aligning himself with the Americans both politically and militarily, Mao sought to isolate Chiang Kai-shek in order to put an end to him altogether. This is what Chiang Kai-shek understood, and this is what the Americans, who are fussing with all kinds of political proposals, are beginning to understand. Chiang Kai-shek knows full well that any concessions to Mao Tse-tung on the part of the Americans will weaken Chungking's authority. That is why he has got Stilwell removed.

7. By aligning himself with the Americans Mao Tse-tung also expected to keep the Soviet Union away from actively participating in the solution of the Far Eastern problems.

The underlying feature of all the contacts between Mao Tse-tung and the Allies is their mutual anti-Sovietism. The Americans at first regarded this unabated anti-Soviet sentiment as a tactical stratagem. At any rate they did not dare to sacrifice Chiang Kai-shek. As for Mao he has given himself away! Basic to any agreement with Mao was his anti-Sovietism ("some sort of national distinction of the Communist Party").

Mao Tse-tung knows full well that the Soviet Union has always been the principal ideological enemy of capitalism in the United States. He knows this and is trying to cash in on the fact. This, however, is merely a skillful stratagem. I know every detail of the talks. In exchange for American weapons and an alliance with the United States Mao Tse-tung promised to make a clean break with Moscow.

8. By making unrealistic demands on the Kuomintang the Chairman of the CCP Central Committee justified his sabotage of the united anti-Japanese front, decried the positions of the Soviet Union and the Comintern on this question, alleging that they had compelled the CCP to enter into an alliance with Chiang Kai-shek (the Sian agreement between the CCP and the Kuomintang signed on September 22, 1937).

9. In all his contacts with the Americans Mao Tse-tung showed up yet another side of his political make-up. He has made it abundantly clear that he is not a Communist but some sort of the "principal national force of the country." His principles have nothing in common with Marxism.

10. Mao Tse-tung is prepared to disavow all commitments and principles if they don't serve his aims. Neither treaties nor traditional international ties nor the suffering of his people mean anything to him. . . . Mao Tse-tung interprets dialectics as freedom of action regardless of principles. In plainer and more precise words his "dialectic" can be described as a mixture of unscrupulous actions and treacherous collusions. . . .

11. Despite the Soviet assistance in the form of arms, money, scholarships for Chinese students at Moscow higher schools of learning and at academies, despite the powerful political support which prevented the more reactionary elements of the Kuomintang to crush the CCP, Mao Tse-tung took a stand bordering on outright betrayal in the years of the war which Nazi Germany waged against the Soviet Union. In the most trying days of 1941–42 when Japan was only hours away from attacking the Soviet Union (it was the courage of the Soviet people that made this attack impossible), Mao Tse-tung was following these developments with callous indifference and even ordered the Eighth Route Army to stay away from active operations against the deploying Japanese troops near the Soviet border. When Russians, Ukrainians, Byelorussians, Georgians, and Armenians were dying on the approaches to Moscow, Leningrad, Sevastopol, and Stalingrad, Mao Tse-tung started a purge in the party, inflicting reprisals on the "dogmatists," Chinese Communists-internationalists.

Soon after he ordered the discontinuance of all combat operations by the Eighth Route Army against the Japanese, thereby allowing them to prepare for an attack on the Soviet Union unimpeded.

12. Mao Tse-tung crushed the "Moscow opposition," slandered the Comintern and its activities from the positions of his own philosophy, the nationalist "Marxism of reality."

13. Mao Tse-tung corrupted the party cadres with anti-Sovietism and nationalism, used terroristic methods in the party.

14. By juggling with false figures he managed to camouflage the true character of the combat operations of the Eighth Route Army (and partly those of the New Fourth Army) against the Japanese, and the true nature of his policy for the united anti-Japanese front.

Now these figures are widely used by the leading news agencies of the world without so much as mentioning the source (Yenan) they have been taken from. These figures have become official. They not only fail to tell the true story about the activities of the CCP in time of war but distort the picture of the true historical processes, their character, direction, and magnitude. And, most importantly, they screen the intentions of the CCP leaders.

The Seventh Congress of the Chinese Communist Party is to open tomorrow.

The congress was supposed to take place in 1940, according to the decision of the sixth plenary meeting of the CCP Central Committee (1938).

The enlarged meeting of the CCP Central Committee in December 1937 was addressed by Wang Ming who spoke about the tasks of consolidating the united anti-Japanese front. His speech was unanimously endorsed by the participants of the meeting. The only person who made some critical remarks on Wang Ming's report was Mao Tse-tung, but after the debates he realized that he risked being left in isolation and finally voted for the resolution which approved the tactic of the united anti-Japanese front as the only correct one in the conditions of Japanese aggression.

Soon after Wang Ming and most of the members of the future "Moscow opposition" left for Hankow where they represented the CCP in Chiang Kai-shek's government, or the "government of national defense" as it was called at that time.

Wang Ming stayed in Hankow right until the capture of this city by the Japanese in October 1938. Mao did not lose time and was busy strengthening his positions and making preparations for cheng-feng. That was the time when Kang Sheng's punitive apparatus was growing in strength. Meanwhile Mao Tse-tung began proving the "invalidity" of the decisions of the meeting of December 1937 and of the CCP Central Committee sixth plenum with regard to the united anti-Japanese front and, consequently, the "invalidity" of the Comintern's position.

So the CCP will open its seventh congress tomorrow!

April 23, 1945

So the Seventh Congress of the Chinese Communist Party has been opened.

The opening speech was made by Jen Pi-shih, member of the Politburo of the CCP Central Committee.

This in brief is what he said:

The twenty-five years of the history of the party is a period of victories and defeats. Great sacrifices have been made over this period. The struggle is continuing.

Our main achievement is the fact that all Chinese people are defending our political line and welcome New Democratism. In the course of our struggle Marxism has been gradually fused with the concrete realities of Chinese life. The banner of Mao Tse-tung has become the banner of the liberation of the Chinese people.

We have entered the period of great changes in the world. Hitler will soon be routed. Democracy will win. In the east the Japanese will be ousted from China in a matter of two or three years. We shall start building a New Democratic China. It is at this particular stage of life that the Chinese people are now.

Jen Pi-shih was followed by Mao Tse-tung.

This in brief is what he said:

The Seventh Congress of the CCP will decide the fate of the 450 million Chinese people. The Chinese people are faced with a choice of two destinies and are about to make up their minds. The congress will have to determine the path the people will follow. The congress will have to unite all people of China and the whole world in order to assure victory for them.

Berlin will soon be taken. In the east the war against Japan is still continuing. But the victory is not far off. It is within our grasp.

The present situation is highly favorable. The people have to decide which road to take: One is light and the other is dark. In the course of the war with Japan our country will be either free, independent, and democratic, or old as China was in the past. It is our task to unite the entire party, the whole of the country, and possibly all the forces of the world to take the road of light and wrest it from darkness. Is such a victory possible? Yes, it is! The Chinese Communist Party is more than 1 million strong. There are vast liberated areas. Public opinion in China and elsewhere in the world is on our side. A few years ago such conditions were nonexistent. (That, however, did not deter Mao from going full hammer toward unleashing a civil war, spoiling for a military conflict with the Kuomintang! A very convincing admission of his adventuristic practices.) We must use these forces for routing Japan and for building a new China.

The twenty-five-year-long history of the CCP breaks down into three stages of struggle: the Northern Expedition, the Civil War, and the anti-Japanese war. Over these three periods in the history of the party we have experienced a lot and learned a lot. The party has become the main liberation force of the Chinese people.

At present the party is working hard to build up a large and strong army.

Despite these achievements, we must be modest, fight conceit, hasty and rash actions. We must also be cautious. We must put our will and our fellow-feelings at the service of the Chinese people. It is only then that we will carry out our tasks.

Next to speak after Mao Tse-tung were Chu Teh; Okano, the representative of the Communist Party of Japan; Liu Shao-chi; Chou Enlai; and Lin Po-chu. All their speeches followed the same monotonous pattern: a short analysis of the international situation, an appeal for the routing of imperialist Japan, a brief retrospective survey of the history of the party, an evaluation of the present situation, successes, the increase of strength, unity.

All the speakers pointed out that in the person of Mao Tse-tung the Communist Party of China has its "leader" and its "banner" which has led them and will continue to lead them from one victory to another. . . .

After that Li Fu-chun read out messages of greetings from the Liberation League of Japan and some other party groups.

Peng Chen told the congress about the results of the verification of the delegates' credentials, the length of their work in the party, the social composition and the age of the delegates, etc.

The length of the party work of the delegates and their numbers: 1921–27—210 delegates, or about 28 per cent of the total number of delegates present at the congress; 1928–37—444 delegates, or 59 per cent of all the delegates present; 1937–41—98 delegates, or 13 per cent of the total number of delegates present.

The age of the delegates: from twenty-three to thirty years old—130 delegates; from thirty-one to forty years old—453 delegates; from forty-one to fifty years old—140 delegates; from fifty-one to sixty years old—24 delegates; and from sixty-one to sixty-nine years old—5 delegates.

Seven hundred delegates are men and 52 are women.

Out of the total of 752 delegates, 401 come from the professional class.

Four hundred and twenty-two delegates have a secondary school education and a college education, 319 delegates have a primary school education, and 11 delegates have no formal education at all.

There are 324 servicemen and 315 professional party workers among the delegates.

Present at the congress are seven officially invited guests and four other persons.

The official guests are representatives of the Korean and Japanese Communist Parties.

Tomorrow Mao Tse-tung will deliver the main political report.

April 24, 1945

After the sitting I was approached by a Chinese comrade who told me that from now on all my notes taken at the congress are a secret document. This comrade said that that was Mao Tse-tung's personal order. He took my notebook and asked me to wait for a while.

Fifteen minutes later he returned and gave me back my notebook.

The cover of the notebook bore a stamp marked "secret," and these words written in a fluent hand: "Comrade Sung Ping, this notebook is a secret document. All the pages are numbered and none of them are allowed to be torn out. The notebook must be handed in after each session and must not by any means be taken out of the hall. After the work of the congress the notebook must be turned in."

Thus I was compelled to hand in my notes, which I will get back only tomorrow, before the next session.

Mao Tse-tung's speech, which I noted down at the congress, has not been included in the official records of the congress. I have no doubts that it will not be made public in its full authentic form. In fact this speech is a secret document. Nobody will know of this speech, besides Mao Tse-tung and the delegates to the congress, and not because it contains any political or military secrets of the CCP. . . .

April 26, 1945

Mao's political report gives a cause for surprise. Some of its theses contradict the actual facts. On many questions theory and practice do not come together at all, as if taking parallel, often diverging courses.

One has the impression that the speaker tried to bypass all key problems of inner party life. His arguments are constantly at variance with the facts. Even a perfunctory examination shows that this report cannot stand up to the practical policy of the CCP leaders. Mao's speech purports to conceal his personal struggle for power under the guise of Marxist slogans, to substantiate his departure from the Marxist theory, or to becloud the unseemly motives and methods of the cheng-feng past. That is why the report sounds sincere, but in actual fact this sincerity is phony. Besides it is highly contradictory and inexact. On the one hand, the speaker proclaimed an irreconcilable struggle with the Kuomintang under the guise of "necessity of hegemony," etc. On the other hand, he says that an alliance with the Kuomintang would be expedient. The question suggests itself if the war with Japan is to be continued, if the congress mobilizes all the forces for the struggle against the Kuomintang. These words should apparently be interpreted this way: The CCP will continue its policy of saving up man power and squeezing out the Kuomintang troops, including the capture of new territories. That is exactly what the speaker said.

Some of the figures in the report are cited as desirable, and then, almost in the same breath, are qualified as actually existing (for example, the size of the population in the CCP-controlled territories).

In general the report has far too many loose ends.

Throughout his whole speech Mao expressed his concern about the party cadres. The damage done by cheng-feng is obviously great. In the theoretical field party workers have been stripped of all initiative. Nobody is even trying to apply the Marxist theory in practical work. There are but a few people in the party who have the right to "hand down" directives for all the others to carry them out. In the complicated political situation charged with an imminent civil war this lack of independent action is fraught with danger. Alien ideology must be dealt with both vigorously and creatively, adjusting to various circumstances. This theoretical laxity on the part of the party cadres has obviously given the Chairman of the CCP Central Committee a cause for concern. On the one hand, Mao cannot disavow the cheng-feng, much less denounce it. On the other hand, though, the negative effects of the reprisals are much too obvious to be ignored. Mao's words seem to be screaming: We will not hurt the party cadres, we shall respect them, we need the cadres!

Many years of sojourn in Yenan have gone by; the World War is drawing to a close. There are many reasons for concern. . . .

This concern underlies the party's promise: no more reprisals against the local party cadres, no repetition of the past. Otherwise it would be very difficult to retain control of the new areas. Mao is trying to assure the local cadres that their services are appreciated and that they have nothing to worry about. He is doing this in order to stimulate their activity. In his personnel policy, just like in the theoretical and practical field, Mao seems to be bent on harmonizing what is disharmonious and reconciling the irreconcilable. He wants to preserve the spirit of the cheng-feng and at the same time to reawaken the spirit of party vigor, comradeship, the feeling of confidence in the future. The question suggests itself: Does Mao believe in what he says?

Mao draws up radiant optimistic plans, little worrying about tying them up with reality. The report is highly pretentious, very cleverly put together, and has conveniently left out all controversial questions.

His harangues about the All-Union Communist Party, about the Soviet Union and the Soviet leadership are nothing but a tactical stratagem and are not tied up with his past deeds. To me they sound like a bunch of empty words.

The aims, tasks, the history, of the united anti-Japanese front, and in the light of this the alliance between the Communist Party and the Kuomintang, are given subjective and biased treatment.

Nobody dares to question or criticize the contents of the report, which has been understood to be a detailed instruction, an order. I can easily imagine that the debate will be a mere illustration of the report.

Also typical are the relations between the top party officials, on the one hand, and file members of the party, on the other. The relations that should normally exist between party comrades are completely nonexistent. The façade of democracy covers up the armylike attitude of superiors to their subordinates. The rapturous servility of the delegates is degrading to their human dignity. Cheng-feng has truly done its job.

It takes a good knowledge of Mao Tse-tung's policy, his devious ambiguous terminology, to understand his speech correctly.

The "mobilization of the popular masses" means preparations for capturing new territories from the Kuomintang and for starting a civil war, in other words a mobilization which has nothing in common with the war against the Japanese.

The "development of forces in 1941–45" should be interpreted as guerrilla warfare, a limited war tactic, the curtailment of the military operations against Japan for the purpose of building up forces for future clashes with the Kuomintang.

"We have set straight the policy of necessary reforms." This means that Mao Tse-tung and his supporters have passed on to the tactic of putting forward unacceptable demands for the settlement of disagreements between the Communist Party and the Kuomintang. This is an admission of a political split under the guise of a class evaluation of the events. According to Mao Tse-tung himself, this tactic goes back to 1938, a tactic aimed at disrupting the anti-Japanese front.

The report is full of such ambiguities and, I would say, insincerities. . . .

April 27, 1945

Mao Tse-tung's speech harks back to the gory events of 1935. Speaking about the military and local party cadres, Mao Tse-tung said:

"The Red Army of the Central Soviet Area of Kiangsi had completed its Long March. On their arrival in the Special Area the party and military cadres, all of them, subjected the local party and military cadres to cruelty and injustice. . . ."

Mao Tse-tung's sham criticism of the shortcomings of the party ("We are Bolsheviks, but we are not free from shortcomings") is meant to cover up the sufferings inflicted upon the local party and Soviet workers of the Special Area. Mao Tse-tung had sent a large army unit to "enforce law and order" there, that is, to liquidate the local Soviet and party apparatus and to set up a new base in the place of the old one. Mao hoped that he would be the lord and master of the new base and that his authority would be unchallenged there.

Kao Kang, and especially Liu Chih-tan, enjoyed the well-earned popularity in this area and were looked up to as popular heroes. In the face of the Kuomintang blockade and the long-standing national strife, they created and strengthened a Soviet base area near the town of Pan-yen (a short distance from Yenan), in the course of a long guerrilla war.

In October 1935 the advance task force of Mao Tse-tung put Shansi to the sword. All local party and administrative workers were arrested. The commanders and soldiers who stepped in to defend their leaders were savagely murdered.

The massacre continued with the arrival of the main forces headed by Mao Tse-tung. The main force of the Red Army arrived in North Shansi in November 1936.

The punitive actions of the task force and the Army caused strong indignation among the members of the CCP Central Committee. Mao Tse-tung was considered responsible for the reprisals, for there was no doubt in anybody's mind that it was he who had given the order. . . .

In this situation the Chairman of the CCP Central Committee chose to put the blame on the military commanders who had led the punitive expedition. Kao Kang, Liu Chih-tan, and all the other survivors of the massacre were rehabilitated. . . .

The perpetrators of the punitive action had arrested Kao Kang, Liu Chih-tan, and their comrades-in-arms in winter. As a torture they kept the arrested men out in blistering cold. When Kao Kang, Liu Chih-tan, and other comrades dropped down half dead with fatigue, they were forced back on their feet with blows and kicks and made to run the gauntlet.

Back in the Futien days Mao Tse-tung's henchmen had made wide use of torture by fire.

This time, they did the same. The arrested men were tortured by fire.

All these years Kao Kang has said nothing about what he was forced to go through, that in the course of such torture sessions the flesh on his right thigh had been burned down to the bone.

Mao's typical artifice: to deal mercilessly with leading party workers who show too great a measure of independence and whose authority is too great for comfort and then to disassociate himself from the reprisals and blame them on their technical perpetrators.

The same thing happened after the Futien reprisals and also after the "case of Kao Kang and Liu Chih-tan." . . .

The same thing happened after cheng-feng, when the whole blame was put on Kang Sheng and some of his associates. . . .

April 30, 1945

Chou En-lai made a report (or rather a co-report):

1. On the united front: the Communist Party—the Kuomintang.

2. The lessons of construction (its party and foreign-policy aspects).

The main conclusion of this part of the co-report: Our slogan at the beginning of the war has not changed: "Set up a coalition government."

Chou En-lai then confirmed the correctness of Mao Tse-tung's critical views on the "two-line policy" (they were dealt with in detail earlier in the co-report).

Chou En-lai dwelled on the relations between the Communist Party and the Kuomintang in various periods of their development:

1. Prior to the Sian events. The period of the mobilization of the masses for the struggle against Japan and against the Kuomintang.

2. The Sian agreement, the creation of the joint anti-Japanese front. On September 22, 1937, the CCP published a declaration on the agreement reached with the Kuomintang. On September 24, 1937, Chiang Kai-shek made a statement formally confirming the existence of this agreement. The slogan of the day was: "Law and order in the country come first!"

3. The period prior to the loss of Hankow (Hankow was captured by the Japanese at the end of October 1938).

4. The period from 1939 until 1944 (prior to the session of the National Political Council).

5. The present period (the situation is fully reflected in our demands).

———

Worthy of note is the emphasis laid on the fourth period in the relations between the Communist Party and the Kuomintang (1939–44), the period when, on Mao Tse-tung's orders, the troops of the CCP began to scale down the military operations against Japan, despite the Hundred Regiments Campaign.

This was a period of deterioration of relations with the Kuomintang, and Chiang Kai-shek was not alone to blame for it. It was early in this period that Mao Tse-tung's policy graduated to splitting up the joint anti-Japanese front.

In 1939, after the abortive Japanese offensive on Changsha, the relations between the Kuomintang troops and the CCP forces took a turn for the worse, which chimed in with Mao Tse-tung's plans. He went right ahead with his plan to wreck the bloc with the Kuomintang which he alleged had been forced upon the CCP by the Chinese liberals and the Comintern, although even then he continued to pay lip service to the idea of the Sian agreement.

This period ended in 1944, which was no mere coincidence. The thing is that in April of that year the Japanese launched an offensive from the Kaifeng area which toward the end of the year brought China to the verge of military disaster.

Thus the year 1944 saw the end of the wait-and-see tactics, Mao Tse-tung's main doctrine disguised as a guerrilla warfare tactic.

The power of the Central Government had by that time been greatly undermined by a sweeping Japanese offensive. Now Mao Tse-tung saw his chance for the sake of which he had refused to join in the active struggle against the Japanese, having thus turned the joint national front into a hoax. The Chairman of the CCP Central Committee now felt that the time had come to act. The power struggle now held out clear and realistic prospects for him. Chiang Kai-shek's troops had been drained of strength, and the government apparatus disorganized. The forces of the political ally in the joint national front had been brought to exhaustion. The chances in the event of civil war were now about even.

Chou En-lai has undergone a remarkable evolution.

Right until July 1943 Chou En-lai was at the head of the CCP mission in Chungking.

Mao Tse-tung described his place in the opposition as that of an "empiricist." By doing so he included Chou in the group known as the "Moscow opposition," which he actually belonged to, since he shared the views of Wang Ming and supported the decisions of the Comintern.

In the course of the cheng-feng struggle Mao Tse-tung sought to defame some members of the "Moscow group" while trying at the same time to win others over to his side. Judging from the facts, it was Chou En-lai whom Mao wanted to make into his ally, for he had left open for him all the avenues for repentance, as well as for subsequently aligning him with the "Marxism of reality."

Acting under pressure from Mao Tse-tung and Kang Sheng, Chou not only dissociated himself from the Wang Ming group but also denounced the activities of the Comintern.

He thus grew from Mao's opponent into his most zealous supporter. At the end of 1943 he began carrying out Mao's most delicate missions, such as adjusting Mao's conflict with Wang Ming.

All of Mao Tse-tung's important projects bear the mark of Chou's handiwork. He was the main initiator of contacts between the leaders of the Communist Party and the Americans. In general he is one of the Chinese who like the West.

Chou took a most active part in the talks with the Americans. It is he who stands behind all important actions of the CCP's foreign policy. Chou supported Mao Tse-tung's stand on the question of the maximum isolation of the Soviet Union in solving the Far Eastern problem. As is known, their reliance on the United States was rather short-lived, which was not their fault anyway.

Chou En-lai hates Kang Sheng (Chou suffered from cheng-feng).

Chou En-lai's daughter and Su Fei [Ma Hai-te's wife] are friends.

Chou has a rather sober approach to various problems. He is very cautious; rather talkative but is at the same time very close-mouthed. He can easily adjust to any circumstances; has his men in the administrative, party, and military apparatus. These people seem to make up an independent organization loyal to him.

He is well informed and politically flexible to the point of being opportunistic. It seems to me that opportunism is the leading trait of his political make-up.

Chou En-lai is one of the few men who have been made privy to the personal affairs of the Chairman of the CCP Central Committee. In fact, Mao sometimes turns to Chou for help in settling a minor family problem. . . .

Chou is capable of carrying through his own decisions and always does so, but presents them as "Chairman Mao's thoughts."

He is always affable with us.

There is more European than Chinese in his temperament, character, education, and behavior.

He is much more gifted than Mao Tse-tung, although he skillfully hides his talents. . . .

Chou En-lai's friends undoubtedly include Yeh Chien-ying and partly Chu Teh. But his greatest friend, to whom Chou is very attached and devoted, is Teng Ying-chao, who married him when she was about sixteen years of age.

May 1945

May 1, 1945

Chen Yi and Kao Kang spoke at the congress. . . .

Despite his tragic past, Kao Kang is sociable. Not a shadow of gloom or distrust in his relations with people. He appreciates and is ready for jokes.

His remarkable tenacity is striking. Not endurance, but tenacity. . . .

In the Kang Sheng commission he displayed restraint that verged on passivity. . . .

Lo Fu is one of the top functionaries of the Chinese Communist Party, its member since 1925. In 1931 was elected a member of the Politburo of the CCP Central Committee, and in 1935 the general secretary of the CCP Central Committee. A cultured party worker with an engineering, literary, and sociopolitical education. A translator of Lev Tolstoi, Turgenev, Wilde. . . . A former book publisher. Later the editor of the main organs of the CCP Central Committee—*Red Flag* and *Struggle*. For several years he studied in Moscow. . . .

He was an active member of the "Moscow opposition" and was subjected to purge in 1942–44.

May 2, 1945

Lo Fu was the first to speak at the congress.

The second speaker after Lo Fu was Kang Sheng.

Kang spoke on two questions: (1) on the peasant question (as central at this stage) and (2) on the special question: (a) on the military intelligence activities of the Japanese against the CCP bases; (b) on the Kuomintang intelligence; (c) on the collaboration between the Kuomintang and the Japanese in the training of spies; and (d) on the collaboration between the United States and Kuomintang secret services.

I am the only Soviet observer at the congress. And the present congress of the CCP is a special one! From the outset it has been clear that it is to establish the undivided rule of Mao Tse-tung. . . .

The German radio has reported about Hitler's death. If this is true, then there is some injustice in that. The worst criminal escaped the peoples' trial.

May 3, 1945

Po Ku made a speech at the congress. Then Peng Chen delivered a co-report. It was on the work in the cities and the transfer of work from villages to cities.

At present there is no time for a detailed analysis of Lo Fu's speech.

But the first sketchy conclusions can be made:

1. Cheng-feng transformed the consciousness of Lo Fu in the spirit of "Marxism in practical life." ("Earlier my prestige was conditioned by my petty-bourgeois base. . . . This is connected only with cheng-feng. . . . I studied thoroughly the style and the ideas of Comrade Mao Tse-tung.")

2. His speech gave a very clear picture of the intraparty struggle. Everything is here: the anti-Li Li-san campaign, the struggle against the Futien opportunism of Mao Tse-tung, the temporary success of the internationalists, the systematic suppression by Mao Tse-tung of "dogmatism" in the CCP for the sake of "Marxism in practical life." ("The struggle against the so-called counterrevolution was conducted in a wrong way . . . ," etc.)

3. The disgraceful condemnation of the role of the Soviet Union in educating internationalist cadres as a reflection of the views of Mao

Tse-tung. An attempt to curry favor with him by abusing the Soviet system of education, that is, a denial of any value whatsoever of the experience of the All-Union Communist Party ("I mastered the dogmas . . . ," etc.)

4. The proclamation of the "Marxism" of Mao Tse-tung as the only revolutionary philosophical system acceptable for China. Identification of Marxism and Maoism. ("I shall not be able to be a pupil of Comrade Mao Tse-tung. And anyone can then regard me not as a Marxist. By reading in the past the works of Marx, we deceived others. In the future I shall be giving very careful attention to the teachings of Comrade Mao Tse-tung. . . .")

5. The justification of all the repressive actions of Mao Tse-tung (from Futien to cheng-feng)! Mao Tse-tung could hardly have expected more from the general secretary of the CCP Central Committee, a former outstanding internationalist, a comrade-in-arms of Wang Ming.

6. But the most striking thing is the proposal of Lo Fu for a "permanent cheng-feng in the party," a continuous cheng-feng in the name of the triumph of the ideas of Mao Tse-tung. ("I thought that the mastering of the ideas of Comrade Mao Tse-tung would be easy. In practice it all proved to be different. I have all the time, step by step, been persistently mastering the ideology of Comrade Mao Tse-tung. . . .")

7. Lo Fu deals a blow to his own friends. A malicious, unjust blow! Not only does he condemn Wang Ming and his former friends, but he also sets the party on them. ("People like myself had a common view of the leaders and of the problems of the Chinese Revolution. This was the way that sectarianism emerged. . . . They will seek to split our party and achieve what the Kuomintang's special services have failed to achieve. Evidence is the documents on the presence in our party of a trend directed against Comrade Mao Tse-tung.") Lo Fu means the letters of Wang Ming and Wang Chia-hsiang to the Seventh Congress of the CCP.

8. He distorts the party's history to please Mao Tse-tung.

9. He affirms a new character or relationships in the party (which has in fact been taking shape over the last few years). This is a spirit of toadyism and humiliation before Mao Tse-tung and his followers. A call for the renunciation of human dignity for the sake of the "eternal righteousness" of Mao Tse-tung. Thus, Lo Fu comes to the point of regarding Mao Tse-tung a "genius," who has no equal in the history of the Chinese Revolution.

10. He belittles in every way the value of Marxism, which he alleges is fruitless for the Chinese Revolution without the "ideas of Mao Tse-tung." ("What does it mean to study the writings of Comrade Mao Tse-tung sincerely? . . .")

11. He resorts to a forgery. He makes a typical petty-bourgeois ideology and simply the loss of personal dignity pass for a "proletarian spirit" in the CCP. Among the delegates there are practically no people related to the working class. Therefore, the talk that the "proletarian spirit began to grow and took root in me" is nonsense! It is the ideas of Mao Tse-tung, not Marxism, that have been growing and taking root.

12. A result of cheng-feng—the striking spiritual fall of man, the impoverishment of the individuality, which is in general characteristic of cheng-feng (the "spiritual purification").

———

There goes a constant silent rivalry between Liu Shao-chi and Chou En-lai. Both are not too scrupulous, at that. It is a cruel struggle for power, with the tacit connivance of Mao Tse-tung. If there is anything that unites Chou and Liu, it is the enmity toward Kang Sheng, an enmity verging on disgust.

———

Stout Ho Lung has put on even more weight. Inborn good nature thrives in this man together with a legendary courage. People who have seen him in battles say that he knows no fear at all.

You will hear his loud voice and laughter before you see him. He is an avid card player and often stays up all night through, and drinks, makes merry, and is full of jokes. He is terrible when angry but lets up very quickly. He will readily choose a good storyteller from among his men and appoint him a commander or his attendant.

And at any moment this desperate lover of poker is ready to take off and go to battle. He keeps his troops in strict discipline. He is one of the most loved senior commanders in the Eighth Route Army.

May 4, 1945

According to foreign radio reports, Berlin fell on the night of May 2. The German troops in Italy surrendered on May 3.

The international conference in San Francisco continues. Its aims are creation of a united nations organization and approval of the members of an international military tribunal for the punishment of the major fascist war criminals.

Broadcasts from all countries of the world are repeating over and over again about "Hitler's death." His powers have been invested in a German admiral.

The first speaker at the congress today was Nieh Jung-chen.

In 1919–21 Nieh Jung-chen studied in France and Belgium. Later he completed a short course at a military academy in Moscow. Now he is the commander of the troops positioned in the Shansi-Hopeh-Chahar border region. This is the strongest CCP base, which has been considerably expanded recently.

The next speaker was Yang Shang-kun.

Yang Shang-kun was a close associate of Wang Ming's in the past. After graduation from Sun Yat-sen University he returned to China. He held major political posts in the Army. For some period he was the acting chief of the Political Department of the Chinese Red Army. Now he is the secretary of the party bureau for North China.

Chen Yun spoke after Yang Shang-kun.

Chen Yun has been a member of the Politburo of CCP Central Committee since 1934. He has been in the Soviet Union several times. At present he heads the Organization Department of the CCP Central Committee.

May 5, 1945

The speeches of Lo Fu, Nieh Jung-chen, Yang Shang-kun, and Chen Yun lead one to definite conclusions.

The Chairman of the CCP Central Committee derived all the possible benefits from the self-dissolution of the Comintern. That decision, based as it was on the revolutionary maturity of Marxist-Leninist parties, had actually untied the hands of the nationalistic elements in the CCP.

After the self-dissolution of the Comintern every independence of the internationalists was suppressed.

The situation of World War II and the inevitable decision of the ECCI on self-dissolution under these conditions had sharply enhanced the chances of Mao Tse-tung in the struggle for his own line in the CCP.

The Comintern decision on self-dissolution was received by Mao

Tse-tung as the opportunity for implementing with impunity any political decisions designed to strengthen his personal power.

This became particularly clear in the raging of cheng-feng, the unseemly behavior of the CCP leaders during the negotiations with the Americans, and now in the speeches at the congress. . . .

World War II, with all its hardships and ordeals, was for Mao Tse-tung personally a real blessing in disguise. Conditions were created for a rapid ideological transformation of the CCP, covered up as it was with sets of slogans about the national liberation of China. In fact, "Marxism in practical life" matured and crystallized then. Virtually each speech at the congress confirms my conclusions.

On the other hand, this decision of the Comintern on self-dissolution revealed sharply the essence of Maoism. The secret policy of sectarianism and division was now at will and began rapidly to reshape the party.

The powerful popular liberation movement in China is an important factor influencing the stand of the Soviet leadership. This struggle of the people of China cannot be left without the support of the Soviet Union. Mao Tse-tung understands this too well and has made it an object of speculation.

The present congress has convinced me finally of the cynical calculating nature of Mao Tse-tung.

World War II has been a disaster for all the peoples of the world, including China. But for Mao Tse-tung it has been a blessing. In the grief, troubles, conflicts, and political crises the political aims of Mao Tse-tung have more easily been making their way. A way to power!

The ancient Greeks wisely said that man is the measure of all things. In this sense Mao is with the utmost precision producing his own world (by politics, tricks, and lies). A joyless world in which there is nothing but nationalism and its inherent appendage—violence. . . .

———

On the speech of Nieh Jung-chen.

The Japanese started their operations to seize Hankow, Hanyang, and Wuchang in May 1938. However, the battles assumed a protracted and bloody character.

Then the Japanese changed their plans and attacked Canton. On October 22 Canton was taken.

The Munich agreement in Europe raised in the Japanese military the hope to achieve the same in the Far East, that is, to get the consent of major world powers to the partition of China in the interests of Tokyo.

The Japanese fascists expected that the Chamberlains and Daladiers in the East, too, would manage to persuade the government of China into capitulation. Tokyo banked on the anti-Sovietism of capitalist world powers ready to go to any lengths, if only Germany and Japan could be set on the Soviet Union.

However, the fighting in China continued.

At the end of October the Japanese rushed into Hankow. The government of Chiang Kai-shek was forced to leave the city. Shortly after, Chungking became the temporary capital of the Chinese Republic.

In November 1938 the second session of the National Political Council of China issued the call for total mobilization. The "eastern Munich plan" had obviously failed. The people of China would not accept Japanese servitude. The government of China, despite the intrigues of the right-wing elements in the Kuomintang, was compelled to reckon with this.

The big losses sustained by the Japanese Army during the operations to capture Canton and Wuchang slowed down the offensive, but it was not this that was the main cause. Having got hold of the richest regions of China, Japan was now preparing for a war against the Soviet Union. The Soviet Far East and Siberia attracted her. Toward Japan certain capitalist powers were continuing the same policy of appeasement as toward fascist Germany. The plan for crushing the Soviet Union simultaneously from the west and the east exceedingly suited them. In the west the Munich agreement had untied Hitler's hands. Chamberlain and other reactionary politicians had no doubts that Hitler would now go east.

In its turn, Japan began to curtail its military operations against China, releasing forces for an attack on the Soviet Union. . . .

Nieh Jung-chen from the platform of the congress of the Communist Party of China declared that it was a mistake "to link political and military questions." Military operations should not have been conducted after 1938 when Japan had sharply reduced her military activity in China. It was precisely then that the notorious provocations by the Japanese militarists followed in the area of Lake Khasan and on the Khalkin-Gol.

Nieh Jung-chen declared that this was in the "interests of Munich," that is, of some other states, and said "we should have ceased the fight against the Japanese and reduced it to guerrilla actions," as was even then insisted upon by Chairman Mao. That is, the military operations of the Eighth Route and the New Fourth armies were not necessary, nor later the Hundred Regiments Campaign.

Let the Soviet Union extricate herself the best way she can—that's what his statement meant. This was said about a very tense period in Soviet history—the eve of the Great Patriotic War.

On the other hand, Nieh Jung-chen deplored that "we then did not listen to Chairman Mao." The CCP should have left it to Chiang Kai-shek to fight the Japanese. The Chinese, according to the theory of Mao Tse-tung, should have ensconced themselves in their bases, waiting when the main political forces would bleed themselves white in the struggle. And this about the years 1938 and 1939, when Japan was probing the strength of the Soviet borders near Lake Khasan and on the Khalkin-Gol.

The Hundred Regiments Campaign was carried out in North China by the Eighth Route Army. It was undertaken without notifying Chiang Kai-shek's general staff, contrary to the agreement on joint actions against the Japanese and participation by the units of the Chinese Red Army as part of the Central Government's troops.

The Hundred Regiments Campaign began on August 20, 1940, and lasted till December 5 of the same year. The Eighth Route Army and guerrilla detachments attacked the Japanese in the northern provinces of Hopeh, Shansi, and Shantung. The attack was repulsed by the Japanese, with great man power and territory losses for the CCP.

The official story coming from Mao Tse-tung is that the Hundred Regiments Campaign was undertaken to prevent a "second Munich" (to isolate the capitulationist right-wing elements in the Kuomintang) and to frustrate the new Japanese attack that was supposedly in preparation.

The initiator of the Hundred Regiments Campaign was Mao Tse-tung, who had informed the Comintern of the plan of the operation.

Now, after hearing Nieh Jung-chen's speech at the congress and many years of my acquaintance with Mao Tse-tung, and proceeding from a number of other facts, I have come to the firm conviction that the operation as conceived by Mao Tse-tung had the following two aims:

1. To expand the existing and create new CCP bases, which could not but affect the firmness of the alliance between the Communist Party and the Kuomintang. Not without reason were the preparations for this operation kept so carefully secret from the military command

of the Central Government. Even a favorable outcome of the operation, once it had not been agreed upon with Chungking, would have inevitably led to a split in the united national front, since in it there were elements of a civil war which took on different forms.

2. To discredit the policy of the Comintern toward the anti-Japanese united front and, consequently, undermine the positions of Wang Ming and the other internationalists.

The operation had been prepared rashly, without proper planning or due account of the forces and means. In fact, from the very first day of the fighting it was doomed to failure. Understanding now what great importance the Chairman of the CCP Central Committee attached to the struggle against the Comintern and the "Moscow opposition," I have almost no doubts that the operation was a conscious provocation by Mao Tse-tung against the united national front and the tactics of mobile warfare, that is, the active resistance to the invaders. Yesterday this was almost word by word admitted by one of the most prominent military workers of the CCP (the half-hints of Nieh Jung-chen: "not to confuse political and tactical tasks . . . An answer to Munich").

The setbacks of the Eighth Route Army in the Hundred Regiments Campaign gave Mao Tse-tung the chance to switch over from the tactics of mobile warfare to guerrilla warfare. He now had the necessary justification. . . .

This political and military aim was achieved by Mao Tse-tung at the price of the defeat of the Eighth Route troops who heroically fought against the Japanese invaders. But the heroism of the Chinese Communists, commanders and soldiers, meant nothing for Mao Tse-tung —it was merely a component part of his plan. . . .

Thus, Mao Tse-tung made his own degree of modification to the struggle of the Chinese people and the CCP for the independence and freedom of their country necessary to fit it into his own "revolutionary plan."

Condemning the mobile warfare of those years, Nieh Jung-chen and a number of other speakers have tried to justify the guerrilla tactics of conducting the struggle against Japan. But, frank as they were, they forgot that the author of the operation was Mao Tse-tung himself. So the soul of this operation, whose faultiness, from their point of view, was known beforehand, was the Chairman of the CCP Central Committee himself. The wisdom of the Chairman of the CCP Central Committee in reality proves to be baseness. Of course, the speakers did not want to say this, but it came out by itself, as if to confirm the old truth that there is no secret that sooner or later does not become known to people. . . .

Then Mao Tse-tung put the blame for the failure of the operation on the Comintern, the "Moscow opposition," and the main commanders of the Eighth Route Army.

The speeches at the congress, in spite of "Chairman Mao" and through the thoughtlessness of his supporters, for the first time revealed most fully the provocative role of Mao Tse-tung as organizer of the failure of the Hundred Regiments Campaign. This operation was a stage in his personal struggle for power.

The speech of Nieh Jung-chen has laid bare the speculative character of Mao Tse-tung's arguments about the technical backwardness of the Army and the shortage of arms as the main reason for guerrilla tactics. It was not at all because of the lack of arms or the superiority of the Japanese that Mao Tse-tung switched the Army over to passive defense. He had his own plan for dividing China, weakening it as a result of the Japanese invasion, and preserving his own forces for the purpose of entering the struggle for power in the ensuing period. The interests of the struggle of world forces against fascism, the sacrifices of his own people, the destruction of cities—all this was a part of his plan. A detail of his plans. And the heroism of the soldiers and Communists and the hardships—these were also just a detail of the same plan. It was for this purpose, not for the struggle against the Japanese, that he demanded arms: Without arms this plan was unrealizable.

All these years Mao Tse-tung has adhered to the principle that he who is able to wait wins the game. The price of waiting plays no role. . . .

May 6, 1945

The congress has gathered all the major party, government, and military leaders together. It is a rare and, I would say, sole occasion to see them all at close quarters.

Virtually each hour I have interesting meetings, conversations, introductions. . . .

On the speech of Yang Shang-kun.

1. He recognized the correctness of cheng-feng.
2. He issued the call for cadre training in the spirit of Mao Tse-

tung's ideology, declaring that neither Marxism nor the experience of the All-Union Communist Party had any practical value for the training of Chinese cadres.

3. To the ideas conned by mistake Yang Shang-kun refers, among others, the following: At the Sun Yat-sen University they underestimated the revolutionary role of the peasantry. They only taught the "backwardness of the peasantry, which cannot do anything by itself." This is an extension of Mao Tse-tung's view of the special role of the peasantry in the Chinese Revolution, a denial of the leading role of the working class, and the affirmation of a peasant ideology in the party.

4. To the ideas conned by mistake Yang Shang-kun also refers the alleged "postulate" of Moscow education that the "reactionary camp is a single entity" and that "in Moscow they fail to see the contradictions in it."

Yang pursues an aim—to justify Mao Tse-tung's contacts with the Americans, behind which there was something more than normal allied relations.

5. In upholding the "value of the intermediate elements for the CCP," Yang asserted the legitimacy of the existence of petty-bourgeois elements in the party. This thesis is another aspect of the same process: the degeneration of the party into a typical peasant party, despite all the Marxist phrase mongering. The report of the chairman of the mandate commission, Peng Chen, confirms my conclusions. Of the 752 delegates, 401 are representatives of the intellectuals and 324 are career military. All these people come in the main from among the well-to-do strata of society or the peasantry. Party workers who come of the workers or of intellectuals having close lifelong ties with the working class constitute an insignificant number at the congress. This explains why Peng Chen avoided a class and social analysis of the composition of the delegates in his report. But even without such an analysis it is clear that the delegates are mainly people from among the peasants and intellectuals with no links with the people, and also career military. This again suggests the idea about the degeneration of the party into a peasant party. I have been led to this conclusion by the speeches of almost all the delegates, despite all the references to Marx and Lenin.

6. Yang said it plainly that there can be no Marxism in China without Mao Tse-tung.

7. Yang from the congress platform admitted that he had been informing on his party comrades. His own guilt Yang lays at Moscow's

door. In 1928 in the Bolshevik Party there was a struggle against Trotskyism which threatened to split the party. Yang knew that perfectly well. He consciously distorts it, in order to justify the ideological tenets of cheng-feng.

8. Yang was right in one thing—when he called himself an opportunist. What kind of opportunism—left or right—it makes no difference in this case. The point is that he betrays Marxism for the sake of the cheng-feng "Marxism in practical life."

May 7, 1945

On the speech of Chen Yun.

In his speech, member of the Politburo of the CCP Central Committee Chen Yun was out to prove the correctness of the principle of the "priority of countryside over town."

The report of Peng Chen and other statements on the inevitability and necessity of the spread of revolutionary work from rural areas to cities are a reflection of the objective side of another process. Without control over the cities there can be no victory. But Mao Tse-tung's thesis about the role of the peasantry is being carefully defended and preserved as the main ideological plank in the CCP program. The speech of Chen Yun has clearly revealed another aspect: the ideological community between Mao Tse-tung and Kang Sheng, their view of the role of the peasantry in the revolution. So it was not only the preparedness for reprisals that brought Kang Sheng and Mao Tse-tung together. . . .

Admissions of this kind on the role of the peasantry in the revolution reveal the process that has been gradually transforming the CCP—its growing peasant in character and principles and the deformation of Marxism for the sake of this process in the party. . . .

The unpleasant side, against which Lenin once fought, is the obligatory laudation. In this case—of the "wisdom of Chairman Mao." . . .

Lenin said once about this kind of phenomena in our party: "Where does it come from? I wonder. All our life we have fought against glorifying the personality of one individual, we have long ago settled the question of heroes. . . . It is no good. . . . I am like all other people. . . ."

The praising of Mao Tse-tung has a special flavor, however. There is the claim to the right of "Chairman Mao" to interpret arbitrarily this or that aspect of Marxist philosophy.

May 8, 1945

Hans Frank, former German governor general of Poland, has been captured in the area of Berchtesgaden. In Frank's house, £ 12.5 million worth of paintings and other works of art amassed by robbery in Poland were discovered. In the same area Hitler's former aide Colonel Wilhelm Buchner has been detained in a hospital.

French troops have taken prisoner the son of the German Kaiser, former Crown Prince Wilhelm.

Baron Konstantin von Neurath, a German minister and former ambassador to Britain, has been arrested. This baron was an SS Obergruppenführer, the chairman of the Privy Council, and an imperial minister. It was he whom in September 1941 Reinhard Heydrich replaced as "protector" for Bohemia and Moravia. Von Neurath opens the list of war criminals, which has been handed over to the United Nations War Crimes Commission.

British troops have discovered the body of Field Marshal Fedor von Bock, who two years ago was the commander of the German troops on the eastern front.

Three salutes at once were fired in Moscow on May 8. At 2000 hours, to the troops of the Fourth Ukrainian Army, which took the city of Olomouc; at 2100 hours, to the troops of the First Ukrainian Army, which took the city of Dresden; and at 2300 hours, to the troops of the Second Ukrainian Army, which took four cities at once.

The British and American radios have more than once repeated an announcement on Germany's surrender. What kind of surrender is this, on which the Soviet Government makes no announcement? And how can the surrender of fascist Germany be accepted without a Soviet delegation? . . .

I get tired to exhaustion. I have to make abstracts of all the speeches at the congress: to translate and put them down on the spot. What dialects do the speakers not speak! How difficult it is to translate the expressions peculiar to these dialects!

Besides, I must also make out what is going on at the delegations' meetings. . . .

More than half the speeches have been made at the congress. I may make the first conclusions.

In a sense, the Chairman of the CCP Central Committee is "right" when he says that Moscow trains "dogmatists." Precisely so: Moscow firmly adheres to the Marxist positions. For Mao this creates difficulties in transforming the ideology of the CCP—implanting in it "peasant Marxism," this intellectual twin brother of "Marxism in practical life."

Therefore, not only do the positions of the Comintern and the All-Union Communist Party irritate Mao Tse-tung. They do not agree with the concepts of his "peasant Marxism." He hides his irritation beneath nicknames like "dogmatist," "empiricist," "subjectivist," and even "Menshevik."

The direction of the ideological process in the CCP has revealed itself most obviously at the congress—the transformation of the CCP into an agrarian party, the desire to fit, or, to be more precise, adapt Marxism to the ideology of an agrarian party. The working class as such is not represented at the congress at all.

Mao Tse-tung has grasped the essence of the processes that have been taking place in China over the last ten years. The agrarian crisis, which once also dominated the life of Russia, is dominant in China today. But in Russia the proletarian party led by Lenin headed the peasant masses, whereas in China the Communist Party accommodates itself and slides back to the level of the consciousness of these masses. It becomes a typical agrarian party.

Having grasped the essence of the trends in the country, Mao Tse-tung began to seek, and has already achieved to a certain extent, an appropriate transformation of the party. The speech of each delegate is a testimony to this. . . .

But the CCP emerged on the basis of the ideas of the October Revolution; it reflected its principles, ideas, and methods. Mao Tse-tung has devoted himself to the struggle against this historical past of the CCP. And he has been waging it in the name of the revolution, using Marxism as a cover, in order to avoid self-exposure. This self-exposure, at one stage, threatened him with expulsion from the CCP. Both the disguise and the actions were subtler then. Later, when he had strengthened his positions, it was advantageous to maintain contacts with Moscow for tactical purposes. . . .

Mao Tse-tung is dodgy and resourceful. Beneath the simplicity of this flabby and sluggish person lies an enormous purposefulness and a clear awareness of his aims and, consequently, of his enemies and allies. . . .

Delegates' speeches reveal another feature. The various "points of theory" (thought) of Mao Tse-tung have always to a certain extent been in each of them, getting on with Marxism in some unnatural manner, being a part of their own convictions. Now, repenting, they confess this not only because of fear or a desire to earn pardon. No, in most of them it's a part of their own true convictions. Fragments of these persuasions are scattered in all of them. And only in Mao Tse-tung they are brought together. Each of them, so to speak, supplements his philosophy of "Marxism in practical life." . . .

The talk of the fallacy of Soviet education does not survive a comparison with the facts. The Soviet people, brought up on the principles of Marxism, have held out in the war and routed fascism. Victory is just a few hours away. . . .

In my opinion, the fault lies elsewhere. The education of Chinese comrades in Sun Yat-sen University did not affect their petty-bourgeois essence; it became engrafted only formally. They really did not "mature ideologically." The level of ideas did not correspond to the peasant environment, in which they later had to work. This environment began slowly to absorb them. Marxism in their consciousness became transformed into a petty-bourgeois "peasant Marxism," whose outstanding exponent was Mao Tse-tung. . . .

It's right indeed, as some of the speakers have admitted: To have knowledge is not yet enough to consider oneself a Communist. . . .

May 9, 1945

The news came straight and clear: At a suburb of Berlin the act of unconditional surrender of the German armed forces was signed!

On the Soviet side the act was signed by Marshal Georgi Zhukov, on behalf of the Supreme Commander of the Allied Expeditionary Forces by Air Chief Marshal Arthur W. Tedder, and for the German armed forces by Wilhelm Keitel, Hans Georg von Friedeberg, and Hans von Stumpff.

In Moscow Stalin made an address to the Soviet people. From now on, May 9 has been proclaimed Victory Day.

At 4 A.M. May 9, Prague and many other Czech cities were freed from the German invaders.

Hermann Göring and Albert Kesselring have been taken prisoner.

The "Dönitz Government" at Flensburg endorsed the act. It was also endorsed by Reichsminister Ludwig Schwerin von Krosigk.

To mark the victory over Germany an artillery salute will be fired in Moscow, on May 9, at 2200 hours—thirty salvos from one thousand guns.

The surrender of Germany has, over the past several days, been the main news of all foreign radio stations. Andrei Yakovlevich would ride to us on horseback every evening to listen to our radio set. He would often doze away in the radio room and then hurry off to his patients.

Victory at last! No more Hitler, no more fascism in Germany! And none, we hope, in the future!

We shouted with joy, and frightfully alarmed the Chinese. . . . We filled our mugs with undiluted alcohol and drank to the victory, to our people, and to all those who had fought against fascism. We embraced one another and we even sang. . . .

My country has held out and routed the Nazis! Our land was the scene of the greatest and the fiercest battles of this war. . . .

Victory!

The great triumph of victory!

The war has taken the toll of death in practically every Soviet family. . . . The image of everyone killed during the war is forever etched in our memory. . . .

Victory!

Down the road of immortality did we go, challenging death!

May 10, 1945

The congress was addressed by Lu Ting-i.

He must be as old as I am. He finished Sun Yat-sen University in Moscow. At first he worked in the youth section of the Comintern. Then he was a party official responsible for the work among the youth. Now he is a deputy chief of the Political Department of the CCP armed forces.

Next to speak was Liu Po-cheng.

Liu Po-cheng is the commander of the troops stationed in Shansi-Hopeh, in the Hengyang border area. The main fighting unit of the armed forces of this area is the 129th Infantry Division (under the command of Liu Po-cheng).

Liu Po-cheng has been a member of the party since 1926. He finished the infantry school and the military academy in Moscow. In 1932 he was appointed chief of the general staff of the Red Army of China.

The last to speak today was Chi Jui.

Chi Jui spoke about the mass party work in Shantung and the military actions there.

On Lu Ting-i's speech:

He stressed that Mao Tse-tung had created a doctrine of his own. ("Now we have a leader and a doctrine. . . .")

He specially distinguished cheng-feng as the correct political line of the party.

He has in fact called for a permanent cheng-feng, for an uninterrupted cheng-feng campaign; this can be achieved by a drastic reshaping of the system of inner party education. ("We did not think about what was understood and comprehended and what was not. . . .")

He called for a still more rigid party purge; warned everybody about the danger and harm of excessive inner party democracy.

Throughout the rest of his speech Lu Ting-i echoed statements made by Lo Fu, Yang Shang-kun, and partly Chen Yun.

On Liu Po-cheng's speech:

He admitted the fact that the war against Japan had been slow and sluggish. ("We have always used guerrilla warfare in the struggle against the Japanese and regular, conventional warfare only when we fought with the Kuomintang.")

He confirmed the fact that regular warfare, conventional warfare, was spearheaded against Chiang Kai-shek.

He confirmed the tactic used by Mao Tse-tung in 1941–45 as a wait-and-see tactic aimed at keeping the CCP troops at their bases. . . .

May 11, 1945

Another speaker at the congress was Ku Ta-tsun.

Ku Ta-tsun is one of the organizers of the Chinese Red Army. He spent most of his life in guerrilla units.

Next to speak was Li Fu-chun.

It took so many years of bitter struggle inside the party to reduce it to a "common denominator," the "Marxism of reality"!

The Chairman of the CCP Central Committee regarded Wang Ming not so much as his comrade in the party as a popular leader who threatened his (Mao's) popularity. This may not be the main reason, but at least one of the reasons for persecution of Wang Ming. . . .

May 13, 1945

So the debates on the report on the war with Japan and on the analysis of the international situation have come to an end.

Taking part in the debates were representatives of the so-called "petty-bourgeois opposition," including Lo Fu, Nieh Jung-chen, Yang Shang-kun, Chen Yun, Lu Ting-i, Liu Po-cheng, Po Ku.

They admitted their mistakes, which boiled down to a dogmatic approach to Marxism-Leninism, to losing touch with the masses in their practical work, to underestimating Mao Tse-tung.

Those who had studied in Moscow (Lo Fu, Yang Shang-kun, etc.) made critical remarks in their speeches about the fallacious methods used in the education of Chinese comrades in the Soviet Union. All of them admitted that they suffered from "dogmatism," "sectarianism," "subjectivism," "empiricism," and confessed to having a petty-bourgeois character. . . .

All the speakers showed a dual attitude to the Soviet Union.

Almost everybody hailed the Soviet Union as a mighty ally of the Communist Party of China.

At the same time all the speakers manifested anti-Soviet sentiment, in one way or another. This self-flagellation for "dogmatic," "empirical," and other mistakes is in actual fact spearheaded against the ideological principles of the All-Union Communist Party. At the same time it amounts to a renunciation of these principles and affirmation of a new philosophy for the Communist Party of China (the "teachings of Comrade Mao Tse-tung").

This duality reflects first and foremost the attitude of the CCP Central Committee Chairman to the Soviet Union: to lean on the might of the Soviet Union and make political capital on this might, on the one hand, and to denounce and suppress "dogmatism" (which is meant to cover up anti-Sovietism), on the other.

Mao Tse-tung adores flattery, which is particularly noticeable now, at the congress, and can be judged from his reaction to the speeches of delegates.

Each speaker glorified the Chairman of the CCP Central Committee without fail. The many years of cheng-feng, cramming of various documents ("The Twenty-two Documents" and the like), the endless mulling of the same old truths dished out as some sort of Marxist education and "inculcation of the proletarian spirit"—all these left their marks.

There are many things in these speeches that could have well been left out: Why should they be repeated over and over again if they are clear anyway? Nevertheless, the ideas drummed into their heads in the course of the "spiritual purification" are conscientiously repeated by everybody. The speakers invariably praise not only Mao Tse-tung's report but all of his other statements. Everything coming from Mao is "wonderful," "profound," "meaningful," etc. Listening to this, Chairman Mao himself smiled approvingly at the speaker from his seat.

Ubiquitous references to theses in the works of "Chairman Mao" are used not in support of some point or some conclusion, but for showing off the speaker's "cheng-feng beatitude" before everybody, and especially before the CCP leaders.

It took Mao Tse-tung many years of inner party struggle, merciless purges, political adroitness, to make sure that the congress would come off the way he wanted it, and finally to call this congress. . . .

May 14, 1945

The report on changes in the party rules was made by Liu Shao-chi.

At 3:15 Liu Shao-chi mounted the rostrum holding a thick folio (his report) in his hands.

By way of preamble to his report Liu Shao-chi said: "From now on the Chinese Communist Party must be regarded as a new party. The CCP is a new type of party!"

The introductory part of Liu Shao-chi's report consisted of comments on Mao Tse-tung's report.

Liu Shao-chi said that in his speech Mao Tse-tung had provided a profound analysis of the international situation. Comrade Mao Tse-tung had formulated conclusions on the state of affairs in the party and on its tasks.

"The twenty-four-year experience of struggle has shown the vitality of the organizational forms of our development. It is our task to retain and preserve them, to deepen and supplement them, in the light of the objective conditions of our time. Ours is a Marxist-Leninist party. . . .

"The changes must affect (1) forms of organization, (2) methods and forms of work, (3) forms of inner party life. The form of organization is changing, for the situation, conditions, and tasks are also changing. Our forms of organization have not changed since the Sixth Congress, despite the tremendous changes. . . ."

Tomorrow Liu Shao-chi will continue his report.

On most of the questions (even the most insignificant ones) Mao Tse-tung takes decisions personally. The Politburo only approves his proposals. . . .

According to Andrei Yakovlevich, Mao Tse-tung's frequently changing spells of nervous excitement and depression stem not only from overwork and angioneurosis but also from his family troubles. . . .

May 15, 1945

Moscow continues to broadcast Informburo reports. This is what today's report says: "The handing over of German prisoners of war on all fronts has been completed." This looks like the last wartime report. . . .

Liu Shao-chi proceeded with his report at the congress.

I am still thinking about his statement that the CCP is a party of a new type. What type is that?

Has the process of transformation of the party gone so far that the CCP leadership considers it complete?

At any rate this statement of the chief (after Mao Tse-tung) party theoretician testifies to the clear-cut understanding by the CCP leadership of the ideological processes taking place in the party. This admission is more than significant considering the events preceding the congress!

Liu Shao-chi seems to have summed up the results of the inner party struggle of 1935–45. As the result of this struggle the CCP is a "new type of party."

There are thirty-two American observers in Yenan.

Every day American airplanes shuttle between Chungking and Chengtu bringing medical supplies, oil drilling equipment (oil fields near Yenan and Yanchang, etc.), for the Special Area, also for the American personnel here.

The same planes bring American information personnel, oil engineers, ore specialists. Despite the cool reception the Americans receive from the local authorities, the Americans are unceremoniously settling down in the Special Area.

The Americans have brought powerful radio equipment, are putting their meteorological service on a solid footing, and are setting up a large information center.

The Americans take advantage of the fact that the CCP leadership is hoping to receive more material aid from them and are busy making contacts with the local population, with military personnel and party workers.

May 16, 1945

The real aims of the Chinese Communist Party, and not just officially proclaimed ones (agrarian reforms and national liberation), only partly represent the program of any true Marxist-Leninist party. To my mind, the CCP is not a Marxist party. In this aspect it is indeed a party of a new type. This can be borne out by its practices over the past decade. . . .

Now this is a typically agrarian party disguised as proletarian. Its leaders, despite all their declarations, regard the peasants and the bourgeoisie, and not the proletariat, as the main driving force of the revolution. All they do is camouflage their activities with endless discourses about the bourgeoisie-democratic stage of the Chinese Revolution (the "New Democratism" of Mao Tse-tung).

The Chinese Communist Party was gradually severing its historical ties with the Comintern.

The Comintern was opposed to the development in the CCP of peasant ideology which is the source of anti-Sovietism, chauvinism, orientation toward capitalist America. Hence the struggle against Marxism, a struggle camouflaged with a highbrow terminology ("dogmatist," "empiricist," etc.).

There is a peculiar eclectic mixture of the Marxist ideology (remnants of the former influence of the Comintern) with the petty-bourgeois ideology. In other words the CCP leaders are trying to artificially wed Marxism to petty-bourgeois philosophy.

The national liberation struggle has turned the CCP into an objective revolutionary force. The Communist Party must stand at the head of an agrarian revolution and direct its course. This, however, it must do from the positions of a Marxist party. I witness the evolution of the CCP toward an agrarian party of the socialist-revolutionary kind.

The struggle against "dogmatism" is the main theoretical and political stratagem of Mao Tse-tung.

No self-respecting Marxist will ever try to dogmatize Marxism. The Marxists have only one way of dealing with dogmatism: to be confirmed dogmatists in their antidogmatism.

I would say that in theory Mao Tse-tung is disarming the party, by replacing the clear-cut working-class criteria of struggle with pseudo-patriotic and in actual fact nationalist criteria. Really, this is not a great achievement for a Marxist, much less a "new style of Marxism applied to Chinese reality."

Mondays, Wednesdays, Saturdays . . . I am swamped with congress material. Orlov is coming every night to help me copy some documents . . .

May 17, 1945

Some questions discussed at the congress:

1. On calling a conference of delegates from all the base areas of the CCP and on the formation of a joint committee of all these areas.

2. On the attitude to the United States.

3. On the attitude to the Soviet Union.

On April 22 a Yenan newspaper announced the establishment of a commission for the organization of a joint professional committee of all the CCP base areas. The paper also announced the establishment of a commission for the creation of a women's organization which will represent all the base areas.

On May 3 the same newspaper announced the setting up of a commission for uniting all the youth organizations in the liberated areas.

Thus an important step was made on the way to the setting up of a government of the liberated territories which bears the name of the Joint Committee of the Liberated Areas.

This question has always been of prime importance to the CCP leadership, but the uncertainty of the situation prevented it from its practical realization. All these weeks and months, however, the CCP leaders have not had time, building up public opinion in support of their aims.

Now that the attitude of the White House is clear and Mao Tse-tung has no second opinion about who the Americans will support, the CCP leaders are taking concrete measures to set up the Joint Committee of the Liberated Areas.

The implication of the formal establishment of such a body is quite clear. This will be a Mao Tse-tung government; this is a step toward a civil war, a step calculated to enlist the support of the Soviet Union, a step which would be impossible without its support because without it this step would be nothing but a mere hoax. What would this committee-government, with its limited resources, be like in the face of the Kuomintang, which is backed by the power of the United States? Obviously, the CCP leaders are banking on the Soviet Union, its assistance, and the widest possible support. . . .

That is why the Chairman of the CCP Central Committee has told the delegates that the question of the setting up of a joint committee must be resolved without delay. He proposed to start by calling a conference of the liberated areas. This conference will announce the establishment of a joint committee. The Chairman of the CCP Central Committee has called this body the Joint Committee for the Liberation of the Chinese People. He emphasized how important it is for the CCP to have its own government. At the same time he forbade use of the word "government" in reference to this body. He requested all the delegates to think about the best name for this organ.

The government question is the most burning for Mao Tse-tung. He warned the delegates that in the present conditions it could hardly be possible to hold elections on democratic principles.

The very fact of the creation of a joint committee and the election of delegates to a constituent conference might elicit curses, calumny, and threats from reactionaries of all kinds. "There is no reason why we should back down," said Mao Tse-tung. "For we are acting in the interests of the people, and ours, no doubt, is the right cause."

Thus, the setting up of a joint committee in a short period of time is a foregone conclusion. Now Mao Tse-tung has turned from words to action. By calling for more caution he gave the world to understand that on the question of power, the CCP has decided to act promptly. (This question was discussed by the five top members of the party.) Yet, in the course of debates the top five disagreed on the question of formation of a joint committee. Some of them were all out for the creation of such a committee. In fact, they demanded that such a committee be set up immediately. They favor the idea of waiting for the conclusion of the Sixth Congress of the Kuomintang, but insist that preparatory measures be taken now! In fact, this group is for acting, regardless of any outside circumstances: to take a short cut toward the proclamation of a joint committee for the liberation of the Chinese people! This line of argument is upheld by Chou En-lai, who stands for the most resolute action. Chou En-lai warns that it will be rather late to start forming a joint committee after the Soviet Union has begun military operations against Japan (besides, Moscow might be put in an awkward situation). If so, the governments of the countries concerned might reproach the Soviet Union for interference.

Their opponents said that it was untimely and risky to set up a joint committee. These comrades insist on necessity to obtain an exhaustive knowledge of the inner political situation in China. It is necessary, they reason, not only to wait for the conclusion of the Sixth Congress of the Kuomintang, when the opinions of the two sides take shape, but also to know the Kuomintang's attitude to the convocation of the National Assembly on November 25 this year. It would be too premature to act without taking the positions of all the sides into consideration.

The Chairman of the CCP Central Committee is vacillating and prefers not to express his views on the matter outright. On the balance the situation is more and more taking a turn in favor of Chou En-lai. It is quite possible that the top five have already adopted the Chou En-lai line.

Mao Tse-tung seems to be preoccupied most of all with the problems pertaining to convocation of the National Assembly.

May 19, 1945

On the attitude to the United States.

The arrival in Yenan last year of a group of foreign correspondents and later the American Observer Group instilled in the leaders of the Special Area hopes for getting arms and ammunition from the United

States. This, in turn, gave rise to all sorts of wild plans for rearmament, etc.

Hurley's press conference dashed their hopes on this score. The Americans have by now taken a clear-cut attitude to the Kuomintang and the CCP. This reflected not only on the mood of the CCP leaders but also on that of the entire population of the Special Area. The former friendliness toward the Americans is deteriorating very fast.

These sentiments found their expression at the Seventh Congress of the CCP. Many of the speakers emphasized the need for maintaining the wartime alliance with the United States and Britain, but these done for appearances only.

The stand of the Communist Party on relations with the Kuomintang has taken quite a definite form.

They may either lead to a civil war or still take a peaceful turn and be quite tolerable. In this case efforts must be made to form a coalition government. This solution of the problem will be the only correct form of political alliance with the Kuomintang.

However, with all the alternatives suggested with regard to relations with the Kuomintang, this by no means is the whole truth spoken by the CCP leaders from the congress rostrum. There is still a third way! There is no doubt that the offensive against the Japanese will be mounted from south to north. In this case, the chances are that the Allies will make numerous landings on the southern, northern, and central coast of China. And they will try to transfer the troops of the Central Government and its administrative and police organs to these areas. The Americans will do exactly this. Moreover, the American landed troops will not allow the New Fourth Army and the Eighth Route Army to obstruct the progress of the troops of the Central Government. In that case conflicts with the Americans and with the Kuomintang troops are inevitable. The Eighth Route and the New Fourth armies have no other way out but to hold on to their territories, to do it at any price, so as not to let in the Americans and the Kuomintang troops. Then the Kuomintang Government will try to show to the whole world that these really necessary measures of the CCP military command are nothing but a provocation. The press will mount a vicious campaign against the Communist Party. The party might even be accused of playing up to the Japanese. The Central Government in Chungking will do its best to use these facts in an effort to isolate the Communist Party. Drawn into the campaign of isolation of the Communist Party will be all international reactionary forces. (The Soviet Union will use its prestige to silence this hullabaloo. This is the unspoken opinion of the CCP leaders.)

The Chairman of the CCP Central Committee has declared (and many delegates repeated his words in their speeches) that the Soviet Union is the only true friend of the Chinese Communist Party. The worth of the other Allies has been shown by history itself. Britain, for example, is trying to strangle freedom in Greece. Others are ready to perpetrate similar crimes here, in China.

The news about the routing of the Nazi garrison in Berlin and its surrender was greeted by the delegates with a loud hurrah. They also chanted slogans in honor of the glorious Red Army and Stalin.

In his military report Chu Teh repeated the thesis of the Chairman of the CCP Central Committee about the attitude to the Allies. Couched in different words, this thesis was repeated by many other delegates. . . .

As for the character of development of relations with the Kuomintang, the leaders of the Communist Party do not rule out the possibility that the Soviet leadership will mediate in the creation of one single coalition government of China. The Soviet Union must balance out the influence of the United States.

Be it civil war with all its variants or the allied landing operations aimed at depriving the Communist Party of its initiative, the United States is invariably assigned the role of suppressor of the struggle waged by the Chinese people for their freedom.

All the speakers were sure that while fighting Japan the Soviet Union would find the means of protecting the Communist Party of China. The Soviet Union will not let the Communist Party be destroyed.

The third course the events in the country may take—that is, allied landing operations on the coast of China—has not been openly discussed at the congress. This is broadly implied, although not spoken of.

All speakers stressed the democratic nature of the policy of the Soviet Union in Poland, Hungary, Bulgaria, and other liberated countries.

All the speeches are filled with confidence that the Soviet Union will open military operations against Japan. This mood has given all the delegates, party, military, the administrative personnel of the Soviet areas, a fresh lease on life. It happens, however, that the Soviet Union is near and dear only when certain aims are to be served. This is just about the only angle at which the practical value of the Soviet Union is determined.

My conviction is sustained by the attitude of the delegates to the three variants of the development of events in China. No matter what course the events might take (coalition government, civil war, landing of allied troops on the coast), the Soviet Union will be held responsible for the outcome of any of them. The mood prevailing in Yenan is that of a parasite. It is only in words that the congress is calling upon the party to fight against Japan, to defend its gains, while in actual fact they have placed all their hopes on the Soviet Union.

The wait-and-see tactics, instead of the mobilization of the forces of the party . . .

In the speeches made at the congress these sentiments are not voiced as clearly as at the seminars arranged for the delegations. But especially frank on the score are the delegates in private talks.

Mao Tse-tung has told me that from now on China has become a center of interests and contradictions of world politics. In Europe, he said, only some questions of limited significance are being settled. . . .

May 20, 1945

The Kuomintang congress in Chungking was addressed by Chiang Kai-shek, War Minister Chen Cheng, and the chief of general staff, Ho Ying-chin. . . .

The Americans display a keen interest in the natural wealth of the Special Area, especially oil. Many American geologists are sizing up the oil deposits in the areas of Yang-chang and Yang-chuan. . . . Their interest seems to be purely commercial, practical.

The Special Area has almost 50 per cent of China's oil resources and about 30 per cent of coal.

My feelings at the congress are most contradictory. Many of the delegates here are soldiers, veteran party members with a record of underground revolutionary activities. They took part in the hard fighting. . . . This is the cream of the party, its hope and its future. But they, too, have been affected by cheng-feng. . . .

Nobody understands internationalism other than in terms of its advantage for the Special Area. To them internationalism means the consent of others (including the Soviet Union, of course) to extend assistance to the CCP. This feeling is at the basis of the general mood prevailing among the delegates.

But it was not only cheng-feng that affected the people here. The long years of life in the mountains, the shortage of Marxist literature, the lack of any other sources of information besides those controlled by the Chairman of the CCP Central Committee, the semifeudal style of life of the local population, and the material difficulties have left their indelible imprint . . .

Marxist phrases are more often than not used as camouflage. The more references to the creators of the Marxist doctrine and the more often their names are used, the more such speeches are valued, even if they are empty of meaning. . . .

Mao Tse-tung is not a bad psychologist. The principles he is defending are loaded with what he alleges to be Chinese and patriotic. But what is apostatic about being a patriot?

The suppression of the democratic forces of resistance in Greece by the British gives no peace to the CCP leaders. Military intervention is a new, unexpected, and very dangerous enemy.

That is why the CCP leaders have placed their fondest hopes with our support and direct assistance. Mao Tse-tung is trying hard to show me his friendly feelings toward the Soviet Union. He says that it is the Soviet Union alone that can help the CCP in the face of the imminent armed conflict with the Kuomintang backed by American military interference. For the first time a more or less correct evaluation of the role of the Soviet Union for the CCP and that of a just solution of the Far Eastern problems have found their way into his line of argument.

May 22, 1945

The congress of the Kuomintang ended in Chungking yesterday. Chiang Kai-shek had turned down the idea of forming an alliance with the Communist Party which, he believed, does not recognize the authority of the Central Government and does not observe its commitments.

The first speaker today was Lin Piao.

Lin Piao took part in the Long March led by Mao Tse-tung. He commanded an army corps, then the 115th Infantry Division. A member of the CCP since 1926. In Tsunyi he played a prominent role, actively supporting Mao Tse-tung. He took his studies in Moscow from 1939 to 1941. His wife once suffered from Kang Sheng's reprisals. Lin Piao hates the Ching-pao-chu chief bitterly.

Lin Piao and I are almost the same age. Yesterday he gave me his photograph with the inscription: "To Comrade Sung Ping. I am shown here a short time after I was wounded."

This is what he said, in brief:

"I shall speak about the report of Comrade Mao Tse-tung; on Marxism and its application to the concrete realities of China's life.

"On the work among the masses.

"On this question Comrades Mao Tse-tung and Liu Shao-chi stated their views correctly and concisely. This question is of importance to the party and especially to the Army. Work among the masses is the basis of all party work. One of the basic features of our party's activities is armed struggle. . . .

"Thanks to our armed forces, we managed to hold out successfully at the time when we were fighting against Chiang Kai-shek; later, in the period of the anti-Japanese struggle, we were able to retain our military strength and, thanks to this, to increase our combat capability. . . . There is nothing like this in other parties.

"Our Army has the best traditions. Our tactic is superior to that of the Kuomintang or the Japanese. . . .

"Dogmatism has done us a great deal of harm. We would develop much better without dogmatism, and our successes would be much greater. . . .

"Very often we have carried out operations not according to plan. There were cases when we failed to draw on the masses or local army units for support. We have long since been suffering from militarist sentiments which came into being because of our poor work with the masses.

"We are building up cadres from among our ranks and from among the masses!

"We are not sufficiently aware of modern warfare, and herein lies our serious shortcoming.

"The weak ties with the people may badly undermine the might of our armed forces.

"We must make use of the veteran army officers who have joined our Army. . . .

"Analyzing all these shortcomings (weak ties with the people, underestimation of the importance of army officers, insufficient knowledge of modern warfare), we can say that all these shortcomings stem from the semifeudal order existing in our country, from the semifeudal world outlook, from the semifeudal past. . . .

"A good deal of responsibility for these shortcomings rests with the high per cent of petty-bourgeois offspring both in the body of the party and in the leadership.

"The fact that we have to maintain an army points to a major weakness in our work with the masses. This weakness in the CCP's work among the masses stems from the presence of the armed forces. These armed forces have been impeding the progress of the party's active, life-giving work among the masses. Our reliance on the armed forces has overshadowed our work among the masses, particularly that in the cities. . . .

"We must follow the example of the Soviet Union, where the Army, the party, and the people are one indivisible whole. It is this unity that enabled the Soviet Union to put Nazi Germany to rout. . . .

"We must draw on the peasants for support, although this does not mean at all that our movement is purely peasant by nature. . . .

"How shall we rouse the people to action? Only by way of improving their living standards! This does not rule out all the other organizational forms of party work. . . ."

———

Liu Lan-po spoke for the delegation of Manchuria.

He said: "Our delegation represents the people of Manchuria at this congress. We have not been in our home country for ten years now. . . ."

Liu Lan-po analyzed the economic situation in Manchuria and convincingly illustrated it with figures. He said that the first several groups of Manchurian Communists have gone to Manchuria to join the local underground.

———

Brief analysis of Lin Piao's speech:

Lin Piao has in effect admitted the fact that the CCP has for many years been "stewing in its own juice." It has very limited connections with the outside world.

He spoke with anxiety about the weak links between the Army and the people.

He warned the congress: The CCP is being militarized, the CCP is a militarized organization; the party is being threatened with total militarization.

He criticized the "dogmatists" and their leaders.

Lin Piao is one of the most talented commanders of the Chinese Red Army. He called the attention of the party to the threat of its deterioration into a military organization. He also pointed out the danger of its insufficient links with the people. . . .

Lin Piao's speech was among the most sober of all those made at the congress, although he also kowtowed to Mao Tse-tung.

May 23, 1945

The first speaker today was Chang Ting-cheng.

A career officer. In 1934 he was a member of the Central Executive Committee of the Chinese Soviet Republic. Commanded a division in the New Fourth Army.

Chang Ting-cheng spoke of cheng-feng and party education, the influence of the backward semifeudal ideology on the party masses, and the necessity of overcoming it by the cheng-feng methods.

He made a brief historical survey of the development of the Chinese Red Army.

The next speaker was Fu Chung, deputy head of the Political Department of the joint staff.

A member of the CCP since 1921. In 1925 at the Fourth Congress of the CCP he was elected a member of the CCP Central Committee. A major political worker in the Army.

Fu Chung subjected to criticism one of the operations of the Army under Chang Kuo-tao.

The analysis of the question of the unity of the people was the main theme in Chung's speech. He spoke about the importance of party unity and the profound correctness of "Mao Tse-tung's thought."

Fu Chung pointed out as a major shortcoming the *shan-tou-chung*, that is, the element of separateness in the life of CCP bases. This *shan-tou-chung* harms unity. Hence the isolation in work, the separatism which takes on the most diverse forms (factionalism, localistic tendencies).

About the *shan-tou-chung* he said: "Figuratively speaking, our bases are like a mountain isolated from a mountain. But even such a mountain has its own hills. . . ."

A brief record of Yeh Chien-ying's speech:

In the first part of his speech Yeh Chien-ying analyzed the situation in Western Europe after Germany's defeat: The Soviet Union has come to the fore as the first power in Europe. The Slavs have rallied around the Soviet Union. Now in Europe the Soviet Union plays the leading role; small countries have linked up with it. . . .

Then Yeh Chien-ying spoke a great deal about the might and prestige of the Soviet Union and the leading role of its Communist Party.

He stressed the weakening of Britain as a result of the last World War.

May 24, 1945

Japan can conduct military operations against the Allies if communication between her and China via Manchuria is maintained.

Chu Teh acquainted me with captured documents, from which this frame of mind of Tokyo becomes obvious. The command of the Japanese land forces believes that, despite all the bombings and sea blockade, it is possible to continue combat actions against Britain and the United States on the mainland. The documents stress the importance of securing a line of communication between the metropolis and the mainland: Korea-Manchuria-China. To preserve it, the Japanese command would fight to the last man.

May 25, 1945

At a formal reception in the Kremlin in honor of Soviet military leaders Stalin proposed an excellent toast to the health of the Russian people. . . .

An avalanche of events: the heated debates in San Francisco, the speeches of De Gaulle and Tito, Truman's message to the Congress, the fuss by Polish reactionaries in London, Spain hiding Pierre Laval, Heinrich Himmler's suicide, the arrest of one of the main fascist anti-Semites—Julius Streicher . . .

Reports from the Soviet Union are devoted to the rehabilitation of the country's economy. Again, as after the Civil War, almost everything has to be built anew: cities, villages, factories, mines.

_____

The Chairman of the CCP Central Committee devoted a special speech to the forthcoming elections to the party's Central Committee.

He proposed that the number of Central Committee members be increased considerably, both by addition of new comrades enriched with practical experience and by inclusion of old members who by their work had proved that they were worthy of such honor. The main criterion in the choice of candidates should be the full confidence that the elected comrades would be upholding the political decisions of this party congress. . . .

Drafts of election rules were twice rejected by the delegates. Finally, the last formulation was approved by the congress today.

May 26, 1945

In North Italy the Allies arrested Palmiro Togliatti (his party pseudonym is Ercole) for his "utterance of unpermitted speeches."

Joseph Stilwell now holds the post of commander of the U. S. Army ground forces. In my own way, I was interested in his fate. I learned about Stilwell's new appointment from a member of the U. S. Army Observer Group.

General Wedemeyer is distinguished in China by a more reactionary course. The general is anti-Soviet. . . .

Among the information received from Yeh Chien-ying there is a report claiming that the British embassy in Chungking received a telegram from London about the government's decision to change its policy toward the Soviet Union.

The British Government intends to go over to a policy of pressure on the Soviet Union and a gradual refusal to co-operate. . . . Well, the old Churchill policy of hatred toward the Soviet Union tells again. . . .

_____

Yesterday the Chairman of the CCP Central Committee spoke on the question of election of members of the CCP Central Committee. Here is the record of the speech:

"I. On the main line in our elections.

"Elections of the leading body of our party, which will be the instrument for pursuing the line of our congress and the party's policy for a period between two congresses, are a most responsible matter. It can now be seen how seriously our comrades approach this question—and this is already good.

"In the elections we must have a definite criterion. What sort of criterion is this? The criterion must be the guarantee that the decisions of this congress will be implemented. Only such a criterion is correct.

"Whom should we elect?

"A. First of all, we should elect from among the old members of the Central Committee. Of such, there now remain twenty-five comrades. The absolute majority of them are worthy of being elected. They have proved this in practice, by leading successfully our party.

"B. We should also elect those who in the past were not members of the Central Committee of our party. These must be comrades that have proved themselves to be worthy of election to the Central Committee. They have a rich practical experience. This experience must be incorporated into the new Central Committee.

"The new Central Committee must be larger in number. It must be neither too big nor too small.

"There are many different opinions concerning candidates for Central Committee membership. Nevertheless, whom are we to elect?

"A. Is it worth electing those who have made mistakes? Some hold that it isn't, others stick to the contrary.

"B. Should we, in the elections, adhere to the principle of proportional representation of all the areas of the country? Some say we should; others argue against it.

"C. And are we to form the Central Committee from among people with different standards of knowledge and professional training? Again some are for, and others against.

"To elect a Central Committee from among people who have made no mistakes is a fine ideal. And that delegates care about this is good. But ideals may happen to be unrealizable in practice.

"Is it good if we shall begin to elect those who have made mistakes? No, not very good.

"Let us turn to historical facts.

"Our Sixth Congress decisively rejected the election of Chen Tu-hsiu to the Central Committee. From today's point of view, that was correct. However, the nonelection of Chen Tu-hsiu proved no guarantee 'against the overturning of the wheelbarrow.'

"At the fourth plenary meeting of the Central Committee Li Li-san was excluded from the Politburo. He was removed from the leadership. However, without him mistakes were made all over again.

"Well, here is a third example—the conference at Tsunyi. Ten years have passed since then, but we have made fewer mistakes during this period. Yet the majority of the comrades who actually worked in this period was elected at the fourth and fifth plenary meetings of the party's Central Committee, while of those elected at the Sixth Congress, there remained only four people. [Here Mao means the following: After Tsunyi Lo Fu, Po Ku, Wang Chia-hsiang, and others, i.e., all the opponents of his policies, were left in the leading bodies, and yet fewer mistakes were made. Consequently, there should be no fears now, either.] And the Tsunyi Conference itself would not have been crowned with success were it not for the comrades who had made mistakes. Or, for example, let us regard the sixth plenary meeting of the Central Committee, at which the same comrades worked.

"There has been much progress in our party since the start of cheng-feng. Changes have taken place in the party.

"In the past, we used simplified methods in solving problems. In the last ten years our stand has been that of tolerance. Experience has justified this method. A person made mistakes, then decided to rectify them. Well, it is good. And so, comrades who made mistakes in the past have now admitted them and are determined to rectify them. It will be correct to elect them to the central organ of the party. And this is a very good ideal.

"We may be called ideal realists or revolutionary realists, for we combine our ideals with the realities of life. Therefore, if we adhere to the above-mentioned principle, we shall exactly be able to combine our aspirations with concrete reality. Otherwise we might overlook an important circumstance and prove wrong. Incidentally, all the comrades here do not want to make a mistake.

"The situation is like this. Some comrades are guided by emotion and do not want to elect those who have erred. But if based on reason, they must elect the given comrades, despite their past. It is necessary to combine emotion and reason. This can be done. It is a recognized necessity.

"I think that we shall be able to co-operate with the people who in the past lapsed into basic errors, but on condition that they acknowledge their mistakes. We must train ourselves and learn things at the same time.

"Examples.

"When Marx was founding the First International, he was compelled to limit his program to a level acceptable to the anarchists in order to co-operate with the anarchists of Italy, Spain, etc. Marx did so because a sizable part of the masses then followed the anarchists. Later on they refused to co-operate. Well, they did—and who cared? That in no way told on Marx's aims or the line of his movement.

"Lenin and Stalin co-operated with members of opposition in the past. It was at the time when the latter were at the head of certain currents in the working class. But when these currents dried up, they broke with the oppositionists.

"Now the Comintern does not exist. It looks as though there is no single guiding center of the world Communist movement, but actually this is not so.

"The Communist parties of the entire world are looking toward their leader and listening to everything he is saying. The Communists of the entire world are giving enormous attention to each word of this leader and are guiding themselves by these words. These guiding ideas are a course which the entire world follows. I am one of such Communists.

"There are no opposition trends in our party now. Of course, it is good that we now stand on the positions of unity and co-operation.

"That's all that I wanted to say on the first question.

"I go over to the second question.

"The election of only those who are suitable, disregarding territorial representation, is a good idea. However, the ignoring of territorial representation has its own negative aspects. It is not we who are responsible for our areas being scattered and isolated. This is the result of the specific social and economic conditions, the handiwork of the enemies and ruling classes. The fact that in such conditions the comrades are doing work—this is the revolution. This must be borne in mind. Today we have bases—and this is remarkable. This is the revolution.

"Revolutionary bases are a remarkable thing, but the *shan-tou-chung* [isolation, separateness, localism] is a bad thing.

"The Chinese Revolution is the creation of bases. In the future these *shan-tou-chung*s will die away of themselves under certain conditions.

"In China there are many various associations of countrymen, unions, and other organizations. There are many of them in each city and in each province. This phenomenon has its social causes: language, morals and manners, mode of life, traditions, etc. Under socialism all this will be gradually overcome.

"It is necessary to take the principle of territorial representation into account in the elections. It will secure a stock-taking of the revolutionary forces of all the areas which must be represented in the highest organs of the party.

"On the third question: Is it necessary that each member of the Central Committee should possess a comprehensive knowledge?

"This would be a good idea, but practically it is impossible.

"The Central Committee of the Communist Party of the Soviet Union is made up of people with different specialities. We should not demand of a person a comprehensive education. It is necessary to strive to ensure that people possess a knowledge in several fields. Then people of all learnings and professions will be represented in the Central Committee. Now, the knowledge of each member cannot presently be comprehensive, nor will it be such in future. Consequently, the Central Committee cannot now be omniscient. We should elect also those who will study and master knowledge.

"Thus, the list of candidates for the party's Central Committee should include a large group of people who did not make any mistakes in pursuing the party's line in the past. Then there should be included a group of people who made mistakes but wish to rectify them. We should also include a group of people popular throughout the country or who can become popular. Finally, we should include a large group of those who possess knowledge and experience in various fields, and an insignificant part of those who possess knowledge only in some fields.

"Such a make-up of the Central Committee will correspond to the present stage of development of our party. It will be able to pursue the congress line and exercise a positive influence on the development of our country.

"But won't such a make-up prove too motley? In the last stage of our Great Revolution, the party was motley [Mao means the field of ideology]. In that period, we were not yet through with Chen Tu-hsiu. In the period of the Civil War, we had not done away with the line of Li Li-san, and because of this the party's line was motley and mistakes were made. In the last period of the Civil War, we had not done away with Chang Kuo-tao's line, and the party sustained great losses. After the conference in Tsunyi, we were not yet through with these mistakes. At the sixth plenary meeting we summed it all up, and then we were through with them.

"Later we went through the three-year period of cheng-feng.

"Thus, from the Tsunyi Conference to the present period, having passed through several stages, the party has lost this heterogeneity.

"Can mistakes be repeated? [Mao means the mistakes that were already made.]

"The comrades who made mistakes have regretted them. They have addressed the congress. One of the points in their speeches is the request to all to help them. I think we must help them. It is very likely that for this reason there will be fewer mistakes. This can surely be guaranteed. But it cannot be claimed that no mistakes will be made altogether.

"That's how matters stand: Those who in the past 'overturned the wheelbarrow' will in future be more prudent, but those who in the past did not 'overturn the wheelbarrow' may become conceited and begin to plume themselves. If so, then the wheelbarrow will necessarily be overturned. We cannot guarantee that there will be not a single man who has not overturned the wheelbarrow. Among several dozen people there will be one who will lag behind. But in this case his comrades and indeed we all shall pull and push him. This can guarantee that the fall of a man will be prevented.

"Finally, will there be some degree of injustice [during the elections]? It is necessary to take all the circumstances into account and react accordingly. It is necessary to elect a large group of people possessing an all-around learning and a group of people who possess a knowledge in just some fields. It is possible that in this approach a measure of injustice will be there, because it might happen that even better comrades will not be elected. In this case I hope that these comrades will not take offense after the congress. On the contrary, they must explain it to others.

"II. On the number of members of the Central Committee, my opinion and the opinion of the Presidium.

"The Presidium's view is that the Central Committee should consist of about seventy members. Opinions differ about this. Some say there can be more; others say there can be fewer. If more, how many, then— one hundred? The Presidium was at first of this view, but later gradually lowered the figure to seventy. If fewer, how many then— thirty to forty? I think that this would be too little. Such a make-up could not represent our party today. The old make-up—twenty-five people—plus five already amounts to thirty. It is said that a small make-up will be flexible. But our party is now large, and it will continue to grow in future. Of course, I do not say that twenty-five people will not be able to lead the Chinese Revolution. But in order that the make-up of the Central Committee should meet the situation today, the number of about seventy is the most suitable.

"The Kuomintang at its Sixth Congress elected a forty-six-strong Central Committee. This is significant in preparing for the Civil War. The Sixth Congress of the Kuomintang elaborated many political plans. We must pay attention only to one point: 'indivisibility.' All this so-called indivisibility in the field of administration, military policy, diplomacy, economic policy—all this is directed against us.

"The Central Committee of our party is the highest leading body of our party. It is the revolution's motive force which will direct and guide the revolutionary movement. I hope that a relatively numerous and powerful Central Committee will be elected."

––––––––––

Thus, Mao's two-hour speech yesterday came down to the following:

—Those are to be elected to the Central Committee who will ensure the carrying out of the main policy of the congress.

—Most of the members of the previous make-up of the Central Committee are worthy of being elected—they have in practice proved that they can lead the party.

—The congress is to elect new comrades who have been enriched with a valuable practical experience.

—In number the new make-up of the Central Committee must be much larger.

––––––––––

Lately Mao has been trying to impart to our relations the character of personal friendliness. Ever more frequently he is inviting me to come around for conversations tête-à-tête. . . .

May 27, 1945

Concerning Mao's speech in connection with the elections to the Central Committee.

Mao is busy trying to pull through the members of the "Moscow opposition" into the Central Committee. He prefers to have morally shaken people in the Central Committee, those who have lived through a harsh purge. On the other hand, his speech was a continuation of the same curtsying before Moscow, in hopes of getting various advantages from the Soviet Union's entry into war. He is bending every effort (resorting even to demagogical arguments along the lines of "overturning the wheelbarrow") to push through to the Central Committee the members of the suppressed "Moscow opposition" who have renounced their former convictions.

Mao's mentioning of cheng-feng is noteworthy. Its real meaning is not quite clear to rank-and-file Communists. The ideological struggle was concentrated mostly in the upper crust of the party. There the CCP's ties with the Comintern and the All-Union Communist Party were condemned, the Soviet Union's authority undermined.

As far as the rank-and-file members of the party are concerned, cheng-feng is a means of inculcating belief in Mao and introduction of chauvinistic elements into the party ideology under the guise of patriotism and loyalty to Marxism-Leninism.

In this light it is clear why the majority of responsible CCP workers have this respectful attitude to their "Chairman." They respect Mao Tse-tung above all for the fact that he allegedly defends precisely the interests of the Chinese Revolution, that he is a "Chinese in the international Communist movement," that he has succeeded in gaining independence for the CCP leadership from the former Comintern. For most of his colleagues this is unquestionably to Mao's advantage, determining his authority of leader of the national(!) revolution.

That ground has been laid for the further flourishing of non-Marxist views is obvious. . . .

In his speech of May 25 Mao had a few words addressed to Stalin. Knowing well Mao's cynical statements about Stalin, I find it impossible to believe his sincerity. For me this duality of Mao is not something very new. Simply, the Special Area will not be able to withstand the coming Civil War without the Soviet Union's assistance.

But in Mao's panegyric one could detect his concealed claim to as great authority as that which Stalin enjoys. Really this Hunan guy's pretensions are limitless!

I know the Chairman of the CCP Central Committee well enough not to have any illusions on this score. The people here, at the congress, reiterate just what he would very much like to hear. Lo Fu has stated in plain words: There is neither revolution nor Marxism-Leninism without Mao Tse-tung.

May 28, 1945

Now it becomes clear why in Tsunyi Mao pulled through Lo Fu instead of Po Ku to the post of first secretary (general secretary) and took the post of Chairman of the CCP Central Committee he had created for himself.

Lo Fu became first secretary because of the services he had done Mao Tse-tung in the struggle for the post of the CCP leader.

It was Lo Fu who in December 1934 began to talk about the necessity to have an enlarged plenary meeting of the CCP Central Committee and started organizing a group of responsible military and party workers who began to demand that a plenum be held immediately. That was the most important service to Mao Tse-tung. . . .

As the developments in Tsunyi have shown, as well as Mao's struggle against the "Moscow group" and the "dogmatists," Chou En-lai had always capitulated before Mao, and not just capitulated but adapted himself to Mao more and more all the time. . . .

It is so easy to believe that the leaders of the CCP are renowned and heroic individuals!

I realize that my opinion is in glaring contradiction with the set image. But it was I who witnessed this image being built. I witnessed these "heroic individuals" putting the people's genuine heroic struggle to their own credit; putting the outburst of wrath and hatred of the insulted and humiliated people to the credit of their leadership.

I cannot write about it and not feel pain. When I hear such things said, I cannot. I have informed Moscow about it in one way or another. Maybe some things are beyond my understanding, but I called them their proper names.

Can I deceive my party? Can I make do with the clumsy, official versions of Mao Tse-tung?

On May 25 Colonel Wilbur Peterkin, the new leader of the U. S. Army Observer Group, accompanied by Army Air Corps Captain Charles Stelle, called on the chief of staff of the XVIII Corps.

Yeh Chien-ying received them and had a talk with them.

May 29, 1945

During the meeting of May 25 Stelle emphasized its unofficial character.

The gist of the talk was the Americans wanted to obtain permission from the CCP leadership to develop the network of their military intelligence bases on territory controlled by the CCP.

Stelle acted in the spirit of his predecessor Service. He reported that the Chungking headquarters of the allied command were allegedly of the opinion that it would be possible to conduct joint military operations with the Eighth Route and the New Fourth armies. They were allegedly inclined toward co-operation with the CCP forces. Such was the essence of Stelle's statement.

Stelle warned that at first such co-operation would naturally be limited.

The Americans are mainly counting on an expansion and consolidation of their intelligence centers. They are ready to supply them with the latest equipment. These centers will serve the CCP armies as well but on one condition: The Americans alone will be in charge of their material and technical base.

Stelle proposed that a network of radio stations be set up. And again on the same condition: The personnel is to be wholly American. . . .

If you stumble into Hsin-hsi-chan, you feel the overpowering odor of sheepskin, soy oil, stale garlic. . . . The odors described in Teddy White's story. . . .

In pouring rain the house is droning. The valley becomes gloomy. A stifling bathhouse air is creeping up through the open door.

May 30, 1945

The congress Presidium is sitting at an ordinary cloth-covered, long table with flowers on it.

Mao Tse-tung and all the other party leaders are wearing dark *tan-is* cut in exactly the same way. Mao Tse-tung has tea in an enamel cup in front of him and a pile of papers. Now and then he peeps into them or makes a remark right from where he is sitting or bursts into a laugh which is immediately echoed by all of the audience. In general, he feels perfectly at home sitting there. Chou En-lai, beside him, is neat and young-looking as ever. Chu Teh is not quite his usual self, and when he reads papers, he puts on his glasses. Liu Shao-chi is reserved and unruffled.

Kang Sheng is very much around during the breaks between the sittings. Like all the leaders, he is also wearing a *tan-i,* only his is perfectly tailored and ironed. The jacket is slightly narrowed about the waist, and the sleeves are not hanging loosely as in most cases. Kang has not changed much over these last few years. Perhaps his hairline has receded a little more and his face has become slightly thinner.

The speakers at the congress were Liu Shao-chi, Chu Teh, and Chou En-lai.

Chu Teh's closing speech was a call to study Mao Tse-tung's military ideas.

Chou En-lai spoke on the current stage of the Chinese Revolution, the need to unite all forces to defeat the Japanese, which called for a temporary abandonment of the open struggle against the Kuomintang. "Our slogan is the setting up of a coalition government!"

At present there are about 350 infantry and cavalry divisions and about 180 tanks and 250 planes in the Chinese Army.

The CCP troops are something like 616,000 men—15 infantry divisions, 76 infantry brigades, 2 cavalry brigades.

The Japanese have 32 infantry divisions in China and 1 tank division—nearly 1 million officers and men in all. The retreat of the forces from the region of the South Seas has increased the strength of the Japanese expedition troops in China by almost one-third.

Chou En-lai is very communicative. He works almost eighteen hours a day. Is in enviable health. Seems to be the only confidant to Mao Tse-tung's personal affairs. Chou's main feature is his skill in getting on with people, even those whom he hates, without betraying his own feelings. He is always courteous and well meaning.

May 31, 1945

Stettinius declared on the radio: The Soviet Union has never been an economic competitor of the United States anywhere; the struggle for markets and raw materials has never come into the Soviet-American relations; paradoxically enough, the basic socioeconomic differences in the Soviet and American systems have never interfered with mutually advantageous business relations.

The foreign press is full of arguments concerning Hitler's generals not being under jurisdiction. But the German generals are not merely "technical experts." They are the support of the entire military-fascist system of Germany. They are not obedient executors of the Führer's will. The Wehrmacht, headed by the generals, is already an ideology of professional killers. These generals should be tried as war criminals. It is on their orders that cities were wiped off the face of the earth, that mass executions of civilians were perpetrated. . . .

Chiang Kai-shek has left the post of chairman of the Executive Yuan. He is being succeeded by T. V. Soong.

T. V. Soong (Sung Tsu-wen) comes from the wealthy Sung family, the finance oligarchy of the country. Chairman of the board and director of the Bank of China. Was born in 1894 in Shanghai. Graduated from Harvard University in 1915. One of the most important financiers closely associated with American bankers.

Mao Tse-tung made the closing speech at the congress.

In the section dealing with general subjects Mao Tse-tung touched upon the scale of mobilization of the masses. Chiang Kai-shek would interfere with the mobilization and organization of the masses, with the strengthening of the armed forces and with expansion of "our regions." . . .

Now it was time to swing one's arms. But that did not mean adventurism. How was one to swing one's arms? One had to strike with advantage for oneself. This was the meaning of his speech.

Then Mao Tse-tung went over to the mistakes of the Second International. They boiled down to the fact that the Second International did not follow the line of the First International, that it would not "swing its arms" (meaning would not organize the masses). The Russian Bolsheviks and the Third International acted differently. They mobilized the masses with great "swing." That was why the Russian Bolsheviks overthrew the czar and smashed the capitalists.

Chu Teh and Liu Shao-chi described this course enthusiastically.

After that Mao Tse-tung spoke at length on the international situation, the conference in San Francisco, China's situation, and some ideological and political issues.

June 1945

June 1, 1945

Chu Teh's military report was actually a repetition of the main ideas of the political report made by the Chairman of the CCP Central Committee. Liu Shao-chi's report on the changes in the party rules was equally "original." Each of them repeated the ideas of Mao Tse-tung in the light of their own reports.

The question of the election of members and alternate members of the CCP Central Committee is still undecided.

The most important event of the congress is Mao Tse-tung's political report. It exists in different versions.

The first version ("On Coalition Government") is that which the Chairman of the CCP Central Committee delivered at the congress on April 24. In it all things were called by their proper names. Mao avoided any ambiguity and outlined his views and assessed events openly. He also analyzed the shortcomings of party work.

The second version will be circulated only among party members. It doesn't differ essentially from the congress version, but its wording is considerably milder. Chiang Kai-shek is not mentioned at all. The shortcomings in party work are mentioned in passing and in the most general terms.

The third, official version is designed for the public. Compared with the first two, this one is even less sharp. All the main stipulations are glossed over carefully. The head of the Central Government is not mentioned.

The last version of the political report has already been published in the Yenan press.

The key reports were those made by Mao Tse-tung, Chu Teh, and Liu Shao-chi. They were discussed, and they will provide the foundation for the basic decisions. . . .

The Chairman's face is puffed and grayish, and his eyelids are inflamed and swollen. . . .

Chiang Ching complained to Andrei Yakovlevich her husband didn't sleep and chain-smoked at night. . . .

"He has vegetative neurosis and, as a result, insomnia and all the rest of it. But he is all right. It's just a functional disorder, and nothing else," Orlov told me.

American lend-lease deliveries have undoubtedly helped the Soviet Union in its struggle against Hitler's Germany. However, they were not the main factor of victory so much spoken about by foreign correspondents. In the critical years of the war the Soviet Union withstood and routed the Wehrmacht striking force practically alone, without any substantial assistance from other countries. It might be said that the lend-lease told on the duration of the war, reducing it in one way or another. However, the destiny of fascist Germany had been sealed by the struggle of our Red Army. . . .

June 2, 1945

The main results of the Seventh CCP Congress:
1. It summed up the results of the inner party struggle;
2. Outlined the policy in respect to the Kuomintang;
3. Urged the mobilization of forces to defeat the Japanese;
4. Approved the policy of territorial expansion of all its regions and bases and the strengthening of the Army;
5. Planned to shift the focus of CCP activities from villages to towns;
6. Proclaimed the necessity to change over from guerrilla tactics to mobile warfare tactics;
7. Warned the party against the possibility of American

"Scobieism" (American imperialism's use of armed force to do away with the CCP);

8. Expressed its attitude to the Soviet Union—the Soviet Union is the only friend and ally of the CCP.

The most important result of the congress was the summing up of the results of the inner party struggle. Nobody spoke on the subject at the congress. Everything had been settled at the plenary meeting which witnessed tears and curses in Kang Sheng's address. . . .

The congress settled the most important question—it recognized that the Chairman of the CCP Central Committee's inner party course had been correct. Only this time it came about a little differently than at the plenum. This time they only repented . . . and confirmed the absolute truth of Mao Tse-tung's views. No analysis was made of party affairs or of cultural and economic development in the liberated areas. Most of the speeches were merely superficial reviews. Not a word about the vicious struggle in the Communist Party between the sixth and seventh congresses. Only repentant speeches. . . .

The Chairman's political course, expressed in his concepts of the "Marxism of reality" and "new democratism," was fully triumphant.

Mao Tse-tung, the "banner of the Chinese Revolution," the "leader recognized by all"! All speeches, even the opening statements made on the first day of the congress, began with compliments to the Chairman of the CCP Central Committee.

The opposition was destroyed completely. Its leaders had publicly recognized their mistakes more or less eloquently.

Mao Tse-tung was especially pleased with the repentant letters of Wang Chia-hsiang.

The Chairman of the CCP Central Committee had reason to believe that a firm foundation for unity had been laid. The opposition had been practically defeated on all questions and in the party organizations of every echelon.

The congress called for a consistent inculcation of "Mao Tse-tung's ideas" in every Communist.

Nevertheless, Mao Tse-tung said that complete unity was still far ahead. At the moment the unity of the party was relative. He warned the party that complete unity would require a long struggle yet.

The CCP Central Committee Chairman said that every military unit, every Soviet region (even a big, well-organized one), behaved as a self-contained entity. Everyone lived as he wanted. The single organism was looking, and the center's guiding role was not felt. All were preoccupied with their own affairs.

The struggle for the complete unity of the party was still ahead, said Mao Tse-tung. . . .

Chiang Ching calls on me now and then. Always with guards. Several soldiers remain outside, but one resolutely enters the house. He is followed by Chiang Ching, slender, delicate, and smiling.

Chiang Ching avoids discussing politics. She is lively and gay. She looks concerned only when she complains about her husband working too much.

They are strange conversations. At the door the guard stands at attention (Chiang Ching doesn't always send him out). In the yard, dark-tanned, brave-looking fellows with Mausers. The undersized horses are sweating in the sun. . . .

June 3, 1945

The second important question was the attitude to the Kuomintang. The way in which it would be tackled could have been foreseen. The ideas of the Chairman of the CCP Central Committee were laid, finally and irreversibly, at the basis of future relations with the Kuomintang.

The congress denounced all who for the sake of alliance with the Kuomintang allegedly hampered the national liberation movement, hindered the growth of the liberated areas, avoided "frightening the Generalissimo away," saw only the positive aspects in the Kuomintang, fawned upon Chungking, adapted themselves to the Kuomintang to the detriment of their own forces, and did not conduct a consistent struggle against the Kuomintang's reactionary features.

However, the slogans "Down with the Central Government!" "Down with the Kuomintang!" "Down with Chiang Kai-shek!" were, at the moment, erroneous and even dangerous.

The Communist Party wanted to try to wash the dirt off Chiang Kai-shek's face, Mao Tse-tung said.

The Chairman explained this as Yenan's desire to work for reforms. The risk of a civil war was feasible. Chiang Kai-shek was preparing for it in every way. The Communist Party's task was to struggle against all attempts to unleash a civil war. Talks with Chungking were still possible and they could not be ignored.

The main demand (which will require every effort) is the formation of a coalition government of China, and the main task (not to spare means and forces for its attainment) is to prevent, frustrate, preclude, any possibility of convening a national assembly.

In his political report the CCP Central Committee Chairman said that the Communist Party should concentrate at least five sixths of the political means (in the broadest sense of the word) for the merciless criticism of and resolute struggle against the Kuomintang. One sixth of these means should be kept in reserve for maneuvering.

The situation at the congress was openly anti-Chiang Kai-shek.

Practically all speeches were reduced to the damnation of the Kuomintang. All curses addressed to Chiang Kai-shek or the Kuomintang were enthusiastically applauded by the delegates.

An analysis of Mao Tse-tung's report, other reports, and speeches leaves no doubt that one of the congress' objectives is mobilization (all-around, energetic preparations for a civil war). The demands to set up a coalition government and not to convene a national assembly are only stages on the road to a civil war.

The Kuomintang and Chiang Kai-shek will not agree to form a coalition government. Yenan is prepared for such refusal. If things take this turn, there will immediately follow the proclamation of the CCP government (the Joint Committee of the Liberated Areas). After this, civil war will become a reality, since the gap between the sides will be growing in the course of fighting against the Japanese.

To all intents and purposes, the CCP's entire policy proceeds from the fact of an early and unavoidable civil war. This is proved by the combat operations of the 7th and 2nd Infantry Divisions of the New Fourth Army, preparations in Shensi, the transfer of troops from the Special Area, the simultaneous departure of a group of military and party comrades in the same direction, and the character of the Communist Party's activities in Hunan and Honan provinces. All this is nothing but preparation for a civil war. . . .

June 4, 1945

The congress discussed the expansion of the bases of the Communist Party. The delegates unanimously voted for the policy of expansion. All pin big hopes on the growth of the Communist Party's armed forces. The task is to drastically increase the strength of guerrilla units and people's volunteer forces. The build-up of the armed forces and the establishment of new bases were the main points in the speeches of most delegates.

Combat operations against Japanese militarists were also discussed, but all speakers without exception, having forgotten about the necessity to fight the Japanese, defamed the Kuomintang. Everyone who began to speak about the struggle against Japan ended with calls for the struggle against the Kuomintang.

The sun blazes down on our little squat house. It is exposed to the sun on every side. It becomes very hot inside by midday. The ceiling and walls radiate heat. . . .

Waves of hot air flood the valley. The sun scorches the sparse grass. On the mountain slopes the leaves on brushwood have withered. The river has become shallow. . . .

June 5, 1945

There are disputes in San Francisco because of the Western powers' biased interpretation of the decisions of the Crimean Conference. . . .

In his election speech on the radio Churchill said that socialism allegedly was closely interwoven with totalitarian ideas and a disgusting worship of the state. . . .

American radio commentators shamelessly claim that Russia is eager to conquer the world. The American senator B. K. Wheeler makes anti-Soviet speeches in Italy. . . .

American Secretary of Commerce Henry A. Wallace said the enemies of peace were those who deliberately tried to spoil relations between the United States and the Soviet Union. . . .

The Japanese expeditionary forces in China are commanded by General Yasuji Okamura. . . .

One of the results of the congress is the decision to step up party work in towns. Mao Tse-tung said that the party must be as successful there as in villages.

The party has strong positions in the countryside. The view that we are "land kings" is justified. We are the true masters of the Chinese village. The peasantry is our unshakable and the most faithful support. However, it would be a blunder to persist in this line. We must become the masters of the town as well. We have no longer the right to be preoccupied only with the countryside. This contradicts Marxism. We shall not have it. However, party members should not fall into the other extreme and forget our reliable support, the peasants, and, consequently, the work in villages. . . .

On this subject Peng Chen made a long speech which could be regarded as a co-report.

The conclusions to be drawn from the political report and Peng Chen's co-report: Emerge from the countryside to lean upon the workers. Indisputably, these are correct and very important conclusions for the CCP.

However, what is also interesting is Mao Tse-tung's admission that the party has been an agrarian party, leaning upon the peasantry and deriving its strength from the peasantry. The peasant ideology in the CCP is what Mao Tse-tung has tried carefully to conceal and what the Comintern has fought persistently. The indisputable Marxist truth is that the peasantry is "everywhere the carrier of national and parochial narrow-mindedness." . . .

Lenin warned against the danger of introducing this peasant narrow-mindedness into the ideology of a proletarian party. He stressed that Russia, being an agrarian country with considerable elements of serfdom and feudalism still surviving, vividly manifested the peasantry's primitive, spontaneous revolutionism which told on the working class connected with it. "This revolutionary sentiment undoubtedly expresses a general democratic (which in essence means bourgeois-democratic) protest, rather than proletarian class-consciousness," Lenin wrote.

In this sense the admission of the Chinese Communist Party's leader, "We are land kings," explains many things and expresses the essence of the highly important events in the history and daily political activities of the CCP. . . .

The Chairman of the CCP Central Committee said further:

"We must foresee that this turning point in our party's politics will cause misunderstanding and friction in some part of the membership. We must foresee and be prepared for that."

Mao Tse-tung's last remark is not accidental and deserves attention, since it is impossible to deny that the petty-bourgeois, peasant stratum predominates in the party.

Nothing was said at the congress about the social composition of the party. However, in the section of his report devoted to the character of the party Mao Tse-tung said: "A considerable proportion of our party comes from the nonproletarian medium. Does this mean our party is nonproletarian? . . . No, by no means. Our party is proletarian, and a proof of this is its program. . . ."

(As far as I know CCP affairs, the program to which Mao Tse-tung referred was not discussed at any of the congresses and therefore simply does not exist.)

The fruitless stay of the Observer Group is a laughingstock. However, the Americans treasure this reconnaissance outpost and calmly do their business.

The Chairman of the CCP Central Committee does not intend to rupture relations with the Allies till the Soviet Union's entry into the war against Japan. . . .

By "Allies" I mean Americans.

The Americans have firmly taken the place of the British in China. As far as the British are concerned, most of the "fighting" in China is done by London correspondents. . . .

June 6, 1945

The declaration on Germany's defeat and the take-over of supreme power in Germany by the governments of the Soviet Union, the United States, France, and Britain was signed in Berlin on June 5. The plan of the zones of occupation will be published in newspapers. The region of "Greater Berlin" will be divided into four zones of occupation.

The declaration was signed by Marshal Zhukov of the Soviet Union, General Eisenhower, Field Marshal Bernard Montgomery, and General Jean de Lattre de Tassigny. . . .

Chiang Kai-shek rejected the Japanese request to send their representatives to conduct peace talks.

June 9, 1945

Today the congress is electing the members of the Central Committee. Of the seventy-nine nominees, forty-five are to be elected. . . .

June 10, 1945

Prime Minister Admiral Kantaro Suzuki said in Parliament that Japan would resist despite everything. If the war spread to Japan's territory, the country would use all the advantages of its location.

Today at the congress Mao Tse-tung had spoken before the elections of alternate members of the Central Committee began.

This is a summary of his speech:

"The members of the Central Committee of the party have already been elected. This is very good. But the election of the alternate members of the Central Committee also has great importance. Under certain circumstances they will be made full members of the Central Committee. I ask comrades to devote serious attention to today's election.

"In his letter to the Presidium one of the delegates wrote the congress should elect those comrades who can guarantee the conduct of our congress' line. This is absolutely correct.

"What do I want to say? Why should the question be posed this way?

"1. Because there are people among the nominees who do not enjoy wide popularity. There are also those who had shortcomings in the past. Despite this, however, these comrades can conduct the line of our congress or ensure the conditions for its conduct.

"I think such people can be elected alternate members of the Central Committee. However, today I cannot guarantee that some of them will not be lagging behind.

"2. Comrade Wang Chia-hsiang was not elected to the membership of the Central Committee. He had made mistakes in the past. At the same time he is a merited man. He is a capable worker.

"The line of the fourth plenary meeting of the party Central Committee did not correspond to the line of the party [should be understood as "Mao's line"], but Wang Chia-hsiang supported the military line and resolutely carried it into life. This made it possible to repulse successfully the first, second, and third marches of the Kuomintang armies.

"Another fact: The conference in Tsunyi was very important. But for the support of Wang Chia-hsiang and Lo Fu, the conference would not have been such a great success. This happened because they had already begun departing from their erroneous line. When we came to northern Shensi, Wang Chia-hsiang was sent to the Comintern. On his return from Moscow he correctly reported on the line of the Comintern. At that time the situation in our party was difficult (he meant differences with the internationalists). The Comintern line was procapitulationist. Wang Chia-hsiang was correct.

"Comrade Wang Chia-hsiang is the author of four Central Committee draft resolutions: on the development of contact between military cadres and civilians, etc. This does him much credit.

"3. This time we must elect by all means the comrade from Manchuria. This is very important for our future, because our party will grow in Manchuria as well."

Following Mao Tse-tung's speech, the election of alternate members of the CCP Central Committee took place.

How significant are the statements made by Mao Tse-tung on May 25 and June 10!

Mao said, "Beginning from the Tsunyi Conference and up to the present time, having passed through several stages, the party has lost . . . its diversity."

This should be interpreted as follows: All views and opinions not coinciding with Mao Tse-tung's line have been suppressed in the CCP. Consequently, "the party has lost its diversity" to assume one color, that of Mao Tse-tung. This is the result of the Tsunyi Conference, the struggle against the Comintern, and the three years of cheng-feng. This is the unity of the party according to Mao's pattern! There can hardly be more convincing proof! . . .

What was new for me was the explanation of the aims of Wang Chia-hsiang's trip to Moscow. He proved to have been Mao's envoy. At that time the new party leader had trusted him with collecting materials about the Comintern's "procapitulationist activities." Already at that time(!) Mao Tse-tung had begun preparing for a decisive struggle against the Comintern and its followers in the CCP. Since the Tsunyi Conference Mao Tse-tung had been conducting his own course.

These speeches vividly illustrate Mao's tactics—disuniting his opponents and suppressing nonconformists with the aid of their own former supporters. He has been using this method all these years.

Now Mao fears that the new members of the Central Committee

have not been indoctrinated to the standard of the twenty-five members of the previous Central Committee and might "begin to think too much of themselves," that is, will express their own opinion and thus "upset the cart."

What fierce struggle these short statements betray! Mao has only lifted the curtain a bit off the political struggle in the party.

What a picture is revealed by this very short digression into the past! How intensive the struggle! What sinister colors!

I do not think Mao has ever expressed himself so frankly in his public statements. But as a matter of fact he can afford it now because he feels himself the full master of the party.

June 11, 1945

The results of the elections have been announced.

The congress has elected forty-four members and thirty-three alternate members to the CCP Central Committee.

At the election of the Central Committee, Mao Tse-tung received 543 votes, Chu Teh 543 votes, Liu Shao-chi 543 votes, Jen Pi-shih 543 votes, Lin Piao 541. . . .

Wang Ming had 321 votes and Po Ku 275 votes.

Po Ku and Wang Ming were elected to the Central Committee.

Also elected were Hsu Teh-li, Chang Ting-cheng, Chen Yun, Lu Ting-i, Li Fu-chun, Teng Ying-chao, Lin Po-chu, Yeh Chien-ying, Nieh Jung-chen, Liu Po-cheng, Chen Ying, Kang Sheng. . . .

The alternate members of the Central Committee include Ku Ta-tsun, Wu Lan-fu, Tan Cheng, and Chen Po-ta.

Mao Tse-tung, Chu Teh, and Liu Shao-chi spoke at the concluding sitting of the congress.

The Seventh CCP Congress closed with the singing of the "Internationale."

Now a few words about the debate at the Seventh CCP Congress.

Twenty-four delegates spoke in the debates. They include Chou En-lai (co-report on the united front and its lessons), Chen Yi (co-report on the situation in central China), Peng Teh-huai (co-report on the situation in northern China), and Kao Kang (co-report on the Special Area).

All speeches can be divided into two groups:
1. Speeches by former opponents of Mao Tse-tung's course.
2. All other speeches.

---

1. Concerning the speeches by former opponents of Mao Tse-tung's course:

A. Statements by Lo Fu, Po Ku, and Yang Shang-kun.

Of the statements of those three comrades, the most dignified was Po Ku's.

The congress showed tolerance in respect to Lo Fu's speech.

Lo Fu and Yang Shang-kun openly begged Mao Tse-tung's forgiveness of their past "sins." Their statements were a humiliating examination of their "mistakes" by stages, self-flagellation, denouncement of their "petty-bourgeois views," references to Moscow, where they had allegedly learned dogmatism and opportunism, reproaches to the Comintern leadership which had made mistakes (Lo Fu), substantiation of the correctness of "Comrade Mao Tse-tung's line," and eulogy of Mao Tse-tung.

Po Ku did not praise Mao Tse-tung and behaved with dignity.

B. The speeches by Chou En-lai, Peng Teh-huai, Nieh Jung-chen, and, partly, Chu Teh.

They spoke of their mistakes with restraint without indulging in self-flagellation. The congress was dissatisfied with Peng Teh-huai's speech.

C. Wang Ming and Wang Chia-hsiang did not speak at the congress. Instead, they wrote letters recognizing their alleged party mistakes.

Kai Feng refused either to speak or to write, although he was a major figure who had set himself in opposition to Mao Tse-tung.

2. Other speeches.

These comrades did not indulge in the examination of their mistakes, the demonstration of their theoretical inconsistency, or substantiation of the correctness of "Mao Tse-tung's line."

Each of them spoke of concrete work, mostly related to the past, less to the present, and hardly at all to the future. Exceptions were made by Li Fu-chun, Yeh Chien-ying, and Lin Piao.

The theoretical and cultural standards of most of the speeches were very low.

Kang Sheng concentrated on two questions: the party policy in respect to the peasants and the activities of his department.

Kang Sheng could gain from the peasant question because this was where Mao Tse-tung's opponents had made most of their mistakes. . . .

The Ching-pao-chu chief did not spare pink colors to describe the state of the intelligence and counterintelligence services. He didn't say a word about the mistakes made during the cadres' screening or cheng-feng outrages, although Mao Tse-tung had admitted in his report the mistakes of the party cadres' screening commission and the congress was awaiting Kang Sheng's explanations.

Right after his speech the congress Presidium was showered with notes demanding that Kang Sheng explain why he had silenced his mistakes.

The Presidium proposed that Kang Sheng either speak up or write a statement to the Presidium. The Fall Minister refused bluntly and said he was "conducting Mao Tse-tung's line"(!).

You should have seen Kang at that moment! He was a picture of an offended intellectual: expressively raised eyebrows behind the spectacles, delicate, refined gestures, pursed lips. . . . The very innocence offended!

This compelled the Chairman of the CCP Central Committee in his concluding speech to condemn, once again and with a heavy heart, the mistakes made during the cadres' screening. However, that didn't raise Kang Sheng's prestige among the delegates.

Names were not mentioned in the statements devoted to the mistakes of Mao Tse-tung's opponents. Only Liu Po-cheng made a slip and mentioned Wang Ming. A very noteworthy "slip"! . . .

In private talks Mao Tse-tung often resorts to caustic remarks about the "Anglo-American military," the "treacherous policy of imperialist America," and the "Chungking duet: Hurley/Chiang Kaishek." . . .

June 12, 1945

Mao Tse-tung spoke at the congress on the following occasions:

1. At the opening—his speech "Two Destinies of China"—April 23.

2. The report "On Coalition Government" (the Political Report of the CCP Central Committee to the Seventh Party Congress)—April 24.

3. On the election of the CCP Central Committee—May 25.

4. Concluding speech—May 31.

5. Before the election of alternate members of the CCP Central Committee—June 10.

6. Before the congress closure (his speech "Yu Kung Moved the Mountains")—June 11.

Besides, Mao Tse-tung frequently spoke at the meetings of delegations from different areas and had long night conferences with Liu Shao-chi, Chou En-lai, Jen Pi-shih. . . . And shortly before that he had conducted the seventh plenary meeting of the CCP Central Committee! An impressive piece of work! Well, the fifty-two-year-old Mao cannot be denied the temperament of a political leader. . . .

Now concerning the elections to the CCP leading bodies.

Relevant preparations had been made well in advance of the congress. Their main task was to prevent passions rising high and pull through Lo Fu, Wang Ming, Po Ku, Wang Chia-hsiang, and Kai Feng into the CCP Central Committee. . . .

By May 25 it had become clear this aim was not attained. Most delegates were for a small Central Committee and against the persons named above.

This compelled Mao Tse-tung to take the floor on May 25. For two hours he spoke about the principles of elections, the selection of candidates, and the necessity of electing those comrades who had erred.

Persuading the congress, Mao went so far as to assert that the persons who had made mistakes were more valuable(!) because they would not repeat them, remembering their bitter experience (that is, they have become trained enough by now), while those who hadn't erred might easily make mistakes because of self-confidence.

At the same meeting Mao made another move by proposing to fix, tentatively, the numerical composition of the CCP Central Committee (both members and alternate members). Mao proposed forming the Central Committee of about seventy members. The congress, naturally, agreed.

The list of nominees was drawn up. It included ninety-four persons, but Yang Shang-kun, Lo Mei, and Kung Yuan were not on the list. Their inclusion seemed to be altogether hopeless.

Acting as he did, Mao emphasized, as it were, the necessity of electing Lo Fu, Wang Ming, Po Ku, and Wang Chia-hsiang, who were included. Also on the list was Li Li-san, who is in Moscow now.

Scheduled for May 20 or thereabout, the elections took place on June 9–10. This is because arguments arose. The delegates demanded that biographies be compiled of every person on the list, different questions explained, and so on and so forth. . . .

The election thus acquired the character of a purge (it should be remembered that the cadres had been reared in the cheng-feng atmosphere). Lo Fu, Po Ku, Wang Ming, and others again began to be discussed and maliciously defamed at the sittings of delegations.

Then came the turn of Ho Lung (militaristic manners, incorrect style of work), Kang Sheng (cadres' screening), Peng Chen (cadres' screening), Peng Teh-huai (military mistakes and lack of self-criticism), Kao Kang (falsification of the history of northwestern China and self-praise), Chen Yi ("intriguing" against his commissar and organizing a group against him), and others. . . .

The political struggle around the elections gives an idea of the inner party situation and the worth of the CCP's unity of which Mao Tse-tung never tires talking.

June 13, 1945

According to the resolution of the Seventh Congress, the Central Committee was to consist of forty-five persons. During the election of the Central Committee members the delegates voted against Teng Fa, Wang Chia-hsiang, and Kai Feng.

The resolution set the number of the Central Committee's alternate members at thirty-three.

Forty-four comrades were elected members of the Central Committee.

The failure of Teng Fa and Kai Feng only annoyed Mao, but he was really distressed over Wang Chia-hsiang's failure. It was practically beyond hope to retain Kai Feng and Teng Fa in the party's leading bodies. However, Mao decided to pull through Wang Chia-hsiang into the Central Committee's membership. That was why the congress did not elect the last member of the Central Committee. Mao Tse-tung exerted undisguised pressure on the delegations' leaders and members.

Besides, he proposed that the congress put Wang Chia-hsiang on the voting list of alternate members of the Central Committee.

The day before he asked the delegates not to elect the forty-fifth member of the Central Committee.

Before voting on the list of alternate members of the Central Committee the Chairman of the CCP Central Committee made a speech in which he emphasized to the delegates Wang Chia-hsiang's services to the party.

Wang Chia-hsiang was not only elected an alternate member but drew the second largest number of votes!

A plenum of the new Central Committee is scheduled to take place in a week's time. Mao Tse-tung will lord it over there. No doubt that at the subsequent plenums, if not at the first, Mao Tse-tung will succeed in co-opting Wang Chia-hsiang into the party Central Committee.

The ideological instability of his opponents has permitted Mao not only to suppress them but later, acting together with some of them, also to discredit the political significance of the Comintern and the experience of the All-Union Communist Party. The giving up of their positions by the "Moscow group" gives Mao Tse-tung an opportunity to revise Marxism with all the ensuing consequences. . . .

June 14, 1945

At present it can be said with confidence that Mao Tse-tung's struggle against the Comintern began in January 1935 when he became the leader of the CCP. Mao's speeches on May 25 and June 10 leave no doubt on this score: The Tsunyi Conference marked the beginning of the radical turn in the CCP course. Previously Mao Tse-tung had avoided speaking of this in public. At this congress he said, yes, since the Tsunyi Conference he has been struggling against the Comintern's "procapitulationist line" (that is, against the Marxist-Leninist policy of the Third Communist International founded by Lenin).

On June 9, 10, and 11 Stelle, Domke, and Swenson, representatives of the Observer Group, called separately on Mao Tse-tung, Chu Teh, and Yeh Chien-ying. They motivated their visits by Wedemeyer's order to fly to Chungking.

In their conversations with the Americans Mao Tse-tung, Chu Teh, and Yeh Chien-ying said that irrespective of who helped the Chinese people—the United States, Great Britain, or the Soviet Union—they would be regarded as friends, whereas those who would be against such aid would be considered enemies.

The Americans were told that until the agreement on military cooperation between the American command and the CCP military command was signed there could be no talk of Americans being sent to bases in the enemy rear, weather stations, etc.

Stelle said he was informed of the supreme American military authorities' intention to send their man to Yenan.

Yeh Chien-ying reiterated that the CCP leadership would welcome this official in Yenan if he would negotiate large-scale co-operation and not discuss small, private affairs. . . .

A new operating room, a stone extension of one of the caves, has been built at Orlov's insistence. It makes it possible to perform up to six operations simultaneously. At present 75 per cent of the operations are performed by the surgeons trained by Andrei Yakovlevich. Two cases of smallpox have been registered in Yenan, let alone other infectious diseases. . . .

Mao Tse-tung spoke on June 11, the closing day of the Seventh CCP Congress.

A summary of his speech:

1. "The congress continued fifty days. It settled major questions, determined the party line, and elected the new Central Committee. The congress' work can be divided into three stages: the precongress activities, reports and debates, and elections.

"The thorough precongress preparations have ensured its success. The delegates spoke well and were self-critical. There was neither much nor little self-criticism, but there could be more of it. The cohesion and unity of the congress became possible on its basis.

"The elections to the Central Committee passed excellently.

"After the congress many delegates will immediately leave for home, and there they must conduct large-scale explanatory work and propaganda of the congress decisions among party members and the population at large.

"There is no doubt the congress line will be approved by the absolute majority of the party membership.

"There are persons who will conduct their splitting activities.

"There are some who will regard the congress as something nonexistent, as it were, and its decisions not binding on them. They will continue to work in accordance with the old course and views.

"It is necessary to take every measure to preclude discords in the party. A major effort is still necessary to strengthen the unity of the party."

2. "Concerning our relation to America.

"In general, we are for co-operation with it, but on certain terms agreed upon."

Mao Tse-tung further described his talk with the Observer Group's representatives leaving for Chungking.

The Americans are permitted to have their people in Yenan and the area of dislocation of the 129th Infantry Division.

"Capitalism has been weakened by World War II. Europe has entered a peaceful stage of development.

"What about the future? Two ways are possible: a revolution or a war."

3. About the position of the Soviet Union.

"The *Izvestia* critical article 'The Kuomintang Congress and Chinese Reality' of June 3 fully reflects the interests of the Chinese people and the CCP."

4. On the development of the Chinese Revolution into a socialist revolution.

This process will be protracted because of China's specifics.

The possibilities for the peaceful development are very big. However, there is also the prospect of a hard, bloodthirsty struggle (speaking of the development, Mao Tse-tung means seizure of power in all China).

"The development depends on the will of the people. If the people are for it, nobody will be able to hinder the process. If the people are against it, the Communist Party's wish will not suffice. I have written about it in my work *On New Democracy*. I have stressed it in my speeches and explained it to the correspondents who visited Yenan last year. . . ."

5. Mao Tse-tung ended his speech by resuming the question of the party unity. He said that the people who had their own views as regards the unity of the party should understand the congress decisions. "But above all it is necessary to pursue the line of the congress. Following this political line, the Chinese people will achieve victory!"

June 21, 1945

At the Seventh CCP Congress Mao Tse-tung said:

—It is premature to reject co-operation with the Kuomintang.

—It is necessary to criticize it, disperse the illusions the people may have because the Kuomintang's influence is still very great; it is much greater than the influence of the Communist Party. . . .

—100 per cent of the officers and men of the Central Government's armies are the Kuomintang party members, while Communists number only 50 per cent of the total strength of the Eighth Route Army and the New Fourth Army. . . .

At present the CCP controls some twenty anti-Japanese democratic bases. . . .

The heat is intolerable—the summer seems to have decided to kill all and everything. Loess dust radiates heat and burns my feet even through the shoes. . . .

In the rays of the setting sun mountaintops become yellow, then pink, and finally deep red. The moon is coming out. . . .

June 25, 1945

A bill has been adopted in Japan under which the government is empowered to mobilize all men between fifteen and sixty and women between seventeen and forty.

The latest statements of the Chairman of the CCP Central Committee have corroborated some of my conclusions. Since the Tsunyi Conference (1935) he has been struggling against the Comintern as a force which influenced the CCP. This fact was proved by Mao's statement before the election of the members and alternate members of the Central Committee.

He regarded the Comintern as his ideological opponent. That is why he began with a rupture of ties with the Comintern. This struggle led him to the revision of Marxism and the development of his own petty-bourgeois philosophy—the "Marxism of reality."

The continuation of the struggle was the rejection of internationalism, betrayal of the Soviet Union in its war against Hitlerism, the rupture of spiritual ties with the All-Union Communist Party under the pretext of the struggle against "dogmatism," and the promotion of a chauvinistic ideology in the CCP.

China's domestic situation, his fear of "Scobieism," and his own selfish interests make him our ally now. Only an ally; not a brother in the class, ideological struggle. He seeks advantages from the alliance with us. He is guided in all his actions by cold calculations. This has more than once led to clashes between him and the living forces of the party no matter what "spiritual purification" they might have been subjected to. Mao's whole life is maneuvering. Not a consistent implementation of Marxist principles, but a rejection of them under the pretext of "national specifics." Hence the continual terror against his own party. He has to uproot the shoots of Comintern influence in it.

June 26, 1945

A magnificent victory parade has been held in Moscow. The parade was commanded by Konstantin Rokossovski and reviewed by Zhukov. Captured fascist banners were thrown on the ground in front of the Lenin Mausoleum. . . .

The San Francisco conference has ended. The Charter of the United Nations has been signed.

The heads of the delegations made concluding speeches.

The American President said that fascism had not disappeared altogether, that it was easier to remove tyrants and destroy concentration camps than to kill the ideas which had brought them forth and given them strength. . . .

Andrei Gromyko spoke on behalf of the Soviet delegation. . . .

Mao Tse-tung's main aim is to seize power in the country disregarding the cost. The party interests him only as far as it can ensure him this power. Hence, the set of outwardly justified slogans and phrases and references to Marx, Lenin . . .

June 28, 1945

Ho Ying-chin, head of the Chinese general staff, said:

—Unless the Americans land in mainland China, the Chungking troops will not be able to drive the Japanese away.

—To chase the invaders away with American aid will also require much time despite the fact that the naval communications between China and Japan may be broken off.

—Relying on Manchukuo's military resources, the Japanese troops will be able to resist stubbornly and for long. . . .

I'm hardly able to continue my diary. When I do have free time, I have no strength—I sit at the desk and fall asleep immediately. When I wake up, my candle is gone and a black smoldering wick is crackling in a small pool of paraffin. . . .

June 30, 1945

Speaking at the French Communist Party Congress in Paris Marcel Cachin said that the Soviet Union was not after territorial acquisitions; it only wanted to destroy fascism and guarantee itself from an aggression such as Hitler's. . . .

A National Unity Government has been formed in Poland. . . .

Stettinius has resigned. James Byrnes has been appointed the new American Secretary of State. Truman's people gradually replace Roosevelt's comrades-in-arms and associates.

Moscow plays host to T. V. Soong, chairman of the Executive Yuan of the National Government and the Minister of Foreign Affairs of the Republic of China. On the threshold of decisive events in the Far East the Kuomintang is trying to develop relations with its mighty neighbor. . . .

The CCP Congress means preparations for a civil war. Whatever the delegates spoke about, in the final run everything was reduced to the struggle with the Kuomintang. . . .

The congress followed in Mao Tse-tung's steps—this is the result of the brutal suppression of the "Moscow group" and rupture with the Comintern's ideological principles.

During the years of the Soviet Union's life-or-death struggle against fascist Germany, all CCP activities served the good of the Japanese militarists. However, at present, when the solution of the Far Eastern problem depends upon the Soviet Union and when the "Scobies" have nothing against crushing the Communist Party, Mao Tse-tung pretends to be a true internationalist and a friend of my people. Well, the political situation in China and on the world scene does not leave any other choice for this great master of destruction of unity. . . .

July 1945

July 2, 1945

Today Orlov congratulated Mao Tse-tung on the twenty-fourth anniversary of the CCP. Mao Tse-tung replied crisply: "If there were no Soviet Union, there would be no Chinese Communist Party!"

Orlov spent the night at our house.

Toward morning I heard somebody's footsteps. I got up and went out into the corridor. It was Andrei Yakovlevich. He tapped me on the shoulder, said "I'll tell you later," and was gone.

It was still and dark outside. In the radio room at the table Kolya was tapping out by candlelight my message to Moscow. There came the usual rattling sound. . . .

Andrei Yakovlevich was out "looking for daybreak." Dawn comes swiftly here, in Yenan. Day replaces night within minutes. But even from the mount over our house Andrei Yakovlevich failed to see it. Where the sun should have appeared the sky began to gray. The contours of the mountain ridge became visible, and shadows began moving down in the valley. The air was brightening with each instant, and it looked as though a fire were flaming up in the mountains. Then the edge of a yellow disk emerged, and a few minutes later the heavy and molten sun hung over the ridge. And immediately a multitude of swallows went scurrying over Yenan. . . .

July 3, 1945

Mao Tse-tung's speeches at the elections of members and alternate members of the CCP Central Committee have buttressed my conviction that ever since the days of Tsunyi Mao Tse-tung has treated with distrust and hostility both the Comintern and the Soviet Union. For him Moscow has had (and, of course, continues to have) value only as a force which must help to overthrow Chiang Kai-shek. . . .

The combat skill of the troops of the Special Area has grown during the past year. Great attention was devoted to doing away with guerrilla methods. . . .

There is a lot of talk about the Soviet Union's victory over Hitler Germany, but from all this the unambiguous conclusion follows that the Soviet Union is the "friend who will help the CCP to gather the strength and power to destroy Chiang Kai-shek's regime." This is not said openly, but all mean it and are looking forward to the start of a war between the Soviet Union and Japan. . . .

Po Ku is one year younger than I. A member of the CCP since 1925. From 1932 to 1934 he was the acting leader of the CCP Central Committee. In January 1934, at the fifth plenary meeting of the CCP Central Committee, he was elected first secretary of the Central Committee. . . .

Mao Tse-tung shows no special liking for Po Ku. In our conversations Mao has tried to evoke in me a feeling of hostility for Po Ku.

The most vexing of all states: There's so much that must be put down, for memory won't be able to keep it all, but tiredness suddenly gets the better of you—and you fall asleep at the table with a pen in the hand. You pour cold water over your head and have a smoke, and you think you have driven sleep away and are again able to work, but in just half an hour the lines and characters again fade into nothingness. . . .

That's exactly how I often fall asleep. In an hour or two I wake up in the darkness. The candles burned out long ago, and only the dense smell of wax lingers on. If there's time left—I undress and go to bed. . . .

I write a lot. The right hand grows numb during sleep. I shift it with the other hand, as though it were dead. . . .

And in the morning once again I have to be clean-shaven, fresh, and braced. To be each instant on the lookout. . . .

July 4, 1945

In a conversation with me Mao Tse-tung declared that the Seventh CCP Congress was the most successful in the party's history and that, undoubtedly, it would have a deep impact on the party and the people.

Here are the words of Mao Tse-tung:

". . . The congress safeguards the party against corruption by anti-Marxist ideas. . . .

"Political capitulationism was to be found in our party, but it was finally overcome during the preparations for the congress. Political views in the party have become uniform. . . .

"The congress approved new party rules which will keep in sanctity the purity of the principles of Marxism-Leninism, but with due consideration for the specifics of Chinese reality. . . .

"Of the total number of 1.21 million members of the CCP at present there remain no more than 1,000 people who joined the party in 1921–27, and no more than 20,000 who joined it in the period of 1927–37. . . ."

Conditions for reinforcement of the proletarian party are absent in the Special Area. Of what proletarian steeling, then, can there be any talk here? And the nucleus of the party has been here for eleven years now! . . .

At other CCP bases the situation is no better. The same kind of remote rural regions in the mountains . . .

July 9, 1945

At a recent party Mao told much of his youth story. He remained sitting almost all the while. Screwing up his eyes and looking around absent-mindedly. And, as always, smoking heavily.

Chou spoke of Chungking affairs. His vigorous speech contrasts sharply with Mao's ponderous manner of talking.

There was much laughter. Here they like to laugh. Maybe because they drink and smoke so much. Chou eats almost nothing. He has time to be everywhere and with everybody.

All slowly get drunk, except Chou. He always keeps his head in hand.

Of political topics, they prefer Chungking news, rumors. . . . Serious matters are dealt with at a different time and without witnesses. . . .

Mao drinks less than he did three years ago when I arrived at Yenan. For several months now he has been suffering from recurrent fits of general weakness, of which he has kept complaining to Orlov. . . .

The one subject that always interests Mao is the rule of Chiang Kai-shek and Chiang Kai-shek himself.

Stubbornly inclining his chin to his chest, Mao is ready to criticize him at any moment. And each time Chou can report something new which always perfectly fits Mao's mood.

Here only Mao is relaxed. The rest continue the game. Each against all. Except Chou, who firmly believes in his right to be here. . . .

Cigarette ends die out on the ashtrays. The light grows dimmer and dimmer and the night deeper and deeper. . . .

The simple tastes of Mao have well been learned by his entourage. The servants silently move about catering to them.

"Chiang Kai-shek is no speaker," stated Chou. "He is a master at asking questions, and he can listen. And he absorbs other people's thoughts. . . ."

Chou speaks rapidly, smiling, touching my shoulder or hand. I see that at the same time he listens to and hears all those present. He misses not a single word or gesture.

The CCP mission in Chungking is located in the Tseng-chiai area. Wang Ping-nan and Chen Chia-kang maintain contact with the American military attaché.

Kang Sheng is a true politician. He does not change, whatever the circumstances. Only instead of haughtiness, suaveness and good nature now prevail in his manner. Kang was in the Soviet Union for about five years. Since 1937 he has been in Yenan without leaving. He has held the post of the chief of the Ching-pao-chu since 1938.

"Tai Li is the head of Chiang Kai-shek's secret service. Nobody has ever seen him. An elusive man . . . ," said Kang.

Mao peacefully enjoyed himself. Leisurely, relaxed gestures. A round, slightly wet, kind face. Mao's mouth can smile, but his heart—never.

"You are becoming Chinese," Mao said to me. "Your mood tells nothing even for your friends."

A distinct smell of tobacco smoke and wet land pervades the system of Mao's underground rooms. Mao does not want to live in a usual house. They could build it for him within weeks. But Mao prefers this underground dwelling. It is inaccessible to weapons, to anybody's eyes. Here he feels in absolute safety.

A glass window that covers almost the whole of the wall. A gray summer twilight.

On the table stands a forgotten Gramophone and a heap of records. In the ashtrays, plates, spittoons—everywhere cigarette ends . . .

In his attitude to Marxism Mao Tse-tung strongly reminds me of Menshevik Fëdor Dan, who was so well described by Maxim Gorki: ". . . Fëdor Dan speaks in the tone of a man to whom genuine truth is his own daughter; he gave birth to and reared it, and he is still rearing it. As for himself, he, Fëdor Dan, is a perfect Karl Marx incarnate, and the Bolsheviks are smatterers, indecent fellows, which is especially clear from their attitude to the Mensheviks, among whom are 'all the outstanding theoreticians of Marxism.' . . ."

"Marxism in practical life" is the truest philosophy of opportunism. The high-sounding phrases so typical of this super-"revolutionary philosophy" are excellently laid bare by just this characterization given by Lenin: "Revolutionary phrase-making, more often than not, is a disease from which revolutionary parties suffer at times when they constitute, directly or indirectly, a combination, alliance, or intermingling of proletarian and petty-bourgeois elements, and when the course of revolutionary events is marked by big rapid zigzags. By revolutionary phrase-making we mean the repetition of revolutionary slogans irrespective of objective circumstances . . ."

July 10, 1945

Armadas of "flying fortresses" are bombing Japanese cities into ruins day after day. B-29s are practically out of the reach of Japanese fighter planes. They release their bomb loads over targets in formation, as if in a fly-past. . . .

On May 31 at the congress Mao Tse-tung in his concluding remarks spoke of the checking of cadres and the struggle against espionage.

Here is a brief summary of the related part of his speech:

—In this work there have been many achievements and many serious mistakes. . . .

—What are the causes of these mistakes? . . .

—We should have done this work according to the principle of less, but more thoroughly. . . .

—Whereas we did more and negligently. . . .

—We must turn the given mistakes into our weapons; corporal punishments have long since been prohibited; evidence should not be taken lightly; we must approach everything always with caution. . . .

—But we must also stimulate a serious attitude to matters; we must not tolerate liberalism, for liberalism is harmful. . . .

Thus, Mao Tse-tung from the rostrum of the congress declared to all in the party that the ideological essence of the "spiritual purification" and all the other repressions is impeccable.

He issued the call to continue to punish mercilessly the dissidents and to make the repressive methods of the cheng-feng a rule of party life. And to "reassure" the delegates, he hypocritically promised them greater "objectivity and discrimination" in the torture chambers of Kang Sheng.

July 11, 1945

The Americans regard the fate of Japan as predetermined. It may take one, two, or three years, but she cannot escape defeat. Japanese industry is destroyed, and the merchant marine of this maritime nation is practically no longer in existence. And yet, despite the flaunty tone of the broadcasts, one can discern in them uneasiness over the future of the invasion. The average figure of their own losses the Americans put at 1 million men and officers. They invariably call this forthcoming invasion a "bloody" invasion. . . .

The congress worked for fifty days. A very long time. But not at all was it due only to the complexity of problems solved. These long weeks were a reflection of the former intraparty struggle.

No, the delegates were quite obedient. But they had to be allowed to say their say so that their repentances and censure might be used to testify the triumph of the course of "Marxism in practical life." This method was consciously chosen by Mao Tse-tung.

In the procedure of elections, too, there was a relapse of the recent bitter intraparty struggle. And again the delegates were absolutely obedient to Mao, but it was necessary to keep down their hostility to members of the "Moscow opposition" and get all those "dogmatists" and "empiricists" into the leading bodies of the Communist Party. This required time, quite a lot of time.

The internationalists had been discredited so much that Mao Tse-tung had virtually to talk the delegates into heeding his recommendations. In the new situation he badly needs them, these "dogmatists," "Moscow people," "empiricists," and "capitulationists." They provide a screen for his political course and are disciplined in the bargain. . . .

And that's how week after week the fifty congress days added together!

July 12, 1945

In the hell of cheng-feng the Communists underwent a tough training in the spirit of Mao Tse-tung's thought. The Seventh CCP Congress ideologically summed up the achievements of "Marxism in practical life."

Most of these Communists are under thirty. They are already the cadre of the party, and, as years go by, they will rise in the party's peck order. The future in the party belongs to them.

The worst thing in all this story is that Mao Tse-tung is being identified with the revolution, and truth in general. For party members Mao Tse-tung is the apostle of their revolutionary belief; he is infallible. Here reason is replaced by an instinct, a blind instinct, a kind of religious dogma! They believe without understanding because it comes from Mao Tse-tung. . . .

The belief of a revolutionary and the belief in a kind of wonder-worker come into conflict. . . .

I involuntarily turned to my philosophical notes. In this respect very significant is the letter of Friedrich Engels to Laura Lafargue. In it Engels writes about the extreme "revolutionariness of the Paris workers"—"Boulangism"—after 1871.

"No, the cause of this surfeit of Boulangism lies deeper. It is chauvinism. . . . And the necessary consequence of this French patriotic aberration is that the French workmen are now the allies of the Czar against not only Germany but against the Russian workmen and revolutionists too! . . . But it is the third time that such an aberration occurs since 1789—the first time Napoleon I, the second time Nap[oleon] III was carried to the top by that wave of aberration, and now it's a worse creature than either—but fortunately the force of the wave, too, is broken. Anyhow we must apparently come to the conclusion that the negative side of the Parisian revolutionary character—chauvinistic Bonapartism—is as essential to it as the positive side, and that after every great revolutionary effort, we may have a recrudescence of Bonapartism, of an appeal to a savior who is to destroy the vile bourgeois. . . .

"So, I shall welcome any revolutionary spurt the Parisians may favor us with, but shall expect them to be again robbed afterward and then fly to a miracle-performing savior. For *action* I hope and trust the Parisians to be as fit as ever, but if they claim to lead with regard to *ideas,* I shall say thank you."

The overthrow of the monarchy in 1911, the continuous agrarian agitation, the revolutionary upheavals of 1925–27, and the bloody excesses of the Civil War—and as a result the same kind of belief, a desire to believe in a "wonder-working idol"—Mao Tse-tung . . .

I derive certitude in the correctness of my words from my longstanding acquaintance with Mao Tse-tung and his creation—chengfeng. Sometimes it seems to me that I myself passed through this severe spiritual purge here. A purge that helped me to see the danger of nationalism, of a blind belief in a leader, of the substitution of dogmas, political talmudism, and distortions for the living thought of Marxism . . .

Chauvinism in the CCP is one of the tragedies of the development of China's national consciousness.

After all these years in Yenan Marx, Lenin, and Engels appear before me in all the brilliance of their intellects, the breadth of their foresight, and their great humaneness. These ideas have fostered the Bolshevik Party. Herein lies its great viability. And the earnest of its victories . . .

Party workers reared in Yenan go away group after group to the most remote regions of the country. They go away to provide leadership to the party masses in the localities. They go away, sacredly believing in the revolution, the truth, the country, and Mao Tse-tung. . . .

Where reason gives way to a blind instinct, dogmas become the justification and the purpose of life. The dismal dogmas of "Marxism in practical life."

Instead of a living word I always hear a set of standard phrases in answer. It's an unpleasant feeling: Different people look as though they were all alike in face. Truths of "Marxism in practical life" serenely learned by rote . . .

The laudation of Mao amounts to a kind of mysticism, unhealthy exaltation. This dangerous process leads, as the congress showed it, to the loss by party members of their independence beyond certain instructions of Chairman Mao and the loss by the party of its activity. This results in the replacement of the brains of people by the single "infallible wonder-working brain of Chairman Mao." . . .

The study of Mao Tse-tung's reports convinces me how skillfully he corrupts the party masses by his distortions of the past of the Communist Party, the revolutionary struggle of the Chinese people and the present events, and by his tell-tale approval of the actions of cheng-feng. . . .

July 13, 1945

There is a distinct and important difference between parties of the national liberation movement and Marxist parties. It is not without reason that Mao so readily agrees before the Americans to change the party's name. In this case it is not a matter of tactics at all. Mao Tse-tung regards Marxism as a "unique cover" for shaping a social movement entirely independent of and different from the Marxist movement. History gives him no other choice: The Communist Party arose not by his will, and Marxism is too popular in the world to be ignored. And so he has worked out his own philosophy, "Marxism in practical life," using the very Marxism as a cover. This explains why the power struggle in the CCP was so hard and bloody. For it actually was a struggle for supremacy between two ideologies in the CCP: Mao's ideology and that of Marxism. No wonder, then, that for ten years the party went through fierce clashes, not always obvious to an outsider, but nevertheless unabating, persistent, and taking on the most diverse forms (down to the fight for the "purity of literary style"). It was a class struggle within a party, a struggle of ideologies, a struggle that was continuously stimulated by the mounting movement of national liberation so pliable to chauvinistic sentiments.

At the congress this struggle culminated in the triumph of Mao Tse-tung, although, in his own words, "genuine unity is still ahead." The revolutionary upsurge in the Chinese national liberation movement as a result of Japan's defeats brings substantial changes into the relationship of the internationalist-Marxist forces and petty-bourgeois "Marxism in practical life" in the CCP.

The fact that Kang Sheng was dropped and new people promoted to leading posts in the CCP is an indication that concessions, even if of a formal nature, have been made to the advanced elements in the CCP. In a word, the struggle for "genuine unity is still ahead.". . . Not everything goes as Mao wants. Herein shows the logic of historical processes. . . .

On the battlefield the Japanese continue to be a formidable force. The Allies have to fight hard for each Pacific island. Japanese garrisons are resisting to the last soldier. The Americans are worried about what reception the Japanese will give them on their own islands. . . .

July 17, 1945

Unfortunately, the CCP leadership also includes people who vacillated between the Comintern and Yenan, trying to guess which line—the internationalist or Mao Tse-tung's—would prevail.

In Moscow these people agreed with the Comintern's recommendations, but accommodated to Mao Tse-tung back in Yenan. Here they, though with caution, would call the very same line of the Comintern with which they had agreed in Moscow a line "procapitulationist and foreign to the national features of China," etc.

Masks! They simply changed masks! And on and on did they do so until the cheng-feng tide swept away everything that the Comintern had tried to uphold. . . .

Mao is having more frequent spells of depression which also tell on his physical condition. He then feels slack and is quite unable to work.

July 21, 1945

A conference attended by Stalin, Truman, Churchill, and their foreign ministers has opened at Potsdam. . . .

In Rome they are going to celebrate the anniversary of Franco's revolt against the Spanish People's Republic. What impudence!

Eight German criminals have been executed in the United States.

Fascist terror reigns in Greece.

An indictment has been brought against former marshal of France Henri Pétain. He is being charged with conspiracy against the state's internal security and links with the enemy.

Today Mao Tse-tung told me how highly he valued the role of the Soviet Communist Party and the Soviet Union in the struggle of the CCP to bring about the triumph of the Chinese Revolution. . . .

The paper windows hardly let light in. And when the weather is bad, it is quite dark in the room. Just as now: It's noon, but it's raining, and so I have lit up a candle.

It's the first relatively free day that I've had for many months.

Streams of rain are pattering on the oiled paper in the window honeycombs.

I am dreaming of the day when in Moscow I shall turn in my mission papers, hide my fountain pen, and, free from thinking about anything, go to my house on foot. . . .

And no longer shall I have to bend till morning over urgent reports, translate long Chinese texts, try to get from the notes of talks the meaning of reservations made, disentangle the lies, and seek the truth. . . .

And, finally, after many years I won't have to be constantly on my guard. . . .

July 27, 1945

Churchill has lost elections. In Britain a new Cabinet has been formed which is led by Labourite Clement Attlee. Churchill is in a humiliating position—having to pack up and leave Potsdam at the height of the conference.

The trial of Pétain, the main traitor of France, has begun.

The Japanese Cabinet has declared that Japan will wage the war to the very end.

In Yenan there operates a group of observers which is a center of the American information service in the Special Area. The group is made up of thirty-two people (eight information service workers, nine radio operators, etc.). The head of the group is Major Peterkin.

Besides, workers of the American information service are here and there at various CCP bases.

Two are in the Shansi-Chahar-Hopeh region (under Nieh Jung-chen), two in the Taihang region, and two in the New Fourth Army.

The Chairman of the CCP Central Committee is restoring his forces, taking into consideration the future events in the country and the Soviet Union's entry into the war against Japan.

The Soviet Union will defeat Japan, it will not allow the Americans to take action against the Special Area, Soviet troops must help and cover the capture of China's northern provinces by the CCP armies, and the Soviet Union will render material and political assistance to the CCP—such is the line of thinking of the CCP leadership, and in some way or other these thoughts were repeated by congress delegates.

This is precisely why Mao Tse-tung has removed Kang Sheng from the forefront of the political life of the Special Area. This man—the closest and most faithful assistant of the Chairman of the CCP Central Committee—is too notorious in Moscow for his anti-Sovietism. . . .

Mao Tse-tung has only warded off the blow aimed at Kang Sheng. . . .

Mao Tse-tungism will be gradually overcome by the Communist movement in China. But for its development there was and there is a number of objective prerequisites—material, ideological, and cultural. In some form or other its resurgence is also possible in the future—and herein lies its dangerous historical precedent for China. . . .

August 1945

August 1, 1945

Japanese Prime Minister Admiral Suzuki said, "We will resolutely go along the road toward the completion of the war."

Pétain is on trial. According to journalists, since his arrest the former marshal has been showing shameful cowardice.

Information Minister Wang Shih-chieh has been appointed China's Minister of Foreign Affairs. . . .

The CCP leadership does not want to break relations with the Americans, despite the exposures of the American imperialist policy in China.

In actual fact, this is a "long-range policy" designed to ensure strong ties with America at a time when the situation in China and the Far East is still uncertain. CCP leaders hope for a clash of United States/Soviet Union interests. In that case it's highly probable they will receive arms and other aid from one of the sides, it doesn't matter from which. . . .

In Orlov's opinion Mao Tse-tung's periodic depressions are a result of the overstrain of the central nervous system.

August 2, 1945

Yesterday the Americans used aircraft groups of eighty-nine machines each to bomb Tokyo. In the course of twenty-one days the Allies sank and put out of action 1,035 small Japanese landing craft and shot down and damaged 1,278 planes.

Fighting continues in Lower Burma.

Laval will be extradited by the Spanish Government.

Pétain delays the beginning of his trial.

By decision of the Sixth Kuomintang Congress, the political organs of this party in the Army are being disbanded.

On July 31 China's Supreme National Defense Council recognized the United Nations Charter. This decision is subject to endorsement by the Legislative Yuan (Parliament).

The Americans delay the repatriation of Soviet citizens.

Chungking troops have stepped up operations on all fronts. . . .

The Japanese defense line is being curtailed. Their combat formations are concentrated in smaller areas. As a result, the Japanese resistance on land does not slacken. The Japanese fight for every important position.

Tokyo's plan is clear enough—to force its enemies, through stubborn resistance, to give up the demands of unconditional surrender. The Japanese military fears the destiny of fascist Germany and its leaders.

The Allies are alarmed over the "bloody" invasion. Now they put the losses they suffered during the invasion at 500,000 to 1 million officers and men. The Americans are worried about the price of the final victory. The Japanese fight desperately to the last soldier. The Allies threaten Japan with an even stronger blockade.

"The Japanese suffer and will suffer even more from malnutrition and hunger!" is the tone of American radio programs.

August 3, 1945

The Potsdam Conference of the Three Powers ended yesterday. Its main subject is measures to eradicate German militarism and Nazism and specify postwar frontiers in Europe.

Another outburst of terror against the democrats in Greece.

The trial of the double-dyed bandit Draža Mihajlović has begun in Yugoslavia.

Chungking troops have captured the town of Ping-lo (Kwangtung province). The Japanese offer stubborn resistance.

The Americans reported the test of their jet aircraft which showed a speed of 550 miles per hour.

August 5, 1945

General Wedemeyer, American commander in chief in China, said the Chinese landing troops were completing combat preparation.

For the past few days Tokyo hasn't broadcast its usual war reports.

The calling of a national assembly in November is one of the permanent subjects of Chungking newspapers. Observers say the assembly would work out a constitution to put an end to the one-party system. The observers express the viewpoint of the government.

The official course of the Chiang Kai-shek government is the convening of a national assembly. . . .

Love, hatred, and tolerance are determined by the advantages of trade, investments, and profits—this is the immutable principle of American diplomacy. Mao Tse-tung willingly accepted this approach of the Americans to matters. This is proved by Mao's talk with John Service and other frank talks which the Chairman of the CCP Central Committee had with the Americans. Moreover, Mao Tse-tung is prepared to guarantee the political interests(!) of the CCP's alliance with America!

Mao Tse-tung is feverishly trying to sound out Moscow's intentions and, simultaneously, compel Moscow, in some way or other, to actively interfere in China's domestic affairs during the future war against Japan. His dream is to use the Red Army to destroy the Kuomintang military and administrative apparatus in the areas bordering on the zone of combat operations. He wants to draw the Soviet Union into the conflict with the Kuomintang. If this plan fails, he wants to build up, behind the back of Red Army troops, new CCP armies, re-equip his armed forces, and occupy new vast areas of China. All these variants presuppose, in one way or another, the Soviet Union's military conflict with the Chungking Government.

For Mao Tse-tung we are not ideological allies, but a tool he wants to use to attain his own aims. In talks with me the Chairman of the CCP Central Committee emphasizes that we are "an interested side in the settlement of the Pacific problems."

Behind all this is the danger of the Soviet Union's clash with the United States.

Mao Tse-tung is intoxicated by a situation in which, he believes, it is possible to move rapidly toward his own aims. . . .

August 6, 1945

The war in the Far East is nearing the end, and this means that I'll be back home soon. . . . What a wonderful day!

Soon I'll embrace my boys and Maria. When I left, Yura was quite young, just past six years. Will he recognize me now?

Only once during these four years I received letters from my family. . . .

August 7, 1945

All American radio stations report: The first atomic bomb was dropped on Japan yesterday. It is equivalent to twenty thousand tons of TNT. President Truman warns the whole of Japan will be in ruins.

The bomb was dropped on Hiroshima. An impenetrable cloud covered the city after the explosion.

A pitifully low theoretical level of the speeches made at the congress returns me to the conclusions I made during the "spiritual purification" climax [1942].

The cultural standards of the CCP cadre leave much to be desired. There can be no talk of well-founded education. The principles of Marxism-Leninism are accepted formally. This is not education, but rather the hasty theoretical training (coaching) of a very superficial character. Most of the workers are content with primitive schoolchildrenlike drilling. At the same time, "Mao's ideas" are absorbed organically, naturally, and enthusiastically. This is because they are the essence of the petty-bourgeois medium which prevails in the country.

The victory of the October Revolution and the activities of the Comintern led to the establishment of the Chinese Communist Party. However, later the Comintern constantly met with the active opposition of different kinds of petty-bourgeois friends. Of course, there were socioeconomic reasons for this. However, the fatal role was also played by the total illiteracy of the population and the centuries-old backwardness of China which imperialism turned into its colony. . . .

As for the CCP, it was weak, shaky ideologically, and by no means united. . . .

The main ideas of Marxist philosophy are learned by heart here, learned dogmatically as something abstract. Only a few persons in the party have the right to interpret Marxism as "applicable to the Chinese Revolution." For the rest Marxist philosophy is a kind of psalm book. As a result Marxist ideas are assimilated with elements of nationalist, anarchist, and petty-bourgeois views.

China lacks the party intelligentsia which played such an important role in the spread of Marxism in Russia.

Education in schools and universities bears an imprint of China's feudal backwardness and is still permeated with the survivals of the past. Here, by tradition, in the course of centuries every living thought was killed for the good of dogmas.

To some extent, all this predetermined the misunderstanding of the Comintern's activities, led to their distorted understanding.

That different kinds of opportunist trends shot deep roots in the CCP was promoted by the specificities of the situation which developed in China and the world at large. Japan's long aggression against China and the current World War have extremely hindered the activities of the Comintern and, on the contrary, promoted the flourishing of various opportunist theories, the falling level of Marxist thought, the utilitarian understanding of Marxist philosophy and its vulgarization.

August 8, 1945

Countless comments on the results of the Potsdam Conference. . . .

On August 6 the Americans used an entirely new weapon, a super-bomb, against Japan. Truman and Attlee spoke on this occasion. From morning till night all radio stations speak of the atomic bombardment of Hiroshima.

American radio stations say the city has been fully destroyed!

Japanese positions on the Chinese coast are attacked by planes operating from allied aircraft carriers.

The International Military Tribunal has been instituted.

T. V. Soong, head of the Chinese Government, accompanied by the Foreign Minister and a group of highly placed officials, went to Moscow yesterday again. Stalin received Soong. . . .

Mao ascribes "big changes in the party" to the cheng-feng.

In his May 25 speech he mentioned the "three-year-long cheng-feng."

This means the Chairman of the CCP Central Committee considers this campaign of repressions continued throughout 1942, 1943, 1944, and up to the congress. This also means I was right—he also used cheng-feng for the "spiritual purification" of the congress delegates.

The course toward Mao Tse-tung's glorification becomes increasingly apparent. He is now called the "banner of the Chinese revolution," the CCP's deliverer of "petty-bourgeois scab." . . . More than that, all disagreements with him are regarded as anti-Maoism subject to unconditional suppression. In his May 2 speech Lo Fu left no doubts on this score. It is only the "systematic study of works by Comrade Mao Tse-tung" that makes it possible to master revolutionary theory and will "foster proletarian spirit." It is only works by Mao Tse-tung that are important for studies! . . .

The Chairman of the CCP Central Committee may take pride in this congress. . . .

———

Mao Tse-tung is an actor by nature. He knows how to conceal his feelings and cleverly play the role he needs even before people he knows well.

Sometimes he plays a trick on a person in a quite serious manner and after that asks whether he was a success. . . .

———

Had a talk with Mao Tse-tung. Went out into the street. Mao is content, squinting his eyes in the sun. . . . He is in a good mood after the congress. The collar of his jacket unbuttoned as always, he deliberates on the unity of the party. . . .

This "unity" formula is used by Mao Tse-tung to cover up, among other things, his cruelty in the struggle for power. . . .

August 9, 1945

Yesterday the Soviet Government told the Japanese ambassador in Moscow that as of August 9 the Soviet Union considered itself to be in the state of war with Japan. . . .

In mid-July the Japanese Government requested the Soviet Union's peaceful mediation in the Far East. The ambassadors of the United States, Britain, and China in Moscow were informed of this request of the Japanese Government.

———

The land question continuously generates the revolutionary situation. The Kuomintang does not want to, nor will it, encroach upon the property of landlords. This means that the agrarian revolution is imminent. Mao Tse-tung takes this into account. . . .

August 10, 1945

Our troops have crossed the Soviet-Manchurian frontier on a broad front. The Japanese ferroconcrete defense line has been broken through in the Maritime Province. In the Khabarovsk area our troops have forced the Amur and the Ussuri in fighting.

The Mongolian People's Republic has declared war on Japan.

Yesterday the Americans dropped another super-bomb. Nagasaki is also in ruins now!

The emergence of this new devastating weapon will radically change the character of war. . . .

————

The Soviet Union's entry into the war has caused confusion in the CCP leadership. Nobody here expected such a rapid transfer of Soviet troops from Germany to the Far East and the colossal might of their blows. Red Army troops have crushed Japanese defenses.

This confusion vividly revealed the CCP leadership's old "disease" —the underestimation of the Soviet Union's possibilities. This is not a delusion but the "disease" which has its roots in ideological foreignness to internationalism and the negation of Soviet reality.

The CCP leadership evaluated the Soviet Union's chances purely arithmetically—the U.S.S.R. has suffered heavy losses in the war against Germany. This means that the Soviet Union has been bled white and cannot prepare for a war with Japan in a short time. The qualitative characteristics which distinguish the Soviet system from any other were disregarded in this respect.

August 11, 1945

Our troops push their way through the taiga, roadless terrain, hills, and waterless steppes. The Kwantung Army has been demoralized. . . .

Eisenhower came on a friendly visit to Moscow.

————

The Red Army offensive in Manchuria and Transbaikalia area paralyzes the will of the Chairman of the CCP Central Committee. In view of the radical change in the situation in China it is necessary to take urgent and important decisions while the Chairman of the CCP is completely at a loss, bordering on prostration.

These days are an especially clear illustration of Mao's cowardice, his characteristic feature. He has retained nothing of his usual emperorlike grandeur. I see a little weak-willed man who, judging by everything, suffers from "bear's disease." . . .

August 12, 1945

Through its mission in Bern Japan has declared its unconditional surrender to all countries struggling against it. . . .

_____

In a talk with me Mao Tse-tung said the Soviet Union should render the CCP gratis aid now and in the future. It is on this that the relations between the CCP and the AUCP(B) depended and would depend. . . .

Mao Tse-tung has an organic dislike for the Soviet Union. Despite all his assurances of friendship, he regards the Soviet Union as his ideological foe. The dislike for the Comintern and the AUCP(B) is neither a whim nor a personal offense. It is important to know that this anti-Sovietism has a ten-year history. It goes back to the time when he sent Wang Chia-hsiang to Moscow to clarify the "procapitulationist" sentiments of the Comintern. Mao Tse-tung considered the Comintern and Moscow were engendering "dogmatists." Gradually, step by step, since the Tsunyi Conference Mao Tse-tung had been driving a wedge between the AUCP(B) and the CCP. He was transforming the CCP in accordance with his plans.

He saw the main revolutionary force in the countryside, and here he disagreed with the Comintern. And he attained his aim—the CCP settled in rural areas. Here the process assumed its logical character. The CCP began to degenerate into an agrarian party with its distinctive ideology. All this was taking place, naturally enough, not without the struggle between the internationalist and nationalist, Marxist and petty-bourgeois trends in the CCP. It might be said this struggle has not yet ended.

In this way, the "Marxism of reality" is not a result of activities of a lucky politician. This is a philosophical system leaning upon a firm ideological and economic basis. Whatever was spoken at the congress about proletarian spirit, there is no trace of it in the party. Here proletarian spirit is interpreted as soldierly obedience to the will of Mao Tse-tung. Thus, the circle has closed. The village has "eaten up" the CCP. Mao Tse-tung has indeed become the leader, but not of a vanguard proletarian party. Everything went in accordance with the classical formula—"being determined consciousness."

To sum up, the "Marxism of reality," this cheng-feng-type "Marxism," is not a whim of history, but a reflection of objective processes. These processes have worked, do work, and will work. And they stem from the way of life of a country, its economy, the correlation of classes, traditions, etc. It is from the medium, formed by these factors, that the CCP received and receives its replenishments.

This explains why not only Mao Tse-tung but also all other party rulers have a dislike for the Soviet Union, the Comintern, and the All-Union Communist Party. They do not move history, but are moved by the objective processes at work in this vast peasant country. In this case it is beyond their power "to direct their steps" because they are the concentrated expression of the medium which prevails in the country. They are an extreme expression of the philosophy of the petty owner with all his nationalistic ambitions. This process of the CCP's transformation may take different forms without changing its essence and directions.

I know their true attitude to the Soviet Union and the AUCP(B). Even in the current atmosphere of forced good will, their utterances about Bolshevism and their behavior bear a surprising resemblance of a restaurant scene during a meeting of German Social Democratic leaders, the scene which was witnessed and described by Maxim Gorki: "Drank Rhine wine and beer; the wine was sour and warm, the beer good; Social Democrats spoke of the Russian Revolution and of the party also sourly and condescendingly, but about their, German, party, very well! In general, everything was very self-content and it was felt even the chairs were content with being burdened with the respectable back parts of the leaders." With their "Marxism of reality" the CCP leaders poison not only their party and people. . . .

I evaluate the "Marxism of reality" from the position of orthodox Marxism because I do not recognize any other philosophical approach. The foundation for my conclusions was provided by facts, not words or such works of Mao Tse-tung as *On New Democracy*. . . .

Here it is pertinent to recall what Rosa Luxemburg said of the opportunists: "You do not stand on Marxism, you sit and even lie on it. . . ."

I would use even sharper words in respect to Mao Tse-tung and his supporters in the CCP. . . .

August 13, 1945

A rapid advance of Red Army troops in Manchuria and the Transbaikalia area and collapse of the Kwantung Army, a formidable and invincible force in the eyes of the CCP leaders, are a complete surprise for them. Here again they underestimate the military and economic potential of the Soviet Union.

Mao Tse-tung is so stunned that it is hard to understand whether or not the Chairman of the CCP is glad to see this course of developments. . . . He now only signs the instructions to his assistants.

The troops of Ho Lung and Nieh Jung-chen were ordered to capture Taiyuan (the capital of Shansi province) and move in the northeastern direction and toward Peiping.

August 14, 1945

On August 13 Soviet troops continued the offensive in Manchuria. . . .

Tensions do not slacken in Greece.

Chiang Kai-shek sent a telegram to Mao Tse-tung, proposing a meeting in Chungking to settle the disagreements which arose in the course of combat operations against the Japanese.

Systematizing of the materials of the Seventh CCP Congress takes all my time, since I was the only man from the Soviet Union at the congress. There can be no doubt that not all which took place at the congress will become known to the public in full. The CCP leadership will "pass through a sieve" the necessary documents and formulas to be incorporated in the future press report. They don't think much about such things here. . . .

Chairman Mao via the Secretariat of the CCP Central Committee supplied me with the following closed documents:

1. Wang Ming's letter to the seventh plenary meeting of the CCP Central Committee.
2. The resolution on some questions of the history of the party.
3. The report (parts 1 and 2) on amendments to the party rules.
4. Po Ku's statement.
5. The draft of new party rules.
6. The report on the organization of the Army.
7. Wang Chia-hsiang's letter to Mao Tse-tung.
8. The joint letter by Wang Ming and Wang Chia-hsiang to Mao Tse-tung.
9. Congress decisions on some questions of the history of the party.
10. Another variant of the draft of the party rules.
11. The material on the negotiations between the CCP and the Kuomintang.
12. Mao Tse-tung's report (with the classified introduction) to the Seventh CCP Congress.

These documents cover the entire history of Mao Tse-tung's struggle for unlimited power, beginning with Tsunyi and up to the recent congress. It would be foolish to conceal them from me. And, in Mao Tse-tung's opinion, not quite sensible in view of his current game with Moscow. Besides, I heard everything at the congress (and partly at the sittings of delegations).

Mao Tse-tung believes the future is with him, only with him. . . .

I saw a stage in the struggle for the future.

Chang Tien-i wrote: "Believe me there are people in the world with whom the future lies!" And this is not Mao Tse-tung, Kang Sheng. . . .

I believe and see that such forces do exist. Persuasion through force and the arbitrariness of the cheng-feng do not become nor can be their faith. Grains, small particles, crystallize into truth, the truth before which violence was, is, and will be impotent. . . .

One can tell lies a year, ten years, twenty years, but not always! . . .

The Chinese people are seeking the truth. The great revolution which is shaking China consists of a search for the truth, and the people will obtain it. . . .

And I again write down these words: "Believe me there are people in the world with whom the future lies!"

August 15, 1945

Moscow confirmed Japan's unconditional surrender.

Japan adopted the Potsdam Declaration's conditions: unconditional surrender. Suzuki's Cabinet resigned. Suzuki said the Japanese people will never forget the day of defeat. War Minister Korechika Anami committed suicide yesterday. . . .

The treaty of friendship and alliance with the Chinese Republic was signed in Moscow.

The CCP Central Committee has finally adopted a directive in connection with the Soviet Union's entry into the war against Japan. The directive describes the state of the party and its present-day and future tasks.

Along with other tasks, the directive emphasizes the necessity of consolidating the newly liberated areas and giving assistance to the middle peasants because they "constitute the main group in the village."

Application of the policy of ground rent reductions to the kulaks has been recommended. The landlords should be given an opportunity to exist. Land confiscation and redistribution are premature. In places where this has been done it is necessary to maintain the status quo. However, the landlords should be supported—they should not be allowed to perish.

Thus, it is necessary to win over the kulaks and actively support those middle peasants whose households are in the state of decline.

Moderation is recommended, but only in Yenan, as regards the criticism of the United States and the Kuomintang. The Americans in distress should be helped everywhere.

The bases and troops must be ready to help the Americans in their future landing operations.

To express sympathies in respect to the American people and the democratic elements in the United States Government.

Tension grows between the CCP and the Kuomintang because of military frictions in the areas being liberated.

The CCP leadership has been staggered by Japan's surrender. In their opinion Japan should have been on defense for several years more (at least two years, in any case).

August 16, 1945

The parasitical features of the Yenan leadership have fully revealed themselves.

The party leaders do not know what to do. You can feel faint notes of discontent with the actions of the Soviet command. The CCP leaders expected the blow of Soviet and Mongolian troops would be directed at Inner Mongolia, at Kalgan, if not at Paotow and Kueisui. . . .

However, their hopes collapsed. Red Army troops inflicted blows, proceeding from military considerations—the complete defeat of the enemy with the least losses.

The Communist Party leadership considers the Soviet Union has betrayed the interests of the CCP and its armed forces by choosing Manchuria as its only area of military operations. There is no end to grumbling in this respect!

In the reply telegram, Chu Teh has declined, on behalf of the CCP's leadership, Chiang Kai-shek's proposal concerning the meeting.

The civil war is the main subject of talks among the CCP leaders. . . .

General Chennault told a New York *Times* correspondent the Soviet Union's entry into the war against Japan was the decisive factor which rapidly led to the end of military operations. The result would be the same—Japan's immediate surrender—irrespective of whether or not the atomic bombs were dropped! . . .

Chennault is right. The Red Army troops have broken the backbone of Japan's resistance—its mainland bases (in Manchuria and Korea) with their big military and economic potential.

August 18, 1945

The Japanese continue to resist on our fronts. However, in some places they have already begun to surrender. . . .

Individual Japanese garrisons continue resisting in Burma as well. Top rankers of the Japanese Army and Navy commit suicide.

Prince Naruhiko Higashikuni has been appointed Prime Minister of Japan. This prince is not from the cohort of peacemakers. Born in 1887, he graduated from a military academy and spent seven years in France. In 1937 he headed the air force branch of the Japanese armed forces.

A trial of war criminals has begun in Austria.

De Gaulle has commuted the sentence of Pétain, who was condemned to death. The former French marshal will be sent to a fortress for life imprisonment.

I read by chance a telegram from the staff of the New Fourth Army. This staff report makes it absolutely clear that there is permanent contact between the Communist Party leadership and the supreme command of the Japanese expeditionary forces.

The telegram left no doubts that the reports about contacts with the Japanese command were regularly reaching Yenan.

Later I established that this contact between the staffs of the CCP troops and the Japanese forces had been maintained for a long time. The end points of this contact were Yenan and Nanking.

August 19, 1945

Yenan issues orders one after another. The Eighth Route Army, the New Fourth Army, guerrillas, and militia move into the areas occupied by the Japanese. The enemy is demoralized and doesn't resist, sticking to strongholds.

The military apparatus of the CCP Central Committee is feverishly active. Yenan hasn't a wink of sleep. . . .

The only aim is to outpace the Kuomintang and capture new areas and Japanese weapons depots as well as to bar the way to the Central Government's troops at any price.

Yenan's secret order: to destroy all Kuomintang units which show persistence in moving forward and, wherever possible, to kick them out of new areas.

Groups of military men, party and Soviet workers, depart from Yenan one after another. . . .

August 20, 1945

Japanese troops do not surrender on the Chinese front. They don't fight, but they don't receive Chinese representatives either.

Ho Ying-chin, chief of the general staff of the Chinese forces, flew to Yu-shan, a small town, for talks with General Okamura, commander in chief of the Japanese expeditionary forces in China.

Chen Yi seems to have flown together with Ho Ying-chin.

Fearing reprisals, the Japanese refused to surrender until the act of capitulation has been signed. . . .

August 21, 1945

The Kwantung Army has ceased resistance in most sectors of the front. Units and formations of the Kwantung Army surrender to our troops. . . .

Our fronts continue to advance in the preassigned directions.

———

Yeh Chien-ying told Mao Tse-tung that I knew the contents of the telegram from the staff of the New Fourth Army. For a long time the Chairman of the CCP Central Committee explained to me the reasons why the Communist Party leadership had decided to establish contact with the command of the Japanese occupationist forces.

A shameful fact, and that was why Mao Tse-tung tried to provide convincing arguments for his explanations.

The talk showed how unseemly all this was. The relations with the Japanese command had been established long ago under great secrecy. Only a few persons from the CCP leadership had known about it. Mao Tse-tung's agent (or a "liaison man" as Mao called him) had been attached, as it were, to General Okamura's staff in Nanking. Whenever necessary, he, carefully protected by the Japanese counterespionage service, had shuttled unhindered between Nanking and the staff of the New Fourth Army.

The necessary information from the Chairman of the CCP Central Committee had awaited this agent (Japanese by origin) in the staff of the New Fourth Army. In the staff of the New Fourth Army the agent's information had been immediately coded and radioed to Yenan.

———

Mixing and clashing, the troops of the CCP and the Central Government are spreading all over the country.

The Yenan-Chungking relations have drastically aggravated. Reciprocal reproaches in the press. . . .

The situation is worsening practically with every hour. The threat of a military clash between the Communist Party and the Kuomintang is growing rapidly. . . .

General Ho Ying-chin receives the surrender of Japanese troops in Hunan (Chih-chiang locality). All Japanese units were ordered to concentrate in that place. The official ceremony of the surrender of the Japanese Army's commanding officers is also taking place there.

August 22, 1945

The Americans guess at Japan's political future. All commentators are unanimous in that Japan must never again become, nor will it be, an American military adversary. This will be a country surrounded with the military might of the United States which "assumes upon itself the mission of peace in this part of the world."

The Americans say they have come to stay in the Pacific islands for a long time and the future of Japan ultimately depends upon them. . . .

Mao Tse-tung receives from Chiang Kai-shek repeated invitations to meet in Chungking to discuss disagreements and work out an agreement. . . .

Mao keeps silent. He now reminds me of a man who, disregarding the wind, fans the flame without caring which direction the flame will take.

August 23, 1945

On August 22 in Manchuria and on the southern Sakhalin Red Army troops advanced in the preassigned directions.

Our aircraft landing parties landed in Dairen and Port Arthur and began to disarm the Japanese garrisons. . . .

The Japanese surrender to our troops also on islands south of Kamchatka. Prisoners of war and weapons are collected everywhere. . . .

On August 21 our troops took as prisoners 71,000 officers and men, including 20 generals. . . .

The act of Japan's surrender will be signed on board the American battleship *Missouri* in Tokyo Bay on August 31.

On America's behalf the surrender of Japan will be received by General Douglas MacArthur. . . .

The first allied landing in Tokyo is planned for August 28. . . .

The traitor Ante Pavelić will be extradited by the Allies to Yugoslavia for trial. . . .

Chiang Kai-shek sent, one after another, two invitations to Mao Tse-tung to meet in Chungking. The country is on the threshold of a civil war.

The Chungking press painfully reacts to Mao Tse-tung's refusals. By Chinese standards, to decline personal invitations on two occasions is more than just an insult. Newspapers say " 'Communist No. 1' [Mao Tse-tung] has decided to send, instead of coming himself, 'Communist No. 2,' his right hand, Chou En-lai. However, Chou En-lai has already been in Chungking many times, where he spoke on countless occasions, arranged press conferences and all kinds of meetings, and everything to no avail."

In reply to Chiang Kai-shek's invitations Radio Yenan demanded that Chungking give up "the one-party dictatorial regime."

In his second telegram Chiang Kai-shek proposed an urgent meeting with Mao Tse-tung. This meeting is necessary in view of Japan's surrender and the aggravation of relations between the CCP and the Kuomintang.

Until the Seventh CCP Congress the military and party cadres had disagreed in their views as regards the Army. What was more expedient—a regular army or guerrilla units?

Up to the recent congress army formations had existed as self-contained units in their own, sometimes large, areas. Even Mao Tse-tung was compelled to attract the military leaders' attention to the "militaristic smell" typical of their style of work and behavior. This was confirmed in his congress speech by Lin Piao.

The Seventh CCP Congress decided gradually to change over from the system of guerrilla units to strong regular formations. This reconstruction was made necessary by the coming collapse of Japan and the course toward a civil war, the course which was practically endorsed by the congress.

Chu Teh was appointed commander in chief of armed forces. Peng Teh-huai was made deputy commander in chief, Yeh Chien-ying, chief of staff (general staff), and Wang Chia-hsiang, head of the Political Department.

Official data on the CCP armed forces: 10 infantry divisions, 3 columns, 7 groups, 10 sections, and 1 cavalry group. (A column equals a division, and a group and a section equal an infantry regiment.)

1. The present-day official strength of the Eighth Route Army:
    The 115th Division—60,000 troops
    The 120th Division—110,000 troops
    The 129th Division—100,000 troops
2. Nieh Jung-chen's army—95,000 troops:
    The Hopeh-Honan Column—25,000 troops
    The Shantung Column—50,000 troops
    The Cavalry Group—6,000 sabres
3. The official strength of the New Fourth Army:
    The New Fourth Army proper—90,000 troops
    Self-contained units—36,000 troops
    In the Japanese rear—36,000 guerrillas

The combined official strength of these armies is about 600,000 troops.

However, the real, not officially inflated, strength of these armies is about 380,000 troops.

The guerrilla units number about 80,000 fighters.

August 25, 1945

On August 24 in the Far East Red Army troops moved in the preassigned directions.

In the Mukden area our troops liberated a camp of allied POWs where the Japanese kept 1,670 officers and men and 28 generals.

On August 23, 14,000 enemy officers and men were taken prisoner. . . .

Churchill spoke in the House of Commons in connection with the expiration of the American lend-lease bill. The former British Prime Minister said: ". . . I cannot believe that such a great country, whose lend-lease policy I characterized as the most unselfish act in history, would act so abruptly and grossly to cause harm to its faithful ally. . . ."

Chiang Kai-shek gave a long speech. . . .

The CCP leadership did not think events would be developing so rapidly in the latter part of 1945. This characterizes not only the CCP leadership's political shortsightedness but also its attitude to the Soviet Union. . . .

"Chairman Mao" had abandoned his second wife, Ho Tzu-chen, during the Long March. Abandoned when she was ill. He left his five children in the care of peasants. . . .

At the Fifth CCP Congress he had no right to vote.

At the Sixth CCP Congress Mao Tse-tung was not present at all. . . .

Following the decision of the December 1938 plenum to convene the Seventh Party Congress, Mao Tse-tung realized he was in isolation and the congress would most probably elect a new Chairman of the CCP Central Committee—Wang Ming!

That was why Mao decided to remove Wang Ming. This was a struggle for power and, simultaneously, the struggle for his ideas. . . .

After his speech at the December meeting of the CCP Central Committee in 1937 Mao Tse-tung found himself in isolation. This staggered him! Kang Sheng came to head the Commission for the Review of Party Cadres and Nonparty Personnel, and after that Mao let cheng-feng loose! . . .

August 26, 1945

Chungking newspapers reported another Chiang Kai-shek invitation to Mao Tse-tung to meet and discuss disagreements.

"The future of the nation depends on these talks," Chiang Kai-shek said.

Chiang Kai-shek ordered a Chinese Air Force plane sent for Mao Tse-tung.

The Central Government's armed forces have entered Shanghai and Nanking. Skirmishes between Kuomintang and CCP troops take place all over the country.

Japanese Prime Minister Prince Higashikuni urged the people "to maintain supreme tranquillity and discipline."

Foreign radio stations continue to comment extensively on the results of the atomic bombardments of Hiroshima and Nagasaki. Radio Moscow reports the progress of economic rehabilitation.

The Soviet Government's decision not to interfere in the domestic affairs of China has been brought to the attention of the CCP leadership.

Mao Tse-tung was compelled to agree to a meeting with Chiang Kai-shek in Chungking. This was the third invitation from the head of the Central Government.

A list of demands was compiled which Mao Tse-tung will put forward at the negotiations:

—the recognition of the government elected by the people (the Joint Committee of the Liberated Areas);

—the earmarking of the areas where CCP representatives could independently receive the surrender of Japanese troops;

—the severe punishment of traitors; the immediate disbandment of all party troops;

—the reorganization of the armed forces and demilitarization of the country;

—the official recognition of the status of all parties and groups;

—the abrogation of the laws limiting the freedom of assembly, the press, etc.;

—the liquidation of secret political groups;

—the liberation of political prisoners;

—the immediate calling of the conferences of all parties, organizations, groups, and nonparty people to discuss the problems of China's postwar setup;

—the elaboration of a program of democratic reforms;

—the establishment of a democratic coalition government.

These demands are also to be broadcast by Radio Yenan.

Behind a number of just demands there are also those to which Chiang Kai-shek would not agree. This is perfectly understood by Mao. He has a faint hope that the situation will possibly change and then the course of events will develop as he wants. . . .

Moscow's decision concerning noninterference means the rejection to back Mao Tse-tung's adventurous policy which generated a situation fraught with the world conflict.

At present the problem has gone beyond the purely national limits of China. Mao's actions have actually created prerequisites for a military clash between the United States and the Soviet Union.

Moscow has resolutely refused to be drawn into such a conflict. This frustrates Mao Tse-tung's personal plans and upturns his strategy to use other people to fight and act for him, disregarding the existing situation. In the obtaining situation the Red Army and American troops are finishing off with the remains of Japanese forces in China. In this situation the continuation of Mao's policy inevitably leads the CCP to a clash with the Kuomintang. The United States stands behind the Kuomintang. Concluding the treaty with Chungking, the Soviet Union proceeded from the prevailing situation in China and the world at large.

Moscow declared it would keep to the treaty concluded with the Chinese Government in July this year. This is a blow to Mao!

What he expected was the freedom of action ensured by the Soviet Union's military might. Moreover, he had dreamed of the conflict-fraught situation which arose at the moment.

Contrary to the wish of the Yenan Government, the past two weeks have laid bare the background of its political tricks. We were being pushed to a fight. Everything was being done for this fight to become unavoidable. Yenan didn't care less that this fight would be nothing but a world war.

Moscow's approach considers the real situation not only in China but also elsewhere. This is a resolute rejection of a new world war. . . .

Mao Tse-tung is also alarmed over his personal security during the negotiations. He believes Chiang Kai-shek's invitation is a trap, and he fears for his life. . . .

Chou En-lai is also active, preparing documents, giving orders, and co-ordinating all matters. Mao Tse-tung is completely confused and practically keeps away from all affairs. . . .

August 27, 1945

The Chairman of the CCP Central Committee has accepted Chiang Kai-shek's third invitation. Chungking had been informed of this earlier, and General Hurley, the American ambassador in China, came by an air force plane to Yenan today. General Chang Chih-chung, the Chairman of the Central Government, arrived jointly with Hurley.

General Hurley looked tired, although during the meeting with Mao Tse-tung he was, as usual, unconstrained and gay. He had a long talk with Mao, but, to the best of my knowledge, this was a mutual sounding out of sentiments. Hurley didn't say anything definite but expressed a desire to see, finally, Mao Tse-tung and Chiang Kai-shek at one table to settle disputes.

At the banquet the guests limited themselves to common talk. For

Hurley the agreement between the Communist Party and the Kuomintang is also a very important personal question. His entire career is at stake. In this respect he made big blunders, and now the situation gives him a chance to rehabilitate himself.

All attempts to find out what Chiang Kai-shek had brought in his political bag to the Chungking talks were unsuccessful. The guests said they knew nothing.

Radio Yenan enumerates the demands without the satisfaction of which an agreement is impossible. . . .

Mao Tse-tung asked once again to confirm the Soviet Government's readiness to guarantee his personal security in Chungking. He requested, if his security was threatened, a refuge in the Soviet Military Mission in Chungking. I confirmed that his personal security was guaranteed and that he could count on a refuge in the Soviet Military Mission. However, all doubts are superfluous, as Chiang Kai-shek would not dare encroach upon his life. This is Moscow's firm guarantee. . . .

The Chairman of the CCP Central Committee, accompanied by Chou En-lai and Wang Jo-fei, will go by plane for talks in Chungking tomorrow.

At Chungking Airport Hurley said:

"I am going to Yenan by agreement with Chiang Kai-shek and at Mao Tse-tung's personal request. I must return with Mao Tse-tung and his associates. . . . I am glad. For a year we have been trying to tell the Central Government to avoid a split and a civil war. The field for discussion is wide. However, the leaders can come to agreement. This gives rise to bright hopes."

August 28, 1945

A funny sight at Yenan Airport. The tall gray-headed Hurley (some ten cm. higher than Mao) in an elegant European suit with a bow tie and a fashionable felt hat. Next to him is Mao Tse-tung in a bulky dark blue field jacket and a cork helmet. I saw such a helmet only in Chiang Kai-shek's pictures.

Mao Tse-tung was smiling, but I know what his mood was these days. Circumstances compelled him to agree to the talks. All these years the aim of the policy of the Chairman of the CCP Central Committee was to prevent any talks. . . .

It looked as if he was going to his Calvary. . . .

The plane with the delegation and guests landed in Chungking in the evening.

August 29, 1945

Tens of thousands of Japanese soldiers surrender to the Red Army troops. Advancing, our forces disarm one garrison after another and liberate more and more Chinese cities. . . .

Americans have landed in Shanghai.

An allied armada is cruising off Tokyo. . . .

In the Kurils the Japanese retain only one island. All others have been captured by our troops.

Yesterday in Chungking Mao Tse-tung made a statement to the effect that unity at home was a "task of paramount importance, an urgent necessity."

"I have come to Chungking at the invitation of Mr. Chiang Kai-shek, the President of the national government, to discuss important questions of unity and national reconstruction," Mao Tse-tung said. "Now that the war against Japan has ended triumphantly, China is preparing to embark upon the stage of peaceful transformation. The current moment is exceptionally important. At present the guarantee of peace and the effecting of democracy and unity at home are questions of paramount importance demanding immediate solution. The numerous urgent political and military questions, which arose in the country, should be solved on the rational foundation of peace, democracy, and unity of the entire country so that it would be possible to build a new independent, strong, and prospering China. We hope all anti-Japanese political parties and patriots of China will pool efforts and struggle jointly for the implementation of these aims. I express my gratitude to Mr. Chiang Kai-shek for his invitation to come to Chungking."

Chiang Kai-shek gave a dinner in honor of Mao Tse-tung.

Yenan newspapers say, "We are fully determined to conclude an agreement with the Kuomintang and other democratic parties in order to promote an early settlement of different problems. We must build a strong alliance with the Kuomintang for a long time to come, the alliance which will make it possible to realize Sun Yat-sen's three national principles. . . ."

As the indispensable conditions for the conclusion of an agreement between the Communist Party and the Kuomintang, Yenan newspapers insist on the fulfillment of the selfsame points of the program: the recognition of the government of the liberated areas, the formation of a coalition government, etc. . . .

Behind all this is the hope for a change in the situation, a sudden change in Moscow's mood.

However, today the Soviet Government reiterated its resolution to abstain from interference in China's domestic affairs and to observe the treaty with the National Government of China.

———

Ma Hai-te has become a "contact" between the CCP leadership and the Americans. Each side treasures him. Ma Hai-te is outside the sphere of activities of Kang Sheng's counterespionage service. Ma Hai-te has developed close friendship with many workers of the general staff.

August 30, 1945

The list of the main war criminals has been published. It includes the group of persons to be brought up, in the first place, before the International Military Tribunal.

The battleship *Missouri* came into Tokyo Bay yesterday. Massive American landings have begun near Tokyo.

Chen Kung-po, the head of Nanking's puppet government, committed suicide.

Negotiations began in Chungking on August 29. The Kuomintang Government is represented by Chiang Kai-shek, Wang Shih-chieh, Chang Chih-chung.

Mao Tse-tung and Chiang Kai-shek met at the dinner on August 28. According to Chungking newspapers, their previous personal meeting took place exactly twenty years ago, when the Kuomintang and the Communist Party still co-operated.

The country is in an acute political crisis. The troops of the CCP and the Kuomintang continue to compete in seizing Japanese arsenals and new areas. Skirmishes do not cease between the Eighth Route Army, the New Fourth Army, and the Central Government's troops.

August 31, 1945

Only a few of my comrades had been in the Special Area before 1940. However, between 1940 and 1944 there were non-Chinese there, including some representatives of other Oriental nationalities (Mongols, Japanese, Koreans, etc.) and a few foreign doctors.

This enabled the Chairman of the CCP Central Committee to organize, in a secret way, the cheng-feng and the measures to misinform the public of other countries of the character of the war conducted by the CCP army (especially the Eighth Route Army) against the Japanese invaders and the sabotage of the united anti-Japanese front. It should be said, however, that from time to time this sabotage was covered by patriotic articles in *Liberation Daily,* mass meetings, and public statements. In the Special Area itself, since 1941, the anti-Kuomintang policy had become an important constituent of the CCP leadership's policy.

No information leaked out, against Mao Tse-tung's will, from this little closed world. Even now when Yenan is visited by numerous foreign correspondents, military and political leaders, the strict control of Mao Tse-tung and Kang Sheng over every party member and soldier makes it possible to successfully continue with misinformation activities. It is only duly prepared "men from the people" that are allowed to answer the questions of foreign reporters and politicians. All others keep silent or answer with crammed slogans. Full submission, the fear to show one's independence, has taken the place of revolutionary democracy. All these years the real situation on the front and the true direction of the CCP policy have been carefully concealed from us Soviet people—although it was persistently demanded that the Soviet Union support this policy in all cases.

Violence was committed here, the truth of which the world will, perhaps, never learn in full (if it learns anything at all). Nobody can learn the full truth of the Seventh CCP Congress which exerts and will indisputably exert a tremendous influence on the CCP. The official reports carried in the press did not reflect reality. A number of statements, including those made by Lo Fu, Yang Shang-kun, Mao (on a number of questions), and others, were withdrawn from the minutes. Other statements were printed with significant cuts, representing the work of the congress in an entirely different line.

At the congress I was the only non-Chinese (with the exception of a few Japanese, Koreans, and Mongols). The Chairman of the CCP Central Committee is confident I didn't learn the main thing—the backstage struggle to persuade and pressurize delegates, the struggle permeated with sharp anti-Sovietism, nationalism, and opportunism.

Already now the history of the congress is interpreted in the spirit which has nothing to do with reality. To put it mildly, this interpretation doesn't correspond to facts. Things are slurred over by vague formulas, forgery, and big cuts in shorthand reports.

Judging by the attitude of the Chairman of the Central Committee, he thinks that since 1944 I have been fully under his influence, that I understand and support his policy. He is confident nobody knows about his sabotage of the united anti-Japanese front and the struggle against the Japanese, his constant misinformation of Moscow, bargaining with the White House, and attempts to isolate the Soviet Union in the sphere of the Far Eastern politics.

The Ching-pao-chu spared no effort to ensure the "hermeticism" of this little world, cultivating the "Marxism of reality." Incidentally, this is one of the weighty reasons why Mao doesn't part with Kang Sheng.

Mao is firmly convinced there are no persons who saw what was taking place here! Cheng-feng helped to effect the purge of thirty thousand cadre workers. Everybody was in sight. Every word became known to the secret service. For most this ended with "spiritual reforming." . . .

Wang Jo-fei is a veteran member of the CCP. In the early twenties he participated in setting up CCP sections in France. Jointly with Chou En-lai he participated in all important talks with the Kuomintang. He is a member of the CCP Central Committee.

September 1945

Soviet troops have fully cleared the Kurils.

The Japanese are still offering resistance in Singapore.

Foreign radio stations repeat over and over again that World War II has brought Russia to the height of power. The tone of these broadcasts is openly provocative. . . .

The situation at the talks in Chungking is gradually changing. The press even reports about a friendly atmosphere.

Chungking's press writes ironically: "Now Mao Tse-tung calls Chiang Kai-shek a president and not a 'fascist reactionary dictator.' The government he now calls a national government and not 'Chiang Kai-shek's regime.' " . . .

A feature of the Yenan policy is to squeeze all possible economic and political advantages from the sides concerned. Ideological considerations are being disregarded. The purpose is to squeeze everything out of the situation. . . .

September 2, 1945

British ships have entered Hong Kong Harbor.

General Chennault has said that he doubts whether even now Japan considers herself defeated.

Hitler's Field Marshals Erich von Manstein and Heinrich Brauchitsch have been arrested.

Vidkun Quisling's trial is under way. The public prosecutor said that not only had Quisling helped the Germans, but he had actually set them to the seizure of Norway, dreaming of becoming a Norwegian führer.

Captive Japanese officers do not think that the war has been lost because of the morale factor. The morale of the Emperor's army has always been high. . . .

But these statements do not hold water. The Soviet Union's declaration of war on Japan caused panic in Manchuria which mounted with each passing day. By the way, the Japanese themselves have admitted it.

––––––––

In August 145 operations were performed at the central hospital, mainly by surgeons trained by Andrei Yakovlevich. (In the whole of 1941 only 400 operations were performed at the same hospital!)

Orlov already speaks Chinese fluently and writes quite well.

––––––––

The Joint Army of the Special Area is commanded by Ho Lung (the chief of the staff is Chang Ching-wu, the commissar is Kao Kang, and the chief of the Political Department is Tan Cheng).

The headquarters of the Joint Army is in Yenan.

All the military units of the Special Area are subordinate to it:

1. The separate 1st Brigade (under Kao Hsin). It is deployed in the Suiteh region.

2. The protective 2nd Brigade (under Wang Wei-chou). It is deployed in the San-pien region.

3. The protective 3rd Brigade (under Ho Chin-nien). It is deployed in the San-pien region.

4. The 358th Brigade (under Chang Tsung-liang).

5. The remnants of the 359th Brigade (under Wang Cheng), deployed in Nanniwan. The brigade itself with Wang Cheng at the head last year left for Hunan, where it established a new base of the CCP.

6. The New 4th Brigade (under Wang Ti-shan). The brigade is deployed in Chuang-chun.

Other military units . . .
The total strength of the Joint Army is 76,518 men.

On the eve of his departure for Chungking Mao Tse-tung told me about his dream of writing a book on all the phases of the Chinese Revolution and about his intention to visit the Soviet Union.

In the absence of Mao Tse-tung, having pushed Kang Sheng aside, Liu Shao-chi is in charge of all party and administrative matters.

Orlov speaks of Kang Sheng as one of those people who prefer to be a big fish in the pond, rather than a small fish in the ocean. Nevertheless, despite the fall of his prestige, the chief of the Ching-pao-chu remains in power.

Largely owing to Mao Tse-tung, the anti-Japanese united front in the country was practically broken down.

The deepening of the division between the Kuomintang and the CCP puts China on the verge of a national catastrophe. The military operations in the last few years developed in a tragic way and presaged a victory for fascist Japan. But this turn of events did not alarm Mao. Taking into account the political situation in the world, he had concentrated all his efforts on the seizure of power in the country and shifted the trouble of defeating Japan on to the shoulders of the Soviet Union and the Allies. Mao was maneuvering politically and did not engage in an active struggle against the occupationists, waiting for the moment when after defeating Germany the Soviet Union and the Allies would bring to bear all their military potential against Japan. The country was being ravaged by the occupationists, the people were in plight and died of hunger, but Mao was waiting for his hour when he would fling all his military forces into the bid for power.

The defeat of fascist Japan mainly by the United States and the Soviet Union removed the threat of China's enslavement by the invaders and eliminated the dangerous effects of the tactic of breaking down the anti-Japanese bloc. But this unscrupulous policy of Mao's cost dear the Chinese people, who suffered a tremendous loss of life and incalculable devastations as a result of the connivance at the Japanese invasion. . . .

September 3, 1945

Yesterday the act of Japan's surrender was signed on board the American battleship *Missouri*.

The first to sign it was Foreign Minister Mamoru Shigemitsu, and chief of the Japanese general staff Umezu was the second. . . .

Lieutenant General Kuzma Derevyanko signed the act for the Soviet Union. . . .

A great reception was given yesterday at the Soviet embassy in Chungking on the occasion of the conclusion of a Sino-Soviet treaty of friendship and alliance.

The reception was attended by members of the National Government of China and also by Mao Tse-tung and Chou En-lai.

September 4, 1945

The economic position of Japan is difficult, the Allies say in broadcasts, and will remain such for many years to come.

According to a report from Chungking, Chiang Kai-shek and Mao Tse-tung have reached mutual understanding on a number of political questions.

Now it is very likely that I, too, shall be recalled to Moscow. For me, a military correspondent and a messenger of the former Comintern attached to the CCP Central Committee, the war has also ended.

Today for the first time I have sent a telegram to Moscow asking for permission to return. Why, I have lived in China for many years. . . .

Suggestions for Further Reading

The most recent and comprehensive history of the Chinese Communist Party is James P. Harrison, *The Long March to Power* (New York: Praeger, 1972). Consultation of this very readable work would provide background on many events, such as the Long March, the Tsunyi Conference, and the New Fourth Army incident, which are alluded to but not fully explained by Vladimirov.

An in-depth treatment of the Communist stay in Yenan is Mark Selden, *The Yenan Way in Revolutionary China* (Cambridge, Mass.: Harvard University Press, 1971), which among other features provides historical background and a good description of the geography of the area. On particular subjects relating to the Yenan period which occupy important places in the present volume, see: Chalmers Johnson, *Peasant Nationalism and Communist Power: The Emergence of Revolutionary China, 1937–1945* (Stanford: Stanford University Press, 1962), on military and propaganda matters; Boyd Compton, *Mao's China: Party Reform Documents, 1942–44* (Seattle: University of Washington Press, 1952), on the rectification campaign; and Lyman Van Slyke, *Enemies and Friends: The United Front in Chinese Communist History* (Stanford: Stanford University Press, 1967), on the history of Mao's shaky alliance with the Kuomintang. The role of the United States, as well as the general situation in China during these years, is treated critically in Tang Tsou, *America's Failure in China, 1941–1950* (Chicago: University of Chicago Press, 1967).

Several good biographies of Mao Tse-tung are available, among which are Edward C. Rice, *Mao's Way* (Berkeley: University of California Press, 1972), and Stuart Schram, *Mao Tse-tung* (New York: Simon & Schuster, 1967). A number of Mao's speeches and writings dating from this period may be found in *Selected Works of Mao Tse-tung*, 4 vols. (Peking: Foreign Languages Press, 1961–65). Capsule biographies of many other individuals mentioned by Vladimirov are available in Donald W. Klein and Anne B. Clark, *Biographic Dictionary of Chinese Communism*, 2 vols. (Cambridge, Mass.: Harvard University Press, 1971).

Finally, several personal (and often highly political) accounts have been published by Americans who visited Yenan and are mentioned by Vladimirov. Among these are David Barrett, *Dixie Mission* (Berkeley: University of California Press, 1970), and Theodore H. White and Annalee Jacoby, *Thunder Out of China* (New York: William Sloane, 1946). The wartime dispatches of John Service have been edited by Joseph W. Esherick and published as *Lost Chance in China* (New York: Random House, 1974).

INDEX

519